BURNING
RAINBOW
FARM

By the same author

I *Am a* Bullet
Ray Gun Out of Control

BURNING RAINBOW FARM

How a Stoner Utopia Went Up in Smoke

Dean Kuipers

BLOOMSBURY

Grateful acknowledgment is extended to the following for permission to reprint
copyrighted material:

"I-Feel-Like-I'm-Fixin'-to-Die Rag," words and music by Joe McDonald, © 1965
Alkatraz Corner Music Co., renewed 1993. Used by permission.

Photographs on pp. vi and 364 by ElVee.

Published by Bloomsbury Publishing, New York and London
Distributed to the trade by Holtzbrinck Publishers

All papers used by Bloomsbury Publishing are natural, recyclable
products made from wood grown in well-managed forests.
The manufacturing processes conform to the environmental
regulations of the country of origin.

Library of Congress Cataloging-in-Publication Data

Kuipers, Dean.
Burning Rainbow Farm: how a stoner utopia went up in smoke / Dean Kuipers.—1st
U.S. ed.
p. cm.
ISBN-13: 978-1-59691-142-0 (hardcover)
ISBN-10: 1-59691-142-5 (hardcover)
1. Crosslin, Tom. 2. Rohm, Rollie. 3. Rainbow Farm (Campground : Vandalia, Mich.).
4. Marijuana—Michigan—Vandalia. 5. Drug control—Michigan—Vandalia.
6. Government, Resistance to—Michigan—Vandalia. 7. Drug legalization—United
States. 8. Marijuana—Law and legislation—United States. I. Title.

HV5833.V36K85 2006
364.1'77—dc22
2005036030

First U.S. Edition 2006

1 3 5 7 9 10 8 6 4 2

Typeset by Westchester Book Group
Printed in the United States of America by Quebecor World Fairfield

For Meg and Spenser

and for Robert

Rollie Rohm, left, and Tom Crosslin, Roach Roast 2000

CONTENTS

ONE August 31, 2001

And there are no descending circles and only one flame in Hell. But it is a beauty.
—Robert Penn Warren

I can't believe they haven't killed you boys already.
—Merle Haggard, first time meeting Tom Crosslin and
Rollie Rohm on Rainbow Farm, July 2000

RAINBOW FARM CAMPGROUND WAS empty on the Friday morning Tom Crosslin burned the place to the ground. Two teenage lovers named Omar Alham and Vanessa Hunckler had been the last to leave, taking down their tent two days earlier, but that red morning they were flying toward it again, fishtailing down the dirt road, dust billowing in a monster ecru cloud behind. Tom hadn't really told them why they had to leave, he'd said only "stuff's happening," but they'd taken that as enough of a statement from a place that had been a living statement for years. Omar had been crashing at the farm on and off since the fourth of July, along with a lot of other people, and Nessa—she shortened it to Nessa—had just returned to it in a kind of pilgrimage. Tom's eviction had been direct, but in his eyes they saw a glimmer of the generosity and hope that had caused people to gather on his property for years, and that would bring them back one more time. They knew Tom and Rollie were in some kind of trouble. So Omar's big car bounced through the swamp bottoms of southwestern Michigan at eighty miles per hour while Nessa clung to the door. The baby blue 1987 Mercury Grand Marquis barely hit its top range as Omar took the back way to the farm, Fox to Quaker to Kirk Lake Road, where there were never any cops. Orange caution tape wrapped around the car sizzled and fried at speed, and the front bumper rattled where it hung by duct tape. The campers at Rainbow Farm had called the car the Hempulance because Omar took the county roads like he was operating an emergency vehicle. He drove fast as a point of pride, and the Hempulance carried the weed, always arriving just in time with the antidote to ordinary blues. Many were saved, and many believed the cannabis plant could save the world. But now it seemed like it was Rainbow Farm that needed saving.

On any other Labor Day weekend, as many as five thousand people would have been pouring through the Rainbow Farm gates for Roach Roast, the annual fall campout where Tommy Chong or Merle Haggard or Big Brother and the Holding Company would play on the big stage and the best-known hemp advocates in the country would preach the legalization of marijuana. It had been that way since 1995, when Tom Crosslin and his lover Rollie Rohm had begun hosting festivals there.

Omar and Nessa raced to aid their friends. They weren't too certain of the details, but they knew Tom and Rollie had been busted in May for growing some pot, and they were in a big feud with the county prosecutor. The Memorial Day festival had been canceled but the Labor Day blowout had still been a go. It had been a go all summer; it had been a go until a few days earlier, when suddenly Tom shut the gates and started talking about how he and Rollie were going to be heroes.

It was still early when Omar and Nessa spun through the gate. They had waited at the home of Omar's mom in Cassopolis as long as they could, but their curiosity was powerful and it was only eight a.m. when the car slid to a stop in front of the campground store in a spray of dust and gravel.

Tom was sitting on a picnic table in front of the farm's coffee shop, under a wooden sign that read The Joint, burning a fattie and drinking coffee with Rollie in the shade of the building's long porch. This was

the morning ritual, and the men shared the ease of having been together for eleven years. But both were also dressed in newish camouflage fatigue shirts and pants, still a little cardboard-stiff, and new boots,
and the look didn't suit them. Tom was forty-six and normally wore
jeans, running shoes and a T-shirt with a windbreaker. Sometimes he'd
choose a tie-dye when Rainbow Farm festivals were on. Longhaired,
skinny Rollie was younger than Tom, only twenty-eight, and still looked
like a kid. He was partial to T-shirts and Levi's and baggie genie pants.

Tom didn't smile. The summer had run him down. His weight had
dropped on his medium frame from about 230 to 210 or so, but his
face was still round. His thin brown hair was clean and lay flat on his
skull, and his pale blue eyes had a friendly droop at the corners. Tom
was typically a fast talker, a charismatic man, but he was quiet now. He
was hungover. Rollie seemed similarly preoccupied.

Jimmy Lee "Jimbo" Collett sat with them, too. A powerfully built
man of forty, he worked at the farm and lived some of the time in a
travel trailer on the back side of the big camp store. He shaved his head
to accentuate his muscular bulk and had a little black goatee, and was
also wearing camo. Omar and Nessa were his friends, and in a moment
of quiet inspiration he'd given the Hempulance its name.

"They knew we were coming back that morning," Vanessa told me
later. The night before, the two had been at the farm, partying with Tom
and Rollie and a couple other people, and Tom had promised Omar he
could have two cans of Day-Glo paint, pink and green, that had been used
to paint the farm's 1932 Farmall tractor. The psychedelic tractor had become an icon, a symbol of Rainbow Farm, especially after farmhand Travis
Hopkins had appeared that summer on the cover of the regional paper, the
South Bend Tribune, perched atop the tractor giving a defiant, raised-fist salute.

"We had no idea what they were gonna do," Nessa said. "We didn't
even know that they was supposed to be going to court that day. But
there was something in the air."

Even then, the two eighteen-year-olds wondered why anything had
to change. The place looked the same. From the gravel parking lot where

they stood talking, the building that held The Joint and the big camp store and the shower rooms stretched away to the north. To the west, gravel paths and two-track farm roads led back through acres of grass campsites to the ten-acre festival field, a kind of natural bowl where a covered wooden stage poked off the top of a hill. To the south, directly across the parking lot, was a large, comfortable two-story farmhouse where Tom and Rollie lived. Sided in light green and trimmed in cream with a gray-green roof, the house grabbed mention as having been beautifully redone. Behind it to the southwest was a seven-acre marsh, part of which was dug out as a pond.

Chickens were burring low in the henhouse in the backyard, and red-winged blackbirds set up their electric whirring on the pond. Omar and Vanessa swatted at early morning deerflies. The place smelled and sounded right, but something dark had opened up in its heart, a presence that made the two teenagers nervous. They didn't understand who was coming to take this all away, but Tom kept saying, "All they're gonna get is ashes."

For a couple days they had watched Tom turn festival guests away from the campground, saying, "The farm is over," and "They've messed with us too long, and we just can't do it anymore. You guys are gonna have to go home." The people who'd showed up were travelers and Rainbow Family crusties, union workers, libertarian fomenters and conspiracy theorists, blue-collar weekenders, academics and spontaneous dancers, all looking for space and amplified music. They came to remote Cass County, Michigan, from just across the state line in Elkhart, Indiana, and as far away as Oregon, Oklahoma, Florida and Quebec. Almost everyone who came to the festivals was looking to smoke grass and promote its legalization. But this time they had to just burn one and split. Tom let them take a free T-shirt or a pack of Rainbow Farm rolling papers or any sodas that were left in the store, then he closed the gate behind them.

Nikki Lester, who managed the camp store, had stopped by the day before and left with a "bad feeling." One of Tom's best friends from the village of Vandalia, Dwight Vowell Sr., had been there that same day with a truck, and Tom had told him to take everything of any value out of the store—groceries and camping supplies and the espresso machine and the hot case for the nacho cheese dip, plus the glass cases that held the extensive headshop and all the Tommy Chong bongs, pipes, urine test kits and Rainbow Farm lighters and Frisbees that were left. Travis Hopkins said he knew that "shit was coming down." The farm's former manager Doug Leinbach, who had known Tom for thirty years and over that span had been his most trusted friend, was there on Wednesday afternoon and said Tom wasn't acting normal and seemed "desperate." "Just like if you back a wild animal up into a corner, you're going to see them react differently than when they're free to roam about the land that they're used to."

Tom thrived on conflict and brinksmanship, so no one knew for sure where any of this was leading. The state was going to prosecute him and Rollie, and Rollie's twelve-year-old son, Robert, who had grown up on Rainbow Farm, had been put in foster care. Tom had lots of lawyers and had survived many legal battles on his properties in the past. He'd worked for eight years outfitting Rainbow Farm with stages, a store, equipment and staff. He'd spent hundreds of thousands of dollars, and now he'd stripped it all away in the space of a week.

Omar noticed the flags on the flagpole had changed since the night before. There had always been an American flag, a rainbow flag that symbolized gay unity and a small white flag bearing a red cross to recognize medical marijuana. Now the American flag flew upside down, a universal symbol of distress.

Omar and Nessa got the paint, but stayed less than fifteen minutes. "Tom wouldn't let us stay," Omar said. "They were puffing a bowl, and I was like, 'Hey, I want to stay and smoke one more bowl.' He was like, 'No, you can't. You gotta go.'"

"'But,' Tom said, 'watch the news tonight,'" added Nessa.

They were all crying, except for Rollie, who wasn't much one for tears.

"Tom didn't say what he was gonna do," added Omar. "They kept saying they were gonna be heroes. Tom didn't say it first. Jimbo was crazy, I bet he said it first. Rollie wasn't saying a lot besides, 'It's time for this to end.' "

Omar honked and spun the tires of the Hempulance as he gunned the car out of the gate. He looked in his rearview mirror. "They were standing there and Tom gave me a Nixon, you know what I mean? Two victory signs; two peace signs."

Heavy rains in August had broken a three-month drought. That summer in the Michiana area, the borderlands between southwest Michigan and northern Indiana, had been one of irrigating struggling crops and keeping cool while a breeze heated to ninety degrees Farenheit would lift an odor of melted asphalt and pig shit into a kind of slow scirocco. It was lake effect in reverse: Chicago, only two hours to the west, was having its second wettest August since 1895, but Cass County, Michigan, was dry. The soil temperature in southwest Michigan was sixty-nine degrees. The fruit agent in neighboring Berrien County reported that the drought conditions in June and July accounted for some poor size in the peach crop, but generally fruit size was good. The blueberry crop was about over and McIntosh apples would begin picking September 2.

Hog prices, a number used to measure the overall economic health of Cass County, were up 10 percent over the previous year. People liked to say that there were more hogs than people in the county, and they must have liked to say that a lot because they were saying it all the time.

Tom Crosslin was one of the people who would say those things. He embraced the country life. He had raised hogs and turkeys and cows and even painted a cartoony pig on his mailbox. He had trucked extra produce from his big gardens to soup kitchens. Like a farmer, he was in the habit of rising at dawn, always the first one up, making strong coffee to go with a little green bud from the Tupperware dish they kept in the kitchen. Most of the stash was Mexican that summer; he and Rollie had to cut back. They couldn't afford the hydroponic smoke they called "lawyer bud" anymore unless a friend gave them some, which was the only charity Tom Crosslin would abide. He'd caffeinate and marinate, then walk the two-track that circled his 54-acre farm with his dog, a gentle rottweiler named Thai Stick, making notes on improvements.

Building improvements were his money business. During the summer of 2001, he still owned seven of the many properties he'd purchased in the area, most of them in the nearby village of Vandalia and thirty miles away in Elkhart. Over the years, there had been so many properties, even his bookkeeper lost count, but one court survey indicated that at one point he'd owned at least fifty-two and he may have owned as many as eighty—rental units, single-family houses, commercial spaces—a good number of which he'd sold off in order to build Rainbow Farm.

Around noon that Friday, he scuffed through the wet grass with Thai Stick, his pockets filled with matches and lighters. He was a man who lived large, a man with a thousand friends, and a man who knew the power of symbolism and large gestures. Using that power had come to matter more than anything.

He stopped at a newish, double-wide modular building set on cinder blocks beside a line of walnut and cherry trees. This was the farm's production office, where entertainment coordinator Derrik DeCraene had kept sound equipment and hour upon hour of audiotape—all the speakers, all the bands, the whole recent history of a place that had become the center of the marijuana movement in Michigan.

Far off, a dog barked on Black Street and Thai Stick turned her head. Over the cornfields to the west, a black cloud of starlings formed and reformed, jerking through the air. The morning heat lifted the hovering insects, a kind of suspended tonnage in mosquitoes, deerflies, gnats and no-see-ums waiting to add their chitins to the earth.

Tom opened the door to the production office. It was packed with bales of dry straw. He nudged the dog out of the way and ignited the golden hay. Once it caught, it went up with a sickening thud, like a body hitting a wood floor. As the flames licked out the windows and consumed the building, he calmed the dog and walked toward the pump house in the field. That would be the next to go.

It is indicative of how the situation at Rainbow Farm had decayed that when Buggy Brown saw the smoke from the fire, he did not call the fire department. He had originally moved to Vandalia to be part of the farm's activism, and in the last few days he had been afraid of something like this. He also made a point of not taking the roads when he drove over there that morning, because he knew someone coming down Pemberton Road might get shot. Instead, he took the dirt lanes between cornfields and entered through a farm gate off the back of the property.

Buggy and his coworker Richard Deans were milking cows at the farm of Ann File, the matriarch of a prominent local family whose several connected hog farms butted up against Rainbow Farm to the southwest. Neither Buggy nor Richard were employees at Rainbow Farm, but the venue's pro-pot campaign was one of the reasons both of them worked nearby. Buggy was thirty-four and his girlfriend was Nikki Lester, who worked in the camp store. Richard, whose nickname was Rainbow Richie, was a gay teenager, and he considered Tom and Rollie to be role models.

"When I got back there, the only thing I saw was Rollie at the house," said Buggy. Rollie told Buggy that Tom was "unavailable." Rollie was also carrying a new Ruger mini-14 assault rifle with a 30-round clip full of .223 ammunition. "At that point, it was the band VIP trailer that was on fire, and I went up to Rollie. And he said 'It was time,' and that I needed to leave. Rollie was always a mellow individual. And his temperament and personality did not change at all, anytime, during any of this. I asked him if we had time for one more bowl. I went and got my bowl and we shared that a little bit, and I gave him a hug and I left. I went back out the back way."

Rainbow Richie was scared. When Buggy came to get the pipe, he told Richie not to get out of the van, and that suited Richie just fine. He wanted to tell Rollie he loved him, but he didn't know what was going on. As a gay kid who felt misunderstood at home, he was afraid to lose the two men who made him feel safe and accepted.

Seeing Rollie with a gun confirmed Buggy's fears. Rollie was slight and emotionally fragile, not given to a lot of dialogue. He was also not in the habit of carrying guns around the farm; in fact, weapons had always been forbidden there. But he had one then, a strange new accessory in a summer that had seen his genial, go-along demeanor turn profoundly sad and stoic.

Buggy had only lived in the area for about fifteen months, but during that time the farm had become the center of his life as it had for hundreds of people in the community, farmers and workers from the Elkhart trailer plants, teenagers from Cassopolis and Marcellus and Dowagiac, passers-through and eco-freaks and political junkies and confused kids who didn't know what they were, just that they needed relief from life in Cass County. It was a private farm but a public refuge, with an espresso machine, two pool tables, a jukebox and what Tom liked to call "the best coin laundry in the county." Other than a local bar, there was not another place to hang out in the area. The farm was a licensed campground, so anyone who cared to could grab a patch of grass and pitch a tent.

With its nationally advertised hemp festivals and voter registration drives, Rainbow Farm had also become the center for cannabis activism in the state of Michigan. The farm and its employees were founding sponsors of the Personal Responsibility Amendment, an initiative that was close to having enough signatures to get on the ballot in 2002 and behind which the movement to legalize pot in Michigan had surged to new prominence.

This was something Buggy believed in, and he didn't want to see all that work fouled up with guns. When he got back to the Files', Buggy called sheriff Joe Underwood, a big, even-tempered African American man widely respected in the community. They had never talked before. Buggy told the sheriff not to send anyone out to Rainbow Farm, that the fire would burn itself out safely. He told him the men were armed.

Buggy kept this phone call a secret for many months, for fear that others in the community would think him a traitor. But others had made similar phone calls.

Scott Teter was the prosecuting attorney for Cass County. At one thirty p.m. on August 31, Grover Thomas Crosslin and Roland Eugene Rohm were due in county court for a hearing with Teter where it would be decided whether or not they'd have their bail bonds revoked on the drug charges from their May bust. They were scheduled to meet with their lawyer at twelve thirty. They'd never turn up.

Buggy explained, "On my way out, my mind started thinking: If they were taking a stand, if the fire department or law enforcement were to go back there and unintentionally cause a conflict—I was afraid of bloodshed. The farm had done so much for the marijuana movement. But the stand they were making was personal—having been railroaded by Teter. The two issues are the same, but separate."

County Prosecutor Teter sat in his tiny, windowless office that morning in the Cass County courthouse cobbling together the paperwork that would put Tom Crosslin and Rollie Rohm back in jail to await trial. He had more than enough cause to revoke their bond, but for months the news traveling through the briars was that Tom and Rollie weren't coming out. What that would mean was anybody's guess. A protest? A massive occupation led by the Michigan Militia? Whatever it was, Teter could only assume that the last days of Rainbow Farm would be something potentially bad or humiliating for him and his office. Just about everything Crosslin did turned out that way.

As far as he was concerned, he'd given them enough rope. They were supposed to be staying off the weed as one of the provisions of bail, but Tom hadn't even tried. And although Rollie had been attending the drug treatment meetings mandated by the Family Independence Agency as a condition for getting his son Robert back, he was still using. Teter might have let even that go, if Tom and Rollie hadn't attempted to have that pathetic little impromptu hemp festival in August, at which about two dozen people, two of whom were narcs, drank beer and smoked pot.

Teter had also made a big play that week, a heavy-handed move to lock up the situation at Rainbow Farm. He had filed to seize Tom Crosslin's farm under state drug asset forfeiture laws. These civil statutes allowed law enforcement to seize any property—land, houses, farm equipment, cars, including all the stuff in them—used in a drug offense and were originally written to cripple the big-money operations of organized crime. But in the early 1980s, President Ronald Reagan unleashed a feeding frenzy by letting federal, state and local law enforcement agencies keep the profits from seized goods. By the mid-1990s, it had turned into a billion-dollar annual racket nationwide. Fighting these seizures required posting huge bonds, and the civil proceedings were so stacked against the defendents that the property was almost impossible to recover. Most of those subject to forfeiture simply walked away from their property, even if they beat the charges—or even if, as was the case 80 percent of the time, they weren't charged with a crime—simply because reclaiming it was too expensive.

Teter had only to get a judge to sign the forfeiture order and even if Tom and Rollie went free Rainbow Farm would cease to exist. He had been threatening to do it for four years but hadn't had a shred of truly damning evidence. That day, he was going to get it done.

Teter knew Tom's lawyer, Dori Leo, a former prosecutor herself from Kalamazoo County. Her firm, Vlachos & Vlachos, could mount a substantial fight. He also knew that Tom could sell properties to pay for his defense and that he wouldn't go down without a slugfest in court. Tom had been sued, enjoined, arrested, convicted and even jailed a few times and had come out okay. He had ranks of lawyers who handled different matters for him. Teter had gained the upper hand by filing for the forfeiture months before it was expected.

But he was anxious and the office felt it. Teter had dealt with Rainbow Farm nearly every single day since his election in 1996, and even before then, when he was an assistant prosecutor. In his opinion, the rural county's worst problems were child abuse and drinking and drugs, and here were these hillbillies Tom and Rollie promoting marijuana, a Schedule I narcotic under the U.S Controlled Substances Act. Worse, the pair had at least some contact with the Michigan Militia.

Michigan state Attorney General Jennifer Granholm, a Democrat and future governor, had her eye on Rainbow Farm, too. Teter had asked for her help to bring state resources to bear on the place, like state police roadblocks during the festivals and undercover narcs from the SWET— the SouthWest Enforcement Team, also known as the "Dope Team." He had organized a task force devoted to shutting down Rainbow Farm. That task force included Teter; Granholm; Sheriff Underwood and some of his staff; agents of the FBI, the ATF (the U.S. Bureau of Alcohol, Tobacco and Firearms), and the federal Drug Enforcement Administration; the Michigan State Police and county prosecutors from around the state. Teter had played a leadership role on the drug issue and he felt like he had to deliver.

The civil forfeiture suit sat like a bomb on his tiny desk. All he had to do was get Tom and Rollie in front of county judge Mike Dodge without incident.

But he wasn't that lucky. When the phone rang, it was Joe Underwood telling him that Rainbow Farm was burning.

Perhaps the last campers to see the farm before the fires started were David Guest and a man who will be referred to as Jerry Stone. Tom and Rollie had asked them to witness a pair of simple, hand-scrawled wills.

Scratched on a plain piece of printer paper in shaky block uppercase letters, Rollie's will has his name at the top and reads, with no punctuation: "Last will I Roland E. Rohm give my entire estate to Robert Lee Michale [sic] Rohm my son + child everything is now Robert L. M. Rohm to do with as he sees fit to do with"

The paper is dated 8-31-01 and signed on a line next to an X. Below appear the names and signatures of "Witnesses" Jerry Stone and David

M. Guest. It was stamped by the Cass County probate/family court and was accepted as a legal, uncontested will on September 24, 2001.

Tom's is exactly the same, except slightly more hurried. He misspells "Michale" the same way, with evidence of correction, meaning Rollie probably told him to change it, calling him "our son + child." He also gives his entire estate to Robert, right down to the houses in which some of his employees were still living. The boy had just turned twelve in August and had lived on Rainbow Farm since he was four.

Robert had celebrated his recent birthday in foster care. Prosecutor Teter and county probate judge Sue Dobrich had ordered the Family Independence Agency to remove him from his middle school classroom on the day the farm had been raided in May. This was questionable and far from routine: Marijuana cases were not regularly found to meet state criteria for "abuse and neglect." In Robert's absence, the mood on the farm grew dark and explosive.

Jerry Stone, a gay man in his fifties who was a friend of both Tom and Rollie and of former manager Doug Leinbach, drove the wills to Sharon Keener, Tom's friend and secretary for more than a dozen years, who lived in Elkhart. Keener notarized them.

David Guest was only eighteen when he witnessed the wills. He was a friendly and perhaps troubled kid from the village of Jones who smoked weed as a kind of prophylactic against harder drugs and who, like Omar and Vanessa, Travis, Nikki, two travelers named Shayla Salzman and Casey Brown, a longtime camper and farm supporter named Hippie, Rainbow Richie, and scores of others who came and went, hovered around the farm because it offered a sense of hope.

On that Friday, they all blew around the county like birds in a tornado. Omar and Nessa vanished and reappeared, driving up and down the county roads, not knowing what to do. They stopped at the trailer in Cassopolis owned by Omar's mom, Nancy Bugajski, and stood on the lawn clutching one another, sobbing. The man who lived in the neighboring trailer came out and teased them, "Y'all stop that." They took to the roads again.

On Thursday night, Tom had written around the gas cap of Omar's car: "The rainbow lives in all of us." Rollie had written: "Live free, die young, keep the spirit alive" and "Rainbow Farm lives in your heart."

Jimbo had scrawled on the rear bumper: "If you can read this you're too fucking close. Back up."

They passed by friends in Elkhart. Finally, they ended up at the home of Omar's older sister, Shimaa Bugajski in Cassopolis. She said their mother was in a panic and they needed to go home. Omar called there and asked if something was wrong, and Omar's mom said, "Well, watch the news."

Tom held a Ruger mini-14 identical to Rollie's by the stock, watching for desecrators, for defilers, for the first flashes of paperwork waved by an army of clerks coming to take his farm away. Nothing moved. Tom, Rollie and Jimbo all predicted that the cops would put a spotter on the highest point on the property, the hill directly south of the house, which festivalgoers had christened with a little wooden sign that read Mount This. The farm's own Peace Police had put a camp up there during shows for the same reason—it provided a view of Pemberton Road in both directions and it overlooked the house.

Rollie and Jimbo stood in the house watching the TV news. Fire trucks and squad cars amassed at a roadblock where Pemberton met Black Street a mile away. Jimbo was nervous about whether or not he should stay. He had a wife and two kids living in Cassopolis, and he'd already had a string of trouble in his life. Thai Stick paced and would not settle.

Worry tended to drive Rollie into resolute silence, but Tom was the exact opposite; he was coming out of his skin. One thing he did not abide well was waiting. He preferred driving, driving and talking, lighting out in his tired 1976 Rolls Royce or in Big Red, his Ford F-350 diesel crew cab four-by-four pickup with the cap on the back. He'd run any errand just for the drive, going the long way down back roads, seeking out tractors bearing For Sale signs, stopping at estate sales and asking the people gathered there what else they'd heard was going on, where the action was. Across Big Red's rear cap window would be the slogan from his latest hempfest adorned with pot leaves professionally applied by a sign company in Elkhart that traded him the service for ten festival tickets. That's the way Tom preferred to do business: face-to-face, having fun.

Tom snatched up the Ruger and called to the dog. He stopped in the doorway and made sure there was a round in the chamber, then stepped out to take a look around. The pump house and a series of small wooden cabins were burning, too. Choking black smoke poured like a funnel cloud into the gloaming noon. But just beyond the smoke, the sun lay warm as ever on the pond and the high bank of woods.

Growing up in Elkhart and the flatlands of Indiana, this feral, glacier-scarred bit of Michigan wilderness was full of possibilities to Tom. On the map it's a green zone, a staggered cluster of ranger-station colors indicating state game areas—mostly sprawling swamps and protected hardwood breaks. On Cass County's intermittent high prairie, agriculture is king, but everywhere else it's camp country, a place of homespun resorts and pine cabins and weedy lakes where city girls got out of their clothes and into bikinis and cigarettes and beer. There was a time when it was all about those girls for Tom, but it had always been about the boys who chased them, too. People like himself vacationed here, working-class people, lots of them with heavy accents from Kentucky and Tennessee and southern Indiana. Though Michigan is a heavily populated state, the eighth highest in the nation, Cass County is dotted mostly with farms and tiny crossroads towns built around gas stations and generic ciggies. The county sits in the southwest corner of the state, just beyond the heavy industrial zone of Gary, Indiana, and the megalopolis of Chicago. It's an unassuming resort area with small-time RV parks and lake cottages where snowmobiles and Jet Skis could be run, white-tailed deer could be killed or guns shot regardless, and Bibles could be cracked in relative seclusion.

The names of the dozen or so camps and retreats held the promise of Native American fantasy and hot nights in musty pine bunkhouses: Wakeshma, Tamarack, Tannadoonah, Sun Chi Win. But, increasingly, the trend was toward Bible camps. The biggest one in the county was Friedenwald, a sprawling complex founded by the Mennonite Church in 1951 on remote Shavehead Lake, named after the fierce Potowatomi leader who burned the village of Chicago. Carved out of the woods nearby were Camp Manitou of the Communities of Christ, Camp Wagner of the Seventh Day Adventists, Bair Lake Bible Camp (nondenominational), the YMCA's Camp Eberhart and Living Waters Camp vacation Bible school. Just three or four miles down M-60 to the east of the farm were Camelot and Rogers Resort campgrounds, reposed on the same chain of swampy lakes that ran through Tom's property. The 2000 census found only 51,104 residents in Cass County, but in the summer the population could easily double with the influx of the lake resort crowd.

Rainbow Farm offered something different, a place for people who wanted a vacation where they could freak freely. Tom had always said about it: "This is a place about alternative lifestyles. Being gay is just one of 'em. Smoking pot is just one of 'em. There's a bunch more, and this is a place where people can be free."

This is what separated Tom Crosslin's progressive beliefs from the communitarianism that has come to represent American political life on both the right and the left. He didn't believe in sacrificing some rights, like the right to smoke weed, just for the good of the community. His property rights were an absolute. On this point he would not compromise, and when people were on his property they could do as they pleased. People had to learn to live like adults who could be trusted with their freedoms, no matter how uncomfortable those freedoms made others.

But the state—and Teter—had a more limited view of his rights. Juddering in the ground under his boots, he could feel the heavy knocking of an approaching helicopter.

Not many people knew where to find Doug Leinbach that Friday morning. The forty-seven-year-old former banker had sold his father's house only two days before and moved to a new set of rooms. He'd hung up his photo of The Band from *The Last Waltz*, but he didn't even have phone service yet. Someone banged on the door around eleven a.m.

Standing on the stoop was Jerry Stone in a state of visible distress.

"I have to talk to you about these," said Jerry, walking in holding two sheets of printer paper.

"Whatcha got there," asked Doug, taking them. They were the wills Jerry and David had witnessed an hour earlier. Doug had to fight to get his breath. Everything with Tom had always been symbolic—a hemp festival was a representation of the right to assemble and petition the government, an angry tirade against the government was an exercise of free speech, a gun was a show of support for the Second Amendment. It had all become real in the space of thirty-six hours—the angry tirade, the threats, the gun.

"I don't know what to do," said Jerry.

"What did Tom tell you to do?" Doug drawled in his nasal Indiana accent.

"He told me to take these to Sharon to get them notarized and then get 'em to Joe Grolimund, and only to Joe."

Grolimund was one of Tom's lawyers, his gay lawyer and the one who'd handled the custody battle for little Robert.

"Well, then that's exactly what you're gonna do," said Doug after a minute. "Tom told me he was going to do this. These are for Robert, and if something happens on that farm and we haven't taken care of this, it's on our heads."

"There was more, though," said Jerry, starting to weep. He relayed all the things Tom and Rollie had told him. It became clear that Rollie was staying with Tom.

Jerry was breaking down. He'd never been entrusted with anything like this before. Doug wept with him, and the two old friends held each other. Doug, an openly gay man, understood that Jerry was badly conflicted about this whole situation. Jerry had deep reservations about being identified with Rainbow Farm and yet, there was his signature on the will. There was no getting out of it now. His only choices were to destroy them and dishonor his friend or file them and face the consequences. For him, personally, those could be relatively severe. To many people, including his own mother, he was closeted. She was a religious conservative and held the purse strings to an inheritance that could one day come his way. He was staring at a document that might be his undoing.

After talking for an hour, Jerry came to the decision himself; he had to get these papers to Sharon and Joe. Doug didn't push him, but he was fiercely protective of Robert and he could think of plenty of scenarios where the boy would be left with nothing if they didn't act. Even at that moment, for instance, Robert's mother, Leslie, was living week to week with her trucker boyfriend at the Weston Plaza Hotel, a few miles away alongside Interstate 80. Tom and Rollie knew that if Robert were to inherit anything, at least the boy would have a fighting chance to do better than that.

Jerry left and Doug stayed at the apartment. If for any reason Rollie were to turn up, he wanted to be there. There might be a frenzied drive to the Canadian border or even to Mexico. He turned on the TV. Channel 16, WNDU, had it on the news at noon. As he watched in horror, the dream he'd worked for years to finance and build went up in flames in the shaky aerial shot from a circling news helicopter. The TV reporter kept talking about how no one had talked with the occupants, but that "they were apparently mad because of drug charges."

"You don't know the half of it, you stupid bitch," he said to the TV. Nor did he trust they would ever get the real story.

At about one p.m. he peeked through the blinds to see an unusual sedan across the street, a plainclothes cop. He hadn't even registered his change of address yet with the post office or the DMV. Only his old bank, where he'd deposited the check for the sale of his dad's house the day before and where the tellers all knew him by sight had his new address.

One of the tellers may have dropped a dime on him. Didn't that just beat all. He could imagine the phone call: "One of those farm people was just in here yesterday and deposited a big check." This was illegal, of course, but welcome to small town U.S.A. For the next five days, a cop followed him everywhere.

Omar and Nessa watched the news at Omar's mom's. The farm was burning but some parts looked the same as ever. The big metal pole building that housed the store and The Joint, where they'd partied the night before, was still standing, along with the house and Jimbo's trailer. Rollie's lemon yellow 2000 Volkswagen Beetle was standing in the parking lot.

They wondered if they should tell anyone who was in the remaining buildings, how Tom and Rollie and Jimbo were armed, how the place was booby-trapped and, as Tom had told them, "rigged to blow." They didn't know how to carry this information silently, and it wore at them; maybe telling someone would help keep their friends alive.

The pair talked a bit with Omar's mother without telling her what they knew, just long enough to realize that she wouldn't understand.

When they went outside to get some air, the neighbor was there. "Man, your boy is going nuts," he said. "He done shot a helicopter. Is that what you were boo-hooing about this morning?"

Omar told him, "Yeah, that's it. We knew he was gonna go."

The neighbor continued, "Man, he's not getting out of this one. They done got the ATF, the FBI, the Special Forces out there now."

The helicopter's urgent drumming came closer as Tom walked away from his burning pump house. Embers rained down on the grass amid the RV sites.

Teter wouldn't get his buildings, wouldn't sell them to finance more of his SWET narcs. But Tom's whole identity was wrapped up in them, too. What was left grew more hollow as it burned, a shell. Every moment he had less and less to lose.

Before he got to taking down the camp store, he'd go take one quick look from the top of Mount This. He tromped down the main gravel drive and up through the grass, past the house where Jim and Rollie sat, and across the back lawn. Down a two-track into the trees was a depot crowded with blue recycling barrels in a hollow alongside the road. A line of blaze orange No Trespassing signs were visible in the woods, marching up the steep hill. Tom was sweating in his full camo by the time he reached the top. About ten yards into the dense undergrowth was a rock fire pit where his festival security used to camp. He could hear radios crackle and bark far off, but nothing moved. Tom stood in the keening hush of leaf rustle and tree-frog drill and whip-poor-will moan and watched the emptiness of the road. He knew every creeping grapevine on this spot, every flowering dogwood lurching sideways for a slice of sun shot through the dark canopy.

Suddenly, the helicopter slapped across the treetops overhead, a blue and yellow four-passenger that felt like it was only a few feet from the leaves. He jumped as it whapped into a banked turn over the store, obviously there to look at the farm. He shook off the electric shudder of adrenaline and tried to focus on the chopper. It could be cops. It looked like cops. He stopped where he stood and watched it, fingers tightening around the Ruger. It was the highest spot on the farm, and he'd always had a special feeling about it. It was the exact spot on which he would die.

TWO The Marijuana Capital of America

SONNY: [*patting down FBI man*] You'd like to kill me. Betcha would.

SHELDON: I wouldn't like to kill you. I will if I have to.

SONNY: It's your job, right? You know, the guy who kills me, I hope he does it 'cause he hates my guts. Not 'cause it's his job.

—**Al Pacino and James Broderick in** Dog Day Afternoon

THE SHOOTINGS IN VANDALIA smelled funny the moment I read about them on the cover of the *Kalamazoo Gazette*. The September 9, 2001, Sunday subscription edition arrived at my house in California, and there was the cover photo of Rollie's stepdad, John Livermore, walking past the burned shell of Rollie's Volkswagen under the headline quote: "It Just Doesn't Make Sense."

I'd never heard of Rainbow Farm before that day. I'd grown up just twenty-five miles north of there, in an area surrounded by vineyards outside the rural village of Mattawan, but left Michigan just before the farm was established. Still, something about the information in the piece didn't add up. Here were two gay guys, rich by local standards, real estate minimagnates, philanthropists, Republicans, pillars of the community even, and they had figured their only recourse was an armed standoff with police? Over weed? And they weren't dealers? Even more bizarre, the FBI and the Michigan State Police had taken them off with snipers hidden in the trees.

Even the cant of the piece was weird: The *Gazette* is hardly a liberal paper anymore—it endorsed Bush both in 2000 and 2004, reflecting the increasingly Christian conservative electorate in the area—and yet the lead quote in reporter Barb Walters's story came from a retired postmaster of Cassopolis, a Korean War vet, saying, "The authorities overreacted. I think they could have handled it more diplomatically. The case was not that serious." The piece expressed a conservative anger, captured in quotes from Livermore, a self-proclaimed religious conservative. When it was brought up that Tom and Rollie had grown marijuana in their basement, Livermore was quoted as saying, "But do you shoot somebody for that?"

No, actually, you don't. Even from 2,000 miles away it stunk.

The Mattawan, Michigan, I grew up in was the marijuana capital of America. Not because my friends and neighbors there were growing that much pot in 1970s and '80s. It's not like the Daniel Boone National Forest in Kentucky or Mendocino County, California, where folks grow so much dope they post signs pleading with growers not to shoot at the crop dusters. It was just a place where people smoked a lot of weed, and the conservative position was that it wasn't the government's business if you did. Now, evidently, little Vandalia, Michigan, population 429, had taken the crown.

And the cops still don't give a damn—not about pot smokers. At least, that's what they say, even at this advanced stage of the War on Drugs. When I talked to Captain Charles Bush, the avuncular division commander of the Michigan State Police Criminal Investigation Division out of Lansing, part of whose job it is to reduce the supply of pot in Michigan he told me: "In all my years in the state police, I can honestly say I don't know of a single case where we busted someone, and they went to jail, for simple possession." He went on, eyes twinkling over his gray mustache, "They're *pleading down* to possession. It would have to be for something more."

So I got on the phone to *Gazette* reporter Barb Walters and she told me, yeah, there was more to the story. "And if the editors hadn't pulled me away to deal with all this 9/11 stuff, I'd still be down there," she said.

By the time that *Gazette* had reached L.A., there was nobody on the Rainbow Farm story anymore. Tons of TV had been out there—CNN, Fox, and locals led by WNDU-TV out of South Bend—and the papers and wire services, too—*Detroit News*, Associated Press. *Rolling Stone* even had a guy on it. But two days after that Sunday edition had come out was September 11, 2001, the day Saudi terrorists crashed commercial airliners into the World Trade Center, the Pentagon, and a field in Pennsylvania. It was, in fact, the day of Rollie Rohm's funeral.

September 11 flipped the script on Tom Crosslin. In the space of one day, his superpatriotic stance, which he saw as fulfilling the charge of the Constitution to defend liberty from the tyranny of bureaucrats, was splashed with the fear of terrorism. At that point, it meant something different to be a rural guy with a gun who gets killed by FBI snipers. Almost every publication dropped the story. All except for the *South Bend Tribune* and the Elkhart *Truth*.

But Rainbow Farm's story didn't have anything to do with terrorism— it was a forfeiture case, and an ugly one. Abuse of the forfeiture statute was so rampant in the mid-1990s that it was almost inevitable that sooner or later some regular guys like Tom and Rollie would resist giving up their property. But their protest had descended into violence. Which might explain why NORML, the National Organization for the Reform of Marijuana Laws, was e-mailing news blasts about Rainbow Farm, but neither NORML's head, Keith Stroup, nor anyone from other big drug advocacy groups like the Drug Policy Alliance or the Marijuana Policy Project were winging into Vandalia to be on TV.

I continued to try to get a read on the story and it continued to be muddied. The community seemed to support Tom and Rollie. Protestors had mobbed the place even while the standoff was going on. The *Tribune*'s big Sunday headline read: "More Questions Than Answers At Rainbow Farm." One of AP's wire stories led with: "Standoff Duo Recalled as

Peace Loving." A *Detroit Free Press* header read: "To Them, There Was No Out." Their Hemp Aid 2001 pot fair was still listed in the *Tribune's* summer festival guide.

They didn't sound like two guys who should get shot to death. I grew up in the Michigan woods; out there, you had to bother a lot of people to earn yourself a police sniper's bullet. But Tom and Rollie's farm was isolated; they hadn't bothered anyone—and even people who didn't care for Rainbow Farm said so. Yet there it was in the paper: Two of the state's best-known, peace-preaching potheads shot to death at their wannabe Woodstock. It rang with a kind of moral dissonance. It is one of the hallmarks of our larger identity as Americans that an abuse of power precipitates a crisis of faith. Such a crisis threatened to seize Cass County. This self-doubt became corrosive—what Allen St. Pierre from NORML accurately described as "rust," a slow decay of trust rather than a swift criminal demolition, an outward evidence of loss of integrity.

It was easy to follow the rust: It spiraled up like a funnel cloud of rumors looking for a place to touch down. One of those rumors, for instance, held that Tom and Rollie had been big-time weed dealers, using their sizable hidden profits to hire big names like Tommy Chong and to fuel Tom's penchant for impulse buys like his Rolls Royce or his Jaguar. Then there was the story that they had a ".50 caliber machine gun" and had the farm "booby-trapped," or had a militia that would come to their aid if summoned. Folks heard there were tunnels from the farm to the Bonine Mansion about four miles away on M-60, a stately 1840s manor house that Tom also owned. Or that amid the gay porn found in the house was evidence of a sex-death scheme. Or that Brandon Peoples, an eighteen-year-old neighbor kid, had been pressured by the FBI to walk the farm owner into a crossfire.

But there was no touching down, because none of this speculation turned out to be true. When the *Washington Post* picked up the story in January, Peter Carlson's piece ran with the headers: "Reefer Madness; Marijuana Advocates Tom Crosslin and Rollie Rohm Sensed the Government

Was Out To Get Them. And Then They Were Dead. Was Rainbow Farm Another Waco?"

Carlson decided that it really wasn't another Waco, and I did, too. The name *Waco* popped up in the local papers for months, but it just didn't track. Something else was going on.

What had really happened was that rural conservatives had begun speaking out against the War on Drugs, and two of the loudest had gotten themselves killed. The attitudes hadn't changed much since I'd lived there, but the consequences of the drug war—the forfeiture statutes, the mandatory minimum sentences, the intrusion—had escalated to the point where the old social contracts were breaking down. This war had drawn out the silent rural dwellers who were allergic to politics and reporters and hubbub. The shootings were the result of an uprising of the intensely private people of rural Michigan and Indiana, and their awkward, slightly embarrassed first foray into public activism.

As I began to interview them, it became clear that something had changed in the greasy blue-collar boonies that were central to my own identity. Plain old cannabis had transcended its middle-finger status to become an organizing principle for a real, honest-to-god movement that blurred all political and even religious lines. Thousands of people against the drug war had gathered at Rainbow Farm—Republicans, Democrats, Libertarians, Greens, New Agers, Buddhists, born-agains, Militiamen, UFO enthusiasts, local mayors, police officers, people who called themselves things like The Wood Bitches and Buzz Daily and Cockroach—the vast majority of them responsible adults with children and businesses and churches. Just as the Vietnam War became a central focus for reform movements of the 1960s and '70s, from civil rights to drugs to the new left to radical feminism, the hemp festivals at Rainbow Farm had become a catch-all for discontent. The partiers there were upset about the decay of privacy and property rights and about urine testing in the factories of Elkhart. A lot of them were people with medical conditions like glaucoma and multiple sclerosis and epilepsy who felt they had to fight the pharmaceutical companies to get cannabis restored to them as medicine. They were upset that industrial hemp was illegal even though you couldn't get high off it and it was a potential solution to a raft of environmental troubles. They were against corporate globalism. They were incensed that their government was treating them like infants. Somehow, in the nonsensical and false climate of red-vs.-blue politics, the potent symbol of all their disparate anger was weed.

And Rainbow Farm was minuscule compared to what was going on elsewhere. Every summer the Seattle Hemp Fest drew up to 150,000 people. Another 100,000 in Boston. And tens of thousands in Washington, D.C. There were scores of these "hempenings" across the country every year. Was anyone in Washington listening?

Tom Crosslin wasn't their hero. His was only the worst-case scenario that proved the drug war was out of control. This was the story of two activists who pushed the limits of the First Amendment, who tried to legalize pot through a ballot initiative and ended up losing their rights, all their money, their land, their kid and, finally, their lives. Right there in the marijuana capital of America.

The people left behind were scared. In one of my first interviews, a woman who had a lot of experience with Cass County's foster care system explained how the county could now legally take children from loving homes where the parents smoked weed. I told her I could relate to this fear, since I had an infant son. Unprompted, she immediately started telling me what do when Child Protective Services came to my door. I held up my hands, explaining that marijuana really wasn't my bag. "That doesn't matter," she said. "You're part of this now."

THREE The Office of America

The office of America is to liberate.

—*Ralph Waldo Emerson*

MORNINGS AT THE KC Pizza and Grill, the residents of tiny Jones, Michigan, could be found hunched over a long table stirring the news of the day into their coffee. A small TV yarbled above the cash register, evolving slowly throughout the day from morning talk to soap operas. The sheet-metal diner looked like it had once been a service station, with tables set up in the former repair bay. Scale model electric trains ran on tracks fixed to shelves above the dining room. The regulars were there when the windows ran with air-conditioner condensation in the hissing green of summer and those who didn't snowbird down in Florida or Arizona were there when they were banked with hard blue snow by Michigan's arctic winter wind.

The coffee pot was controlled by owner Rebecca Kitner, a pensive woman with heavy-lidded eyes and a low, softly commanding voice. She had owned the place for six years in 2001, and was still there in 2005, a fairly long run for a rural business dependent on whatever comes down the two-lane blacktop of M-60. It could be tough to make a living off a one-dollar cup of coffee that lasts three hours. There used to be more business before Rainbow Farm closed.

"Tom and Rollie came in here for years," said Kitner, pouring a cup of coffee. "Most people didn't know who they were when they come in to eat here. They didn't try to press their opinions on anybody. They wanted to be let alone."

Rainbow Farm was located about equidistant between Jones and Vandalia, and though Vandalia was the bigger village and had a more formal bar-restaurant called Kulesia's, it didn't have a diner anymore after Joe's Bar burned down. Tom and Rollie sometimes brought a crew of a dozen or more to KC Pizza for breakfast, often including campers. On a bright, warm Indian summer day in the November following the shootings, the mostly older gentlemen at the big table refused to comment on Rainbow Farm with a polite dip of the head. One of them rose, saying, "Well, I got to get back to the house," and grabbed his jacket.

"Let's go outside," Kitner said. "A lot of people don't know what to say, because they aren't for drugs or homosexuality, but they don't like what happened, either."

Kitner's son and coowner, Jerry Cocanower, a man in his thirties with dark hair and features, was outside splitting wood. "Some of us around here hated to see it end like that," he said. "Those two shouldn't be dead. Most of the people who don't want to talk about it never been up there." Cocanower had bought a brand new pizza truck in 2000, at Tom's urging, primarily to make deliveries to the festivals at Rainbow Farm. There had been four big gatherings that year and business had boomed.

The KC sits not far from a building used by the Newberg Township volunteer fire department. Cocanower motioned toward it and noted that the township would run an ambulance up to the M-40 Raceway on weekends and out to Swiss Valley ski area in nearby Marcellus, but they refused to provide ambulance service to Rainbow Farm. Tom offered to donate money to the fire department, but the trustees wouldn't take it.

Tom had tried to bring the community around one person at a time to appreciating his rights. "Tom sat in here one day with the owner of Swiss Valley and said, 'Come up for free and see Merle Haggard,' " said Kitner. "He didn't go up there because he didn't want to have no stigma on him. He was real nice, listened to him, but he never did go."

This, said Kitner, is the country way. Try not to let anything touch you. Avoid anything that muddies feelings or beliefs that were once clear.

"They were going to force people to make a decision about what they believed, in how free people should be, and they didn't like it. They'd rather not make that decision. They'd rather just have them gone and be done with it."

Jerry noted, however, that letting a moral or legal question go unsettled doesn't make it go away and that the people who don't say anything might be afraid of sounding like they supported gays and drugs, or the flipside, might be afraid of sounding like a bigot who thought Tom and Rollie deserved what they got. But mostly they were just afraid. The total violence unleashed against Rainbow Farm threatened everyone.

"There's murderers that get less than what these guys got," he said. "Just because people are doing something on their property that you can't control, that's no reason to kill them and take what's theirs. What's the limit, then, of what they can do?"

Whether or not Tom knew much about the area before moving to the farm, hardcore little Vandalia, Michigan, had been a remote outpost for resistance politics and church activism for over 150 years. The village today is little more than a flashing yellow caution light on M-60 where the road dips down to Christiana Creek. There's the Marathon station, officially named the 7 Days Expressmart but usually called Mr. D's after the old owner; Kulesia's restaurant; an old wooden church on Mill Street that's been converted into a pumpkin orange Buddhist temple; a tiny hunting and fishing store and one hundred or so wood-frame houses, some of them nice examples of prairie Victorian. In the shaded and halcyon otiosity of summer, it's Mayberry all over, an overgrowth of massive maples and old asphalt shingles and derelict Americana. In winter, it's a kind of frozen purgatory of woodsmoke and plastic-covered windows and the discarded stubs from used foodstamp booklets.

Of the 429 residents, more than half are African American, the direct legacy of the Underground Railroad. During and after the Civil War, Vandalia wasn't only a stop on the railroad, it was a terminus, and just beyond where the houses sat was once an entire village called Ramp Town, populated by hundreds of freed slaves.

Freemen and runaway slaves and ex-slaves who'd been freed by the war made their way to Vandalia, and Cass County in general, because they had been welcomed there by land-owning Quaker abolitionists who fiercely defended the pacifism and racial equality espoused by their religion.

The radical history of the county was not lost on Tom after he settled there. He devoured stories about the Underground Railroad and was proud to buy into it when he bought the Bonine Mansion, which had been used to hide runaway slaves. This became part of his deep connection to Vandalia and his friendship with black, five-term mayor Sondra Mose-Ursery, an advocate who helped organize Vandalia's Underground Railroad Museum.

In 1902, educator and black historian Booker T. Washington traveled to Cass County to make a study of a "self-governing community of colored people." His resulting essay, "Two Generations Under Freedom," detailed, farm by farm, the legacy of the Underground Railroad that terminated in the boggy woods around Rainbow Farm.

The family histories of Cass County are pretty well documented, beginning with Zaccheus Wooden, a nineteen-year-old white trapper who wandered through the St. Joseph River country beginning in 1813. He worked the county for two years and only encountered one other white resident, a French trapper named John Kabeau, living with an Indian wife close to what is now Edwardsburg. This was Potowatomi country then, an Algonquin word meaning "People of the Fire" or "Nation of Fire," settled by one of three bands called the Potowatomi of the Woods. Indian villages lay scattered all about the lower end of Lake Michigan, including Pokagon, which stood in Cass County. But the Potowatomi were quickly ceding land and by the 1830s would be removed altogether to a reservation in Kansas.

Among the early colonizers arriving in the fledgling territory in the 1830s were Quakers who had pulled up stakes in the south because, according to Washington, "they did not approve of slavery." Word went out that they would aid slaves on the run, and beginning in 1840, a few escapees began appearing in Calvin and Porter townships, just south of Vandalia. Most of these came from Kentucky, and in 1847 the stream had become such a flood that a well-armed posse rode up from Kentucky to retrieve their property. The local Quakers, blacks, and white settlers were infuriated by this incursion and ran the posse out of town. This established Cass County's reputation as a haven.

Washington came to the area in 1902 because it was one of the first thriving new post Civil–War communities of free blacks. He had been told about it by black workers at the Studebaker wagon factory in South Bend, who said they sold to black farmers in Cass County who were as prosperous as any whites.

In fact, they were more prosperous. In the year of Washington's visit, the biggest taxpayer in Calvin Township was a black man. Black families owned spreads of five hundred acres and were worth as much as fifty thousand dollars. They owned threshing machines, managed banks and ran the local government. Outstanding to Washington was that one community took forty copies of the daily newspaper.

By the time Tom Crosslin came to Cass County, in 1993, Vandalia and Cassopolis had large black populations but the areas were depressed. Kids liked to call it "Cash County," because as farmers sold out and populations expanded out of South Bend and Elkhart there was an influx of new McMansions. But this trend had yet to fully reach Vandalia. According to the 2000 census, 20 percent of the homes in the village had no telephone service. About 15 percent of the people lived below the poverty line. There were a few wealthy folks in town, but the average annual full-time income for men was twenty-eight thousand dollars.

In Vandalia, the radical legacy of the Underground Railroad mingled with some different kinds of resistance. One was a type of rump hillbilly culture, with blaze orange as its flag, lobbing empty beer cans at the encroaching suburbia. The other was a growing string of church camps strung throughout the county. Both bred a deep sense of remove from city life. People like Tom Crosslin, and eventually his dad, Pops, and his brother, Jim, moved to Vandalia for exactly that reason.

Jim Crosslin never went to the war his older brother, Larry, fought in Vietnam; it came to him. The helicopters that buzzed his house in Vandalia seemed like a paranoid hallucination, but they were real. We were standing on the asphalt apron between the house and his barn in November 2001 when one came over, made a big hammering turn over the treetops and buzzed us again. In a half-dozen visits I made to the house during those first years after Tom was killed, the choppers were there on two occasions. Jim said that, for a while, they came every day. They'd make this same loop over the house. They were not news helicopters, and as far as I could make out not marked as police. If they were national guard or federal ships—I never could trace them—they went far out of their way to get to Vandalia.

One of the first times they came, Jim was standing in a mowed patch of yard on the back of his property; there were men in the helicopter who looked like soldiers sitting in the open doors on either side of it. The copter came so close that both Jim and his wife, Miriame, could see their faces, men dressed in camo, holding rifles. Jim pulled his pants down and waved his dick at them.

"I work hard. I *am* the citizen here. I pay my taxes. I support this community. But I'll *die* before I'll let them come up here and take my place, too," sputtered Jim, fixing me in an angry stare.

The deep grouse beat of the copter's rotors faded into the distance after swinging over Jim's place, an aging two-story farmhouse that he had about half remodeled. His was a tidy piece of wooded hilltop on five acres just a quarter-mile across a creek bottom from Vandalia. The helicopter added a certain hyperreal boost to Indian summer, with a hard yellow and crimson in the maples, and the oaks in the big woods behind going to red. The whole world smelled of pigs and burning leaves.

All Jim had done with his life was work and raise a family, and it showed. He was a barrel-chested, if somewhat diminished man of forty-nine when we met. He'd stood clutching a Busch beer in clawlike hands covered in scar tissue layered on by years of physical labor. His eyes and mouth looked like Tom's, though his features had grown sharper where Tom's had stayed rounded. His stringy hair was graying and he had a little bit of a stoop; a few years earlier, he'd broken his back in a fall off the roof. He was the middle brother, and had little time to get involved in politics or growing pot or anything outside of a few turkey shoots or Saturday nights at the car races in Jones. Both he and Miriame had worked for over thirty years in Elkhart's RV and mobile home factories and they were proud of this house.

"A white plane comes over low, too," said Jim.

"They ain't lookin' for pot," said Miriame. "They cut the engines. They stall right over the house."

"God, it's so aggravating, what they're doing to us," Jim seethed.

Their son, Boss, pulled up in his truck and joined the conversation. Then twenty-two, he had short hair slicked to his head and baggy jeans, a country raver aesthetic. He was named after his great-grandfather, the late Boss Crosslin, Grover Sr.'s dad, from Manchester, Tennessee.

Just across the creek, on a half-acre pond, was Grover Sr.'s house, a clean prefab job. Jim and Miriame had been living there for six years in 2001, Grover and his second wife, Mae, a little less. They came out from Elkhart, like lots of other people, to be close to Tom. That's the way it was; wherever Tom went, that's where everybody wanted to be. Tom was the schemer, the fixer. He had a vision for the way he wanted to live, and a knack for making it a material reality. For instance, he scored Jim's garage in a trade—a nice metal pole barn—and gave it to his brother. Tom left that kind of stuff in his wake.

He also left a certain amount of good-natured mayhem. The Crosslin boys had grown up with a kind of brotherly affection for the

fuzz—indeed, many Elkhart cops and sheriff's deputies were their run-
nin' buddies. Tom had bought the farm from a cop, and a fair number
of cops went to Rainbow Farm festivals out of uniform.

But in the end, Tom had been killed by federal agents, and a lot of that
goodwill dried up. Unmarked sedans sat on the road out in front of Jim's
house for months—purposely conspicuous Crown Victorias and other
classic cop sedans in dull colors, the only car sitting on an empty stretch
of country road next to the cattails. The cars had followed them all to
work, and followed Boss to community college and back home again.

Cass County had slapped aside Tom's well-known public persona as
though only the technicalities of misdemeanor pot smoking mattered,
and were a matter of life and death. Jim blamed the Edwardsburg local
who ruined the old rural code, who destroyed the love between the
cops and the people, Scott Teter.

"I don't want to ever *see* that son of a bitch," he spat. "When this gets
to the federal courts, that's when people are going to find out what's
really going on in this county. When I'm done with that son of a
bitch"—he spat again—"he won't even be able to sell popcorn. Ha ha!
He won't even be able to sell popcorn."

FOUR Occult On Wheels

ELKHART, INDIANA, IN 1973 was a leafy mill town of a certain meanness. The war was on in Vietnam, a culture war was raging in the streets and there had been race riots in the schools. If you didn't want to get your ass kicked on the town's working-class south side, you were friends with the Crosslin household on Homer Avenue. Because the Crosslin boys lived to fight. The Crosslin men—Grover "Pops" Crosslin and his boys Larry, Jim, and Grover Thomas, who went by Tom—would fist fight strangers and friends alike in the bars on Friday nights, fight each other in the basement while trading pink slips for cars or listening to the stereo and fight Pops when he tried to keep them in line. Pops ruled the house, but by that summer he didn't challenge the boys anymore; they were too big and too committed to battle. For a little while they ran like a pack.

The cops were always around, and one time that winter they were looking for Tom. He had just turned nineteen and was managing a car wash. Tom's main business then was trading cars, flipping them for cash or barter. Like all four of the Crosslin kids, including his younger sister, Shirley, he'd dropped out of Elkhart High School at sixteen and gone to work. But he didn't approach it exactly like the rest. "Tom wasn't one for manual labor," said Jim's wife, Miriame, who'd known the boys pretty much all her life. "He was always trying to figure out the easiest and the best way of makin' money. Don't get me wrong, though, he did work. They all did."

Tom took one look at Pops working himself to death and decided the problem was not being your own boss. For over twenty years, Pops worked the day shift at Elcona, a well-known brand of mobile homes, then nights and weekends at an Elkhart lumberyard called Pre-Cuts. Tom wanted to be on the side writing the checks. He'd had a paper route and worked at entry-level jobs at Pre-Cuts and a couple of area factories, then he got the job managing the car wash.

It's unclear whether he was fired from that job or whether there had been a dispute over hours, but he hadn't been there too long when the owner shorted Tom's check for two weeks' pay. Tom got a gun and got his money. One of the boys he ran with was the son of Elkhart's chief of police, and Tom reportedly traded the kid a big sack of weed for one of his dad's .38 revolvers. The clerk at the gas station, who knew Tom perfectly well, since it was the gas station attached to the car wash, peeled off the exact amount Tom was owed, and Tom went home with it.

"That's all he took, too, was what they owed him," said Miriame.

"Yep, the chief of police was out at the house, he was wantin' that gun back," laughed Jim. "We come out and there were fifteen or so of 'em, and these guys were pretty well armored, well enough anyway, so they knew the Crosslin name.

"He got six months out of it."

He was convicted of felony armed robbery—later changed to Robbery By Fear—but didn't actually serve much time. Tom got ten months work release, and was back on the street flashing his impish grin. It wasn't the last time he'd have a boss, but it was a good indication of what was to come. It also wasn't the last time he'd be in jail.

The mobile home and RV factories were booming and there was money and dope around. Any line worker who thought he could open a trailer company did so; what the locals call "mafia" money was readily available and underworld connections were only a handshake or two away. Trailer companies would be launched running three shifts, and some would go under just as quickly. The Crosslin boys were boomtown scavengers. They had a line on most everything moving. They were trying to get their share of kicks, and it was a fairly fat share. The Crosslins knew which plants were hiring, where you could get a deal on a set of Cherry Bombs for your Mustang, who to talk to about weed or acid, whose girl was available and who was fighting at the bar. The cops were always there to drive them home or hold them overnight when it came to that.

Pops had come up from Tennessee to work in the Elkhart factories, and he was a hustler. He always had a deal in play for a car or a horse or a broken-down house. He brought a lot of Tennessee with him—a dirt farmer's work ethic, a certain respect for the evangelical, a hillbilly's comic stoicism—and an ever-growing litany of wild tales delivered on a raft of party songs and cuss and whiskey. Other places, calling someone a "hillbilly" might earn you a beating, but Pops was proud of the word. Pops's mother was a Cherokee whose last name was Bess; his birth name was Grover Bess. She had given him up for adoption, or, rather, he had been taken by his grandparents, who were religious and strict, and adopted out. Pops's adoptive parents, Boss Crosslin and his wife, were farmers. They sent him up to Elkhart ahead of his young wife Ruby and the family in the 1950s. Tom was born November 10, 1954, in the house in Manchester, Tennessee.

Even though Pops was strict with the boys, it was pretty common to see the old man stirring up his own trouble down at the B&B Tavern in Osceola or the One Rainbow on Melbourne; he liked to smoke a little Indian hay and had his own circuit of friends and barkeeps who set a chair out for him. At night after work he'd go home drunk. His wife, Ruby, worked a sewing machine at Camelot, which made awnings for RVs, and put up with the drinking partly because she got her licks in, too. "If she was drinkin' at the bar and she didn't like your look, buddy, she come over and change it for you," said a relative.

The house on Homer Avenue lay just inside the Elkhart city limits, going southeast toward Dunlap and Goshen. Back then, the road dead-ended into open fields. They lived on the wrong side of the tracks, on the south side of Elkhart and the St. Joseph River, a neighborhood with deep working-class roots. Elkhart had its share of old money—pharmaceutical firm Miles Laboratories, now Bayer, was formed there in 1884; the town was also known for musical instruments by C. G. Conn, Selmer, J. J. Babbitt and Gemeinhardt. The founders of these companies and their beneficiaries lived in stone mansions occupying the bluffs high above the north side of the river.

The Homer Avenue place was tiny, a two-bedroom wood-frame box that Pops had refurbished. The three boys slept in one room and Shirley slept in what had been a closet.

In blurry Instamatic prints, the boys sometimes looked like cleaned-up working stiffs, sometimes like the Allman Brothers—hair, sideburns and beards swinging in bellbottom glory. In one Christmas photo, all the Crosslin boys are wearing plaid cowboy-cut Levi's shirts and jeans, hair long, faces shaved. In another, when Tom was riding with a biker club, his hair is longer and he's wearing a full beard. They look happy and tough and utterly enfranchised in the neighborhood, where they were kings.

"I don't know how in the world they ever got four kids in that house," Shirley said. "It was up for sale at one point, and I thought, Well I'm gonna go back and check it out. I didn't realize how tiny it was. It was a two-bedroom house, and I remember sleeping in this little bitty room that was like a closet. And you had to go through that to go to the bathroom. The boys used to drive cars out in the field. They loved that. We had a pony named Trigger."

Theirs was a world made by boys as a living monument to prolonged adolescence. Of course there was a treehouse, and of course it was No Girls Allowed, and one time when Shirley was under it crying her eyes out because they wouldn't let her in, it collapsed and a two-by-four split her head open. It was a homosexual world, in the sense that it was of one sex; their peers were men and their experience was measured by men, and even when there were women around they barely made it into the Christmas pictures. Despite Jim's close relationship with Miriame, which started during the early 1970s and endures today, and the women who often held them all together, the boys' club was a dynamic that would last all their lives.

Pops took the boys deer hunting in the fall, which Tom apparently liked more than the others because he's the only one who carried on with it into the 1990s. They shot one or two whitetails over the years and their share of pheasant, quail and rabbits.

The boys had tons of cars, and some of them were nice, like Jim's Mach 1 Mustang, but most of them were just rides.

"They wasn't really so much into cars for hot rods," explained Wright Spry, a plumber and electrician who had worked for Tom and was related to him by marriage. "But they did deals with 'em, swap cars, might swap with you then turn around two, three days later, might swap back. Tom'll swap house with you, he'll go fix that thing up, turn around, you come like it real good, heck, he'll swap back to you and get some more booze off of you, make some more money. He's a hustler."

"And make money on anything," said Wright's wife, Elaine.

"Right," added Wright, fired up by talking about Tom, "and he comes out on top. Believe me, man he can talk you into anything."

The boys would race around the small lot next door, looping into Yancy Spry's yard. Another Tennesseean, Yancy was Pops Crosslin's brother-in-law; his wife, Mary, and Pops's wife, Ruby, were sisters. Wright Spry, who lived not far away, was Yancy's brother. Yancy would get red-faced mad about the boys peeling through his yard, and he finally put up a fence across their makeshift track.

On the phone, Tom's aunt Mary Spry sounded downhearted about Tom, about the way he died and how her sister had to deal with it, but also about the mark he left on their family. "I don't want to do anything to hurt the family or anything," she said quietly, "because my sister was hurt so many times and it's brought up in the papers and things. But Tom hurt my kids and they never really got over it."

Yancy and Mary had six children that were about the same age as the

Crosslins, but they didn't really grow close. With the exception of Shirley, who was friends with the youngest cousin, Betty Marie, they grew apart as they got older

"We couldn't give 'em the clothes, the things that my sister and her husband give to their kids, and we had to live in that little bitty house there . . . and it did really look bad," said Mary Spry, hurt in her voice. "They was always cutting my kids down going to school."

When Tom was sixteen, he evidently stole a moped and gave it to his cousin Bobby, who had to appear in court over it. According to Mary, Pops and Ruby never dealt with it, and the relationship was strained. The two families still saw each other every day, and the kids did talk and hang together at holidays and such, but they weren't best friends.

The Crosslin boys could live with a feud. That was the structure of their young lives. Punching at any moving shadow was a way to deal, in part, with their status as outsiders to the suburban middle-class.

Tom was into grass by age thirteen or so and started having it around in some quantity, when he could get it, by fourteen.

"I remember one time Mom or Dad found a pillowcase filled with marijuana in the closet," said Shirley. "And man, did they raise holy hell. And I know it had to be his. He was thirteen, fourteen, something like that."

For Shirley, the youngest in a clan for whom partying was second nature, pot was always there, as easy to get as cigarettes, if not easier. She started smoking it when she was twelve.

On the occasion of the pillowcase affair, Pops threw out the pot, and Tom and his father fought bitterly about it. Shirley remembers: "The boys argued with Dad more than I did. Dad was pretty strict. We all left home—as soon as I turned sixteen, I got a job, got married and left. I got out of there as soon as possible. Dad used to drink and I remember that him and the boys used to fight."

In 1969, when fifteen-year-old Doug Leinbach and his friends started smoking dope, they would score off of an old Elkhart hippie named

Tree. Doug knew Tom by then; they met when they went to eighth grade together at West Side Junior High. He didn't really run with him much at that time, but the weed was the secret handshake linking one to the other. They'd go out to Tree's place and he'd pull out a coffee can full of brown Mexican dirt weed, put a pile of it on the can's plastic lid and sell them a "lid" for ten bucks. This was not only the key to the underground party but also the height of political engagement in the struggles of the times—when you got high, you belonged, and you knew things about your town. You saw through the bullshit. You got the vision. The straights supported the logic and the raw fear of the war in Vietnam and the murderous repression of radical ideas like civil rights. Everybody could see that was wrong, it was written across the land like a giant skull, but apparently only the heads and politically informed would admit they saw it. Whomever was against this vision, against the truth, was obviously the Man. The Man was not only the enemy of truth, but of life and fun. Smoking pot was still risky, because the pot laws could be hellish if they cared to enforce them. But this gave life a mission and an aesthetic, the whole tragicomedy was laid right out, ripe for the living, with the hilarity of getting stoned all hung like it was with death and lies.

There was hash around, too, and it came from Afghanistan or Morocco or Nepal, places that seemed a lot more exotic than a fetid ditch in Mexico. It was a geography of tastes, and good sweet hash must come from good sweet places. In the summer of 1970, a friend gave Doug just the tiniest bit of a roach and said, "Here, man, smoke this." He had never tasted anything like it before. It was sweeter than hash, expanded more in the lungs and head and instantly had him profoundly stoned. Just two tokes and he was hallucinating.

"Man, what is this?" Doug croaked. "Where'd you get it?" His friend said it was Vietnamese weed and he got it from a guy in Cass County who had just come back from 'Nam. This guy had been mailing it back to himself in the States all the time he was over there. He had it machine-rolled into cigarettes that looked just like regular Pall Mall straights and he was selling them for a buck apiece. The boys could take

one of these machine-rolled ciggies and reroll it into three regular-sized joints. Four people who were used to skunky Mexican sativa couldn't get through one of these joints without putting it out and coming back to it later. This was Cannabis indica, the mystic Asian bud, and they hoovered that up all summer. They'd scurry around collecting beer bottles, cash them in for the recycling deposits and run across the Michigan border to a section of Cass County called Outlaw Flats with ten or twenty dollars until the guy finally ran out.

But there were plenty of veterans coming back from Southeast Asia in the early 1970s, and indica tastes were everywhere. There was Cambodian weed and Thai sticks and Laotian and Vietnamese bud available in abundance, right there in the punk little fist-fighting bars of Elkhart and the woods up in Cass. The smoke itself created an impetus to a sort of protoecotourism, and seekers who were traveling to the Middle East were bringing back a delectation for hash that kept it available, too. Once in a while, there was some good Mexican and Central American weed—Acapulco Gold, Panama Red, or Michoacan—flowing into town with hippies who had gone to the West Coast. It was all good smoke and relatively inexpensive by today's standards.

Weed became an indicator of the political winds and how they blew, and culture followed. After the Vietnam War ended in 1975, the Asian weed dried up around Elkhart. For a few years, there was only Mexican dirt weed again. Middle Eastern hash was still available, but the price was going up. Nixon's antipot crusade had tightened the Canadian border and what did make it to Michiana seemed to be coming via New York instead. Just as the Asian and Middle Eastern flavor of the pot culture began to shake loose from those roots, a new culture leaned in.

Jamaican and Colombian weed started pouring in through Florida, and attention turned to the Caribbean. This bud was a bit more expensive—they had been paying about twenty-five dollars an ounce, but this new bud cost thirty-five dollars—and it wasn't as good as the Asian indica, but it was a lot better than the average Mexican weed. So the reggae and Rastafarian culture of Jamaica came to quickly dominate the scene,

sowing the seeds for the emergence of hip-hop culture beginning in the early 1980s.

Of course, right from the very start, the boys were growing their own. This was an era when bud still came loaded with stems and seeds, and kids from Elkhart had sowed an underground economy that reeked to high heaven out in the cornfields of Cass County in Michigan, and in Elkhart, St. Joseph, and Kosciusko Counties in Indiana. Some pretty good marijuana came out of those cornfields. Tom and Doug were urban dwellers, but much of their life could only be lived out in the wide-open spaces where they grew their weed and crept out in the darkness to sit in cars to burn it.

Tom Crosslin's campground lawyer, Don France, took lots of pot cases in the 1970s, and said that some of the weed was volunteer from the days when commercial hemp was grown in the area during World War II. True enough, Cass County had been part of Michigan's wartime hemp industry along with Huron and Sanilac Counties up in Michigan's thumb. It was widely recalled that Cass County once boasted a hemp processing plant, though ag records on hemp are scarce. Leinbach's Mennonite grandfather, Noah, grew it on his farm in Wakarusa, Indiana. Wild hemp was out there alright, in the ditches and fence rows, but Doug and his pals found out the hard way that it would only give you a headache if you smoked it.

As they roared up and down the dirt farm roads and narrow blacktop where you had to pull over to let another car pass, they flung seeds as a botanical analogue to the jetting overdrive of their sex lives, returning months later in a flash of weed-starved inspiration to see if anything had grown. One of the reasons that Doug knew about the dirt lane called Pemberton Road was that he and his buddies used to roll up and down the lane every October, claiming their ditchweed harvest.

Marijuana's peaceful ethos barely touched the Crosslin boys, except to add a grin to their passion for teenage evil; when they got drunk, they loved to fight, and when they got stoned they just fought a little bit less.

Wright Spry had changed Tom Crosslin's diapers; he and his wife had seen the whole arc of these boys' lives. Wright had hands like Jim Crosslin's, thick and scarred, and walked like him, too, hunched under his gray brush cut. He was in his sixties and a fireplug of a man, quick to laugh, a plumber and electrician by trade. The Tom Crosslin he knew was a rough character—generous, but rough.

By his late teens, Tom had grown into the kind of man that made you glad he was your friend, because you wouldn't want him to be your enemy. He was powerful and seemed to take some pleasure in reaching into deep reservoirs of rage to see what he'd find there.

As was the case elsewhere in America, there were race riots in Elkhart in 1968, touched off by the death of the Reverend Dr. Martin Luther King, and tensions smouldered for years. Phil Overholser, whose mother used to babysit Tom when he was a kid, said that he and Tom's brother Larry were surprised by the rising black consciousness and rage suddenly present among kids they'd known all their lives. They fought the black kids in Elkhart just because Larry "wasn't going to take their shit," meaning their newfound righteous anger. Those fights were something that Phil came to regret later in his life, saying, "I tried to move away from that, to not live like a racist. Larry did, too, but he had other pressures." Overholser, in fact, was thrown out of Elkhart High in the tenth grade after a fight with an African American kid, and when he returned the following year, ran into the kid on his first day of school and walked out, saying, "It ain't worth it. I'm just going to end up killin' him."

Tom took part in the race wars, too. Because they lived on the south side, Tom and the other boys went to Pierre Moran Junior High, which was a predominantly black school. He wasn't far into the eighth grade when he was transferred—or left of his own accord—and went to West Side Junior High, which had only a handful of black students. Tom did his share of fighting there, too, so it's hard to say how much of his anger was necessarily racial; he had loads of black friends later in his life, some of them his most treasured.

Racially, though, Elkhart quivered on a hair trigger. The Ku Klux Klan was active in the outlying areas, and when students from rural junior highs like Brookdale and West Side joined those from Pierre Moran in the high schools, the results were incendiary. From 1968 thru 1970, there was a lot of blood shed in the halls of Elkhart High. Police regularly patrolled inside the school and shut it down on several occasions.

"We went to Garfield one day and, man, there were four black guys over there," Wright Spry said in his thick Appalachian twist. "I said, 'Tom, ain't no way we gonna whip them.' He said, 'Can you handle one?' I said, 'Yeah I'll take that little one.' He said, 'I'll take the other three of 'em.' I went, 'No way.' He went, 'Shoot, buddy—c'mon niggers, come on get us!' They backed off, we started after them, they all run. Believe me boy, that one told another: 'Hey' he said, 'ain't no way we can whip Tom.' "

"Hillbillies got loose in Indiana's what it is," said Wright's wife Elaine with a sarcastic smile.

"Them boys'll give you the shirt off their back. But don't think you can push 'em in a corner and just keep pushing 'em," added Wright. "That didn't work back then, still didn't work up until the day that I can tell you he died."

That went for Tom's brothers like it went for anyone else. His anger ran far below the surface, but when it erupted it was shocking and unpredictable. Once, when Tom and Larry came to blows in the family basement, a teenage Tom descended into an adolescent rage and kept coming and coming at his war hero brother, and Mary Spry said that he put Larry's eye out.

"Yep, with an ice pick, uh huh," said Mrs. Spry. "Larry went spending time in the army, come home, and then they got into it in the basement and then Larry's eye was put out."

Aunt Mary had thought a lot about Tom over the years; it was always Tom who started things. Larry was troubled, but he was older and kept things from the family. Jim was just a steady worker, her favorite. Shirley was a good woman, fighting for attention in that household of men. But Tom couldn't help himself. He was an extreme extrovert; he couldn't live in his own skin, he had to have company, a gang, and if you were hanging around with him it usually meant being an accomplice.

"You know he was gay?" Mary said tentatively.

Jim and Phil said that Tom's homosexuality or bisexuality had never been apparent until after Tom was at least twenty-one or so, but Mary softly said, no, that wasn't true. She was roundabout in her explanation, not wanting to implicate anyone.

"So that's been going on all the times he got up to where he could go out, you know, without having to have his mom and dad there," she said. "He'd go out with the other kids and things. The guys, the boys. He always went around with the boys."

That didn't mean anything. Boys always went out with their troops. That was the fabric of Friday night. And none of Mary's stories re-counted directly how Tom had done anything different than that, but she had seen firsthand Tom's emerging sexuality, both as it pertained to men and women, and she strongly intimated there was more to tell. Tom himself told the story many times at the farm about how he had been molested by an older male relative when he was young, but he made light of it, always adding to the story, "But I liked it and kept coming back for more!" His Aunt Mary was more cagey. This was a matter that none of the other family members really wanted to get into.

Finally, she wrapped it up, as though it were too painful, saying, "And there's other things I know but I'd rather not say."

Tom wasn't too attuned to politics, per se, but as the youngest son he felt the change as Larry and the older boys came back from Vietnam—both dead and alive. As pain settled over the town, the boys' mischievous and good-spirited violence began to turn inward; it drained out of the bars and pushed into the houses, then whole families started turning inside-out across Elkhart. The feeling was raw and vulnerable. The majority of families were caught flat-footed by it and tried to pretend a bitterness and disillusionment wasn't settling over them, not their little burg. But Tom and his boys heard the music, they watched the news, and they knew that their folks might not let them go to the revolution, whatever that was, but it was happening in their backyard—in Chicago, in Ann Arbor, in Detroit.

Larry was three years older than Tom and joined the army in 1969.

"Larry went to the army because he got himself in trouble," said Mary. "They said, 'It's either you go to the army, or you go to jail.' That was the choice the boys had then."

Larry was already married and had a kid on the way. He thought that shipping overseas to the war was going to be alright. His ma, Ruby, was real proud of him, and Pops, too, the way parents had been over the span of then-contemporary memory, in World Wars I and II, Korea, and then in Vietnam. When the first wave of kids went to Indochina in the mid-to-late 1960s, Elkhart felt good about it. This was before hippie consciousness would really hit around 1970. The blue-collar patriots put out flags and ran their cars in the memorial day parade and gave the finger to the few academic peaceniks in nearby South Bend, home of Notre Dame University.

So Larry packed off to the infantry, Army Private First Class Larry Allen Crosslin, a grunt. And a real grunt, at that. He was tough enough and liked to think of himself as well put together; he just liked a cold beer when he could get one. He disappeared in country, into a withering rain of heavy combat in the jungles and rice paddies that didn't let up for a year. He wrote few letters home and made few phone calls.

When he reappeared one day in 1970, back to his wife and child, everybody was glad as hell to see him, and dragged him down to the bar to get loaded. Which is right where he stayed for the next three decades. He didn't want to talk about Vietnam, he said. Jim and Tom were dying of curiosity: What was it like there? Did he kill anybody? What did he think of all the protests? Was it like they saw on the news? Did American soldiers kill women and children and set farms on fire?

"He used to be pretty much an in-charge kind of person," said Phil Overholser, who had been Larry's buddy since elementary school. Phil had enlisted in the marines a year earlier and served in Tennessee. "Then, when he come back, he was more of a follower and seemed like he didn't have the ambition that he used to have.

"To my knowledge, he didn't keep a job for any length of time after he'd come back from 'Nam."

Larry's silence was neither confirmation nor denial. He and a few of the other local boys each seemed to go home to their own private hell and sit stewing in it. Larry came back drinking a little more than before he had left, but overseas his taste for weed had developed, too. Soon it was heavier stuff, whatever he could get his hands on.

Decades later, when Larry was divorced from his wife (who married him twice, trying to help Larry work it out) and estranged from his three kids, Larry Allen, Katina and Benji, he worked for Tom and rented one of the apartments Tom owned on the St. Joe River. "River Larry" used to come up to Doug Leinbach's apartment in the same building and talk.

"He was one of those guys they dropped down into the holes with a gun and a flashlight and said, 'Start shooting, dude,' " said Doug. "They dropped guys down into the tunnels where the Vietcong hung out. He said, 'Shit, I just closed my eyes and pulled that trigger. I'd have it on semiautomatic, just as fast as I could pull it. I'd about shit my pants, but that's all I could do.'

"He talked about wading through rice fields with water up to your chest, holding your gun up above your head, and bullets whizzing past your head.

"In one of the speeches that he gave up there in my apartment, he talked about how he was a proud American and went over to Vietnam and that's when he found out we were all getting fucked," Doug said. You didn't know whether to laugh or cry with Larry.

Larry was decorated, and what he had done was brave, but really it was like surviving a year of consecutive suicide attempts.

Tom tried to make light of it. When Doug asked him during those years, "Man, Vietnam must have something to do with him being a crazy drunk," Tom's response was to laugh and say, "Aw hell, he was a crazy drunk before he went over there. Don't let him blame that on Vietnam."

According to both Jim and Shirley, Larry would remain a staunch anti-Communist, and supported the war in Vietnam and what he had done there as having helped slow the spread of international communism in Asia. He would fly a POW/MIA flag at his house, and Tom would later sell them through Tom's Flag Service. Larry was against the hippies and antiwar protestors, because they lessened support for the soldiers still in Vietnam. He supported Nixon.

He also had nagging health problems. As more and more information came out about the effects of Agent Orange, he began to mention that this might have something to do with his nerves and constant nausea. But the veterans registry and the first government acknowledgment of illness caused by Agent Orange wouldn't come until 1978, and his symptoms weren't recognized by the VA as anything caused by the war. They were recognized as the symptoms of alcoholism.

Meanwhile, political consciousness hit Elkhart. A drastic change was visible in the Elkhart *Pennant*, the yearbook of Elkhart High School— now Elkhart Central—between the years 1969 and 1970. The 1969 book contained no political statements; the least clean-cut of the kids wore Beatles mops. The most outrageous statement of the year was the annual Sadie Hawkins dance, when the students dressed up like "hillbillies," according to the caption, in overalls and straw hats, and the girls brought the boy of their choice on the end of a rope.

By 1970, all this had changed. A double-page spread in the *Pennant* featured a stop sign from nearby Edwardsburg spray painted to read Stop War, an antiwar poster from the school's writing lab and a photo-illustration from *Psychology Today* titled "The Enemy Within," showing a soldier in a gas-mask and helmet covered by the stars and stripes, calling attention to the deadly rise in air pollution. Several pages were dedicated to photos of students painting the interior of the new student center, which came out looking like the psychedelic set of the TV show *Laugh-In*. The best indication of the new attitude is a photo on the last page of the 1972 book: In a house ad that reads "Hang in there with THE PENNANT," a longhair named John Funk, who would have been in Jim Crosslin's class, hangs from a tree by one hand wearing a defiant look on his face, bell-bottom jeans and a sleeveless Elkhart T-shirt and with his free hand is giving the finger straight into the camera.

Jim is the only one of the Crosslin kids to appear in the Elkhart *Pennant*, in 1970, as a sophomore. He looked like many of the other eight hundred students, his hair cut short sides and his bangs combed down to his eyes, he had a smirk on his face and sharp, feral eyes. He'd never finish that school year, but he still got further than the other Crosslin kids. Ruby pointed out with some pride that "I think they all got the GED."

Jim Crosslin was given the same option as Larry—to go to jail or join the army. He took the service, but wasn't gone too long. The army wasn't for him. He went back to Elkhart and married Miriame and buried himself in work.

Doug was fourteen and wondered whether or not he should go to the '68 demonstrations in Chicago. Jim called himself a "part-time hippie." He and Tom went in mostly for the cultural affectations, the weed and the music. With guys like Larry lurking around town, brooding over Vietnam, it was hard to know how to feel about the revolution, except that it was real and the Cold War was real and the country was in a murderous state of disassociation. The nation called its young men to foreign war and high-minded idealists like the Kennedy brothers and Martin Luther King and Malcolm X had called everyone to the battle for the soul and it looked like following either would earn you a funeral.

A song floated through Elkhart the summer Tom was seventeen, turning eighteen, a simple, heartbreaking tune that spun rage into understated beauty.

Mother, mother
There's too many of you crying

Marvin Gaye's "What's Going On" may not have been the kind of song
a fight-crazed hillbilly dropout from Elkhart would listen to, but Tom
had discovered soul music and found this song and hundreds more,
from artists like Otis Redding to Aretha Franklin to the Jackson Five.
Some of this music made its way onto Chicago's monolithic WLS, the
50,000-watt Top 40 AM powerhouse that dominated that whole section of the Midwest, and he'd hunch over his car radio digging Al
Green, the Supremes, or James Brown.

Aside from his love of soul music, which lasted his whole life, Tom
was basically a country hippie rocker, a small-town roughneck who
had enough church in him to make it with the hicks and enough dope
and Detroit slick to wear radical stripes. Both sides of the deepening
culture war claimed that old frontier America of buckskin shirts and
Levi's. Right from the start he had loved the Grateful Dead and Jefferson
Airplane and Country Joe and the Fish, especially Joe's Woodstock anthem, "I-Feel-Like-I'm-Fixin'-to-Die Rag."

And it's one, two, three,
What are we fighting for?
Don't ask me, I don't give a damn,
Next stop is Vietnam;
And it's five, six, seven,
Open up the pearly gates,
Well there ain't no time to wonder why,
Whoopee! we're all gonna die.

By 1972 or '73, the agrarian hippie persona had become more like
him, more confused and prone to punch-outs. The culture had just ab-
sorbed too much death, too much Altamont and Vietnam and overdose

and cult murder. The western look was still as patriotic as an American flag decal, but by the time Tom achieved majority many of the country-rock heroes had darkened considerably. In 1974 Neil Young would offer up his murky commentary on the Tate-LaBianca murders and the end of the Laurel Canyon scene that had nurtured the country-rock phenomenon, singing on "Revolution Blues": "They say that Laurel Canyon is filled with famous stars / But I hate them worse than lepers and I'll kill them in their cars."

But Tom's rural or at least blue-collar identity served other purposes, too. It provided a safe distance from which he could indulge more secret tastes, like glam. He felt drawn to the escapist androgyny filtering in from England in the form of David Bowie's *The Rise and Fall of Ziggy Stardust*, Roxy Music's eponymous debut, and "Children of the Revolution" by Marc Bolan's T. Rex. Lou Reed's "Walk on the Wild Side" made it onto the radio, as did the first singles from Queen. One of Tom's favorite tracks from the period was the Bowie-produced Mott the Hoople song, "All the Young Dudes."

Like so many of the toughs he ran with, Tom was repulsed by the mere mention of homosexuality—calling something "gay" had become an insult—but then, here was this music he loved and that his girlfriends loved, made by fags and poofs. Maybe you had to be this cool to come out. How could a regular guy in jeans and mother-of-pearl buttons just say, "I'm gay"? The local malingerers would tear him to pieces, or worse, turn their backs on him. Rock stars had some kind of street smarts or knowledge that he didn't have, and they had to have cast-iron balls to bring it right out in the open like that.

Little sister Shirley ran off at sixteen with a big, bearded biker named Bob DeWeese, who was known around town as "Wolfman." They were married pretty soon after and Wolfman could safely risk coming around the Crosslin house without the shotguns coming out. DeWeese was a talented machinist and artist who could make just about anything, including most of his own furniture. He also wore biker colors and bombed up and down the streets of Elkhart on a muscular trike he'd made out of a Volkswagen Beetle. Tom thought that trike was about the coolest thing in the world, and it gave him a whole bunch of new ideas.

The Crosslin boys were only part-time motorheads, but Tom couldn't resist the brotherhood that formed around motorcycles. He was driving a convertible Corvair with the flutes of its four-barrel carburetor jutting through the rear hood, and dumped it for a Harley.

Details about Tom's first bikes are thin. He drove Harleys, among other bikes, but no one seems to remember models or which came in what order, because during this same time the Crosslin household was flying apart. Ruby and Grover Sr. split up when they moved out of the Homer Avenue house in 1973. She would later change her life completely and marry a religious man named Luther Batey. For the first time, they all had separate homes. Jim married Miriame and they had a baby boy, Jimmy, and were renting their own place. Larry and his family were struggling on their own. Tom was renting a house two streets east of Pops, over on Kelsey Avenue.

Tom took to motorcycles, but just driving one wouldn't be enough. Other bikers had clubs and gangs and he wanted one of his own. He was lean then, but imposing, with knuckles scarred, and he cut a figure on a bike that fit with the gang image. But he didn't have the colors. So he started a club with an impossibly ridiculous name, Occult On Wheels— sort of a takeoff on the bikeploitation movie, Hell's Angels on Wheels. Tom was the club's president.

Occult On Wheels (OOW!) was just a club, at most two dozen strong, making runs together to the annual Harley gathering in Milwaukee and other biker rallies. Tom's lead rider was a big black man named Ace. They rode a mixed bag of bikes, and they didn't have the apocalyptic gear of biker gangs of that era. No spiked gloves or sawed-off shotguns in saddle scabbards. Some of them did ride with pistols but they kept them hidden. They had colors, but nobody seems to remember what they looked like.

During this time, Tom got two sailor tattoos on his right arm, neither of them that well done: a lion on his shoulder, and an eagle lower down on his arm.

"He used to have big parties, I went to a couple of 'em," said Jim Crosslin. "The gang'd all get together, they'd cook out, drink beer, smoke their pot out in the country somewhere."

"I used to hang around with some kids down on the south side of town," said Doug Leinbach. "All those kids always got excited when Tom Crosslin came around, because there was about 20 to 30 motorcycles with him. They'd roar down the avenue. And there was a house down there that—heh—a doctor lived at. He was never home, his wife was always drunk and—the kids kind of raised their own hell. So Tom would come rollin' in there with a bunch of [his club] from time to time."

The club was benign, but just as a weapon tends to deploy itself, it quickly grew more dangerous. Tom was nineteen or twenty when he formed Occult On Wheels, and he watched his merry band of small-time outlaws move through Elkhart's live-and-let-die society with a certain impunity. He sensed opportunity. In a rented house out on Highway 33 toward Goshen, the club started to move some quantities of weed and other drugs, mostly psychedelics. They also talked a lot about radical political movements like the Black Panthers and the Weathermen, though it's unclear if they ever exercised their politics.

Tom was making revolution, but not with the political design that was then driving the radical left. He was just against hassle. He was really like a Goldwater conservative: against government intrusion into the private lives of Americans and laws governing drugs and helmets and sodomy and guns. He was defending his castle. He wanted to be free to be a complex, sexualized, enlightened adult, and he was a happy warrior in that version of the culture war.

"I remember one time that I pulled up to his house to get something, and people there jumped out of the bushes with automatic weapons and scared the shit outta me," said Phil Overholser. "They were having some sort of war with some other bike gang."

Without prompting, Phil reconsiders. "You know, I ain't too sure that he wasn't into some political thing right then. I know that he got busted living at that house."

Several arrests appear on Tom's record during this era. On August 22, 1974, he was arrested for possession of marijuana. On March 5 of the next year, he was popped for conspiracy to commit armed robbery, later changed to armed robbery. He was convicted, and sentenced again to ten months of work release, probation and fines.

Around 1974, Tom became reacquainted with a biker who would change his life, a petite tomboy with long red hair named Sonny Kay Weaver—that was her legal name, too, a woman with a man's name. Tom and Sonny had met before, but this time she not only caught his eye but captured his imagination. She was riding a Harley-Davidson—Jim said it was a "panhead," which would have been a lot of bike.

"It was green and yellow, we called it the Banana Slug, it was the ugliest thing you ever seen," said Jim. She was from Elkhart, and Tom had known her for years. But she'd grown up into a tough, plain-spoken woman, a partier and the kind to have everyone laughing—the sort of woman Tom liked best. Out in the garage and in the bars, out on the road with Occult On Wheels, Tom had always run with the boys. Not that many women could hang with him, but this redheaded gal could run just as hard as he did. In hindsight, it's not hard to see where Tom was headed, but in his public life at this time there was never any indication that Tom was anything but a hotheaded heterosexual.

Sonny sure thought so, or else was open-minded about his bisexuality. After living together for almost a year, Tom and Sonny got married. They rented a house in Bristol, a neighborhood in northeast Elkhart, and moved in with their bikes and their dogs. Tom raised Doberman pinschers at the time and Sonny had a basset hound she called Freddie the Freeloader.

"She had horses up there [at her parents' house]," said Jim Crosslin. "Her folks always went to the 4-H fairs and stuff and she rode her horses and she'd stay there all week. She's a pretty good gal, she's just a little ornery."

"She tells it like it is," laughed Miriame.

When he married Sonny, Tom quit Occult On Wheels. The club eventually sputtered out, but a few of its members joined nationally known gangs like the Outlaws. As was typical for Tom, he shifted his focus to his next project: the marriage. Tom was making RV doors at Elixir, where Miriame also worked, and Sonny worked at Schultz Insurance. But the pair kept their bikes. Jim and Miriame were always around with their toddler, Jimmy, but Sonny and Tom only babysat him one time, because, according to Jim, Sonny couldn't stand to change a diaper. No children are mentioned in their divorce records, though this fact confused several people close to Tom who had heard they'd had a daughter. Sonny's last residence in Cass County, where she lived up to the time Tom was killed, was just a few miles from the farm on Tharp Lake Road. Today it's a cornfield.

The marriage lasted only two years. Sonny was the first person unrelated to Tom to discover what he himself would not acknowledge: He was attracted to men. In his macho world of blood brotherhood and fighting, he was both ashamed of this and confused. Sonny treated it with either tremendous tenderness or deep shame, because she told no one. Neither Jim nor Shirley would discover until years after the two had been divorced that Tom was gay.

Tom didn't run out and start dating men. He wouldn't get his first openly acknowledged boyfriend until years later, and that would happen out of state. Instead, he closed off parts of himself, again shifted his focus, packed up the candy-apple red Harley Sportster he was riding and moved out. Tom had bought the house they were living in on Hudson Street and he gave it to Sonny because he loved her and thought it was the right thing to do. He had wanted it to work out, had wanted to do better with his family than Pops or Jim or Larry seemed to be doing—they were all embroiled in constant, hair-raising domestic fights—but he didn't feel like he fit in. He was sliding in between worlds again, but this time there was nothing familiar. Being a hick and a dropout in Elkhart's increasingly middle-class, contemporary society had made him enough of an outsider, and his biker mob and criminal record had extended this perception into a radical stance. But this was standard male territory. Tom knew little about being gay or bisexual. He might have feared no man, but he feared his increasing desire.

Tom's ego and confidence took him across this gap in a way that doesn't happen for most people; if his old world was to be shattered by his emerging sexual preference, he would make a new world, an entire universe, that could contain them all—his friends, his family, the people he loved—and anyone else who felt like he did—the freaks and hairies, the ex-cons, dissenters and one-percenters, the dishonorable discharges, closeted gays, potheads and hippies. He began to fantasize about a kind of utopia where he could be surrounded by these people all the time and they would be his new family.

"Tom was going in a different direction," said Jim.

"We didn't even know that was part of the reason that they had split up," said Miriame. "She didn't want to say anything but Ruby kept asking her and asking her, so Sonny finally told her. Otherwise, the family probably wouldn't even have known for sure. There was always people around, but nobody suspected. Actually, Tom used to flirt with me all the time, didn't he?"

FIVE Out in Oklahoma

PHIL OVERHOLSER HAD BEEN Larry's best friend, not Tom's. But when Larry came back from Vietnam, the jungle had him wrapped in its alcoholic tendrils and Phil couldn't reach him. A few years later, around 1977, divorce drove Tom to seek Phil's friendship. They shared a birthday—November 10—with Phil being the older by two years. Other than the fact that Phil wasn't gay, they had a lot in common. Phil was more than just a fellow divorcé, hardcore pothead, biker and ex-con; Phil was the enabler of Tom's next persona. In Phil, a long-haul big-rig driver, Tom saw a clear route to being his own boss at last and getting out of Elkhart. He needed space to figure out what it meant to start dating men without all his Elkhart boys coming down on him, and getting out on the road sounded right. Tom would reinvent himself as an over-the-road trucker.

Phil had come to truck driving in order to make his own escape. He'd been a troubled kid in Elkhart and joined the Marine Corps a few days after his seventeenth birthday, when a judge gave him the choice of either jail or a "government job." He went AWOL from basic training but managed to get back in and serve a year outside Memphis. Only weeks after getting out of the service, he met Debra Joe and got married and had two kids immediately. Then the drugs started kicking in.

"Through my first marriage, I was pretty much stoned all the time," he said, speaking from his home in Rector, Arkansas, where he still parks his truck when he isn't out on the road. "We did anything and everything: speed, PCP, uppers, downers, weed. We did about anything we could get our hands on."

That Elkhart party crew did not include Tom. This was while Tom was out in front of Occult On Wheels, and he and Phil didn't really hang out. If anything, Tom would have gone to Phil to buy weed because Phil was, by his own admission, a regular dealer.

He was working for Terrenda Manufacturing, delivering camper shells in a "dualie"—an oversized pickup truck with dual wheels on the back to pull heavy trailers—and a friend was teaching him to drive a big rig. It was during a run to Wisconsin for Terrenda that Phil's party ended. He'd bagged up a pound and a half of pot and left it at his house with Debra Joe. When he came back, his big-rig friend had left a note on the window of his truck saying "Don't go home. They're looking for you." Debra Joe was already in jail and mad as hell. Phil turned himself in for possession and distribution of marijuana and then bonded both of them out.

"She'd been in there like two days or something, and her mother had the kids," he recalled. "That was about the end of our marriage."

Phil was reeling from this divorce and trying to figure out what would happen with his kids, when he ran into Tom again for the first time in years. Tom had also been driving, making deliveries around Elkhart in a stakebed truck. They tore around to a few bars on their motorcycles. Tom liked what he heard about driving a rig out on the open road, and before Phil was even fully aware that he was doing it, Tom was completing a trucking certification course in Elkhart. They presented themselves as a long-haul team to Sawyer Transportation in Chesterton, Indiana, and were hired.

By the time he got in that truck with Phil, Tom was out as a bisexual. He'd had a few encounters in Elkhart, just enough for the word to get around. Then he got in the truck and pulled away, leaving rumors to linger until his return.

Both Tom and Phil lived out of the truck, and oftentimes they would stay with Herb Phillips for a day or two when they would pass through town. Phillips was a gentle, gay black man with a wicked sense of humor, maybe twenty years older than Tom and the calm center of at least one circle of Elkhart's gay community. They were a crowd who stayed out of the limelight, and since Elkhart didn't have any gay bars in those days—you had to go to Kalamazoo or South Bend or Fort Wayne for that—they weren't all that visible to the public. Phillips had done a four-year stint in the navy and worked since then at Whitehall Labs (later American Home Products), the makers of Anacin and Advil.

"I met Tom, I think it was through Terry Pendel," Herb Phillips said, mentioning another well-known fellow, much more flamboyant, in Elkhart's gay community. Herb had a quick and precise way of speaking, with a touch of southern twang from growing up black on the south side of town. "We were playing euchre, and that's how I met Tom. We kind of gravitated toward each other. When he would come in off the road, a lot of times he'd come out and we'd have supper together. He would say, 'You really should open a restaurant. You'd have all kinda business, because we can't get this kind of food on the road.' "

Herb always had a pot of greens cooking on the stove at his house and could whip up bona fide soul food.

Phil would sometimes crash at Herb's, too, even though he was straight. Phil said he never felt uncomfortable there or anywhere else with Tom.

"We'd come back to Elkhart for like a weekend. I was with Tom, and I don't know if you've ever heard of Terry Pendel—he was a real great guy. I mean, a flamingo. He was flaming," said Phil. The scene at Pendel's house was more outrageous than that at Herb's.

"We called it Pendel's Palace," added Phil. "I didn't really have no place to go, so I went over there with him, and I fell asleep in a beanbag in front of the TV. And I knew where I was at; there was a bunch of gay people there. They knew I was straight and Tom wasn't the kind of guy to attack you or something. But I was awakened by somebody jumping on me. And I came out of there ready to kill somebody."

The molester, however, turned out to be a woman. That changed everything. Tom had called up one of his cousins who thought Phil was cute, or cute enough, and she came right over to even up the odds on everyone getting laid.

"Tom had went and got his cousin for me," said Phil. "I thought that was real nice of him. Give me something to do."

Tom and Phil were driving a cab-over Peterbilt, what Phil's kids called a "flat-face," one of the most powerful trucks on the road at that time, with a 430 Cummins engine and a ten-speed Road Ranger tranny. It had a sleeper cab and they drove hard, rarely stopping for more than a day here or there. They carried broker loads for anyone who was paying, covering the entire lower forty-eight.

For the first time, Tom glimpsed a kind of nirvana that he'd longed for, a way to turn his separateness into a place, into a lifestyle, but not be straight-jacketed as gay or a hippie or a redneck or a criminal or even a stoner. His universe was the truck. He had no commitments except to Phil, total mobility, little regulatory hassle and great ability to slide from one social scene to the next. The pay was decent, there were drugs and there were tricks. Tom liked women and men, but more and more he preferred the company of men.

"Worked out real well, because he could have all the boys, I could have all the girls," said Phil.

They picked up a couple of girls in Vero Beach, Florida, who were walking along with another man. Phil held his bag of weed out the window and yelled "Hey, come and party with us. Forget that old man," and they did, rolling along in the truck for several days. Another pair from Albuquerque didn't last that long.

"I was driving and Tom took one of these big Mexican girls back there in the back, and the next thing I know he's yelling, 'Stop this f-ing truck!' you know? I pulled over on the edge of the highway there and he threw them out. He said it stunk so bad he just couldn't stand it.

"The first time I know of him with men was when we moved to Tulsa and started that pill business down there."

They drove out of Elkhart for six months and then moved to Tulsa, Oklahoma. Phil's ex-wife, Debra Joe, had moved there and taken the kids with her, and Phil wanted to stay close to them. Phil and Tom eventually set up in a nice three-bedroom brick house in Rolling Hills, an area in the town of Catoosa, just east of Tulsa. They drove out of a truck stop nearby and, together with the truck stop manager, ran a booming business in uppers. They were legal pills, actually, maximum-strength caffeine tablets bought from an ad in *High Times* and no different than No Doz or Vivarin, but many of the drivers and trucking companies thought they were prescription. Tom and Phil bought them for $15 to $35 per thousand and sold the same amount for $150. One of the trucking companies kept a bottle on the desk for dispensing to the drivers—"Here, take a handful. They'll get you there."

It wasn't long before Tom stopped driving. His other pursuits—men, drugs and scoping out real-estate—became full-time obsessions. The pill business, which went on for two years, had them flush with cash; they sometimes moved as many as twenty thousand pills a week, shipping them around the country. Tom was looking for better ways to make money and exercise his new persona as a gay man. Cash just bumped up his charisma; if you ran into Tom at an estate auction or the liquor store, you'd be partying at his house that night. He had a 500cc Kawasaki road bike, among other small-displacement bikes which he'd traded for weed and pills, and Phil had a super-fast 1974 Kawasaki Z1R, a 900cc road bike that had been built-out for drag racing. The cookouts and hog roasts that Tom hosted just seemed natural; he felt good with people around. They would argue all night against drug laws and the helmet law in neighboring Arkansas. He hated wearing what he called the "brain bucket" and evangelized that it wasn't the government's place to tell him how to keep his head in one piece. For the first time Tom started to have boyfriends come up and stay at the house, and he was very excited about it—more excited than Phil had seen him with any woman.

"Well, girls had a tendency of breaking his heart or turning him down," said Phil. "He didn't take rejection real well. So he had better luck with the boys. I wasn't around him a whole lot right after his divorce, but I know it did bother him."

Land and houses were cheap in Oklahoma and Tom was on the prowl for a deal. The house in Catoosa was always run through with people, half flophouse and half experimental collective, as he tried to find a way to combine business with family and to stave off loneliness and isolation. Tom's sister, Shirley, was living on a real commune in the south; she and Wolfman traveled down there from Elkhart on ten-speed bicycles on their way to Florida and ended up staying for a stretch. The religious or political ideologies that governed these places might not have sat just right with Tom, but the idea of combining incomes to own land sure did. With dreams of self-sufficiency and evading the scrutiny of the cops and the straights, he and Phil located a piece of remote land in a place called Possum Hollow near the eastern Oklahoma town of Roland.

The thirty-acre parcel was pretty but rugged. It was mountain wilderness with a creek flowing through it and big pines, situated just outside of the Ozark National Forest, which stopped at the nearby state line north of Fort Smith, Arkansas.

"It was way out in the sticks," said Overholser. "At that time, he had a boyfriend and I had a girlfriend. We stayed out there about six months just roughing it. We lived in a tent for a little while, then I got a seventeen-and-a-half-foot camper from my dad and we lived in that. Just basically played the mountain man."

This was heaven. Tom had dreams of improving the place, but he was also trying to run the pill business out of Tulsa two hours away and experiment with his new sexual freedom. Phil laid out a log cabin and began trying to build it, but didn't get very far. Tensions ran fairly high in the little camper and Tom was off a good part of the time in Tulsa with a man who'd become his companion, who we'll call Ray Baker. Phil stayed the whole summer of 1980, however, rooted to the place by a distraction much bigger than any cabin plans, and much more lucrative.

One of their neighbors was a well-respected land baron with twelve thousand acres where he ran livestock and put in a few crops—the most notable of which was a half-acre plot of marijuana. It was worth a fortune and the owner offered Phil a piece of it in exchange for standing watch. Phil dropped everything and camped on the land with another guy whom he called "Mexican Jim"; he was armed with a Colt AR-15 assault rifle and Mexican Jim was carrying an AK-47. As the summer deepened, their paranoia increased to a feverish pitch—whenever they felt stressed, they'd "drop a couple of tops and put them on a bucket and let them dry out." Most of the crop was Mexican skunk, but Jim had located a few plants of a more potent strain and the two men pretty much cleaned those out over the course of the summer. Armed and stoned, they patrolled the patch with radios and shooed away deer and inadvertent visitors, steeped in dread; this was enough pot to put someone in jail forever. It was no joke.

The inevitable happened. Just as the buds were maturing and the eight-foot-tall plants were stinking like a herd of wet goats, a helicopter appeared and hovered fifteen or twenty feet over the patch. "I got on the radio to [the landowner], and he had a truckload of Mexicans out there within a few minutes and we loaded up a cattle trailer full of that marijuana," said Phil. "Before they could get there with their four-wheelers and their posse, we had chopped it down and had it off." They moved the trailer—the kind of double-decked trailer used to haul herds of cattle behind a big rig—to a secret location on the property and proceeded to get the contact high of the century. "We sit inside that trailer for three days stripping this stuff out, burning the stalks and bagging the buds. We had two decks that were stuffed full of marijuana. It might've been a thousand pounds, I couldn't really say." Even at a low-ball estimate of fifty dollars an ounce, this was a million dollars' worth of dope.

Tom wasn't part of this operation—somebody had to keep the bills paid with less risky endeavors—but he lived with it just the same. This mountain of weed had to be sold, and the job fell to Phil, so they all moved back to Tulsa for just a while where his connections were better. The landowner rented them an apartment, then they rented another house in Rolling Hills where they knew the terrain. They were loaded with cash and also just plain loaded. The guns were kept handy, but the house was still full of people at all hours, a lot of them strays. One guy they nicknamed Huff Head and they thought he had brain damage from huffing gold spray paint out of paper bags.

The stress grew to epic proportions. Paranoia and drug abuse and high tensions between the gay and nongay guests had everyone fighting—not to mention the raggedy fringes of Tulsa's criminal underworld dragging through the place like ghosts. Things started to break up. In 1981, Phil got his kids back, who were then ten and eight, so he took a job driving a truck for an Oklahoma City company called Film Transit, running between Tulsa and Fort Smith. Tom and Phil bought a house outside of Fort Smith, up on Wild Horse Mountain about twenty miles west of town, and started partying there—Tom and Ray, Phil and his girlfriend—soon to be his second wife—and the kids coming in and out. A couple of months later Debra Joe and her new husband showed up in Fort Smith, too. In fact, they moved into the house, all of them together. But that soon imploded. Phil's second wife didn't like the fact that Tom wasn't working and that he was bringing boys to the house.

They made a friendly deal. Whomever paid the other a thousand dollars—the down payment money they had in the house—could leave. Phil paid Tom and split, leaving Tom the grow lights for the weed they were raising. It didn't seem like the thirty acres in Possum Hollow was going to be the genesis of Tom's revolution, so he cashed out and headed back to Elkhart—taking Ray Baker with him.

"When he was ridin' with [Occult On Wheels], he hid it," said Doug Leinbach. "He had to hide it. He couldn't live that lifestyle. But he was in Oklahoma with his motorcycle, and I know he changed from having his girlfriend riding on the back of his cycle to young guys riding on the back of his motorcycle. Long-haired, Oklahoma country boys, heh. I know some of 'em, they're good people.

"It wasn't like they were riding around on the motorcycle making out or anything. It's not unusual to see two guys on a cycle. And, to be honest, the sexual end of it probably wasn't that much. Every one of these guys that I'm talking about had girlfriends, or kids, or wives. None of them would I classify as homosexuals. Even Rollie, I would not classify as a homosexual. You would have to call him bisexual.

"Tom and I never had sex together. And we were the closest friends in the world. We tried a couple of times, but it just wasn't meant to be. It was uncomfortable and almost comical. We both realized we were not sexually attracted to each other. Our attraction to one another was much deeper than just sex. It was a true friendship and mutual admiration."

SIX Tom's Services, Inc.

"THEY COME IN AND SAY, 'Well, Tom, you bought all this stuff with dope.' No, nope. I know better than that," said Wright Spry. "He did not buy nothing with dope, because I was the one that got him started on buying houses on land contracts."

The south side where Tom grew up is where he landed again when he came back from Oklahoma, and he started right where Spry lived, on Harrison Street. A canopy of oaks and maples filtered green light over blocks of two-story wood-frame houses in various states of neglect. A couple of corner liquor stores flashed up on Franklin Avenue. This community, about three hundred yards from the bluffs of the St. Joseph River, had the shabby nobility of a place that had once been wealthy, a whiff of aspiration, and this is where Tom had the most social currency.

Tom dropped by to visit Wright one day and asked about getting staked in the real-estate business.

"See, I got eighteen apartment houses and two mobile homes," said Spry. "He said, 'How did you ever get started?' I said, 'Get land contracts.' So I went out and started getting houses for him on land contracts. And then, man, he just flew."

Tom wasn't going to stop smoking or growing pot, but after watching Phil try to move that stash in Oklahoma he wasn't going to deal. Even though the outlaw life suited him—he was able to forge order out of the chaos of fringe living—it just didn't pay. The property they owned in Oklahoma hadn't made them any money; he hadn't been dug in deep enough for it to become profitable. That was a mistake he wouldn't make again.

Land contracts are rent-to-own agreements where the seller's security is the property itself. No banks are involved. A cash price is set for the whole property, usually pretty low, and the buyer makes payments directly to the owner. If the buyer can't make the payments, the property simply reverts to the seller. The buyer has little security, but needs little downpayment—sometimes as little as five hundred dollars.

With no banks involved, it's the kind of business that requires a forceful personality, even a bit of a thug. Sometimes it took muscle to guarantee the terms were kept. This was just the way Tom Crosslin wanted to live his life. It wasn't lawyers or the government that were going to tell him how to treat people; it was the generosity and compassion he had demonstrated in his flophouses in Oklahoma. After a few quick land contract purchases, he started going to mortgages so he could own the houses right away and start extensive remodeling. He was a slumlord when he started, but he immediately established high standards for his properties and his own conduct, and he was an instant success.

Tom felt righteous plunking down cold cash, but Wright coached him in bargaining, and one house he got for three hundred dollars down. People liked Tom and his holdings grew. He was honest, even if he was aggressive, and that kind of attitude goes far, especially among the working poor.

He raised the cash for the land contracts by steeplejacking—putting up flagpoles. He'd worked a short time for a flagpole company out in Oklahoma, then another one in Osceola, Indiana, when he came back, but it wasn't long before he went out on his own and founded Tom's Flag Service. Ray Baker was his first employee. Tom had no fear of heights, and for a big guy he could shinny up those poles like a monkey. Family photos show him putting up flagpoles atop some of the biggest buildings in Elkhart, including the county courthouse and the local Sears store. It's a fairly unusual business, but he could make as much as $350 an hour doing it. He'd bid the job and then race to beat his own bid, often needing just a few tools. When he first started out, he was working from the back of a motorcycle.

For a short time, Tom was employed by an Elkhart service company owned by Bud Keener, a kind of jack-of-all-trades operation that could provide mowing, cleaning, snow removal, light construction and what-have-you. The flag service was headed in that direction. Tom bought a tan and dark brown Dodge van, and his business began expanding. He bought chimney sweeping equipment, then started doing lawn care, fire-damage jobs and board-ups. Whatever problem you had, Tom could fix it. By 1985 or so, he'd changed the name of his company to Tom's Services, Inc.

Morel Yonkers, who is called Moe or sometimes Moses, needed the kind of work Tom did. An ex-military man, an impenitent hippie, a libertarian who needed to own his time, he knew how to do a little bit of everything. "They called me Moses on the farm because they thought I could do anything, I guess," he said. He was a pothead from way back and a tireless worker. He'd swing a hammer all day if he felt he was truly free and if he believed in the project. He was an old-school conservationist, too, and had lived off the land for years. Since the 1970s, Moe had spent seven months of the year camping outdoors, with no permament address.

"Normally, from April first until November first Amy and I live outdoors," said Moe, talking in the small rear apartment he had rented from Wright Spry during the winter of 2001/2002. He was sitting on a couch with his longtime companion Amy Heyd—Tom had given her the nickname Amy Jo and it stuck—both fiddling with a bag of loose tobacco and rolling one cigarette after another. The outdoors had gnarled them both; his thin face looked a touch older than forty-nine, but he was about six feet two inches and wiry and moved like a young man, with a long ponytail flowing out from under a dirty Rainbow Farm baseball cap. He had a brilliant flash of a smile and was quick to erupt in loud laughter. Amy was a petite brunette and reserved until she got rolling, then she was a talker.

They liked their smoke and both of them liked to drink, too. They weren't quite A-Campers—a term used by hippie travelers called the Rainbow Family of Living Light to describe the cheery alcoholic campers, who traditionally greet one another at Rainbow Family gatherings with a hearty "Fuck you!"—but close to it.

Moe had gone to junior high at Pierre Moran with the Crosslin boys. He was Jim's age and had also dropped out, but later got some college education. He became part of Tom's Services crew when business started getting steady.

"I just rung him up, told him I was looking for an apartment and some work and got both of them the same day," Moe said. "That's just the kind of guy Tom was. He said, 'Well, meet me at your apartment and I'll tell you when to be to work.'"

Moe had come out of the Marine Corps, where he was an MP in Norfolk, Virginia, from 1972 to 1974, and moved up to Baldwin, Michigan, a National Guard town known in the 1980s and '90s for survivalists and a strong hunting-meets-military vibe. Moe had been a head since he was a teen, a pot connoisseur. He talked with fondness of 1969 to '70, when he was smoking out of a corncob pipe and the good shit was Acapulco Gold and two-foot long Michoacan buds that came wrapped in aluminum foil. Back then, he had a connection that could score him Nepalese finger hash and temple balls and red hash. "You could buy a quart jar of red hash for a grand," he recalled. "One person could stay stoned on that for a year. You couldn't touch one of them today for five grand—that's if you could find it."

Though he had earned a good conduct medal in the marines, Moe was busted for pot on several occasions and the base commander finally threw him out. In their final confrontation, Moe explained—never at a

loss for dramatic flourish—that he quoted the man—a general—some lines from John Prine's "Great Compromise."

When I opened my eyes
I was a victim of the great compromise

He told the commander that if Richard Nixon could quit, so could he. He got a bad-conduct discharge, but it was later changed to honorable.

He was married then and had two kids, and up in Baldwin he ran a seasonal business called the Deer Yard, selling carrots and apples as deer food for the hunting crowds. In the summers he worked repairing mobile homes.

"You tell people you're from Elkhart, and the first thing they want to know is, 'Can you fix my mobile home?' There was a lot of mobile homes up in Lake County because it was such a poor area, anyway."

When Moe came back to Elkhart in the mid-1980s, he figures Tom had about twenty properties. "And then, in the next couple of years, he bumped it up to around seventy pieces of property, at one point, maybe eighty or ninety. It got to be pretty big. It was a full-time job."

Tom did eventually own a lot of buildings, but never that many at one time. His longtime secretary and bookkeeper, Sharon Keener—his former boss Bud's ex-wife—said usually it was "no more than twenty." His service company had more than eighty employees over the years—again, not all of them working at the same time.

The crew that assembled around Tom's Services, Inc. would be the same one that eventually created Rainbow Farm. The buildings Tom bought were often borderline teardowns that had to be completely gutted and refitted from the ground up—drywall, electric, plumbing, kitchen, roof, the works. The only way that it made any economic sense was for Tom's Services to do all the labor and, usually, live in the building while they did it.

"I mean, he'd take a house in the worst neighborhood in town, make it look like a doll house, and all the neighbors were fighting over who was gonna get to rent it first," said Moe.

Doug Leinbach was a repo man—"managing distressed properties"—at what is now Key Bank in Elkhart when he got a phone call from Tom. Doug was one of the suits there, in charge of resolving foreclosures and damages on industrial property, houses and estates. He managed over thirty accounts with assets totaling more than twenty million dollars.

"Doug, I'd like to come down and talk to you about a business proposition," Tom said.

"Well, does it have to do with my work here at the bank?" asked Doug. He was a very careful person and kept his private life as a gay man and a pot smoker separate from his work.

"Yeah, it does. I'd like to take you out to lunch where we can talk casual."

Over lunch a few days later, Tom said to Doug: "Look, I got a service company, and I know you require people to do all kinds of things for you on properties. I'd like to do some of that work for you."

Doug wasn't one to jump into this kind of thing. He was a year younger than Tom, probably in his mid-thirties at the time of this meeting, but they couldn't have been more different. Doug wasn't an extrovert. He was a kind man with a slightly acne-scarred face and a head of bushy dark hair, extremely careful and detail-oriented, and also very trustworthy once he agreed to a deal. He and Tom had just been reacquainted and Doug was taken with what he saw in Tom: Here was a gay or bisexual guy who lived very openly—smoking dope, drinking in the straight bars, chasing tail, maintaining his connection to a big family and loads of friends and working right out in the middle of a homophobic building trade. Tom ignored the closet. If you weren't charmed by his generosity and good nature, he wouldn't pursue your friendship. If you crossed him, look out for a beating. Tom's outlook

was so different from Doug's that the banker could hardly help but find it attractive.

They worked out a trial arrangement. Sooner or later, banks handle just about every property in town, and when they were burned out, water damaged, left unguarded or just needed the lawn mowed, Tom's Services came in. It was a sweetheart deal but a good one for the bank. A couple of times, management questioned whether Doug was getting too cozy with Tom. Each time, Doug was able to show that he'd tried other crews and Tom's simply did the better job. Tom was busy even without the bank's work, putting up flagpoles all over the state and on the list of bonded contractors to do board-up work and site security for the city.

Doug and Tom had met each other in their postadolescent lives as gay men only a few months earlier, at Herb Phillips's place, and Tom had made an impression. He came roaring up on his motorcycle with a young man who just stopped the party dead for a few seconds.

"He had this long-haired Indian on the back who just took my breath away," gushed Doug. "This was Ray Baker. Ray was very young, sixteen or seventeen at the time, probably.

"I couldn't help it, I was like, [gawking] 'Wow.' And Tom gave me a look like, 'Don't you even think what you're thinking. I'll strangle you,' " Doug laughed. "So I thought, 'Well, okay, I don't want any of that!' "

"Later on, as I got to know Ray, he was just one of the nicest people I ever met in my life. The only time I ever had any trouble with Ray is when he got drunk. Ray was out of the Tulsa area, and he never went anywhere without a Bowie knife strapped inside his pants leg."

Doug explained his connection to Tom one spring day while we drove around Elkhart with pollen raining down out of the trees. They were businessmen and spiritual dreamers, and neither one bought into the stereotype of what it meant to be a gay man.

Doug said of Tom, "He didn't live to be gay. He lived his life, and he just happened to be gay. I'm the same way. Herb Phillips was that way. That's why Tom and I were very close friends. I've just about given up on the gay community in Elkhart. You need fellowship. You need to hang around with like-minded people. But to me, being gay isn't as important as living a good life."

When it came to his sexuality, Tom didn't seem to need labels. His ego didn't abide them. When Tom walked into a room, he was one step ahead of everything you thought you knew about him. You saw the real man and he didn't care how you felt about it. For Doug, that was a kind of power.

J. Moritz "Joe" Grolimund leaned back in his chair and chuckled softly in the cluttered, cat-filled house in downtown Elkhart where he kept his law office. From the outside, the early-twentieth-century brick building almost looked abandoned, but Grolimund was very well known around town; he was formerly a county judge. Joe Grolimund handled some of Tom's most personal matters, including Rollie's custody case for Robert. A large, sympathetic man in a suit, with a head of tousled white hair, he was very much the image of a country barrister.

"As long as Tom did what the city wanted, they were very happy. They gave him plaques, they gave him awards," Joe said.

Tom got two awards from the city for helping to restore historic homes—complete with award-dinner ceremonies—and he displayed them wherever he was living.

Grolimund mentions, though, that this didn't mean the city could push him, and proceeds to tell the story of a house that has become an Elkhart legend. The house was located at the point where Benham Street veers into Third, and the city inspector was insisting it be painted. Tom, however, wasn't in a mood to hear it. He'd been down at mayor Jim Perron's office fighting a trash citation and was in a snit. He and the mayor went 'round and 'round and for Tom it became a matter of prin- ciple. Finally, he received an order from the city saying to paint the house or it would be condemned. So he did.

"There was this house," laughed Joe Grolimund, "atrociously pink." Day-Glo pink. The neighbors were in an uproar. The house made the front page of the Elkhart Truth. It stayed hot pink, with green trim, until Tom sold it months later. The city finally footed the bill for a nice coat of beige.

Some of Tom's other interactions with the city, however, were less genial. In the gritty world of construction work, rivalries festered and threats turned physical. When an Elkhart building inspector arrived at one of Tom's job sites on Garfield Street, he didn't like what he saw and cussed them out, ordering the men to stop work. Wright Spry was there.

"He said to the fellas, 'No, you ain't gonna hit another lick,'" said Wright. "Tom came over and goes, 'What happened?' Boy, he flew right down to that office. He was gonna bust his head, see?"

"He said, 'I got a permit. Anytime you want to talk about one of my jobs, you come and talk to me. Don't go and talk to my men. You come after me if they do something wrong.'"

This was exactly what Tom's men wanted in a boss. Someone who would stand up for them, treat them like they were worth defending.

Later in his life, Tom would become fond of telling people that in the Declaration of Independence, the three inalienable rights of men—life, liberty and the pursuit of happiness—were originally written as life, liberty and the pursuit of property, after the seventeenth-century work of John Locke. For Tom, property was both freedom and happiness, and in it he felt a potential and a responsibility that wouldn't be foreign to the average homeowner. But Tom was a believer, a zealot. Whether or not it is true that, as the influential American psychologist and writer William James once wrote, "the instinct of ownership is fundamental in man's nature," everyone who came into contact with Tom felt a natural order in his organization. His ambition turned it into a private revolution.

All down a string of freshly patched and painted houses on Elkhart's south side, a starry sense of purpose awoke in Tom and his crew. It came like church in reverse. They saved themselves and then God came sniffing around. The cadre of workers had come looking simply for work but in each other they found a kinship that took them all by surprise. Like Tom's biker gang, and his outlaw houses in Oklahoma, a flash of recognition ran among the faces, but this construction crew was different because the business was straight.

So Tom's Services, Inc. became more than a construction crew. It became a kind of loose collective.

Its members had always been separate because their pride and their self-reliance and their fear had kept them behind closed doors. They were dope smokers, gays, ex-cons, vets, one-percenters, GED recipients and survivors of abuse and bad marriages and cults and alcoholism and just plain hard luck. They were blue-collar and working poor who often wouldn't take welfare and wouldn't sacrifice their identity and who usually became visible to the public only when they turned up on a police blotter. They were constitutionalists who believed the government should stay out of their personal lives. They were Johnsons, not shits. In a country increasingly split into haves and have-nots, they were have-nots for sure, but having wasn't as important as being. They wanted to be recognized as good people, honorable people, and though survival had dimmed their vision some, they recognized their own reflection in Tom's eyes.

Tom was only getting rich on paper—there was never much cash around because his daily outlay became enormous and he was constantly giving money away—but he had pulled together a family and identified them by lighting up their pride. When one of the men on his crew would get in trouble, Tom would put his family in an apartment and let the guy work it off. If it got real bad, he'd drop off money and groceries to his wife and children, usually asking them to keep it a secret. "Let that deadbeat go out and work for you," he'd say.

There was also another, more practical matter that drove good workers to Tom: they were angry about urine testing for drugs at the trailer factories.

With the onset of the 1980s and the Reagan administration, pot smokers found themselves increasingly at risk. Ronald Reagan was the second U.S. president to categorically deny the best recommendations of his own medical and scientific experts to pursue an expensive, unwinnable and highly politicized war on pot. The first was Richard Nixon (more on him later). During Reagan's first year in office, 1981, the National Academy of Sciences (NAS), a respected nongovernmental body, released a report saying the federal classification of marijuana as a Schedule I narcotic, with no medical value, was false and harmful to efforts to decrease drug use. But reducing drug use has never been a government goal—increasing the number of criminals is more politically useful. So on the day the report was released, Reagan held a press conference to announce he was ramping up sentences for marijuana possession and instituting federal drug-testing programs. He was, he said, launching an all-out "War on Drugs." He never acknowledged that any such report by the NAS existed and it was his war that made headlines instead.

Every worker in Elkhart soon knew all about the War on Drugs. Evidently, they were the enemy.

Most of Tom's people were refugees from the piss testing that began in 1985. Only 3 percent of American companies were demanding a whiz quiz in the 1980s, but by the time Rainbow Farm got up to speed in the mid-1990s, it was up to 98 percent. In Elkhart alone, thousands were affected. Workers like Moe and Amy and Dayved Watts, one of Tom's carpenters, had seen urine screening implemented in Elkhart's trailer factories and loyal employees ruined. In the vast majority of cases, it played out like this: A worker with a spotless track record had an accident and filed for workman's comp; the insurance company would demand a drug test, and a trace of THC would be found. That did not imply the worker was high on the job—only that he or she had smoked pot in the last several weeks, almost certainly on their own time and in the privacy of their own home. The worker was then fired and all claims denied. This didn't help to prevent accidents; it was simply an insurance scam.

New laws in the 1980s also made it easier to remove children from homes where drug use was known, even though removal solely for smoking pot was still rare. Urine testing, then, became the ultimate threat.

Tom's Services, Inc. sold Urine Luck and Clear Test and other products that helped a worker beat a urine test. Among their biggest customers were railroad workers. The service company office on Indiana Street, a cinderblock garage building with two small apartments on the side, was hard up against the railroad tracks, and conductors would literally stop their trains up above the office and scramble down the hill for a box of pee fix.

Doug would eventually leave his position at the bank when drug testing was implemented for all employees under the level of vice president. The corporate order was to be carried out by a VP at the branch who was known to smoke a joint now and then. He told Doug it was just politics. Doug had made the bank millions of dollars with his careful repo work so he told the VP to shove it up his ass.

Tom reacted to the new climate of paranoia by putting his own neck on the line. He'd hire these people and protect their privacy, and the Orwellian insurance people and pee testers could go to hell. By honoring who they were as people, not the chemicals in their bodies or their sexual proclivities, he inspired intense loyalty.

"They were all hungry people," said Doug. "Some of the guys lived there at Tom's house, and there was a handful of guys in town on the streets, ten to twenty guys, and they knew that if they could get over to his house at seven o'clock in the morning, he'd usually put somebody to work. It was like a Faith Mission. If he didn't, he'd give 'em breakfast or something and send 'em on their way."

Tom's family were pulled into the circle, too, after a string of tragedies. Larry, lost in drink and father to three kids, had a standing offer of work whenever he was sober. Shirley was living alone in Elkhart with her two boys, Jason and Jonathan, after Wolfman's drug problems had driven him to suicide. Jim and Miriame were devastated when their oldest boy, Jimmy, was killed in a car accident. They clung to their younger boy, Boss, and often to Tom with a sense of profound hope and fear. Together with Pops, Tom was now keeping them all looking forward by replacing the old idea of a family—fighting hillbillies, basically—with something completely new.

In the house at 1408 Prairie Street the collective was in full effect. The place was a biggish two-story 1920s or '30s post-Victorian affair with neighbors on both sides, neighbors Tom was constantly courting because he knew his house was too full and too loud. The woman who lived next door let her kids come over all the time; it was fun at Tom's house. The crew pretty much lived to party. Some of the workers rented rooms in the house, but no matter who was living there, after quitting time it was often the end-up for the crew and their boyfriends and girl-friends and families. The music and smoke spilled out onto the porch and into the big dirt parking lot of the adjacent Mennonite church, where Tom kept a fleet of vehicles. Some nights it was just Tom and his tenants, oftentimes it was a crowd of two dozen or more.

When secretary Sharon Keener was working in the Prairie Street house, she and her daughter were often there after work to have a few beers and cook. Tom was the king of the grill, and he was partial to hog roasts. Once he even roasted a goat with the Mexican family who rented his house directly behind on Kinzy Street.

Sharon was another who felt Tom had saved her life. She had been the bookkeeper for her husband, Bud, but when they split up it got ugly. She didn't have the courage to leave and Tom helped her, and afterward Bud was hot. He came over a number of times and slashed Sharon's tires and then Tom's, too. Word from the employees is that Tom had to go over and kick Bud's ass, or threaten to, before he finally slunk off. Later, Sharon developed a heart condition and Tom paid for most of her care. Tom was happy to eat her famous lasagna now and again, but hosting the whole meal was more his style.

"I don't know if he was proud, that was just his nature," she said.

"He always told me, 'If I've got it and they're hungry or they need a place, they can have it.' That means anything—clothing—anything. He said, 'I'll go get me new.'"

You were for sure going to get smoked-out at Tom's house, too—you just weren't sure what you were going to get. Reagan had the squeeze on marijuana, and exotic tastes were drying up. There was Mexican dirt weed around, but no hash coming in from anywhere, and the Jamaican and Colombian connections through Florida had stopped almost cold.

What replaced it, of course, was cocaine and heroin. Crack had always been portrayed as an inner-city drug, but it poured into little Elkhart like water from a fire hose. Tom got into cocaine, and some of his employees got into it heavily, but he saw right away how coke and booze would destroy a man and began prosyletizing for using weed as a means to stay off hard drugs.

Necessity is the mother of invention, and around this time heads all over the country began turning to the ads in the back of High Times and the marijuana seed banks in Amsterdam. The implementation of drug asset forfeiture made growing extremely risky, but even so, indoor hydroponic systems became all the rage and "grow shops" even sprouted up, careful to sell equipment with no mention of or association with pot.

Soon the locals were producing some very high-quality weed from the Holland seed-bank strains like Afghani, Northern Lights and various skunks. The THC content in this dope is much higher than that of the Mexican that Doug and Tom and Moe had been smoking, and even led to claims by the government that this "chronic" weed was so powerful that it lead to serious addictions and had permanent side effects. But in their estimation the new stuff didn't hold a candle to the indica they had smoked during the Vietnam era, and as Doug put it, "We survived the Vietnamese weed, so I am sure we will survive the THC content of Northern Lights #2 and its kin."

The downside, though, was the cost. The killer Vietnamese bud used to go for twenty-five dollars an ounce. The new hydro was ten times that, and today goes for around four to five hundred dollars an ounce.

After one of Tom's German shepherds ate up about fifty sprouts he had sunning in the backyard, he turned to hydroponics. Jim Crosslin said, "He used to have a little growing machine over there—that's about first when hydroponics was coming out. I remember he talked me into it, when I was living over there on Penny Lane—I had a basement that nobody could get to, it had a hole-in-the-floor trapdoor. He says, 'Well, you oughta be growing this shit, it's easy.' I ended up renting a chainsaw and cutting a hole outta the floor to make it so we could grow the pot. I bought a system off of him, and me and him and Rollie took off to Chicago to get all the nutrients and stuff. We're sitting out there waiting for them to open up, we forgot they were an hour different, and we were out there smoking a joint and they got cameras out there. I said, 'Oh, no, boy.' "

A little paranoid, Jim got cold feet by the time he got the stuff installed.

"That was the last time we ever grew it," affirmed Miriame.

"Yeah, I sold it back to Tom," Jim said. "I didn't want to take any chances. He knew how to do it, though."

The Prairie Street house wasn't the only place the gang was partying. Tom would get in a mood and throw everybody out, but the smoke rolled on. The success of Tom's Service, Inc. was a validation of the appetites that had set this crew apart in the first place, and they were hungry for more—more exotic tastes, more laughs, more buildings, more freedom. In another house at 1024 Main Street, the crew would spill back and forth across the street to Louie & Kelly's Bar. The only rule was no hard drugs—no coke or crack, no heroin, no meth. The crew would get you to rehab if you had a problem, but Tom would throw you out if you couldn't hang—and Tom was a gourmand among them.

The ever-present bankroll in his hip pocket had given him rapacious habits, even if it was a roll of singles. Ray hadn't stayed with Tom that long once he arrived in Elkhart, although he did stay on the crew for a while and remained Tom's friend. Ray got a job elsewhere and met a gorgeous woman—the two of them were the town's most handsome couple—and had children. The boss man's appetites had him on the lookout for fast-moving tail where he could get it. As in Oklahoma with Phil, and later up at Rainbow Farm, Tom kept his sex life behind closed doors. Unless he was hitting on you, which he might after a lot of beer, you'd never know he was gay.

However, a few men had been put on the crew with motives other than work in mind, including a teenager we'll call Joey.

Joey may or may not have been sleeping with Tom, but he played a crucial role in Tom's life. Joey lived in one of Wright Spry's houses on Harrison Street and he became friends with a down-on-his-luck kid on the streets of Elkhart, a sixteen-year-old longhair named Rollie Rohm. He came to share a room with Joey in the house on Harrison, and though he worked every day at a Burger King and then at an RV parts manufacturer, Rollie seemed pretty fragile. He had just split up with his wife, was a new father and was lost.

Tom came by the house one morning—it was directly across the street from a house Tom owned on Harrison—and Joey introduced his new friend, Rollie. The sight of him immediately had Tom's nose open. He was everything Tom loved in men—young, lithe, long-haired, a rock 'n' roller wearing a version of a mullet. He was a little tough, a little dirty, a little damaged. Tom was a respectful person, used to handling his business discreetly, but the room seemed to constrict around Rollie. Tom was in the grips of an instant crush. Joey laid out Rollie's circumstances. From the description of his wife and new child, it was clear Rollie wasn't gay. But Joey was, and he was also attracted to Rollie. Tom offered Rollie a job and a place to stay.

SEVEN Rollie

Neither of us would go to heaven unless we could get the other one in.
—*Allen Ginsberg on the promise made with his lover, Peter Orlovsky,*
at three a.m. in Foster's Cafeteria, New York City

"VERY WHORISH," CHUCKLED HERB PHILLIPS, volunteering his assessment of Tom's love life.

Doug laughed. He was sitting with Herb and said, "I've never come right out and said that, but back in those days, he was quite the whore. Let's be honest. And he'd be the first one to tell you that himself."

Herb said, "He would appreciate that. Herb said he was very whorish."

"You can testify to that," said Doug. "But once he met Rollie, man, he changed his ways, did he not? I never saw him out whorin' around once he met Rollie. He told me, 'Doug, I've never been in love before. And I never knew what love meant until this.' He said, 'Now I've got Rollie and that's all I need.'"

"I was really naïve. I still am kind of naïve. I can't believe people get married, have kids and then turn the other way, but Rollie had moved in with Tom."

Gerry Livermore, the woman that Rollie called "Mom," didn't want her son falling in love with a man, but she had a mother's courage to recognize love as love. Tom was good to Rollie, and she was grateful for that. Gerry was actually Rollie's stepmother, but she had raised him since he was five years old and adopted him a couple years later. She never used the term "stepmother." Tom and Rollie both had family who would like to deny the two were lovers. Convictions, though, like appearances, are always more malleable in private than they are in public, and almost all of those who said they condemned homosexuality or bisexuality also admitted some admiration for the fact that these two were bound together by something deep and nameless. They were, in fact, two of the most in-love people you'd ever care to meet. They were inseparable.

"I kept hearing rumors from different people that they were like they were," said Gerry. "And I kept saying, 'That can't be true. Not my son.' Then it was on a New Year's Eve, this [Joey] called me up and talked to me for about two hours about how he was really upset and he missed Rollie and just on and on. He told me that Tom was really mean to young boys and beat him and did all these terrible things to him. And I thought, oh great.

"And then eventually when I met Tom, I realized he wasn't that way. At least, he wasn't that way with Rollie. He was good to Rollie," she added.

"Those two people were in love, and I guess even the county couldn't deal with that. I'm sure their homosexuality or bisexuality played into this," said Derrik DeCraene, Rainbow Farm's entertainment coordinator. "Rollie's family ran him off and he hated [John Livermore]. He wouldn't even let them on their property, you know? His own stepdad."

Eventually, that did change. John and Gerry would come up from Tennessee to visit relatives in Elkhart and stop in at the farm, and in the fall of 2000 John actually went to Rainbow Farm's Roach Roast. There was at least one time—possibly just before John and Gerry moved down to Tennessee with their three other boys—Tom, John and Rollie sat down at the dining room table with a bottle of whiskey. And when they were done with that bottle they drove into Vandalia and got more.

John and Rollie put aside some of their differences then, bonded by the intercession of the whiskey, but not all. On their liquor run, they got pulled over by a county cop. He took one look at Tom, who nobody liked to mess with when he was red in the face, and one look at John, who was as mean looking and as big as Tom and again by half, and decided better than to mess with all that. He gently told Rollie to drive those two to the farm and stay off the streets until they sobered up.

"I can't stress this enough: these two people were a family," Doug said. "When they were trying to get custody of Robert, the Elkhart court sent a woman out from the Family Independence Agency to do a home study on Rainbow Farm. Well, Robert took that lady by the hand and showed her his room, the house, the beautiful grounds, the garden. I think we had some new baby chicks in the chicken coop and she helped him gather eggs. She wrote up that she thought this was 'a wholesome environment for a young person to be raised in.'"

"You know they were gay or whatever you want to call it? I never knew that for a little while, and then it started to dawn on us," said Bob File, a neighbor of Rainbow Farm. "I never judged him for it. I don't know if a lot of people knew it, to be honest with you. He wasn't flamboyant. And neither was Rollie. Rollie was just about partying. That's all Rollie wanted to do. I couldn't really figure it out, to be honest with you—him being a lot younger. But they were both good people, I'll tell you that."

It gets complicated out there, in the sentimental wilderness of jukebox songs and barroom lovers. The circle of adults that made up Rollie's biological family didn't entertain any more or fewer dreams than anyone who lived in tighter nuclear arrangements, they just kept their fantasies closer. Partying evidently seemed worth the costs in marriages and spiritual health. Children got lost. Exposure to the raw weathers of the heart makes for sloppy strategies—every night was one of taking last-minute refuge, tabs extended at the package store, keys borrowed, cigarettes and husbands going to the wrong house. The mornings involve massive reconstruction, a temporarary, febrile universe of restarted cars and loyalties and debts just reaching all the way back to the trailer factory.

Rollie was one of the lost boys. He was seventeen years old when he met Tom in late 1990. Tom was thirty-six. Rollie had not been waiting for a man like Tom, but he craved direction. And once Tom was there he turned, still a child, to see the chaos that was his childhood, and fell back into Tom's arms.

Roland Eugene Rohm was born two days after Christmas 1972 to Elkhart native Robert "Bob" Rohm and his wife Cheryl Lynn. Cheryl already had one child, a daughter a couple of years older than Rollie, named Bethann. Bob and Cheryl were married two months before Rollie was born and only stayed together a few years. By all accounts and for whatever reason, Bob Rohm wasn't one much for kids. He fed and clothed Rollie for a few years but had another boy, Rollie's half-brother Nickolaus, whom he ignored completely. Bob Rohm did not respond to calls and letters regarding this book.

A quarter century later, when Rollie was holed up with Tom in their standoff with the FBI, Bob Rohm turned up at the police barricade on Black Street. Gerry had Nick with her, who was then twenty-one, and said, "Look, Nick, there's your real daddy." Nick hadn't seen him much in his life, and hadn't seen him at all for eleven years. Nick walked over and nervously introduced himself, saying, "You know who I am?"

"No," he said.

"I'm your son," said Nick.

After a minute, Bob said, "Which one?"

Well, as far as anyone knew, there were only two, and the one everyone was talking about was sitting somewhere down that road with a rifle across his knees. Nick just walked away.

According to Nick, the Rohm family was not completely bereft of cultural moorings. He claims that Bob's father was once the Grand Dragon of the Ku Klux Klan in Indiana. The state was once, in fact, the Klan's power base; Republican Klansman Edward Jackson was elected governor there in 1924 and presided over a legislature full of Klan members. The organization's actual financial structure was dissolved by Indiana veterinarian James Colescott in 1944, but the American Knights of the Ku Klux Klan still hole up in Newville, Indiana.

Nick said he and Rollie were "kinda proud" of their grandfather's leadership role. Rollie somehow inherited a photograph of his grandfather in his green robes, and they had talked about it. The photo would later be lost in the fire at Rainbow Farm.

Back when Gerry met him, Bob Rohm had his charm. He was a talker and a schemer—"could sell snow to an Eskimo," she said. He was working in a plastics plant, and she was practically a goody-two-shoes compared to his crowd, still living at home with her parents, who worked at the big New York Central railroad yard. Gerry Hoffer was a diligent student—she had been in Tom Crosslin's class at Elkhart High and knew him—and had gone through three years of college at Indiana University at South Bend, working toward her teaching degree. She was 23 and on her way out of Elkhart's blue-collar bog when she met Bob in 1978, and then, though she continued to kick her feet, she got stuck.

It does get tangled. Rollie was five years old when Gerry met Bob, and she could see the boy was already wounded, and took it on herself to protect him. Bob was a drinker, at best, and Rollie's real mom, Cheryl, had issues of her own. The courts had intervened at one point, and Bethann had already been in foster care for a short while. Rollie was spared the same fate because of Gerry. Cheryl got a new boyfriend, and Rollie had been living with them on and off, but the instant Gerry was on the scene, Cheryl tucked off to Arkansas for a year or two and as far as Gerry knew never said good-bye to Rollie.

Gerry was working full time at Johnson Controls in Goshen, where she stayed for seventeen years, and Bob went through spells with no money, so Gerry bought a house four doors down from her parents' place so she could adopt Rollie. While living in that house, Gerry and Bob had Nickolaus Paul Hoffer Rohm, who is eight years younger than Rollie. All of Rollie's siblings are halfs and steps.

Education was Gerry's specialty, and she found out right away once Rollie started kindergarten that he had a learning disability; however slight, it was enough that he was put in remedial programs. He was diagnosed as hyperactive—now they might say he had ADD—and was fawned over quite a bit by special ed counselors.

"He got along really well in school. He was real popular. But learning was hard for him, and he didn't want to concentrate," said Gerry. "We fought with him all through school."

The teachers sent home notes that Rollie was disrupting class. The cycle of medication went around and around; Bob and Cheryl had partied in order to stave off something ineffable, maybe just the end of the party, and Rollie was gobbling Ritalin in order to shorten that distance again, to keep words from swimming off the page and fantasy from creeping in on him from the fringes of the classroom. Gerry questioned the safety of Ritalin, though, and after reading about it extensively she decided to take him off it. There weren't many therapy options open to her, so she made up her own, using a strict diet to control his sugar intake.

With Gerry's help, Rollie managed to stay in school. For the first time in the boy's life, someone was paying attention. Gerry continued to educate herself on these issues and later in life would become a foster parent. She would also rail against the foster care systems in many states that encouraged parents to put kids on Ritalin as a kind of chemical restraint to dull the rage and fear that drove these kids to act out.

Rollie found safety with Gerry, but not calm, and he would blow out with some regularity. He didn't particularly like any subjects in school, and he fixated on the two things he did like: soccer and girls. Concord Elementary had a soccer program for kids, and he played from a very young age and showed talent. He also always had a girlfriend and clung to them with a kind of ferocity. His fears were deep—abandonment, being a freak to the other kids, poverty—and Bob didn't help reassure him.

Gerry continued to ride Rollie, staying present, keeping him focused. Their battle was epic.

Bob went out alone on New Year's Eve 1986 and then called a few days later to announce that he wasn't coming back. Gerry moved into an apartment with Rollie, then thirteen, and Nick, who was five or six. Rollie and Nick were close then, and Rollie would watch him after school and carry him around on his shoulders.

It was little Nick who first befriended John Livermore, another one of the denizens of the building. Gerry married him six months later. After that, Nick started losing his grip on his big brother.

John Livermore was a giant of a man, physically, and a commanding presence in the home. He had just started a custom metal fabricating business called Plant Machinery, welding parts and frames for the trailer industry, and was doing alright. He had a code. Livermore had been raised along with his many siblings by his father, a lumberjack and single parent, in Michigan's Upper Peninsula. Livermore had turned to religion and strict discipline to help him raise his own two boys, David and Robert, then sixteen and fourteen, respectively, and expected Rollie and Nick to toe the line, too. They had chores, they had rules and they had massive, pitched fights. This wasn't the Brady Bunch. It was tense, and Rollie couldn't take the strain. He resented John at the time and wanted out.

Finally, a year after moving in with John Livermore, Rollie ran away and stayed with his birth mother for a while and then ended up back with his dad, Bob, and Bob's new wife.

Rollie was fifteen. Bob immediately let Rollie drop out of school. He didn't give a shit; the kid was having problems, let him get a job and sort himself out. He didn't really need another mouth to feed anyway. For Rollie, however, this wasn't a bad deal. He got to be with his dad a little bit, which he craved despite their problems, and he got to be alone to withdraw into his own private world. He never went back to school.

Rollie was almost sixteen when Leslie Pletcher moved into the house with them. She was twenty-four, one of Bob's partying friends. Leslie was a cute rock'n'roller with long, straight dirty-blond hair, a good-time girl, going whatever way anyone was going. With her big, unquestioning blue eyes and soft voice, she gave the impression of deep, mysto insight, like she was amused by your thoughts. At the time she met Rollie, she already had one child in diapers, Candy, whom the court later found she couldn't really support, materially or emotionally. Leslie's mother was raising the child most of the time.

Gerry was livid. "Bob, being the bum that he is—none of their utilities or anything was ever in him and his wife's name. So they needed to put electric or something in somebody else's name, and Leslie was a friend of his wife, I guess. They asked her if she wanted to move in there. Well, you've got a fifteen-year-old child, hormones racing and everything else, and one thing led to another. Right in his dad's house."

Leslie Pletcher became pregnant by Rollie in November 1988.

For Rollie, this was his call to some kind of male responsibility, and he heeded it. He rushed out to find a job, finally scoring counter work at Burger King.

Robert Lee Michael Rohm was born August 16, 1989, one day before Leslie's twenty-sixth birthday. He was a good-looking boy, and was instantly the subject of intense adoration on the part of Rollie and Leslie, who were still living in Bob's house.

Gerry was staying far away from the Rohm household and didn't even know. "I was left in the dark. Nick would say something about Rollie's pregnant girlfriend; I thought it was a joke. In fact, Robert was four months old before I ever found out I had a grandson. But they thought that I would have her put in jail if they would've told me. If I would've known then what I know now, I would have."

Rollie never would have seen it that way. He was in love. Leslie liked Rollie's long-haired rocker look and gentle, retiring personality. They were a lot like one another.

"He was very sweet and all that," said Leslie. "He done everything for me. He stuck up for me. He just had a real nice personality. Then, after I'd known him for a year, we got married when he turned seventeen in December. And then in February we separated. So we were only married two months. That's when I found out he was gay."

This, she says, was the cause of their separation, adding, "That Tom, Tom's the one who came over and told me that he's gay."

Rollie's family sees it much differently. Only a few weeks after Robert was born, Bob Rohm threw Rollie and Leslie out—having a grandson around was real buzzkill—and they moved into a crappy apartment in Elkhart. Leslie was flattered and confused by Rollie's doting but pretty much laughing at him all the way. Soon after they were married, Rollie was pretty sure she was running around with another guy.

John Livermore knew Rollie couldn't support a wife and child on Burger King wages so he took him on at Plant Machinery, where he ran a forklift, assisted the welders and swept up. Many days, though, when Leslie came to pick him up in her car, this other guy was with her.

Gerry and Rollie figured out what was going on, but he was too nonconfrontational to risk a big fight and have Leslie walk out on him, because she could have taken Robert with her if she left.

According to the Livermores and members of Tom's crew who knew him, Rollie was fully aware that he was repeating a bad cycle. He had come from a home like this, and was scarred by it, and now he was creating a new one. He confided to Gerry, his only real confidante even then, that he was terrified that Robert would grow up like him—nervous, poor, constantly fighting the pull of self-loathing. He tried not to think about this too much, though; it tended to drive him into deep despair.

"Robert was his number one concern," Gerry said. "And I think it was because of his earlier childhood. He was gonna make Robert's better."

It's unclear whether Rollie met Tom before or after his marriage fell apart, but Rollie fell into a state of depression and confusion and moved back in with the Livermores for what they remember as most of 1990. It wasn't until two years later that he and Leslie actually got a divorce. But right away when he left her, she wouldn't let Rollie have Robert by himself. She would gladly let Gerry babysit every weekend, however. John's religious views were rocked by this rumor of Rollie's emerging bisexuality, but he said later it wasn't as much of an issue as it's been made out to be.

"We had a good relationship," said Livermore. "Just because they're homosexuals, you don't love them any less. They're still your son. Now, if he'd tried to become a deacon in a church or force his beliefs on anybody, I would have felt differently."

The Livermores took baby Robert on vacations and to visit family in Michigan's Upper Peninsula and to Tennessee. Since Rollie was always around, he had his son every weekend.

Rollie cared for Robert in ways his dad never had cared for him. He played with him, talked to him, rolled a ball for him, made sure he had toys. He made Robert laugh, and Robert laughing was one of the few times that Rollie would laugh, too.

Toward the end of 1990, he moved into the apartment with Joey. And there was Tom.

Rollie was an unshorn update on the dungareed greaser in the *Wild One*, torn right out of Larry Clark's *Tulsa*. He was a kid whose beauty hurt men and women alike because underneath his soft skin lay the indelible impressions of distrust and vulnerability. He was a midwestern hesher wearing a Levi's jacket and jeans and Nikes, hair past his shoulders and his tastes in music and the look in his eyes were an accusation—pride mixed with exposed soul rubbed raw. *You won't be the next to hurt me.* He was vain about his hair, which was wavy and light brown, and he knew that both men and women admired it. He was also athletic, and when he and the Livermore brothers would walk through town he would tease them by dashing nimbly through traffic. Though he aped the late-1980s Guns N' Roses look, his tastes were a little more broad, more open to the '90s indie-rock revolution that would bring Nirvana and Smashing Pumpkins to popularity. One of Rollie's favorite bands of the early 1990s was Sublime, a weed-obsessed punk outfit from Long Beach, whose songs mixed reggae's every-little-thing-gonna-be-alright feelgood with hip-hop's gangland posturing. Later they'd have a hit with "What I Got": "I don't get angry when my mom smokes pot / Hits the bottle and goes right to the rock."

Tom put Rollie on a flagpole crew and he took to that. He tried to pull his own weight with child support payments to Leslie, and Tom picked up some of the slack when he fell behind. Not that Tom had any sympathy for Leslie. He was the first one to advocate cutting her off from Robert completely, and she and Tom were bitter enemies almost right from the start.

It may have been the most courtly relationship of Tom's life, but Rollie balked at the sexual advances; this didn't seem like his bag, really, and to make it more complicated, every now and again Leslie would come around and give him a little pussy. Spinning deeper and deeper into confusion, he ran off to the Livermores' a couple of times during the summer of 1991.

"He'd go over to see Leslie when her boyfriend went out of town for work," said Gerry. "Tom even went over there a couple of different times and got Rollie and took him back with him. They were fighting over him."

Tom wasn't about to lose a fight over a lover. Leslie claimed that Tom shoved her off his porch once when she came over to see Rollie at the Prairie Street house, throwing her over a railing right in front of Robert, who was a toddler. She said she filed charges but no record of this appears anywhere.

"There was a knock on my door one morning and Tom was there. I had never met him," said Gerry. "He says, 'Is Rollie here?' I said, 'Yes.' And I hollered downstairs because Rollie was down in the family room. Tom says, 'Do you care if I go down?' I says, 'No, that's okay.' So he went downstairs. Little bit later, they come up and Rollie says, 'We're going for a drive, Ma. Be back in a little bit.' They got back together. I told John they must've had a little lovers' quarrel."

Finally, Rollie moved in at Prairie Street. The collective shifted around a bit to accommodate this new development, but mostly went on just the same, aggregating loose souls. Tom became even more of a big daddy, throwing his arms around this giant family of problem children. Rollie sometimes chafed under his rule like he'd gnashed at John Livermore, but there was a huge difference, of course, and the difference was that Tom was fun. He was in on the joke. In Tom, Rollie not only found his daddy, but found a mentor in a lifestyle that had separated him from other loving figures in his life—smoking, drinking, telling nasty jokes, playing music, getting laid. Rather than judging those things, Tom was a connoisseur, the maximum leader in a band of partiers.

More important, Tom let the kid talk. Rollie had always been so quiet no one knew he had anything to say. Even with Tom, the words didn't come geysering out, but in his own clipped manner he talked constantly with Tom, about everything from music to weed to politics to his greatest fantasies. Rollie's dream was to travel the world on a mission to gather esoteric knowledge and powers, experiencing medicines and rituals that could be used to heal people and make them whole. He watched cable TV programs about ancient sites like Angkor Wat and Mayan sun temples and Machu Picchu and the Buddhist monestaries in Tibet. He confided in Tom that he longed to walk the dirt paths of those monasteries high in the Himalayas, to study with monks, to learn the most important lessons—how to be at peace, how to love, how to attain some moral authority without caving in to the locally oppressive hegemony of the Christian church. Some of these, of course, were the power-trip fantasies of a kid who never had any power. But Tom also gave him a safe place to express concern for others, and to let his goals become more altruistic.

Tom, for his part, wanted a place to house his growing feelings for Rollie. He wanted a farm. Falling deeper in love with Rollie, his utopian dreams began to flower. Being out, and really out, had taken a toll, even if it never showed in his day-to-day behavior—he wanted to get away from the constant threat of being busted for weed and coke, the implied judgment over his relationship with Rollie, the municipality telling him what to do with his property, neighbors with their noses over the fence.

Tom began to take long rides out in the country, looking at houses out there, but the crew gathered at the Indiana Street office every morning and he felt he needed to be there to keep it running smoothly.

His secretary, Sharon, brought about his next move. During her divorce, she'd let her ex-husband Bud keep their house out toward the edge of town on Perkins Street. It was a sprawling ranch home on two and a half acres. The story, according to Tom and Sharon, was that she sold her half of the house to Bud but he just stopped paying her after she moved out. This went on for years, which frustrated Tom to distraction. He couldn't believe she'd let the guy bankrupt her and not do anything about it, but these are the foolish arrangements of the heart.

"Tom and Sharon were very close," noted Doug. "And Bud and Tom didn't get along. Tom would see Bud on the street and call him an asshole.

"So Tom told Sharon, 'Foreclose on that fucker. Take your house back. I'll pay for the fuckin' lawyer.' And Sharon kept saying, 'No, no, no,' but then she'd keep bitchin' about it. And finally, he said, 'Look, I don't want to hear about that house and your problems anymore, because you're not willin' to resolve it.' A week or so later, she said, 'Yeah, you're right. Let's go hire an attorney and foreclose on him.'"

Bud quit the place, but before he did he and his guests destroyed it. Some of the housemates had made a fire on the living room floor for heat, shitting in the unflushable toilet after the water was cut off and wiping with old clothes and throwing them in a closet. The basement was flooded and filled up with garbage and rats. You just wanted to throw a match on the place and burn it.

Of course, Tom took one look at it and saw a palace. Sharon was horrified, and Tom said, "Now, don't worry. This is what I do, take trashed-out houses and fix 'em up."

"Well, I can't afford to pay ya to do all the work," said Sharon.

Tom sized it up and said, "Okay, I'll buy the house from you. We'll do a contract and I'll give you a down payment and I'll make payments to you. I like this house. We'll fix it up and Rollie and I will move in here."

This was Tom and Rollie's love nest, and Tom laid it on with a complete redo. The crew came in and stripped out everything, inside and out, trimming out the skylights in the big living room that Bud had added but never finished. One day Tom rolled up with a big hot tub he'd acquired in a trade somewhere.

"What you gonna do, put that outside your family room?" said Doug.

"No, I'm gonna put it right in the middle of that fuckin' family room," said Tom, and he did.

Doug recalled later: "You could have a blast in that, I mean, that was entertainment. You could sit on the couch and chairs and there's all these people sittin' in the hot tub, drinkin', smokin' joints. They loved it."

This was the start of the real homey relationship between Tom and Rollie. Tom bought Rollie a sporty red Pontiac Fiero and new clothes. Perkins Street was a little less of a party pad, and they bought nice furniture and carpet to array around the hot tub and throughout the house. Moe and Amy were camped across the street in a stretch of woods right on the banks of the Elkhart River during summer months, and they helped the boys put in their first big garden. Not everything had changed: That back lot was the site of a massive Halloween party that year which got totally out of control and had the neighbors calling the cops, drunk and stoned crew members stumbling over the pumpkins, a roaring bonfire throwing light across the thin city stars, music drifting deep into the night.

The house was actually real close to the Livermore's, and once in a while the boys would come down there, especially ten-year-old Nick, but they had to sneak away from John and Gerry, who forbade them from visiting. They didn't approve of either dope or homosexuality, and Nick pretty much lost track of his big brother around this time.

Sharon Keener still came out to the house a lot, running things. Tom bought a house from Doug on Harrison Street and let her live there permanently.

The relative isolation brought Tom and Rollie closer. At night they soaked together in their tub, savoring the fine tastes of some gentle friend's hydroponic, watching TV, Rollie playing for Tom the new CDs he'd scored, Tom rattling on about the changes he would make to the house. More and more, Rollie talked about getting custody of Robert.

EIGHT The Farm

LEAVES HELICOPTERED DOWN OUT of the trees as Doug and I kicked through the lengthening grass on Rainbow Farm in November 2001. On the hillside behind the house, little patches of orange dirt were still freshly turned where .308 caliber sniper rounds had drawn an outline of Rollie under a small pine tree. All that remained of the farmhouse was a strangely unscorched foundation. There wasn't an odor of fire anywhere, and eyewitnesses like Doug said that it had been like that from the minute they were let back onto the property after the shootings. It smelled not of fire but of sassafrass. Not one charred stick of the house remained—the FBI had sucked it all up and carted it away.

Doug could hardly look at it. He turned toward the rolling fields and said, "We were on a mission from God from the very beginning up here."

On their very first visit to Rainbow Farm, Tom said to Doug: "Doug, it's our destiny to own this place. This is the place we've been looking for."

Right from the start, Tom talked about the place collectively. He would own it, but it worked in his life because everyone fell in love with the place just like he did.

In 1993 Doug had secured a good job for Tom's Services, Inc. up in Vandalia. A van-conversion outfit called Bivouac had gone belly-up and Doug was in charge of liquidating the property, a dozen large green metal buildings arranged in rows over five acres, plus a modern single-story office building on the opposite side of M-60. On the backside of the

Bivouac property was a disused but modern elementary school. Equipment and tools had to be removed and cleaned and readied for auction, and the place needed to be secured when no one was around. Tom put some of his crew on the job.

At about this same time, Herb Phillips was in contact with a friend, Maurice Williams, who had property in Vandalia that he wanted to sell.

"He thought he would retire to the farm at one time, but about three different times vandals came in there and just stole and vandalized the place. And so he went, 'Oh, I'll just get rid of it,'" said Herb.

The Files had leased Maurice's farm for years, planting some fifteen to twenty acres in corn. They had offered to buy all thirty-four acres outright, but Maurice didn't like the terms. Evidently, Mr. File had said to come see him only if he really got desperate.

"That's why I told Tom if he wanted to buy it, make it cash money, because I wasn't gonna be sitting around waiting for the next five years to get my money," said Maurice, interviewed on the phone from one of his homes in Calumet, Illinois.

The state had made several overtures to buy the place, too. There had been a house across the street, a nice four-bedroom farmhouse, and the Department of Natural Resources had scooped it up, moved the house and returned the acreage to wilderness. They planned to do the same to Maurice's land, but he wasn't interested in that.

One night at Herb's house, Tom told Maurice about the job they were doing in Vandalia, and that he needed someone with a gun permit to work security. Maurice was an ex-cop, so Tom put him on that job.

Sometimes Tom would come out and do the night shift with him. Talking together, Maurice came to know and respect Tom. They saw eye-to-eye on the way a man ought to be treated. Maurice had put in thirty-five years with the Chicago Police Department, and never sought a rank. A lot of his fellow African American officers were dead, he said, because they weren't supported in the force.

Maurice and his sister, Beatrice Thompson, had owned the farm together since the 1950s, and he had a dim view of Cass County politics. "Republicans owned Cassopolis, and they were backwards all the way down the line," he said. "And Vandalia was like a stagnant town in the lower part of Mississippi somewhere."

Tom, however, struck him as someone who understood. He wasn't a bigot and wasn't allergic to handling jobs out at Bivouac all by himself. He told Maurice that he would farm his place if he'd sell it. Maurice told him to come up with thirty-five thousand dollars in cash—a thousand dollars an acre plus another thousand for the ramshackle house—and he could take it.

Tom went home and hatched a plan. He would sell his office on Indiana Street and it's two attached apartments to get the cash.

"I'll never forget the day he auctioned that place on Indiana," said Moe Yonkers. "I sat there in chairs with Amy Jo and some other folks. Well, that price just kept going up and at one point Tom just turned with a big 'ol smile and said, 'We just got ourselves a farm.' He was ecstatic."

Tom was in as much of a hurry as Maurice. His new life wouldn't wait. The gavel came down and Tom and Maurice signed the papers and by afternoon Moe and Amy had snatched up their camping gear and were sitting behind the farmhouse smoking a bowl, trying to decide where to make base camp.

Maurice had called the place Maple Leaf Farm, but Tom was cornier than that. As Tom, Rollie and the crew on the Bivouac job took lunches out on the hill behind the farmhouse in the wet spring of 1993, another natural asset presented itself. Moe estimates that they went out there eight to ten times in April and on three occasions they saw rainbows.

"I think that it was the third time that we were sittin' on the hill, and it was just a brilliant, brilliant rainbow, aw, it looked like a picture out of a book, and Tom said to Rollie, 'Rollie, I think we ought to call this Rainbow Farm.' Rollie looked at him and said, 'Tom, I think we oughta, too.'

We all got a good chuckle out of it, and thus on, it was called Rainbow Farm," said Moe.

People naturally made assumptions, however, the most common being that they were affiliated with the Rainbow Family of Living Light, a loose but large nationwide network of back-to-the-land hippie activists who made a political and social point of organizing huge annual gatherings in the national forests. Many of the Rainbow Family were travelers who'd once spent months of each year on the road following the Grateful Dead. Tom made the link seem even more intentional by including one of the Dead's dancing bears on the logo for Rainbow Farm Campground. Moe knew something about the Rainbow Family, being a camper, but Tom did not and he insisted this had nothing to do with his choice of either the name or the Dead reference.

A rainbow flag, of course, had also become the international symbol of gay culture. This was why they laughed when they agreed this would be the name. Let people think what they want, said Tom. I'm sitting here with mostly heterosexual people, and mostly heterosexual people will come to this farm. It's an 'alternative' farm and whatever anyone wants to make of that, that's what it is.

It was a working farm when they moved in, with three sections planted in corn. There are mixed reports on whether Tom had ever mentioned making it into a commercial campground. It was supposed to be a family place, a Shangri-la where they could have cookouts and parties like they'd always had, but in more seclusion. Tom envisioned small cabins placed around the periphery of the property, where friends could get some quality R&R. Where they could all do some hunting and fishing, ride motorbikes, build big bonfires, smoke weed, make homebrew and spread out.

Later, when the politics moved to the fore and the festivals were in full swing, the name also reminded people of the Rainbow Coalition, the late-1980s, early-1990s political caucus of South Carolina congressman and Democratic presidential candidate Jesse Jackson, which included progressive voices from labor, minorities, the queer nation, youth and environmental and other liberal advocacy groups. Although the farm certainly became a magnet for those sentiments amid its mishmash of hippie liberalism and country libertarianism, this was not an intentional endorsement.

John Sinclair, the former manager of the MC5 and founder of the radical White Panther Party in Detroit, thought it was a reference to the Rainbow People's Party, which was the next incarnation of the White Panthers after they dropped some of their Black Panther affectations.

The name of Tom's farm wasn't tied to any of these, but neither were they strongly disavowed. Rainbows were the province of all kinds of groups and Tom didn't give a shit what you thought the place was about just so long as you remembered it was his place and offered it that kind of respect.

The whole idea was to be left alone. It sure wouldn't turn out that way. Right from the start, Rainbow Farm riled up the whole county.

Maurice Williams's farm was a complete mess in late April of 1993. The smallish, two-story, fieldstone-foundation farmhouse, which may have originally been constructed in the 1800s, could have been easily torn down and rebuilt, and maybe should have been—some of the ceilings had collapsed; the floor had rotted through; the drywall was decayed and moldy and most of the electrical, plumbing, heating, appliances, cabinetry and windows had to be replaced. The only thing worth keeping were the big floor timbers and even some of them had to go.

Behind the house, on the slight downward slope that ran to the three arable sections then in corn, stood a collection of rusted big-rig trailers and piggyback containers. Incredibly, they were full of blank tombstones. Where Maurice got most of this stuff, and what he would use some of it for, was beyond even his explanation. There were huge sheets of stainless steel and ricks of bricks stacked all over the property (cobblestones, it turns out, originally from Chicago's State Street) along with big stacks of lumber: two-by-fours, four-by-fours, two-by-sixes. Tom's crew would help Maurice move some of this stuff into storage and the rest was sold or dumped or recycled.

Moe and Amy set up a camp next to the old farmhouse and the very first day pulled a Rototiller off Tom's Chevy Blazer and started putting in a hundred-foot by thirty-foot garden behind the house, in a spot out of sight of the road between the house and the seven-acre marsh to the southwest. They'd live out of a tent the whole summer, leveling a spot on the hillside and making a big fire pit for cooking. Later that summer, when four-year-old Robert started coming up to the farm, this would become Rainbow Robert Camp. The house's toilet and shower were repaired first, with planks to walk on so you didn't fall through the floor, but the kitchen was a lost cause so they cooked outdoors all summer and fall.

Moe was sweating over the Rototiller that first day when the File boys dropped by, one in a truck and one on a tractor, with work to do in the fields. "What you doin'?" one of them asked. The sale of the farm was a shock to them, especially later when they found out that Maurice had given it to Tom for a song.

"I'm putting in a garden," said Moe.

"Hell, you can't grow nothing there," they said, pointing out that the soil was all slippery clay.

"Well, I'll give it a shot," Moe replied with his characteristic smile. Tom introduced himself and turned on the charm. The Files warmed to him immediately, sensing in Tom a good 'ol boy, and volunteered their services. "You folks need anything out here," one fellow said, jumping back on the tractor, "you just let us know."

Tom and Rollie had originally planned to just drop Moe and Amy on the farm, like any of their other job sites, but once they had unloaded the camp along with some flats of zucchini and tomatoes and strawberries, they stopped for a meal and a smoke.

"Tom and Rollie and Amy and I sat down at the first campfire," said Moe, "and we fired up a bowl and we didn't get about halfway through the bowl, and Tom looked at Rollie and said, 'Rollie, let's go get our sleeping bags.' Tom and Rollie cleaned 'em up a room, so they could get outta the bugs. And they roughed it right along with me and Amy."

Their affinity for the place was instant and unshakable: This was home at last. From that moment, they would spend as much time as they could at Rainbow Farm. The house was pretty much uninhabitable, so Tom still ran his business every day out of the Perkins Street house. But Rollie, Moe and Amy made steady work of the renovation, working mostly on the house during the week, gutting it, and waiting for the weekends to make big moves on the cluttered, overgrown grounds.

The very first weekend, the collective began to arrive.

This is a remarkable phenomenon in itself: here they were, America's working poor, turning out shift labor all week in the trailer factories of Elkhart, and yet on weekends they'd turn up with tents, kegs and chainsaws to work on Tom's farm for free. Nobody ever told them that this was communal property, and indeed, it was not. It was Tom's home. Yet, before he even owned the place, it was more. It was a dream of disappearance and reinvention, and anyone who wanted to disappear and reinvent themselves and imagine a new world was welcome to do it there.

The first weekend, a few friends and family came by and threw up tents in the yard, including Doug, Moe's brother Mike Yonkers and guys from the crew. Moe's lifelong friend Gene Sanders came, the man who had taught him how to camp as a boy. While they partied they were also pulling out small trees with chains hooked to the bumper of Tom's Blazer and Gene's four-wheel drive, making runs to the dump, and attacking massive, decades-old warrens of brambles and slash. Moe and Amy quickly determined that the Files were right about the soil, so they had folks help them move black muck from the swamp up the hill to enrich the garden. Tom and Rollie kept everyone fed, stoned and entertained. There was always a boom box blasting or someone playing guitar, usually their friend Guitar Joe Mallot.

"It might have been Mother's Day, I believe," said Moe, "and the next morning, when Tom got up, he said, 'Moe, I think we need to find somewhere else for all these people to camp. Look out there in that backyard.'

There were probably eight tents, and three or four cars down on the lane and people sleeping in them, just people who knew better than to drive home the evening before. He let 'em all come in and take showers and we fed 'em all every day."

That day Moe and Amy walked the property, which was like hacking through dense jungle, and found a new spot along the swamp a few hundred yards from the house. It was one of the few places the Files had kept brush-hogged, and was a good area for upwards of ten tents and a big bonfire. The groggy crew descended on it and in a few days it was turned into the Marsh Camp.

With Tom and Moe as guides, both the ethic and the aesthetic of the place were established immediately. This was a working farm where simple labor was a ticket to freedom. No nosy neighbors or cops were coming down on you when you blew your gage, or when you were over-the-line drunk or having a hatchet-throwing contest or getting it on with your old lady bare-assed in the bushes. It was all a stone giggle.

Tom decided to throw the biggest summer party he'd ever had, a pig roast for the coming fourth of July. Moe and Amy found the perfect spot under three ancient cherry trees on the north edge of the property. Farmers had piled fieldstones there for decades so it was dubbed Rock Camp. Moe would give a camp to anyone who would clear one, and twenty people claimed one the first day and the work was quickly accomplished. They hung a horse saddle from a tree for kids to play on and drove a pitcher pump for fresh water there.

They expected about 100 people that weekend and about 250 showed up, some of them people they didn't even know. The vibe, however, was unlike anything Tom and company had experienced in Elkhart; instead of ramping up to a kind of dystopic hysteria, a let's-get-crazy exorcism of urban neurosis that tended to send the city parties into tight and intimate confrontations, neighbor on neighbor, man on woman, answerer of the door on cop, the campout vibe and the big flow of smoke through the crowd put everyone in a pioneering mood. They were people together in the wilderness! Moe's cousin Paul, Doug, their friend Joe Mallot and others brought guitars, and tents were strewn everywhere around the edges of the new corn. They instantly ran out of roast pig, and Tom sent runners into Cassopolis to buy three forty-pound boxes of chicken and more beer and sodas. He didn't mind spending the money, the party was the point, but he related to both Moe and Doug that this gave him ideas. He was always looking for an angle to help pay for things, and he thought if he could refashion these festivals down the line and get ten dollars a head from everyone, they'd have a hell of a good time and even turn a little profit.

To warrant a gate fee, however, it had to be a killer party, and Tom was competitive. After that first fourth of July party, he thought he might try to own that date, throwing a big patriotic bash every year with fire-works and the lot. The very next summer, he would find out the locals had a different idea of entertainment. As his 1994 Independence Day party got under way, their gathering was disturbed by loud music and cheering ringing over the hills. Echoing over the treetops and the pond they could hear the reverberations, a great brutal drubbing of electric bass and drums, like a full-blown Slayer concert going on somewhere beyond the sun-dappled rows of new corn.

"Where the hell is that coming from?" asked Tom, perturbed.

Huge peals of shouting rose up in the trees. It was close enough that individual voices could be heard crying out and cussing. They could only surmise that one of the neighbors was having a huge party—a party bigger than theirs.

"The guys in that trailer at the end of the Pemberton Road are having a hell of a party," one of the new arrivals informed him.

Incensed, Tom and Rollie tried their best to ignore it, but finally cracked. Tom just couldn't stand to be upstaged. They jumped in the truck and sped off to investigate.

Down the road, they found a hillbilly party to beat all hell. The neigh-bors, who worked for the Files and were about to become acquain-tances of Tom's, had set up a boxing ring in their yard and were staging bare-knuckled fights. As Tom and Rollie pulled up, two shirtless men in jeans and boots were whaling on each other to the delight of screaming, drunken, blood-spattered onlookers. Heavy-metal music was blasting out of a giant sound system and the shaded grass was strewn with paper plates and bottles and steak and chicken bones. The party was teetering on the edge of an angry frenzy and, whether or not Tom started anything, their arrival gave it a good shove in the direction of raw id gratification. They weren't there five minutes when it erupted into a chaotic explosion of bloodlust, a massive brawl, and Tom, already in a gathering rage from being outdone on the most patriotic day of the year, waded in with both fists flying.

"When they got back to the farm that night, both Tom and Rollie were cut up, faces all bloodied, clothes all torn and dirty," said Doug. "They'd had themselves a time. And Tom told me then: 'Goddammit, that won't never happen again. Nobody will ever have a bigger fourth of July party than us.'"

They didn't get many visits from the sheriff right away, but the local game warden came around with some regularity. Tom, Rollie and their guests would shoot target practice with their deer rifles now and again, and Jim Crosslin recalls that he was out there shooting with them one time and the warden came by to tell them that the farm was a no-fire zone because of its proximity to the DNR land on their perimeter. Tom decided to ignore this. As farmers, they could get permits to shoot a number of deer on their property during the season, and if they could shoot then, they decided they might as well shoot anytime. They were below the line in southern Michigan marking the latitude above which hunting can be done with high-powered rifles, so any actual hunting that went on at the farm had to be done with a shotgun. Rollie was left-handed, and there were mixed reports as to whether Tom bought him a left-handed shotgun or whether he just shot a right-hander from the opposite shoulder, ejected shell whistling across his nose. There were also mixed reports as to whether or not he could hit anything. Derrik said he couldn't hit the broad side of a barn. Moe insisted he was a crack shot. Rollie bagged his first deer that summer with only Amy there to help him.

"I cleaned Rollie's first deer," said Amy. "He didn't know how to clean one. He shot that in the middle of the summer."

"We applied for permits for the garden, and they told us, 'Well, we're not gonna give you permits this year. Come back next year and show us the damage,'" said Moe. "So on purpose we grew five rows of sweet corn for them, hoping they'd eat it first before the rest of our vegetables. We had enough deer coming out there."

"It was on a hot summer day and he was gonna leave it in the middle of the field 'til these guys got home from town. I said, 'Rollie we can't do that,'" said Amy.

"It was ninety degrees," said Moe.

"The deer will be spoiled by the time they get home."

"He wanted to leave it laying there 'til I got home!" said Moe. "'Have Moe clean it!' Amy says, 'I know how to clean it, let's go get it.'"

"I had him help me hang it up," she added. "He helped me pull the skin off when I couldn't pull the skin off."

It was Rollie's first experience with hunting and with meat cutting, something he later came to enjoy. They ate fresh venison for weeks.

When fall came, Moe and Amy first moved into an old shed that Maurice had bought from the railroad and put on the spot for storage. They called it their "sugar shack" and lived there some of the first winter. Later, they would fix up the cinderblock garage and turn it into their makeshift apartment.

"Moe and Amy used to live in that," marveled Jim Crosslin. "They had 'em a wood burner set up in there and they stayed out there in the wintertime."

Tom and Rollie had the one habitable room in the house, and while they renovated the rest of the place—the furnace and the kitchen first, racing the area's heavy lake-effect snows—Tom began to realize that Rainbow Farm had awakened more than just the party beast within. This place was good, spiritually good, and he felt good in it. Every wild scheme they dreamed up seemed to come to pass, so he began dreaming bigger. He saw that he and Rollie had a real opportunity to get custody of Robert, to make a kind of nuclear family. More than this he saw an opportunity for redemption. In talks with Doug, who was always his confidant for the more contemplative matters in his life, he was dealing with some guilt from his past.

There had been a lot of hell-raising, a lot of petty crime, a lot of spiritual chaos. True righteousness had evaded Tom Crosslin and now he wanted it. He couldn't stand judgment of any kind, and the idea that his behavior might have overshadowed his generous heart needled him. It was corrosive and he worried that his people might see on him the signs of failure. At the dark edges of their lifestyle lay criminality and ruin, waiting there if you went too far. In his own life there had been casualties—Larry's eye; his divorce; men and women who had gravitated toward his biker gang, his weed and his service company and then were quit in various states of addiction and psychosis; young boys taken as lovers and put back out on the street. But these were good people. They deserved to feel better about themselves. They could control their own esteem, and all it would cost is everything. They had to lay it all on the line.

Doug's older brother Mike had given him some advice once and it stuck with him. "He told me a long time ago. 'Don't try and do anything worthwhile in Elkhart, Doug,' " he said, " 'They'll just beat you down. If you've got any aspirations to do anything meaningful, get away from the Midwest, man. Go out West and have fun.' "

But Tom said no. They weren't going to do it out West. This was their piece of the country, this was holy, this was where the family was. So the dirt on Rainbow Farm was where they planted the very best of themselves and it quickly shot up in a riot of green. This time, he was starting with prime material. Rainbow Farm wasn't one of his broken-down southside ghetto houses, with the basement full of bum shit and junkie rigs jammed in the drywall. It was country, it was pure. It was also loaded with fierce resistance—a good deal of it inside their own heads.

"Tom came to me many times and said he wanted to atone for his sins, basically," said Doug. "But he came to me, and he would not say this to anybody, 'I'm sorry about a lot of the things that I did, and you're the kind of person that can help me make some things right.' He wanted to be a good man. But most of his life he didn't know what that was."

Even during their spats, Tom kept Doug close because Doug was the conscience he needed. Doug was averse to trouble, and Tom knew it. Tom could fight, he could curse people he needed in his life, he could make enemies in the local administration, but Doug was looking after his dignity. Because Doug had had enough of heartbreak and shame.

Doug's parents had split up when he was young, and his older brother Mike ended up in reform school. The experience horrified Doug and he vowed to keep out of trouble. It was the height of the hippie era and Mike disappeared into Haight-Ashbury to become a freak known as "Frog," coming back to Elkhart only periodically, and toting a heroin habit. Doug's mom died of cancer in 1976 and Doug begged Mike to leave him and his father in peace, and eventually Frog took to the rails and became a modern-day hobo, and possibly—if it's the same guy—a legend: In 1997 a hobo named Frog was declared King of the Hobos at the annual National Hobo Convention in Ames, Iowa. Doug and Mike's dad died in 2002. Frog might not even know.

"Tom recognized in me someone who at least comprehended the difference between good and bad," chuckled Doug.

NINE Madd Maxx

Homosexuality, dope, uh, immorality in general: These are the enemies of strong societies. That's why the Communists and the left-wingers are pushing the stuff, they're trying to destroy us.

—*President Richard M. Nixon to H. R. "Bob" Haldeman,*
Oval Office tapes, May 31, 1971

MAX BAER ROBINSON KNEW something about laying it all on the line. For years, his rickety personage comprised a big chunk of the pot movement in northwest Indiana. He had worked with NORML, was a friend to *High Times* and their Freedom Fighters, and was a tireless advocate for industrial hemp. "Madd Maxx," as he was called, had made sacrifices in his pursuit of justice—his career, his family, even his home. His cluttered bungalow in Hammond, Indiana, was a smoked-out warren, a momument to a life given over to pushing back against The Man.

He was named after the boxer Max Baer, the world heavyweight champion from 1934 to 1935 and the great Jewish hope who'd beaten Hitler's Max Schmelling with a Star of David sewn on his trunks. This association afforded Max Robinson some chutzpah but couldn't have been more ironic considering his physical condition. Robinson was a smallish and deliberate man with great energy but somewhat disabled by myasthenia gravis (a form of muscular dystrophy, a degenerative nerve disease), which slowed him down and made his voice very nasal and difficult to understand. He also suffered from glaucoma and cataracts.

Like a lot of patients with MD, MG and glaucoma, he used cannabis as a cheap and effective treatment that also enhanced the effectiveness of some prescription meds.

He was a very capable campaign planner with a sharp wit and an unending ability to talk big picture about resisting the drug war—though he did most of it through e-mail because of his voice. The small living room in his house was dominated by two computers and production equipment used to help create his public access TV show: "They're Stealing Your Country—Take It Back!"

In early spring 1991 a few of Tom's crew had seen notices in the *South Bend Tribune* about regular meetings at the public library for those who wanted to "relegalize" marijuana, hosted by then-thirty-four-year-old Max Robinson. Here's a guy with some balls, they thought. Holding pot meetings at the public library. Curious, Tom and Rollie drove out to one of the monthly meetings to check it out.

When they met Max they were even more impressed. Max had been the South Bend organizer for the 1990 Hemp Tour, which brought in Jack Herer, the author of the bible of the industrial hemp movement, *The Emperor Wears No Clothes*, which has sold over 600,000 copies. At that time, Max was on fire and was organizing a 1991 festival. He was doing all this while working as a telemarketer and often living on Social Security disability payments and food stamps when he was too wrapped up in his politics, or held down by his illness, to do anything else. He was a certified welder, a computer freak, and trained in business management, but he didn't pursue these things as passionately as he did pot law reform. Max was an irritating, uncompromising hustler.

He readily acknowledged some of the contradictions in his libertarian positions, too: Here he was, living on Social Security for life, but he was against it in principle. He was also against Medicare and other forms of "socialized medicine." He believed that overregulation and government ties to Big Pharmacy and Big Insurance kept healthcare prices high, and if both would butt out maybe the regular consumer could afford drugs and medical care.

Max's main project—which he also sought to display at the downtown library—was his Hemp Museum. This was a traveling exhibit, modeled after the famed Hash Marihuana & Hemp Museum in Amsterdam, displayed across twenty to forty feet of tables and meant to dispel myths about the *Cannabis sativa* plant. Not only did it contain accurate information about the medical uses of marijuana and the properties of pot's active ingredient, tetrahydrocannibinol (THC), but it also gave a simple history of the cultivation and commercial uses of commercial hemp, the low-THC male plant, used primarily as an industrial fiber over the past millennia.

After 1937 the government had done its best to destroy all evidence that hemp was once one of the top crops grown in America, especially right there in Indiana, where slick advertising photos had once hawked tractor-mounted harvesters and fiber breakers. Many crop records went missing and mention of "hemp" or "cannabis" had been purged from some agriculture records. The government destroyed all copies of the propaganda film, *Hemp for Victory*, made by the United States during World War II to encourage farmers to grow cannabis for military rope and cloth and oil. Jack Herer became a hero when he found the one copy of the film in the Library of Congress, where it had survived only because it had been misfiled.

Max's small Hemp Museum did its best to reconstitute bits of this history, reminding viewers that the U.S. Constitution and the Declaration of Independence were both written on hemp paper, that Washington and Jefferson both recorded growing hemp on their farms—that even President George H. W. Bush, an aggressive antipot crusader, had bailed out of a burning airplane over the Pacific during World War II in a parachute with hemp rigging.

It was a small-scale exhibit, consisting of a lot of Xeroxes, hanks of hemp rope, hemp oil, etc. but it was courageous, and Tom saw the potential. This was a simple visual method to change public attitudes about pot, and in it he saw his first political action. He decided to back Max's Hemp Museum with money and his company's services.

"When we saw his setup over there, we were really impressed," said Moe. "The guy talked real positive. Tom said, 'Oh man, I'm gonna go after this.'"

"One of the things Tom liked about him is that he spoke his mind," said Doug. "He would stand up for what he believes."

Max's aggression is apparent in some of the materials posted to his Web site during his 1999 run for mayor of Hammond as a Libertarian Party candidate, writing: "They lied at Waco, they lie everyday in courtrooms across the country, they lie everytime they tell you they will lower your taxes, they lie, they lie, they lie! Police and government officials are not to be trusted . . . They're stealing your country."

This kind of rhetoric, which Max was already spouting in passionate tirades during the early 1990s, electrified Tom, resonating as a politicized anger and hope which he himself had never been able to articulate. Tom was a stalwart Republican and had voted for Reagan twice and George H. W. Bush, too. Other people on his farm were Democrats and even Greens. But here was a guy who was *saying* all the things about social liberty that Tom and a lot of his crew *felt*. Max *understood*.

What he understood was libertarianism—a conservative political philosophy that had inspired radical progressive stances during the Vietnam War and civil rights era, but never had the same cachet as leftism or liberalism. Though the term had been around since an 1858 journal called *Le Libertaire*, the Libertarian, where it was used in reference to "individualist anarchism" as opposed to syndicalism, the philosophy didn't really come to any prominence until the presidential candidacy of Barry Goldwater in 1964.

In many ways, Max's rap was the language of Goldwater, and his cohorts in the Libertarian Party of Indiana were philosophical heirs of that snarling Arizona senator who took the Republican nomination from Nixon in 1964 and threatened to split the party.

Goldwater was no fan of marijuana, let's make that clear, but he was the kind of conservative who saw the moralistic prohibition of marijuana as a Big Government disaster, a boondoggle filling the jails with

nonviolent taxpayers and packing the welfare rolls, expanding a bureacracy for the sole purpose of expensive and paternalistic meddling.
In the 1960s, "conservative" didn't mean antiabortion and all that, but
rather limited government power. These were people who wanted a return to rugged individualism, at least as an ethos. Goldwater wanted big
corporate power out of the government and wanted the government
out of places like Vietnam, out of the welfare business and out of everyone's bedroom and body. He wanted religious tolerance, not religious
tyranny. (It was Goldwater who said later, in July 1981, when the Reverend Jerry Falwell's activist Moral Majority reared its ugly head during
Reagan's first term, "I think every good Christian ought to kick Falwell
right in the ass.") Goldwater was for freedom on both the personal and
economic fronts, and evidently a lot of people agreed with him.

Not enough, however. Goldwater got hammered by Lyndon Johnson
in the '64 election and was painted as a redneck extremist, but his campaign caught on with many young antiwar idealists who thought the
big leftist movements would only give the government more power.
Among them was David Nolan, a founder of M.I.T. Students for Goldwater and later youth coordinator for the Liberty Amendment Committee,
a "constitutional conservative" group which sought to repeal the federal
income tax and get the government out of all activities not enumerated
in the U.S. Constitution. In Goldwater, and in the take-no-prisoners rhetoric of his speechwriter Karl Hess, Nolan and his colleagues finally
heard a major figure—the Republican presidential nominee!—propose
that the U.S. government had no authority to police personal morality.

Libertarian was not a word that Goldwater used to describe himself,
but Nolan and others picked up on the term as a way to reclaim the
original, free-market interpretation of the word "liberal." In December
1971 they launched the Libertarian Party in Nolan's living room in Colorado Springs, Colorado. It is an optimistic "good neighbor" philosophy, in practice relying on corporations and markets to police themselves,
but one which leaves so much latitude for exploitation and abuse it was
only a sideshow in the revolutionary circus of the late 1960s and early

1970s. It is a sharp critique of both Republican and Democratic admin-
istrations, however, that libertarianism became a call to militants again
in the 1980s and '90s.

This plea comes from the bottom of my heart. Every friend of freedom, and I
know you are one, must be revolted as I am by the prospect of turning the
United States into an armed camp, by the vision of jails filled with casual drug
users and of an army of enforcers empowered to invade the liberty of citizens
on slight evidence.
> —**Milton Friedman, Nobel Peace Prize–winning architect of conservative
> Reaganomics, "An Open Letter to Bill Bennett,"** Wall Street Journal,
> **Sept. 7, 1989**

Tom, in particular, heard a lot of his own beliefs in Madd Maxx's libertarian screeds. Like Max, Tom's position on pot was basically a right-wing
critique: he thought drugs should be legal not because the government
should provide some kind of utopian experience; he thought drugs
should be legal because policing them was unconstitutional.

A lot of Tom's rural and blue-collar neighbors felt the same way, and
this represented a huge change in the movement to legalize pot: instead of being a liberal or progressive or even hippie issue, conservatives had now weighed-in against the drug war, with serious possible
consequences for the interpretation of federal powers. In the early
1980s, for example, both the Green Party and the Libertarian Party put
an anti–drug war plank in their national campaign platforms, though
arriving there via different philosophical routes. For the Libertarians, it
was the bastardization of the Constitution's Commerce Clause that
wrongly gave the feds the power to police drugs. But that particular
bastardization is the underpinning of the whole liberal social safety net.

During the presidency of Franklin Delano Roosevelt, the General Welfare Clause of the constitution was still narrowly interpreted; under the
theory of enumerated powers, the creation of a Social Security Administration, for instance, was not a power granted to the federal government.

Neither was policing drugs. Faced with bringing the nation out of the ravages of the Depression, however, Roosevelt threatened the Supreme Court—once promising to increase the number of judges to fifteen and stack it with his own appointees—until it reversed its position on General Welfare. Born then were Medicare, Social Security, the Department of Housing and Urban Development—the bulk, in fact, of the federal bureacracy and all of the most-prized creations of Progressivism.

That same court then reinterpreted the Commerce Clause to grant Congress the ability to regulate everything "affecting" interstate commerce—which was just about everything imaginable.

Harry Ainslinger, then head of the Federal Bureau of Narcotics, jumped at this opening, proposing to make marijuana illegal as a "tax crime." The 1937 Marihuana Tax Bill sailed through Congress on a wave of hubris and bald-faced lies during the House floor vote. (One of the representatives assured the chair during the vote that the American Medical Association was in "full agreement" with prohibiting pot, though the AMA had submitted, in writing, the opposite opinion.) Smokable pot, cannabis medicine and even commercial hemp were criminalized throughout the United States.

Marijuana continues to fuel the fight over this interpretation of federal powers. In the 2005 decision *Gonzalez v. Raich*, three of the court's most conservative judges ruled that the government had no authority to interfere with state medical marijuana laws—in this case, a pro-pot opinion—but a liberal majority ruled that it did. Justice John Paul Stevens almost apologized for it in his majority opinion, saying it's a shame that cancer patients can't have their dope, but the Commerce Clause had been read this way since the New Deal court. He called it "well-settled law."

When Tom met him in the spring of 1991, Max was planning his biggest event ever: a four-day Fourth of July festival called Independence Camp in recognition of the two hundredth anniversary of the Bill of Rights.

This was to be his crowning achievement, a revival meeting of patriots who smoked dope. It was billed as a "freedom festival"—code that meant it was pot-friendly. Max, like Tom, considered himself a true patriot, a purist, a man who believed the Constitution of the United States was a work of tolerance and liberty and one of the finest documents ever produced by the mind of man. Most hemp rallies across the country took this angle—they weren't generally down-with-the-U.S.A. affairs—but this was especially true in industrial Indiana, where passions for the red-white-and-blue ran high.

But as patriots it was their job to expose the hypocrisy at the heart of prohibition, and Max savored this. He was confrontational. Displays like his Hemp Museum were evidence in a grand and public trial. This was a constitutional crisis, and he needed to rub it in the face of the politicians who carried on about sacrificing freedom for morality. His fest was going to be four days of righteous haranguing with movement heroes Jack Herer and a famous hemp advocate named Chris Conrad, R. J. Tavel from a libertarian court-reform group called the Fully Informed Jury Association, good local bands, lots of smoke and whatever other drugs were around. Max thought they should all be legal, anyway, so he didn't care what people did once they were through the gate.

Through some friends at *High Times* he'd found a site for the camp, a gorgeous fifty-two-acre plot of rolling hills close to Hudson Lake out in rural New Carlisle, about fifty miles due east of Chicago. Max's description really put a spell on Tom: When Max had first gone out to the property, he took the South Shore train. The New Carlisle station was just a whistlestop, and when you stepped off the train you were in open country. He walked a couple of miles down a road shaded by maple trees and then followed a circular driveway to what he described as a "1950s ranch-style dream home." This sat up on the edge of the fifty-two acres, which had woods and ponds. It was breathtaking.

The house and acreage belonged to a guy named Ray Christl, by all accounts an eccentric who ran a Chicago production company renting outdoor stages. One of the other swaths of green in the area was a vast horse farm owned by TV-talk-show hostess Oprah Winfrey.

Christl wanted to call the festival Hempstock USA, but Max thought that was much too similar to the Wisconsin festival called Weedstock, thrown every year by the man Max considered his mentor, Ben Masel. So the press called it Hempstock, but in typical Max fashion, he kept insisting that it was Independence Camp. Even at his own event, he was a contrarian.

Still, Tom immediately committed to helping Max throw this event, and so did Rollie, Moe and Amy. After one of the South Bend library meetings, they went for coffee and Tom pulled out his little traveling sack of chronic. He always had good weed with him, Max acknowledged, and they talked about his vision for the Hemp Museum.

Max was dead set on taking the museum down to Logansport, Indiana, site of a major hemp festival about sixty miles south, halfway to Indianapolis. This would be a warm-up for Independence Camp. But his van had crapped out and he was broke. He was always broke, which, in fact, was one of the things about Max that rubbed a lot of people the wrong way. Besides being very hard of hearing and having a voice that was difficult to understand, he also had a big chip on his shoulder, as though the urgency of his political program meant that the government or big-money political organizations or somebody owed him a break. Derrik DeCraene, who would later work at Rainbow Farm, had been working another hemp-friendly ecofest in LaPorte called Green Wave around this same time where he had already met Max and come to dislike him.

But on the way home that day, Tom decided to fund Max's trip to Logansport. The event was the Hemp and Freedom Festival, opening April 20, 1991. Organizers Geri and Paul Guthrie were putting it on for the second year at Tall Sycamore Campground, right on the banks of the Wabash River. Their 1990 festival had drawn two to three thousand people; they'd had the Green Panthers there and Weedstock's Ben Masel and other pot heroes. Tom took Max down to the print shop and bought him $250 worth of fliers to promote his Independence Camp, then got his van fixed. They were off.

The 1991 event at Tall Sycamore had some problems, which might have put Max on notice as to just how easily his own event could go awry. Tom took note of the issues, but that didn't curb his enthusiasm. He saw that local prosecutors were threatened by these small-town organizers. Plus, the five of them—Tom, Rollie, Moe, Amy and Max—had a ball smoking dope in the open air, camping, and listening to bands and speakers.

"Max became Tom's friend for life," said Doug.

"Yeah, pretty much from that point on," agreed Moe. "Boy oh boy. Tom funded everything Max ever went to."

Max needed a patron, and Tom needed a guru; they milked one another for all they were worth. Tom didn't go overboard, but he was generous with Max when they were getting along. And Max had been around the movement a long time; he knew that Tom's feelings of persecution as a pot smoker reflected a reality in America, that the War on Drugs was increasingly a war on marijuana.

Since 1972 when President Richard Nixon launched the first attack of the War on Drugs (coining the term in an Oval Office discussion with Chief of Staff H. R. "Bob" Haldeman saying he wanted an "all-out war, on all fronts"), an estimated 10 to 15 million Americans have been busted for marijuana, the overwhelming majority, over 80 percent, for simple possession and use. In 1971 at the height of the hippie era, 292,179 people were busted for pot. The next year, as Nixon's war kicked in, that number jumped to 420,700. President Ronald Reagan greatly increased funding for this war—creating the upward spiral that would take public expenditures from $1 billion a year in 1981 to over $20 billion in 2001—and gave police the forfeiture boondoggle. George H. W. Bush ramped up mandatory minimum sentences. By 2001 pot busts would reach 724,000 in a single year. NORML reported that pot arrests have more than doubled since 1991, while busts for cocaine and heroin fell by 33 percent. Already by the early 1990s, America's jails were crowded with potheads, and it has gotten worse every year since.

This was inevitable: Americans, like drug users worldwide, use more marijuana than any other illegal drug—vastly more. Law enforcement needs numbers to validate funding for and spending on the drug war and busting pot users is an easy way to get them. A lot easier than busting crack or meth users. Any cop will tell you that most potheads are nonviolent, smart and don't carry guns—good people.

By the government's own best figures and estimates, Americans smoke mountains of weed. This was already going on in 1991, as Max and Tom talked in preparation for Independence Camp, but in the interest of providing some up-to-date statistics, it's helpful to skip ahead in time. The National Drug Intelligence Center, a clearinghouse for federal data on drug use and crime, estimated that in 2000 Mexico and Colombia produced 7,500 metric tons of marijuana for the U.S. market, or roughly 16,500,000 pounds, and Canada produced another 800 metric tons, 1,750,000 pounds, of which 50 to 60 percent has been reported as being exported to the United States (though federal officials in both countries couldn't verify that export percentage). Federal seizures of both domestic and imported sources that same year totaled 2,614,746 pounds, but that would represent a relatively small percentage of the weed seized by law enforcement, as it doesn't include any amounts nabbed by state, county or local police—agencies that handle amounts of pot orders of magnitude higher than the feds but not generally tabulated state-by-state.

The homegrown market is just as significant, economically, and maybe more so culturally. Since the 1980s, marijuana production shifted stateside and criminalization made it hugely profitable. NORML doesn't compile a domestic crop report every year, but its most recent report estimated that the minimum 1997 domestic U.S. harvest was 5,500,000 pounds. This was a low-ball figure, using counts and per-plant weights less than half of what the DEA uses. NORML figured this crop was worth

$15.1 billion to growers and $25.2 billion at retail. Using these figures, marijuana was the number four cash crop in the country that year, surpassed only by corn, soybeans and hay, and was the number one cash crop in Alabama, California, Connecticut, Hawaii, Kentucky, Maine, Rhode Island, Tennessee, Virginia and West Virginia. If you use the government estimates for weight and street market price rather than wholesale price, as the feds often do, then pot was by far the number one money crop in the nation.

Rainbow Farm was in Michigan, and Michigan, for its prominence in the pot movement, was not high on NORML's list of marijuana producers, ranking twenty-third for the 1997 crop. But the price was high there, averaging $265 an ounce, fourth in the nation, and it's a major transshipment state for "BC Bud," high-THC-content hothouse superbud from British Columbia, plus Quebec Gold and Mexican skunk.

No, Michigan's claim to fame is for being the state where people get *busted* for pot. Radical poet, MC5 manager and White Panther Party founder John Sinclair was set up by undercover agents there in 1967 and served two years of a ten-year sentence for possession of two joints. His arrest drew protest appearances by John Lennon, Yoko Ono, Allen Ginsberg and others. Subsequently, in 1972, the radical bastion of Ann Arbor was the first city in the nation to decriminalize marijuana possession, making it a misdemeanor punishable by a five-dollar fine. The Hash Bash, the first organized public smoke-out, began in 1971 on the University of Michigan campus and inspired a thousand other hempfests that occur now in every state in the union.

In a 2002 "Open Letter to America's Prosecutors," Scott Burns, the White House's deputy director for state and local affairs tells prosecutors that "the truth is that we aren't imprisoning individuals for just 'smoking a joint,'" saying that just .46 percent of those in prison nationwide are in for possession.

I checked this out with Brian C. Bennett, a former federal intelligence analyst living in Barboursville, Virginia. A twenty-year air force intelligence veteran and former senior technologist with the federal External

Affairs Office, Bennett went into the data used by the White House's Office of National Drug Control Policy (ONDCP), the Department of Justice (which includes the DEA, FBI, ATF, etc.), the Federal Drug Administration and other agencies, to look at how they skewed the numbers. The damning results are posted on his graphics-friendly Web site, "Truth: the Anti-Drugwar," at www.briancbennett.com.

Bennett looked into who is actually getting incarcerated in Michigan, breaking down raw numbers used to produce the Uniform Crime Report for the Michigan State Police and sentencing info from the Department of Corrections. For 2001, for instance, the most recent year available, 9.6 percent of all arrests for any crime statewide were for drugs, and 4.1 percent of all busts were for pot. But, of those, 88.1 percent were for the federal categories of simple possession and use—not dealing, not growing, not being a member of the Mexican mafia. Even if you threw out all the other pot arrests in order to eliminate duplications, and figured that pot possession must often be a secondary charge in busts for burglary, car theft, etc., at the very best, police were using arrest for possession as a fallback, and in the end the vast majority of all drug users were going down for holding marijuana.

More important, this wasn't happening in the inner city, but in the rural counties. Not included in the raw data pulled by the Uniform Crime Report statisticians were data for the Ann Arbor, Detroit, Lansing, Livonia and Flint police departments. The numbers we received reflected what was going on out in places like Cass County, places where the cops would routinely say they didn't want to bother the peaceable pot smoker at home.

And it was getting worse. Michigan prosecutors were going after smokers. While arrests of Michigan marijuana distributors and growers stayed flat from 1998 through 2001, arrests for possession increased sharply from eight thousand to over eleven thousand per year in these same rural counties. Meanwhile, all crime in the state was experiencing a steadily downward trend.

The situation in Indiana was similar: Marijuana busts were rising, and activists were getting targeted. Max tried to tell Tom that what they were about to get into was very serious, but for Tom it had become a crusade.

The 1991 festival schedule rolled on and seemed to be building toward some kind of freaky crescendo, with Max in high gear and Tom just getting his footing. Max and Ray Christl took off to circulate fliers up at Weedstock, which was happening over Memorial Day weekend that year in rural Black River Falls, Wisconsin, and invited Tom along. "I don't know," Tom said. "You go ahead and I might turn up there."

Max and Ray got up there and were tripping on acid when, sure enough, Tom and Rollie came rolling up in Tom's big red pickup. Ray, who was not a regular acidhead, was running around naked holding a towel in front of his dick while he stood right next to the public road, spray painting messages in Day-Glo paint all over the travel trailer they had dragged up there. Max got the vibe that maybe Tom and Rollie were avoiding them. But meanwhile Tom was studying the place and Ben Masel's operation.

Weedstock was an annual festival that ran for fourteen years from 1988 to 2001, put together by Masel, a pro-marijuana warrior well known all over the country, head of NORML Wisconsin for several years in the late 1980s and early 1990s and a father figure to the state's pot underground. Tom and Ben would meet, though much later, at either the '96 or '97 Weedstock. Masel was up to something that not many activists had done since Woodstock: he would rent out a piece of private property and turn it into a three-day campout, where heads could listen to bands and pro-pot speakers but stay on site, fed by approved vendors who were kicking back a percentage to Masel and the sponsors.

This wasn't just about pot, it was consumer culture gone feral. For an entry fee of twenty-five dollars, thousands of heads beat paths through the tall grass of Wisconsin's west central country openly smoking the kind bud. The genius of this idea hit Tom like a flash: If Masel wasn't making money, he was just doing this wrong. Masel ran the thing on rented property in order to skirt drug war forfeiture laws, but there was no investment in permanent culture or infrastructure. So there was always a county prosecutor trying to throw an injunction on you for violating Woodstock laws (no overnight gatherings of five thousand or more people), zoning laws, public health ordinances, environmental regulations or what have you but the revolution had no home base and no money.

Tom thought the solution was to run it on private property and keep it small enough so that it would be illegal for the police to enter. You'd take a forfeiture risk, but you'd just have to make some hard-and-fast rules. Masel was moving from county to county every year to avoid injunctions, and as far as Tom was concerned, that just ruined the investment that could make it a permanent protest.

"Hell, anybody could do this," he told Doug and Moe on his return. "Why the hell am I driving all the way out there? All you need is a piece of private property that you own and they couldn't touch you."

Tom learned the rest of what he needed to know from the disaster that befell Max. On the Friday afternoon of Independence Camp 1991, with the stage hot and scores of campers already setting up on the rolling hills and the road heavy with a steady stream of partiers cruising in from all points, Tom and Rollie pulled up to a barricade across the road. LaPorte County sheriff's deputies were standing there with an injunction: the event lacked proper permits. They laid it on right at five p.m. so the courts would be closed for the weekend and it would be impossible to fight.

Max and Ray had argued all week that they didn't need a permit because they were going to draw less than the five thousand people allowed under the Woodstock laws. The county's estimate, though, was over ten thousand. Which meant there weren't enough Porta Pottis, etc.

Max had ordered extras, and just to make his point he had them drop one off for the cops. It was a battle of estimates, so it was a crime that never happened, but a judge was hard to find on Friday night.

Tom and Rollie and their crew had been camped inside for days already and had just made a beer run to town. Tom's huge red pickup was packed with about forty cases of Budweiser on ice underneath a tarp. This was Tom's way: If Max was going to have a festival, he was going to make a buck off it by selling beer.

A cop stepped over to the window and said, "Where are you guys going?"

"Oh, we're farmers," said Tom, indicating they had to get farther down the road.

"You're not here for the Hempstock-Independence Camp deal? That's been closed down by injunction."

"Oh, hell, no. Is that all them hippies and stuff? You'd do me a favor by keeping those fuckers off my farm, okay?"

"Okay, go ahead then," said the cop, and let them pass. Tom rumbled a few yards down the path, then blithely pulled the truck off into Ray's place and gave the cops the finger. His truck had a pot leaf painted on the tailgate.

So, there wasn't any Independence Camp. Instead, there was a media feeding frenzy. Network news trucks and reporters pulled up to the barricade 24-7. It wasn't a pot fest by billing, but that's all the news talked about. Max and Ray and a medical marijuana advocate from Minnesota named Darrell Paulsen, who was in a wheelchair and suffered from MS, talked about pot and hemp 'til they were sick of it. A friend of Max's, Jay Statzer, who was the organizer of the local chapter of the American Civil Liberties Union at Purdue University, came barreling over there with his video camera winking, interviewing the cops on the roadblock. They made the front page of the *South Bend Tribune* for three straight days and TV news at noon, six and ten. It was a hundred times more successful than it would have been if it had just gone off without interference.

When the barricades went up, the judge ruled that anyone inside could stay, but no going in and out. So the party boiled with a militant edge. The oppressors were literally at the gate. Tom and Rollie had supplied a small crew of workers, including Moe and Amy, and they brought a tractor to mow paths through the wilderness and cut some trees away from the stagnant ponds. He had also offered Max five thousand dollars as an "investment" in Independence Camp, but Max didn't like the sound of that. It meant Tom would want a cut of the profits if there were any. So he told Tom to keep it in his pocket and in restrospect was glad he did.

Tom had a powerful need for the beer, but since he had a seemingly endless supply and about a quarter pound of boo, he was locked in for the party. Everything seemed fine that night until Max started messing with the flag.

Up at the barricades, Max was in a frenzy. He had taken down the American flag and was taunting the cops with it.

"Hey you," he yelled to one of the festivalgoers. "Take this flag and go run it back up the flagpole. But put it up there flying upside down."

Tom saw that and came up to the house on the double.

"What the fuck is that, Max?" he yelled.

"It's the flag upside down," said Max.

"I can't be a part of that kind of shit. If that's the way this is going to be, me and my people are out of here."

"It's an international distress signal, Tom, you should know that—"

"It's bullshit, is what it is. It's disrespectful. Fuck you."

Max tried to break in, but Tom was hot and wouldn't hear it. In fact, this really is a distress signal, but Tom the professional steeplejack didn't know that, and it took time for him to cool down enough for Moe and others to assure him that Max meant no harm by it.

Of course, then Max got into some acid and he wasn't much good for anything after that. The weekend still fomented some good, hot political rage. A few bands actually played and Chris Conrad delivered an impassioned fifty-minute tirade about the implausibility that all this cop action could be over a plant as benign as hemp. *High Times* ran a story by a writer who'd been there and painted a picture of apocalyptic paranoia, saying, "I found myself wishing I had an M-16 or AK-47."

Tom and Rollie stuck around all weekend, and Rollie partied to the point that he got sunstroke. Tom was up all night with him in the hospital.

Max ate his acid and snuck back and forth through the woods into town. After a few days, everyone was gone, but he stayed on. In fact, he stayed on the New Carlisle property until the end of the summer, past Labor Day, completely broke and often sitting out by those ponds all by himself.

"We were celebrating the two hundredth anniversary of the Bill of Rights," said Max, "and they put up barricades. So much for the Bill of Rights."

I want a goddamn strong statement about marijuana. Can I get that out of this sonofabitching, uh, domestic council? . . . I mean one on marijuana that just tears the ass out of them.

      —President Richard M. Nixon to Chief of Staff H. R. "Bob" Haldemann,
regarding his own National Commission on Marihuana and Drug Abuse. The
commission, the most extensive government study of marijuana ever
undertaken, would recommend legalization. Oval Office tapes, May 26, 1971.

TEN Long Live David Koresh!

ROLLIE'S EX-WIFE LESLIE PLETCHER wanted to make one thing clear: she didn't want Robert to be a fag. She didn't like how Tom turned Rollie into one, and she didn't want either one of them turning her son into one.

"I always had the fear of [Rollie] turning . . . my son that way," she said. "And Robert didn't understand that until he was about eight or nine years old. He says, 'Mommy, Tom and Dad are sleeping together.' And I said, 'Yeah.' And he said, 'Why are they sleeping together?' And I explained to him, I didn't keep back. He had the right to know. His dad never told him. I said, 'Do you know what the word *gay* means?' He said, 'Yeah, Mom.' I said, 'Well, that's what your dad is and Tom.' And he says, 'Yuck.' It's just like that coming out of my son's mouth, and I knew he was not gonna turn that way. And I told him, 'You ever turn that way, I won't disown you, but I won't talk to you unless you need help.' "

When Tom and Rollie moved to Rainbow Farm, Leslie imagined the worst—34 acres of naked, drunk, dope-smoking chicken hawks disporting all about the hillsides like a riotous reenactment of the medieval Hieronymous Bosch painting, *The Garden of Earthly Delights*. In fact, sitting at smoky kitchen tables all across Michiana were a fair number of citizens who let their imaginings about the place run too vivid. Gerry Livermore, for instance, avoided going up to the farm—she preferred not seeing Rollie that way—even though her own kids went up there on weekends and told her that wasn't how it was. Gerry didn't know what gay people did, really, besides have sex with each other, so that's how anyone gay would be defined, and their Victorian imaginings rendered Rainbow Farm a veritable Sodom.

Tom, for his part, maybe would have liked to see things go a little bit further in that direction for the adults, get some real fun going. Max claims that one of the first times he came up to the farm, Tom told him he idealized Caligula, the Roman emperor who descended into a debauched madness of bisexual and bestial deviancy as well as political conspiracy, and that he would have loved to live like him, wallowing in pure id gratification. But if Tom saw his own farm as being like *Penthouse* founder Bob Guccione's 1970s film *Caligula*, a nonsensical parade of naked beauties, the reality must have been a disappointment. On the weekends, the place might be full of tents, but there would also be Tom's mother Ruby and her religious husband, Luther Batey, Grover and his wife, Mae, business contacts Tom invited up from Elkhart and just plain folks to be fed and attended to. There was usually a joint being passed, but it never quite turned into an outtake from William S. Burroughs's *Wild Boys*.

Robert was four years old in 1994 when Leslie slipped up and he had to go live with his maternal grandparents, the Rogers.

"At one point, Leslie was living with another woman who we believed might have been a dope dealer, as they were making money, people were coming and going all evening, and so on," said attorney Joe Grolimund. "So I went to the judge that was handling that case and told him about it. He said, 'We'll send an investigator out.' So the probation department had an investigator who ran out right away, and came back and made an oral report to the judge that the house was full of cockroaches, it was filthy, it was just no fit place for any children to be."

The place must have been more than "filthy," however, as the judge was moved to swift action. A dirty house is not grounds for removal.

"So the judge issued an order, ordering both children, Robert and the child of the other woman, removed from the home and taken to juvenile court and let them handle it from that point on," Joe added.

Rollie's worst nightmare actually came to pass. Robert, his beautiful boy, whom he wanted to shelter from the dislocation and abandonment that had marked his own life, landed in foster care. Leslie was crushed, too, though she was in deep denial that this was any of her doing.

"Of course, soon as they did that, why, I managed to get Robert with Rollie and Tom," said Grolimund.

This took months and smacked a bit of an inside deal, but the casual and official granting of custody to Rollie was the product of an agreement between judge and attorney: Sexuality wouldn't be a part of this case. Leslie brought up in court that Tom and Rollie were gay and that she was adamantly against Robert going to live in a gay household. But Elkhart County Superior Court Judge David Bonfiglio wasn't moved by this, and could afford to essentially ignore it since her parental rights had been suspended. (They were only terminated years later, after Rollie was killed, so Robert could be adopted.) Grolimund was openly gay, as open as anyone was open in Elkhart County, and had been a county judge himself for many years. He quickly made a convincing argument that there were a lot more pressing issues in the life of young Robert— like a safe and stable home, which Tom and Rollie could provide.

It was not the first time a gay or same-sex couple were granted custody of children in Elkhart—Grolimund had handled similar cases— but they were rare. An investigator was sent out to do a home study on Rainbow Farm in the summer of 1994.

"We had a report from somebody in Michigan, I don't know whether it was a court agency or what," said Grolimund. "But they reported back to us that it's the best possible place for him. He had a horse, he had a farm, he had a nice school to go to, he got along well with their neighbors, he was a good, bright schoolkid. And it would be better than what Leslie would provide, moving from place to place and no permanent residence anywhere."

With Rainbow Robert on the farm, Tom felt his redemption close at hand. He might never be recognized for legalizing pot, or taking care of his employees, or fixing up homes in Elkhart, but he and Rollie could make Robert's life into a boy's dream. A long-legged little towhead in jeans and an electric smile, he would run from henhouse to pig wallow, trying to stay out of the path of their two biting geese, his high-pitched voice echoing back as he called out for Rollie—Dad! Dad! They also had a few cows and turkeys and Moe and Amy's giant five-acre garden. People in Elkhart still talk about the produce they'd give away; potatoes covered two acres alone, and they produced enough tomatoes, beans, squash, pumpkins, corn and the like to keep them canning for weeks and eating for a year. They plunked down walnut trees in the fencerows and raised a dozen pigs for roasting.

Leslie was Tom's enemy, to be sure, but Robert still went to stay with her for long stretches when school was out in the summer, beginning in 1995. Tom didn't like it, knowing that Leslie put poisonous ideas about gays in Robert's mind, but he didn't want to get between the boy and his mother. Robert himself was a little testy with Tom; the boy was desperately defensive of his dad. Tom paid all the fees for the custody case and it wasn't cheap. But it had its rewards: There's nothing that will ingratiate a person more than a promise kept to take care of their children, and Tom had come through. He and Rollie fell even more deeply in love. And Robert blossomed. Pretty soon a gang of kids from Vandalia were over at Rainbow Farm every day, captained by Robert.

When the kids in Vandalia got together to ride their bikes, they'd ride to Rainbow Farm. Similarly, when adults were scared by a layoff or seething over new revelations about the shooting of Randy Weaver's wife and son on Ruby Ridge or giddy because someone just hit a minor lotto, they drove out to the farm. It was the soda counter, the park, the speaker's corner, the nerve center. Someone out there would be ready to smoke a bowl. Someone there would really give a shit.

On the cold spring afternoon of April 19, 1995, Tom and Rollie rolled up to Joe's Lounge in Vandalia with little Robert in tow, taking him into the bar for lunch and looking forward to a Joe Burger. It was the best sandwich in the county, and even though the place is burned down now it's still talked about with some admiration. Joe Evans was the proprietor and familiar to everyone around as he not only owned this bar but worked as a drywall and plaster man. It was a good place for Tom to get away from himself. He felt agitated, on a hair trigger, and in need of a beer.

For one thing, Tom had been on the phone a lot trying to console Doug, who was in a pissy mood over a young man who'd been living at Rainbow Farm. Tom had been getting an earful of the drama. It had begun almost a year earlier, when a boyfriend of Moe's stepdaughter Rochelle turned up in Elkhart needing a place to hide. The boy was only seventeen and had apparently run away from a juvenile detention facility down in Indianapolis, but he got into the Jack Daniel's one night while he was hanging around the Rainbow Farm crew and after that it became his name; his reinvention was a new self named Jack Daniels, or JD. He stayed with Moe and Amy at the house on State and Prairie Streets in Elkhart, then got out of Indiana by working and camping on the farm.

Almost a year went by, and JD became part of the Rainbow Farm household. He stayed in Doug's tepee sometimes, and Doug felt like he got close to this young man. But JD stayed just long enough to turn eighteen and then, after a fishing trip, announced he had other plans.

"Moe and his friend Gene Sanders always had stories about 'Up in Northern Michigan . . . ,'" said Doug. "Anyway, the steelhead runs were coming up in the spring and they'd go steelhead gigging. They got into the whole excitement of doing it illegally at night and not getting caught by the game wardens and coming home with tons of steelhead that they'd smoke—real he-man shit. JD listened to this and they had him hooked."

Moe had lived up on the Pere Marquette River and he knew all the honey holes for "salmon slammin'." "We used to go up there to push-hook for food to bring home. Spearin' 'em," chuckled Moe.

Doug says he tried to talk JD out of it, sensing the kid had one foot out the door already, but on a crisp morning in the spring with the steelhead surging up the rivers in a blind gonadotrophic fury, JD went off with Gene and Moe, happy as a Labrador puppy.

A week later, he came back and immediately moved out of Rainbow Farm. Moe says JD never mentioned any kind of conflict at the farm, and that neither Doug nor Tom ever hinted that there'd been any issues. But JD's rapid departure left Doug with a broken heart. Later that year, JD and Rochelle were married, and both came back to work at Rainbow Farm festivals in 1996 and '97.

Tom had tried to call Doug at home in Elkhart and comfort him, but sometimes his friend wouldn't even pick up. "I was extremely upset over the whole thing," said Doug. "I didn't even go up to the farm for a couple weeks 'cause I was just, 'Fuck it all.'"

Joe's Lounge looked fairly crowded for a Wednesday but then it was one of the livelier village taverns in a county short on nightspots. "What's the word, Tom? Rollie," said Joe, the owner, from behind the bar. He got Robert a soda.

Joe and his burgers drew a uniquely mixed-race crowd. Though there were racial tensions in the area—a couple of years later, nearby Benton Harbor would erupt in two of the worst nights of race rioting since Detroit in the 1960s—they didn't often manifest at Joe's. It was a rural village bar usually half full on weeknights with guys in sleeveless shirts and workboots, ladies with the bangs teased up high having a smoke, and Bon Jovi competing with Young MC's "Bust a Move" for control of the jukebox a dozen years after these songs were hits. This was country but it was no cowboy bar.

"Gimme a shot and a beer, Joe," said Tom. Rollie had his beer, too. That's how it started.

Tom couldn't settle. Rollie sat there tight-lipped and occupied himself with Robert. Tom had been driving around all day, scouting For Sale signs like he did when he was distracted, hardly able to work, bending down to listen to the news on the truck radio. Up on the TV at the bar, the reason for his agitation popped right up. Earlier that day, at three past nine a.m. central time, someone had detonated a massive truck bomb in front of the Murrah Federal Building in Oklahoma City, and every hour Governor Keating was saying at least ten or twenty more people had been killed and hundreds more were missing, including children in a day-care center. The total was already up to around eighty dead.

At that point, no one knew the name of twenty-seven-year-old Gulf War vet Timothy McVeigh. On the TV at the bar, CNN reported over and over that the FBI were fervently scouting the Oklahoma City area for "two or three Middle Eastern–looking men" possibly wearing track suits.

But Tom, like thousands of people nationwide, thought the investigators were way off track. The date, April 19, held the biggest clue as to why anyone would want to bomb a federal building anywhere in the country: it was the second anniversary of the assault on the Branch Davidian compound in Waco, Texas, which had ended in a conflagration that killed self-styled religious leader David Koresh and seventy-five of his followers, including women and children. Four agents of the FBI and ATF, and six Davidians, were killed in an initial firefight that lead to a standoff and the raid some fifty days later.

The siege of Mount Carmel, the Branch Davidian property, had become the single most important inspiration for the explosive growth of an armed militia movement in the United States. The idea that the government would attack religious separatists with a full military raid including armored vehicles and tanks, while the inhabitants were screaming into the phone at the local sheriff that they had women and children taking gunfire, was the long-awaited signal that the government had begun a war against its own people.

Wire reports cited on the TV news wouldn't begin to examine the militia connections to Oklahoma until the last news cycle that night, saying that the Murrah building housed some of the ATF agents who spearheaded the Waco raid. But they did mention the Waco anniversary. By the next morning, not only would McVeigh and Terry Nichols be identified as suspects and linked to the Michigan Militia (a link later found to be tenuous), agents would have a farmhouse surrounded in Decker, Michigan, up in the thumb area a couple hundred miles from Vandalia, looking for Nichols and his brother.

Tom knew a thing or two about the militia. Madd Maxx had long had a militia connection out of South Bend, a "lone wolf" who had fed him lots of literature. Tom got this information secondhand from Max. He didn't believe that the militia would win any revolution against the U.S. military, if it came down to that, but he was sympathetic to their strict constitutional views and their frustrations.

As the gutted Murrah Building appeared and reappeared on the news, Tom drank angrily. He was upset at the government for never admitting wrongdoing at Waco and Ruby Ridge, and he was horrified that this bombing might be the result. By early evening, he was well on his way to being drunk. Rollie stayed relatively sober, fussing over the five-year-old boy as a way to stay out of Tom's path.

Pearl Mills came into Joe's around six p.m. with her two older brothers. She lived close by, only a couple of miles from Rainbow Farm, but she didn't know Tom. The thirty-one-year-old ran a dog grooming shop in Cassopolis, and she had been talking up the spiritual delectation that was the Joe Burger to such an extent that one of her brothers, who worked in a plant down in Elkhart, just had to try one.

They took a booth and Pearl saw the news flash on the TV. Her brothers had been working all day and this was the first they'd heard of the Oklahoma City bombing, so Pearl told them what she knew about it. She was short and frank in her assessment—in her rapid, clipped manner of speaking, Pearl tells it like is—and not withholding judgment on whomever might have set off this hideous explosion.

Tom apparently overheard her and lurched over from his seat to hang over the edge of their booth and fill them in on what they ought to know.

"Fuck the government," Tom growled at the trio. "Long live David

Koresh! They ought to know better than to come down on citizens of this country that way. When people are pissed, they're gonna fight back. This Oklahoma shit is just the beginning. You wait. The people are gonna rebel against the government!"

And so forth. Pearl and her brothers sat back, a little stunned, but Tom was relatively brief, just an angry proclamation of resistance from a drunk at the bar, and they were relieved when he moved back to his seat. They felt a little sorry for Rollie sitting there, who they thought was probably Tom's son, and Robert, who looked like a grandson.

Joe was in the back cooking, and Pearl and her party were anxious to get a few beers themselves. They hadn't even ordered. But Tom was just getting started. As the party in the booth went back to their conversation about Oklahoma City, he swung by the booth two more times in quick succession, prefacing his minidiatribes each time with the proclamation: "Fuck the government. Long live David Koresh!"

On the third pass, Pearl snapped, "Listen. I don't know you, but leave. Nobody asked you here. I wasn't talking to you. I was telling my brothers about it. Now you need to go away."

"You dumb fuckin' bitch!" Tom roared—but that's about as far as he got. Pearl tried to stand up from the wooden bench where she was sitting, intending to deliver the snappy comeback, "Excuse me, did I offend you in a different lifetime?" But before she could get the words out, Tom slammed her into the wooden benches and sent her crashing to the floor. The two brothers were up then and the fight was on. Tom went into his bar-fighting mode, all arms and legs just the way Wright Spry had described him, but the other fellows could hold their own against a drunk and Tom was neither winning nor losing when Joe came flying out of the kitchen and grabbed him.

"I kept telling my brothers, when this big fight was going on, to break it up," said Pearl. "Leave the kid alone—because he [Rollie] wanted to get in it. I said—we had a drunken father at home, too—'Let it go. It's just his kid. Leave him alone.' At this point, we thought it was broke up and Joe had come out of the back."

"I tried to break it up," said Joe. "I pulled Tom behind the bar. I put him down on the floor, where I had some clubs there that I used for unruly patrons." The clubs were really thick hanks of stiff electrical cord, about as big in diameter as a half-dollar, wrapped in rubber. Joe kept these around for protection, because when the patrons of a bar got violent you had to sap them without killing them, generally. Joe and another patron named Mushy helped get Tom down, but the instant they let him go he popped up swinging.

"He saw these clubs, so he grabbed one and started swinging it. He hit Pearl with it," said Joe.

Tom cracked Pearl in the back of the head with the club and blood came streaming out everywhere.

Someone got the sap out of his hands, but Tom's face was beet red by then and there was no satisfying him.

"Fuck all you motherfuckers! I'm going to go home and get an M-16 and none of you fuckers will walk out of here alive!" Tom raged. Then he lurched out the door. It's unclear whether Rollie and Robert went with him but it's more likely they stayed behind. Tom's rage spread through his body like 220 current, like a bitter rush of cocaine. He was not just pissed at the people he'd just been swatting, but at himself and at the shits who were ruining this country. He was angry about JD, about the betrayal by Moe and Gene Sanders. He was angry that someone he trusted would fill the kid's head with judgment and hate. He was angry at ignorance and common apathy. The very sound of Pearl's voice had set him off. As she pointed out, "he must not have been too fond of women."

Tom wasn't happy about a guy like McVeigh and was sickened by the death and destruction he'd caused. But he blamed the government for producing him and despised the tactics they'd used at Waco, killing citizens with impunity. Now other citizens were militarizing in response, and he feared it. He was drunk and out of control, and he was angry at himself for resorting to violence in front of Rollie and especially Robert.

Driving badly, Tom hit Pearl's car with his truck, then careened ten miles down M-60 to Vandalia, veered onto White Temple Road and went into a ditch, wrecking his truck. He either walked or hitchhiked the two or three miles back to the farm, and was on his way back to the bar, being driven by someone in a Chevy truck, when sheriff's deputies pulled him over and arrested Tom. He was recalcitrant, refusing to budge when they demanded he get out of the truck, but it's unknown whether he had managed to find a gun or not. Later he told Doug and others that he had been headed back to the bar to apologize.

If he had, Pearl wouldn't have been in any mood to hear it. Her injuries, it turned out, were severe. The body slam against the benches had herniated two discs in her lower back, requiring a bilateral discectomy—a total of eleven hours of surgery that ended up costing her twelve thousand dollars. The gash on the back of her head bled a lot and hurt like hell, but it healed up without requiring any major treatment.

Tom told people he paid for part of that, and Doug said he delivered a check, but Pearl says what he paid were legal costs. Then again, Tom also told people that he went into a rage because Pearl called him a faggot. She says that never happened.

"I wouldn't have known if he were a faggot or not," she said. "In fact, I thought Rollie was his son. And the little boy that was with them, I thought was his grandson or something. I never knew him."

He spent the night in jail and was arraigned on a felony charge of attempted assault with a deadly weapon. When taking his statement, Tom told the sheriff that the lady had called him a faggot and used other sexual slurs. But the arrest report, which, outlandishly, has a box where one indicates whether or not the person in custody is a "Known Homosexual" is checked "no." The faggot comment was the story Tom told a lot of people, somewhat sheepishly. He confided to a few others about the Waco bit and how angry it made him, but mostly he kept quiet about his pro-Koresh tirade.

In his mug shot, Tom looks as sad as an old Saint Bernard. His hair is so fine and oily that even though it's only a half-inch long it lays flat against his head, and he's wearing a full brown beard and mustache. Tom was forty years old. He posted his own three-thousand-dollar bond, already resolved to plead guilty.

Tom wasn't a militia man. He wasn't even a libertarian at heart; he loved the Constitution and he wanted the government out of his smoke and out of his bedroom, but he also believed that people could band together if they wanted and create farm cooperatives or even regulatory bureaucracies—especially to do good things like protect the environment. It was a matter of free choice. He wasn't a purist looking for a pure system. He loved voting. He was a humanist, basically, and a Republican one. But he was angry about the drug war, and the libertarian ideas that Max had related to him fed into that anger. He grew angry at the Republicans for capitulating to the Christian Right on social issues and for selling off political freedoms to profiteering corporate interests like big oil, pharmaceuticals and insurance as well as the federal prison system.

Tom was just angry enough to get caught up in the fever, as there was revolution in the air that spring. Revolution and fear.

The Persian Gulf War, waged in 1991 to protect Kuwaiti oilfields, was a strangely telepresent exercise during which U.S. bombers and cruise missiles reportedly killed tens of thousands of Iraqis, with only a handful of U.S. casualties, inflaming the Arab world and Jihadist movements over America's naked thirst for oil. Islamists had already made one fairly serious attempt to blow up New York's World Trade Center in 1993. Anger mounted in the United States as globalist corporations and the United Nations seemed to exert undue influence in Washington, D.C. The shootings at Ruby Ridge had happened in 1992, followed by Waco in 1993, then came the Oklahoma City bombing that spring. By May 1995 it had come to light that McVeigh had fought in the Gulf War. He had managed to turn that war inward against the government.

Tom invited Madd Maxx up to the farm and the two of them walked the property talking about the state of the libertarian uprising, such as it were, and where they fit in. Tom felt extremely foolish about his bar fight in Vandalia, but not about the real anger he felt. He faced trial in the fall, but he needed to make a statement. He needed to run up a flag.

The hemp movement meshed perfectly with the work of the patriot and militia movements, despite the apparent clash of values over guns. Max had seen first-hand that the two could coexist peacefully. He'd just attended the Freedom Camp put on by the *High Times* Freedom Fighters that preceded the annual Hash Bash in Ann Arbor in April. The camp was on a piece of state land outside of town, and he went early just to party for a few days—Hash Bash itself only occupies one hour on the Diag in the middle of the University of Michigan campus. The Freedom Fighters and their magazine, *Let Freedom Ring*, were the "party militant" wing of the pot movement who roamed from event to event and brought logistical help, literature and even a well-stocked paraphernalia store to turn any festival into a hempfest.

Max recounted to Tom that he'd pulled into the camping area and right at the gate was Adam Brook—Hash Bash coordinator and 1995 Freedom Fighter of the Year—wearing a tricornered hat like the ones worn by the founding fathers. With him were 1990 Freedom Fighter of the Year, Thom Harris, and *High Times* ganja gourmet, Chef Ra.

"There was a sign that said, Welcome Home," said Max. "You could just feel the love there. And all of a sudden, boom! You were home."

Adam Brook was, by his own admission, a big gun nut. Freedom, for him, didn't stop at the right to smoke pot. It meant the right to bear arms.

Also at the camp was Scott Ploehn, soon to become the commander of the Michigan Militia Corps Wolverines. But he generally preferred not to run around the woods with guns. He was more of a talker.

At the Hash Bash, Max was introduced to Ploehn and immediately got deep into his never-ending questions about how the militia and pa-triot movement were structured, and how it meshed with the efforts to relegalize industrial hemp and repeal marijuana prohibition and all drug laws.

"He was answering questions, but finally he goes, 'Wait a minute, I have something for you,' " said Max. "He turned around and he came back with a big envelope full of literature. He had 'em already made. He said, 'This isn't for the public. You need this.' " The packet included an antigovernment tome cryptically titled: "Operation Vampire Killer 2000: American Police Action Plan for Stopping World Government Rule," published by Police Against the New World Order.

"I couldn't put it down," said Max. "There was more genuine U.S. history and law than I ever cared to learn about when I was in school. Everything I felt began falling into place. Relegalizing marijuana didn't seem as important as stopping the New World Order."

Perhaps that should have been a caution to the Rainbow Farm crew, most of whom were decidedly nonviolent. But Tom wasn't buying everything Max was selling, anyway. Their friend was useful for his connections to the hemp movement, but they took his conspiratorial ravings with a grain of salt.

McVeigh's arrest sent the militia movement underground—the Michigan Militia split in two over it about a month after the Oklahoma City bombing, dumping gun-shop owner Norm Olson as the statewide leader. Ploehn's more media-friendly faction became the de facto face of the Militia in the state.

But the state was humming with the sound of angry rural teeth grinding, and Tom and Max thought this was a perfect opportunity to crank up their hemp festival. They could harness a lot of freedom impulse and direct it at the ballot box.

"Max, when I bought this farm, I partly had you in mind," Tom confessed. "I want you to get your Hemp Museum up here and I want to put on a real festival."

Max's ego took a hundred little hops and he started scheming on how Rainbow Farm could be a bigger, better Independence Camp. Tom needed Max's help to get speakers and pot advocates and bands, the meat of the hemp movement itself, and Max needed Tom's resources. But the two weren't really communicating. What Max wasn't hearing was that Tom was going to invest a lot of money into his property, and it would remain his property.

For being a libertarian, Max worked under a concept of movement politics that came mostly from the Left's swinging sixties. Max's idea of the hemp festival was that Tom would donate his property and the man-power of his staff and probably a good amount of materiel to put on a killer hemp festival and then slice off the handsome profits to the Hemp Museum, to Max Robinson and to organizations like Cannabis Action Network or Max's spin-off group, Hemp Advocates.

Organized right, Tom might even have been able to afford that. But he had a different idea and it involved a more permanent revolution.

Property was Tom's basic organizing principle, and he held an un-shakable regard for the rights of others to do with their bodies and their property as they pleased. It wasn't his duty to share Rainbow Farm be-cause doing so would make him a good guy; on the contrary, he loved to share it because it was *his to share*. It was collectivelike in shape only; Rain-bow Farm was really organized like a company town, and Tom owned the company.

In his thoughtful book *Libertarianism: A Primer*, executive vice president of the Cato Institute David Boaz begins his discussion of rights with the first principles of John Locke, the English philosopher who, in 1690, first turned away from the divine right of kings to propose that the pur-pose of government was to protect "life, liberty and property." The right to property, argues Boaz, is the first of natural rights, an innate under-standing of the way society is structured. "We shall see that all rights can be understood as property rights," he writes. "But this is a con-tentious point, and not always easily understood. Many people wonder why we couldn't voluntarily share our goods and property."

The argument, which Boaz shared with Adam Smith and capitalists ever after, was that if property was sacred then individual rights were sacred, and your life and liberty could never be sacrificed for the good of the whole. You could choose to share it, but any mechanism by which sharing could be coerced would be unfair and subject to almost certain corruption. Tom Crosslin, too, believed that sharing could only happen through what philosopher Robert Nozick called "capitalist acts between consenting adults."

Somehow, Tom and Max never fully talked this out. Tom believed they were building a shining city on the hill, a private Lotusland. Max was under the impression his new sugar daddy would throw it all over for the cause of freedom. They both heard what they wanted to hear.

Their dress rehearsal that took place on Labor Day 1995 didn't really make much of an impact, but Tom felt hampered by his pending sentencing hearing. He couldn't really advertise a big-ass smoke-out, but they put out fliers around Elkhart and South Bend advertising Summer Fest '95 as a three-day party and campout with food and "freedom" for only ten dollars.

There wasn't any stage, speakers or entertainment, but there were a lot of people. Word got around about good eats and killer smoke— strictly BYO—and travelers came from around the country and swarmed up out of Elkhart. Rollie, who'd been getting into the act of slaughtering the hogs, did one up with a lot of squealing and un-vegan mess. The beer was flowing. They hadn't even figured out how to collect from everyone, so Tom walked around, smiling and irritated, shouting to Doug and Moe, "Dammit, I don't think I've collected from everybody at this party! Who out here hasn't paid the ten bucks?!"

Moe's cousin Paul and Doug got out the electric guitars and little practice amps that could run off the cigarette lighters in their cars. It was cold at night and they sat there in flannel shirts with their breath visible in little clouds. That was the music for most of the "festival," but it was enough to focus everyone and give them a feeling something was happening besides the rustling drama of a hundred flapping tents. Boom boxes were blasting and other guitars emerged at the Rock Camp and another little gathering at the Marsh Camp. Tom still lost a bunch of money, but at least he had a nice party to finish out the summer before he had to go to jail.

On September 9 Tom was in court on his attempted assault charge. He accepted his guilty plea without comment. Pearl Mills was there, too. The whole thing was ugly, and neither one of them liked it.

Cass County judge Mike Dodge made short work of the sentencing on October 6, quickly reading through the findings and then giving Tom 210 days (of a possible 365) in county jail, knocked down to 172 by procedural hoo-ha, plus $3,646.76 in fines and $1,170 in court costs. Rollie was the only person from Rainbow Farm at the sentencing, and he sat stoic and grim as ever as Tom was turned over to waiting sheriffs and went straight to jail. He was due to get out March 26 of the following year.

Tom didn't want anybody else there; he was too ashamed. He'd been drunk and out of control, and Rainbow Farm just wasn't going to make it on that kind of behavior. Moe and Amy had to know about the jail stretch because Rollie couldn't be left to run Rainbow Farm and Tom's Services, Inc., by himself, but he asked them not to tell anyone else. So one of the most visible men in either Cass or Elkhart Counties just quietly went away for a bit and everyone thought he was in Tennessee.

It was winter by then, early November, and the cold weather brought on the dormant season on Rainbow Farm. After the brilliant explosion of early color in the maples, the almost unbearable sharpness of crimson and yellow, the big oaks and hickories turned dull brown and then all shed.

Rollie went to visit Tom almost every day, sometimes taking Robert with him. Pops came down there a time or two, but he could be trusted to keep a secret. Ruby never knew, because she couldn't. Later in November, Rollie and Amy finally told Doug, because Tom needed Doug to take care of a couple of things for him at the bank.

"I knew something strange was going on, but I never contemplated he was sitting in jail," said Doug. "I felt sorry for him and Rollie, and I felt hurt because they hadn't told me from the start."

But a guy like Tom wasn't going to stay in prison long. He was a model prisoner, chatting up the other inmates about the drug war and his new political understandings, and the sheriff was only too happy to clear him out. So on November 29 Tom was granted work release and three years probation. He was charged to remain sober for the three years of his probation as verified by random drug tests. But just because he wasn't smoking—at least, not at first—didn't mean there wasn't going to be another Summer Fest. Rainbow Farm was back in business.

ELEVEN Pig Fuckers and the Thin Green Line

MOE AND AMY WERE on the road in Wisconsin just before Memorial Day 1996, headed to Weedstock, held that year in the woodsy corner of Sparta, Wisconsin, on the state's western frontier. It would be a particularly edgy Weedstock that year, with over 3,000 people in attendance and more than one hundred arrests for possession and sales, making the pages of the *Chicago Tribune* and *USA Today*. The smokers were getting more militant, and the cops were getting less tolerant. Moe and Amy would have liked to have witnessed it, but never got that far. They had caught a ride with an acquaintance when they were pulled over by a Wisconsin state trooper. As if a carful of long-haired hippies wasn't reason enough to inspire a search with Weedstock on, the driver had a pipe in plain view. So they got searched, and Moe and Amy waited it out. They had no pot on them. But the trooper pawed obsessively through Amy's purse and—triumphantly—found four tiny seeds the size of green BBs in one of her jewelry pouches.

"I didn't even know they were there," said Amy. "I hadn't been in that bag in a while. They told us how much it was just to let me go. Moe was only short by a few dollars. But they wouldn't take it. So anyway, got me arrested."

Misdemeanor possession earned her a ticket, but attending a marijuana festival would violate terms of the ticket for sure so the pair turned back toward home. This was two years in a row they'd struck out at Weedstock. (The year before they'd been turned away when they tried to sell a thousand hot dogs without a vendor's license.) Defeated, they got a ride back to Chicago, then were dropped at the junction of the Illinois Turnpike and the Indiana Toll Road.

Tom, as he often had to, showed up to bring them home, but he was in a weirdly upbeat mood about it. There was some kind of urgent good news. The two bedraggled travelers jumped into the big red truck. Tom settled in, turned to Amy and said in his nasal Indiana twang, "Amy, you ain't got to worry about gettin' busted no more. You'll be staying at home and having them from now on. We're gonna have our own festival."

He didn't mean a campout. He meant an all-out marijuana festival. Like Weedstock, only better.

"That's the day we knew for sure we were gonna have our own festival," said Moe. "We'd been talking about it for years, with Max and all that, but that was the day we knew for sure we were gonna have one."

Amy sat there holding her ticket and the thought of hosting their own festivals filled her and Moe with just a little dread. They knew what they were in for; Ben Masel's epic struggles with the law were well-documented in the movement. Masel was constantly maneuvering Weedstock to outflank the county prosecutor in a war of permits—then decamping to a different county every year so that they wouldn't get wise. The First Amendment right to free speech and assembly were near absolutes in this country, but when free speech consisted of thousands of heads puffing joints in public there wasn't an official anywhere who wouldn't try to shut it down.

Tom had been talking to his lawyers about that. Rainbow Farm would be a unique situation, and one watched closely by *High Times* and pot advocates across the country. Their strategy would be to minimize the number of arrests, and thus deflate tensions, by making a virtually unbustable scene: Hold the festival on private property and strictly forbid all drug sales. They couldn't risk any felony sale being linked to Tom and Rollie, because the property might then be eligible for forfeiture. Growing and selling dope are felony offenses, but smoking pot is only a misdemeanor. Technically, the cops couldn't come on the property to serve a misdemeanor ticket unless they were in pursuit. Partygoers would be at risk while they were driving, of course, because everyone would be carrying their own bag of dope into the festival. But once they were through the gates they'd be home free. Also, as long as they weren't in the farmhouse, they weren't violating the vague statute against "maintaining a drug house"—the 1980s crackhouse law. There was no such law about open fields. This was the thin green line that Tom drew around his property, and time would bear out that it actually worked.

The in-your-face tactics that Masel often used were dramatic and got press, but they also invited trouble. Masel and other organizers had really clashed with the police that year, calling the arrests the actions of a "Fascist police state" in the press. That didn't really fly in rural Wisconsin, and it wasn't going to fly in Cass County, either.

"We weren't into this style of protest," said Doug. "This was what Max wanted, too: Go to Windy City [Chicago hempfest] with a bullhorn and shout at the police until they arrest you, make a scene. We wanted to change things a different way."

Tom poured out his enthusiasm to Moe and Amy as they bounced along in the back of the king cab, as though he'd just invented the whole idea of a festival himself. By the time they'd gone a few miles they were ready to pave paradise if that's what it took to get Rainbow Farm on the national festival circuit.

They set their sights on Labor Day 1996. It wasn't just going to be a festival, it was going to be the festival, Summer Fest '96, a must-attend for anybody who ever skinned-up from Amsterdam to Arkansas. Moe's tired synapses started firing and he began putting it together right there: He knew bands from Traverse City to Detroit to Chicago to Louisville to Memphis. They could set up vendors with important food, vegans and organics and local pork purveyors. They could advance the movement with top speakers and the best literature. They'd get the coolest jewelry and glass-blowers and hemp clothing. They could launch a ballot initiative and register voters.

And, hey! Tom reminded them, they could make lots of money. If they did it right, they could come out with a tidy profit for everyone to share. That night, Tom put on a hog roast and Amy Jo started thinking she might get Moe out of a tent at last and get that cute little house she'd always wanted—or at least winter someplace warm for a change.

Max thought that the thin green line didn't mean shit. They needed muscle. Armed patriots were riding high and mighty that year and had filled his head with delectable militia conspiracy and, by God, Rainbow Farm would be just their kind of thing. He wanted the Michigan Militia to work security for Summer Fest and got on the phone to Scott Ploehn.

Tom didn't like it. "No, no guns," he said. Guns and drugs were a recipe for sure disaster. Besides the fact that they'd scare away Jack Herer and *High Times*, someone would end up getting shot. Guns were banned from Summer Fest.

But other instances of armed resistance were making national news. On March 25 of that spring, a standoff began between local authorities and a group calling themselves the Montana Freemen on their farm 175 miles outside of Billings. Tom and the others watched this story on CNN as it stretched on until their eventual surrender on June 13. The Freemen case involved a kind of tax revolt—the farm had been taken through foreclosure, and the men there had been indicted for hanging paper (writing millions of dollars in bad checks and money orders), fraud and threatening a federal judge. They claimed the United States had no jurisdiction on their property and that they'd created their own new government and monetary system.

The Freemen case showed that some things had changed: Unlike Waco and Ruby Ridge, the feds were waiting the Freemen out. In a weekly news briefing on Friday, March 29, U.S. attorney general Janet Reno said,

"The government continues to resolve this matter peacefully. We will do so in every way possible. It intends no armed confrontation, no siege and no armed perimeter."

So Max kept on talking with Ploehn and they got another idea: Let the Militia bring video cameras instead of guns, and if the cops raided the farm they'd get it all on tape. Tom liked it. "If they agree to come out here without any weapons, we'll let them do it," he told Max. "They can camp at every gate and they can be armed with video cameras and spotlights if they want."

Scott Ploehn saw the opportunity. After the Oklahoma City debacle, it was just what the Militia needed to reclaim their image in the eyes of Michiganders. Not only would they walk tall among the peaceful hippies, but Ploehn could consummate a marriage between Militia interests and hemp activism, which was definitely a sore spot among the leadership.

Ploehn was a calm, soft-featured man living a Norman Rockwell version of Americana—his reality couldn't have been more different than that of his new acolyte, Max. His oak-shaded two-story house in the outlying Urbandale section of Battle Creek was neatly arrayed with family photos and middle-class furnishings and the trappings of three school-aged kids. He worked nights and his wife worked days to keep the mortgage paid. On the hot summer morning I visited, his smiling fifteen-year-old daughter, Amanda, sat in on the conversation and a golden retriever wedged its head against my knee.

He didn't seem like a military man, didn't have any of the corny tropes toward "yes sirs" and army hickisms. He said he didn't really know an AK-47 from an Uzi. All he knew was his shotguns and the .45 sidearm he'd learned to shoot. But from April 1994, when the Michigan Militia was formed, through 1997, Ploehn was a key speaker for the organization and ran the state's eleventh Brigade, fourth Division, holding his meetings down at Speeds Koffee Shop at the end of his block.

The militia movement had brought Scott Ploehn closer to God. Heavy representation by born-again Christians was somewhat typical of militia movements throughout the country, and the Michigan Militia's first commander, General Norm Olson, was both a gun-shop owner and the pastor of the Calvary Baptist Church in Brutus. For both he and Ploehn, however, this was vastly different than the "Christian Identity" brand of patriots, who advocated white supremacy. Olson preached that racism would destroy the militia. Ploehn simply wanted to emphasize the Christian roots of the U.S. Constitution and the American ideal. At a rally in Battle Creek, he noted that the battle cry of the militiamen fighting in America's revolutionary war was: "No king but King Jesus!"

The Michigan Militia had started as a secret meeting of twenty-eight men out in the woods, but overnight it came right out front as the biggest and best-organized citizen's militia in the country. Technically, the authority to organize a militia rests solely with the states and the federal government, but they counted themselves as part of the "unorganized militia" as mentioned in the U.S. Code, Title 10, Section 311. By 1996, the movement had peaked and the Southern Poverty Law Center, which studies right-wing extremist groups, counted 858 organized "citizens militias" in the United States, operating in every state in the union. The SPLC estimated that the Michigan Militia had 6,000 members then, though the press regularly counted them as 12,000 and militia commanders themselves claimed 15,000.

In the wake of the Oklahoma City bombing, however, Michigan's militia groups split. In fact, when McVeigh and coconspirator Terry Nichols were first tied to Michigan Militia meetings, the press descended immediately on Ploehn's house. He was the one who had to explain to them that the militia condemned the bombing as an act of cowardice. Later, however, Olson made some public remarks blaming the government for producing a guy like McVeigh and even bizarrely blamed the bombing on the Japanese, and Ploehn's brigade, among others, went their own way and formed the North American Militia. Ploehn was elected commander of its newly-named twenty-third Resistance Group, first Detachment, first Battalion.

The meetings down at Speeds were not some kind of child's play; the men attending them were certain the country was headed for civil war. All the signs were there, and the meetings consisted mostly of reading the signs. Theirs was a more hard-bitten version of the antigovernment anger that drove the "Republican Revolution" in the 1994 midterm elections, and at Speeds it wasn't something they had to hide. The diner is kind of a hard-bitten place itself, with tables covered in plastic gingham at which men in sleeveless shirts and a five-day growth of beard bellow over their cigarettes, and families eat ravenously in the smoky pall.

Ruby Ridge and Waco were enough to set the patriots' teeth on edge, but there was more, more evidence that the federal government was overstepping its constitutional authority to wage war on the hunter and the home defender. The 1993 Brady Act instituted a mandatory background check for the purchase of handguns, and the 1994 Crime Bill outlawed some 185 types of heretofore-legal assault rifles. Among supporters of the Second Amendment, it seemed that President Bill Clinton might not stop; the chatter in gun circles was that federal registration of all firearms was right around the corner and private gun ownership might be banned altogether.

This was primal stuff, real god-guns-n-guts material that anyone could understand. But down at Speeds it got more baroque. Bush Sr.'s New World Order was singled out for special hostility and the signing of the GATT and NAFTA treaties blamed for the wholesale export of America's core economy. Conspiracy theories raged: Our military was being surrendered to the control of the United Nations. Those "black helicopters" seen throughout the land were no mass hallucination. UN troops were amassing on the Canadian border! Militiamen and true patriots were ready to die for their country rather than let it become some kind of globalized police state. The fifty or sixty men (and the occasional woman) who crowded the banquet rooms at Speeds sang "My Country 'Tis of Thee" until they went hoarse, as is their right. And Ploehn had his own special message. When he held the conch, he often talked about hemp.

Networking with a group of students out of Michigan State University, home of the state's agricultural school, Ploehn and his friend Kevin Smith organized the Michigan Hemp Coalition, dedicated to ending the prohibition of industrial hemp and marijuana, which they viewed as the prime outcome of FDR's unconstitutional New Deal. One of their members was Tom Ness, who ran Detroit's *Jam Rag* music magazine.

That kind of thing didn't go over so big with everyone in the militia. Olson, though somewhat out of the picture by then, had been against weed from the start. At a 1994 rally he pleaded with potential militia organizers, and Ploehn, "If you're in a household with drugs, please get rid of them. Drugs will discredit the militia."

But like an accidental Rastafarian, Ploehn's weed activism fed into his worship of Yahweh, as outlined in a pamphlet he made and likes to give away titled: *Beware the Serpent; Save the Seed.*

Take heed; of all the seed bearing herbs I have given to thee, only one can provide most of the basic necessities for healthy living. . . . Many times shall this herb give forth sustenance, even as the serpent seeks to destroy it, as he seeks to consume all the good I have done.

That herb, of course, is *herb*, marijuana.

So Ploehn mustered his troops, including then-colonel Ken Carter, who would succeed Ploehn as commander of their group, and they came down to Rainbow Farm a couple times during the summer of 1996.

"I felt the Militia needed the positive PR as much as the movement needed to learn that peace may not be the only answer and to prepare for the worst," said Max.

"This was a one-time deal," said Doug. "We weren't sure if we would go into the future with them or not. We really didn't like the idea of having them there in the first place, to be honest, but we really felt threatened [by the police]."

"They made us a little nervous," said Moe.

"It was a pretty well-organized campground and they were really into freedom," Ploehn said. "They had a nice bandstand. We were really impressed with what they had set up there. It became known as the Mecca for not being bothered by people."

Turns out Max was right about the green line not meaning shit. At least at first.

It was about an hour before sunset on a baking Sunday afternoon in August, and Tom's mother, Ruby, had been over with some of her friends for a cookout. It may have been Robert's birthday, August 16, because there had been a family party of maybe twenty people there. Moe and Rollie were toking up and had a game of horseshoes going—that was about as radical as it got on a Sunday—and Tom was cleaning up after dinner. The stereo in the house was playing one of Tom's Motown tapes when in the gaps between songs they heard a muffled thudding and rattling, the sound of cars rolling too fast down the dirt road.

As Tom stood on the grass of the backyard, dirty plates in hand, the phone rang. "Hey Tom," barked old Butch McDonald, his neighbor down the road, "the cops are on the way down there! They just stopped at my house to look at my marsh!"

Tom didn't even have time to hang up the phone before the din of the marshbirds suddenly shut down, and out of that stillness came a pair of Michigan State Police troopers walking across the side lawn.

There wasn't any of the much-ballyhooed "dialogue" that Tom had hoped to have with the authorities. The Dope Team put Rainbow Farm on notice right then: They only played this game one way.

Rollie and Amy looked to Moe, but slippery Moe was already hiding. Though Moe had no outstanding warrants, he nimbly ducked down behind the chicken coop. But who were these guys? They weren't wearing trooper olive, they were wearing blue jumpsuits with the pants legs tucked into combat boots, Michigan State Police emblazoned on the blue, and carrying pistols in shiny black leather shoulder holsters. It was the state police's SouthWest Enforcement Team, or SWET, a district unit that specialized in drug busts. Other teams around the state were called things like BAYANET and UPSET. The troopers themselves routinely called them the Dope Team. They looked like exterminators. Two more came kicking their way down the hill from the Kirk Lake access road. Another pair came in across the garden plot to the north, along Pemberton Road, all of them scuffing through the weeds and peering into the underbrush, radios coughing and squawking.

A Cass County Animal Control truck pulled into the driveway, and a sheriff's deputy jumped out, an acquaintance of Tom's—Moe called him "the dog-catcher"—hands out and already saying, "I know, I know, let me explain."

Tom was hot about it, but he wasn't red-faced. As long as he wasn't red-faced, it would be okay. "What the fuck is this all about?!" Tom barked at the deputy.

"Tom. Tom. These boys got a tip that there's marijuana growing and they're gonna take a look," said the deputy.

"There's nothing growing down there. Nothing. And I don't approve of a search. I don't want them on my property," Tom said. "Nobody's shown me a warrant."

"At this point, there's not a thing that you or I can do about it," said the deputy.

"Well, do you know that's against the law!?" Tom shouted to the troopers.

"Just let 'em look," said the deputy. "There's nothing I can do, nothing you can do. They're using the Hot Tip."

A Dope Teamer eventually explained that they didn't need a warrant, as they were working off a drug-tip hotline—there were a couple of different ones, 1-800-FON-SWET or even a pot eradication line at 1-800-235-HEMP—anyone could have called and under these programs, state troopers could crash properties looking for drugs with no warrant. The troopers told them, "We had somebody called in that said that marijuana was growing on the pond, here."

"Well, yeah, then why were you just in that teepee back there?" Tom snapped. Since 1994, Doug had weekended in a fifteen-foot-tall custom-made canvas teepee. "There ain't no pond in that teepee."

The troopers at first denied that they'd gone into the teepee, but Moe heard on their radios that they did.

"I heard the one talking about, 'Yeah, it's back here at this teepee. Oh, we got us a pipe back here,'" said Moe. "They found a deer-antler pipe in the teepee."

Tom told them, "The pond's way over there"—motioning to the south—"it's about dried up. Watch the geese. Go and look at the pond and then get out of here."

There weren't many roads on the property yet and the brambles and thicket weren't completely cleared, so a thorough search was going to take days. Evidently, they weren't that interested. A couple of them made it down to the pond, took a quick look around, one of them smoked a cigarette and talked some more on the radio, then they came back by the house and said, "We didn't see anything down there," and moved on.

Two of the officers were standing on the new stage, which Moe and Amy had just completed, and Moe was convinced that one of the cops pulled out one of their fliers and was looking at it. They had fliered Hash Bash and Elkhart and surrounding towns and they were sure that's why the cops were there, scoping it out. The stage hung off the treeline at the edge of a high field and out over a lower, arable field that sloped away into a kind of ten-acre bowl. It rose again on the other side in an even bigger slope, what they'd come to call Deadhead Hill, reaching up to Kirk Lake road on the north edge of the property. Doug's teepee flapped in the hot breeze at the bottom of the bowl, a drop of eighty feet or so. It was a natural amphitheater.

Meanwhile, the animal control deputy tried to do his part by talking Tom down. He was there to check on Thai Stick, which was standard procedure when a dog, especially a big rottweiler, was known to be present. ("That dog was a big sweetheart," said the dispatcher at Cass County's Animal Control office. "Wouldn't hurt a flea. It was just routine.")

"Tom just almost stood there, you know, dumbfounded," said Moe. "I mean, what do you do? All of a sudden you got six state cops heading at you in these uniforms with the 9-millimeters hanging around."

The officers found no marijuana growing anywhere. They never said sorry for the inconvenience or promised Tom a report or any kind of official handshake. Just left, with the implicit understanding that they could come back like this anytime they wanted.

"Well, I'll see you later," said the deputy, packing up after them.

"I hope not," snapped Tom.

A day or so later, Tom went down to the state trooper post in White Pigeon and got a copy of the report on this raid in what Moe said was a Freedom of Information Act response from the Michigan State Police. (My own FOIA requests on this came up empty.) Tom also asked to listen to a phone recording of the tip, but it had been "erased."

Moe said they found out later that the tip was real, and it came from a jealous girl. Her boyfriend was up at the farm camping and didn't come home that weekend to Middlebury, Kentucky, so she called in the tip, thinking a raid would send him home. But he was never searched or harrassed, so kept right on camping.

Tom called Sheriff Underwood and said he wanted a report from the officer working animal control and was told he was off-duty that day. I found the same thing: No county record exists of any on-duty animal control officer going to Rainbow Farm that day, or that year. Whoever went, he was off the clock and in uniform to help the State Police.

That weekend, the crew went down to Farm & Fleet and bought a big iron gate for the entry to the farm. They hadn't needed one before.

The afternoon of the raid, Tom announced, "Fuck this dancing around, calling our festivals Summer Fest and crap like that. They're out here looking for pot, I'm going to give them pot. I'm going to put on a weed festival and I'm going to advertise it as such. The next flier I put out is going to have a big fuckin' pot leaf on it and it's going to be a marijuana festival."

"I'm fighting this," he huffed at Moe. "They'll never do this to me again."

Despite the presence of Colonel Ken Carter and seven of his militiamen from Operation Rolling Thunder—that's what they called their security detail—Summer Fest '96 went off the rails so fast it just about took Rainbow Farm down with it.

Not that it wasn't fun or even peaceful. It's just that it wasn't about hemp. That first night the party in the main festival field devolved into a rowdy kegger not too different from some of Tom's worst biker parties or the July fourth bare-knuckle bloodsport they'd witnessed down the street. In fact, it turned into an actual demolition derby, and it was a miracle no one was killed.

A couple of hundred folks turned up on the Friday afternoon of that Labor Day weekend, paid their thirty dollars (twenty-five dollars in advance) and expected a show. The fliers had promised bands—Evening Rain, Strawberry Larry out of Bloomington, Indiana, Mushroomhead Experience from Indianapolis, Captain Smoothy from Chicago, a popular South Bend college rock band called Forearm Shiver, a bunch of Moe's Elkhart friends called the Zany Bullshit Band, and of course Doug and his cousin Paul (billed as "Breakfast with Doug & Paul"). There were rock bands among the twenty or so listed, but they were definitely going for the Grateful Dead–like jam band vibe.

Evening Rain was the first band ever hired at Rainbow Farm, a group of blues-rockers from out of Elkhart, South Bend and Union, Michigan, that Moe knew through one of its members, a guy named Chuck Black. Tom and Rollie had gone up to Union to see them play before hiring them and struck a deal: They would be the nominal headliner if they'd provide the PA system and the rest of the sound equipment for the show.

Since Evening Rain wasn't slated to play until Saturday night, however, they didn't show up with any stage equipment until Saturday afternoon.

In the meantime, three bands played that first night (according to Carter's notes) using some other system thrown together at the last minute. But there weren't any speakers and it didn't last long. The crowd was just getting fully high by the time it was all over.

Max was committed to getting his acid trip on, although he was nominally in charge of this mess. He was on the Rainbow Farm board, which consisted then of Tom and Rollie (voting as one), him and Moe, with Doug sitting in as a kind of consigliere to Tom. Max was supposed to be emceeing, but his nasal voice and his increasingly distracted state couldn't keep the crowd dynamic from going straight to hell.

As the sun sank behind the trees on File's property to the west, the festival field was packed with tents, smoking campfires and cars. They hadn't designated a parking area, so most people had driven right into the field for a kind of modified car camping. Soon, car stereos were blasting, a competitive sport anywhere in the United States, and that's when the Pig Fuckers showed up.

"In comes this old Plymouth station wagon with all the windows broken out of it, no headlights or taillights, the back roof was cut out, and it was stacked high with camping gear and people, it looked like the Beverly Hillbillies," said Doug, laughing now but not back then. "And at the very top of it was a keg of beer just barely hanging on.

"They came in the back way, down the dirt roads. They were local pig farming kids. The car was all spraypainted on the sides, 'Hog-mobile'— they had all kinds of things spraypainted on the side of it. One was 'Fuck the pigs.' And there was a picture of a cop bent over being fucked in the ass by a big-dicked farm boy. So we were calling them the Pig Fuckers.

"That hog-mobile, they had this fuckin stereo in there—it was very loud. And of course they were all headbangers and it was heavy metal music. People wanted entertainment and were getting drunker by the minute, so their stereo won out."

It turned into a shouting match between metalheads and peaceniks, who were hungry for some mellow reggae or blues that they could dance to and get rid of the hostile vibes. But with every complaint, the Pig Fuckers just cranked up the Slayer and Deicide and Napalm Death and whatever else they had going. They had a hundred-dollar car and a thousand-dollar stereo, and as total drunkeness set in they began driving around the field. They loaded up the keg and drove slowly among the tents, offering beer to anyone who could keep up, and soon there were twenty to thirty people crammed onto the car like a fraternity contest and another cloud of partiers chasing it, beer splashing, people falling down, other campers cursing them and running alongside pounding on the car, trying to get them to stop.

As the chasers fell off, some of them got in their own cars and began driving after the Pig Fuckers, honking their horns and playing their own stereos loud. Then they began bumping into one another, and soon they were smashing into each other on purpose, a smash-up derby, wild cackling and hurled curses punching through the trebley, barely differentiated sheets of guitar distortion. Round and round they circled the periphery of the ten-acre field, headlights bouncing wildly from tents to treetops.

"I just remember saying, 'Somebody's gonna be dead tomorrow,' " said Doug. "Their cars would come crashing into each other, running over tents. I saw a tent just get flattened and I thought, 'God, is somebody sleeping in that tent right now? Somebody just been run over and dead?' And, you know, the next morning we found people laying out in the road and we went and woke 'em up to make sure they were alive. Fortunately there were no fatalities, no serious injuries that we were made aware of."

That night, the Rainbow Farm crew saw the other side of their mission: Not only were they deconstructing straight culture, but they had to replace it with their own utopian construction. People had to get off the juice and on the leaf. They had to get off a definition of *freedom* that meant violent apathy and onto an understanding of freedom as responsibility. They'd been explicit on the fliers: DO NOT BRING: Fireworks firearms, hard drugs, nitrous or bad attitudes. PLEASE, NO BOTTLES and ABSOLUTELY NO DOGS!!!" But clearly they'd have to model those ground rules themselves, to establish a culture on Rainbow Farm, a set of cues about how things were supposed to run so they weren't shut down by an injury lawsuit or kids selling tabs. Personal responsibilty— Tom's mantra—had to shine in some way.

The "Theater Command" of Operation Rolling Thunder, for its part, reported Friday as an "uneventful evening." But they were off on the perimeter, hidden in camo, visible only by the laser spotting glasses and infrared sensors on their hats that identified their positions in the dark. It gave some people the willies to see their little lights bobbing all over the farm like laser rifle sights, sometimes from up in a tree.

They were to pass a significant test that night, however. It was an event that colored all the interactions with the police for the remaining days of Rainbow Farm, and left a lot of people wide-eyed with fear and joy.

At about three a.m., a female state trooper wheeled her cruiser through the main gate and drove right onto the property unannounced. There were still plenty of people up and the Rainbow Farm Peace Police chased after her, yelling for her to stop. Somebody radioed Moe, and he got Tom on the horn. He was up at Vendor's Row and started storming down to- ward the gate. He caught up to her car at the ticket booth, which was Jerry Stone's old motorhome with its license plate High 1, and slammed his hands right down on the hood.

"Oh, she was coming right at us," said Moe. "Me and Tom are both standing in the street and Tom said, 'Stop that fucking car now!' And she put on her brakes and I walked in front of them, and Tom walked up to her window. He said, 'This is private property. Do you have a warrant?' And she said, 'I can come on any piece of property in the state of Michi- gan I want.' And he said, 'Not on private property. There was a sign out front, and you have to have a warrant to come in here.' She rolled her window up, and in the meantime I got on the radio and here they come—[the militia] had like jet-landing lights hooked to these giant batteries on the back of these four-wheel buggies. These weren't little videos, these were real TV cameras on their shoulders."

Militiaman Randy Graham, who was the "rover" that night on his red Quad, pulled up and poured extra light into the car. Other militiamen came hustling up with their video cameras. It turned out they didn't have either "jet landing lights" or TV cameras, but their lights were bright and they got the whole interaction on tape.

"I was there," said Wright Spry. "She was bumping Tom with that car, pushing him. And he had his hands on the hood of that car, stopping her. But, boy, them militias come down on her like a ton of bricks."

"She rolled up her window, grabbed her microphone, put it in reverse and backed up," added Moe. "So the guys with the cameras jump off, and the guys with the spotlights, they're following her all the way out the gate. I said, 'Five miles an hour,' because that was the rule out there. And I look up and coming out of Vendor's Row is Rollie with about fifty people. They're all coming out cheering: 'Get out of here! Go home! We're peaceful! We don't need you here!' It was just like, wow, you know?"

Like, wow. The lady trooper left without incident, and Rainbow Farm had its thin green line back. She must have called for backup, because in the road out front two more cruisers pulled up, and after a brief conference they rolled down to the intersection of Pemberton Road and Black Street to set up a roadblock. Even at that late hour, people were rolling in, and when the Militia put a man down there to observe he reported they searched thirty to sixty vehicles despite protestations forbidding those searches and then turned them away. At about five a.m., one of the attorneys representing the event—almost all the speakers were attorneys—presented the troopers with the 501(c)(3) paperwork that made this an "educational" event (thus, not subject to Woodstock laws, either) and they left.

When Tom rose as usual at the crack of dawn the next morning, walking the periphery of the property with his coffee, the place was calm enough. But the camping field was torn up and rutted around the edges like the beginnings of a quarter-mile dirt oval racetrack. There were complaints, but no deaths. Some trekked down to Kirk Lake to clean up. The vendors that were there did a brisk business in eggs and bacon and burgers and tacos and whatnot. Bob File was there with his festival wagon selling barbecue pork sandwiches. His whole family was there, camping even though they were only a half-mile from their beds, and he'd be out there at every festival they ever had.

The dank smell of marijuana smoke lay in the shady bowl of the field like an inversion layer, gradually lifting in the morning sun. This was a crowd that liked to wake and bake. Tom and Rollie stopped to smoke with campers at their morning fires. Some of the hemp clothing vendors and jewelry makers set out their wares.

By mid-afternoon, Evening Rain finally rolled in and the festival entertainment came together, such as it was. The first song jangling through the crowd hit it like a magnetic field, orienting everyone at last—oh, I see what this is about—and chilled the weird rumblings from the night before.

The speakers got up between bands to do their bit, too. Top billed was attorney R. J. Tavel, Max's contact and the Indiana coordinator for the Fully Informed Jury Association, or FIJA. He and his Indiana group were the tax-exempt sponsor for the Summer Fest, and he spoke to the crowd about another freedom-loving cause: jury nullification. Under this little-known quirk of America's trial-by-jury system, a jury can vacate a prosecution if they disagree with the law under which that person is charged. It's not used much, but Tavel wanted to change that, and the application for pot violators was clear.

Indiana Libertarian Party gubernatorial candidate and NORML coordinator Steve Dillon spoke, as did Ploehn. But the Rainbow Farm heads were most excited about having on hand Elvy Musikka, a nationally known musician and pot advocate who was one of only eight people in America who received, by order of the Florida Supreme Court, medical marijuana from the federal government to treat her advanced glaucoma. That's right, grown by the feds on their own experimental farms and sent to Musikka as little packages of nicely rolled cigarettes.

The hemp agenda began to emerge from the get-drunk-and-fight agenda, but Max's idea of how to handle a stage was still shoddy at best. One of the partiers who came up that Saturday was Derrik DeCraene, a musician, environmentalist and publisher of a hemp-eco-science-fantasy 'zine called *Head Gear* who had been the entertainment coordinator and emcee at the Green Wave festivals in LaPorte. It was his first time at Rainbow Farm. Watching the long set-up times between bands, the lack of speakers or even banter, he was less than impressed.

"It was a fucking disaster," Derrik said, interviewed at his house in nearby Edwardsburg. "They didn't have good stage management, they didn't have anyone on the mic giving it a sense of continuity, keeping people pumped."

During a set change, Derrik hunted down Doug and Moe. "Man, you guys need an emcee," he said. "You also need a stage manager, a talent coordinator, a sound man, some lights, all that stuff, but mostly you need someone on the mic to keep things moving."

"That was like the most welcome thing I'd heard all weekend," said Doug. "This was how it worked up there: when we really needed something done, someone would step in and just start doing it."

They introduced Derrik to Tom. He told Derrik to go ahead, and if they liked what he did, he would be put on the payroll. In minutes, Derrik stepped up to the front of the stage with a mic in his hand. "Alright, all you hippies, I'm Derrik DeCraene, some of you may remember me from the Green Wave (shouts of recognition), and I'd like to welcome you to gorgeous Rainbow Farm. We've got some important work to do here." Derrik was wired pretty tight but he was chatty, had a strong emcee persona and voice and he looked alright—a tall, athletic guy in his late twenties with a good build and a long ponytail and a cocky blue-collar sensibility. He was meticulous about details and categorical in his thinking. By the end of Saturday night, Tom came to find Derrik and said, "You're hired." Derrik would be their Bill Graham, their promoter and hustler and onstage huckster, for the next five years.

By the time the cars bounced out of the field on Sunday night—none of them were sad to see the Pig Fuckers pull out—Summer Fest '96 had lost a fair bit of money. Even with bands playing for free and almost all services donated, the costs of Porta Pottis, feeding the crew, paying for a medic to be on hand and a raft of unforseen costs just blew out the thirty-dollar entry fee by a mile. There was nothing left to donate to the Militia or to R. J. Tavel, which rubbed him the wrong way, and even worse, there was no donation for Max's Hemp Museum. The Militia wrote it off as a training weekend, so that was fine, but Max in particular was pretty bitterly disappointed, and said so. Funding his activism was meant to have been the whole point, wasn't it?

Max tested the nerves of some of the crew, but Tom still felt indebted to the guy. The next festival, they all agreed, was going to make bank. Max and R. J. agreed to postpone feeling really shafted until then.

The Militia, strangely enough, had sort of won the day. Their presence put off a lot of hippies—Elvy Musikka was really uneasy about them lurking in the woods—but they'd stood their ground against the state police. And apparently without pissing them off too much. Late on Saturday night, Scott Ploehn had all kinds of car trouble and was broken down on the side of the road. It being Labor Day weekend, state troopers were swarming up and down M-60 in the vicinity of Rainbow Farm, and each car stopped and ran a check on this dude in full camouflage uniform and hat, carrying the ridiculous rank of "general." Finally, Ploehn asked for a ride back to the farm, and who turned up to give it but the same lady trooper who'd been run off the night before.

She frisked him twice and ran his file again through the computer, then gave him a ride. On the way, he says, they had a good talk. "We talked about freedom and stuff like that," Ploehn said. He told her about the Militia and how they were organized and that they were un-armed at Rainbow Farm. They talked a little constitutional absolutism, and he apologized for having run her off the night before, but said she could come in anytime she wanted without a gun "and she'd have to buy a ticket." He decided she was a real nice lady and gave her his card so anyone at her post could call him if they had any questions.

Just to make his point to the Rainbow Farm crew, Ploehn asked her to pull right up to the gate. The same kid doing security from the night before came up to the car, asking, "C-can I h-help you?" Ploehn jumped out then and gave them all a good shock. But when he was saying good-bye, she told him not to worry about seeing them again.

"She didn't really assure us that nothing would happen but she said, 'There's no big plans in the works to raid you or anything like that.' Whether I could take her word for it or not, I didn't know," he said.

TWELVE The Pantagruel of All Time—
Or: Marijuana Can Save the World!

In defense of the Pygmies, perhaps I should note that a friend of mine who has spent time with them says that for such activities as the patient stalking and hunting of mammals and fish they prepare themselves through marijuana intoxication, which helps to make the long waits, boring to anyone further evolved than a Komodo dragon, at least moderately tolerable. Ganja is, he says, their only cultivated crop. It would be wryly interesting if in human history the cultivation of marijuana led generally to the invention of agriculture, and thereby to civilization.

—**Carl Sagan,** The Dragons of Eden, 1977

JACK HERER WASN'T TALKING about God, bless his heart, when he stood up on Rainbow Farm's graceful little wooden bandstand and continued with his lifelong mission to untell "the Lie." The Lie was his enemy, the hypocrisy at the root of prohibition which had become, by that Sunday before Memorial Day 1997, a metastatic, nation-devouring parasite that took up residence in the bodies of politicians and caused them to jail and destroy over the specter of marijuana, seemingly helpless to stop themselves. Halting that Lie was the reason they were all there, about three thousand of them, camped on every available patch of grass and hooting at beefy Jack Herer, their frizzy-haired, Abbie Hoffman–like hero. He wasn't talking about God, but God was on their lips. The struggle drove people deep into their religious personas. Like the Vietnam War or the denial of suffrage to blacks, to them it was a deadly wrong that had so hurt the nation it required divine intercession.

Chris Conrad, the ebullient author of *Hemp: Lifeline to the Future* and *Hemp for Health*, was a former seminarian himself and howled from the stage that day with a near-Pentecostal fervor, "we shall build as Gandhi, and Martin Luther King and Jesus Christ, and all those who've gone before in the name of peace!" Marvin Surowitz, who was one of the founders of the Hash Bash and called himself Marvin Marvin, blessed them all as God's people and explained in an interview with *SLAM* magazine's Jay Statzer that hemp was the flower of his church, which was called Earth Community. R. J. Tavel busted out with the "justice" passages from his Bible concordance: "Follow justice and justice alone," (Deuteronomy 16:20) plus that old Sunday morning standard, Micah 6:8, "And what does the Lord require of you? To act justly and to love mercy and to walk humbly with your God." Tavel's point was that putting pot smokers away for long stretches was depraved. Scott Ploehn was ready to quote you one of the early American heroes like Patrick Henry in building a Christian case for strict constitutionalism ("It cannot be emphasized too strongly or too often that this great nation was founded not by religionists but by Christians, not on religions but on the gospel of Jesus Christ. For this very reason, peoples of other faiths have afforded a solemn prosperity and freedom of worship here.") and an end to the drug war. In fact, he'd brought along a married couple who set up in Vendor Row with their church literature and tabled for Christ all weekend.

Friday and Saturday had been wet and the campground reduced to muddy pathways. Cars were up to their axles in muck and volunteers circled with tractors cracking bales of straw to help sop it up. But then the storm broke and the sun came out on the sabbath and God smiled on them.

But no, Jack Herer, the man Tom Crosslin wanted to appear on the Rainbow Farm stage more than anyone else, didn't have to talk about

God, because he had marijuana and he had acid. Or rather, he had his own skeptic brain and one fateful day twenty-four years earlier he had bathed those lobes in LSD and he had seen a truth about marijuana.

He stood on the little fifteen-by-fifteen-foot stage, just big enough for a four-piece band, covered with a rented tent because Moe and Amy didn't get to building the roof yet, and in an expletive-laced tub-thumping he told the crowd about one night in 1973 when he was with his best friend Captain Ed Adair. They had been researching the industrial uses of hemp for quite some time then, years, and they were on acid. Jack said:

We read all these things about marijuana once being paper, once being fiber, once being fuel, and Ed! Captain Ed, he just wrote: "Marijuana grows from the equator to the Arctic Circle, from the desert to the sea, from the mountains to the valleys. It grows the biggest, the best, the healthiest, the strongest of every-thing that grows on this earth. *Marijuana can save the world!*"

On acid, we dreamt up that marijuana was going to save the world. It was going to come back and be the Pantagruel of all time! It was going to be the greatest thing that ever existed on the planet Earth and save all of the Earth from death!

This proclamation was met with huge pealing roars of approval. And it wasn't just wink-wink code, like getting the all clear from the big guru to honk down more weed. This was an aspect of grass that had been hidden from most of them, too, and hooray for this guy for ex-posing "the Lie." The way he was talking, it was like the government was trying to sweep manna under the rug. Jack continued:

Of course, we knew we were going to come down from the acid, But when we came down from the acid, it was still true, and it's still true today some twenty-four years later. Marijuana, and only marijuana, can make the paper, fiber, and fuel, the food, the protein, the medicine and best of times every-where. Marijuana can save the world.

Sweet Jesus! Tom Crosslin watched from alongside the stage, sitting on a golf cart, his usually wry smile spreading into an irrepresible gap. This day, this event, this electrifying realization were what he had been waiting for since he'd met Max and started fumbling down his activist path. Everything that Herer said resonated in the dirt beneath his running shoes. The thousands of tenters and Good Sam Clubbers and hemp jewelers and NORML pamphleteers were here because marijuana could save the world. They drove thousands of miles, some of them, and risked arrest because marijuana could save the world. Hell, if one of the topless girls waiting for the next band were to throw down a pot seed among the trilliums, and it were to grow there unseen because that's what seeds do, the laws were written in such a way that Tom could lose his entire farm. The risks were insane and yet here they were, toking up out in the open, blowing smoke in the faces of the narcs. His crew had worked like mush dogs and now they were soaring on an altruistic rush because marijuana could save the world. The Michigan Militia were up in his trees not because the government was evil but because *marijuana could save the world.*

Hemp Hemp Hooray! Hemp Hemp Hooray! Shouted the crowd.

Herer carried on like a revival preacher, shouting and barking himself hoarse. The information he had found about hemp was pretty well known in 1997, thanks mostly to his proselytizing, but in 1973 it was a miracle he'd stumbled across it.

It may have seemed a digression in the war against the War on Drugs, but the history of hemp was the backbone to "the Lie." To dope smokers in the late 1960s or early 1970s, it seemed that pot was vilified just because it got you stoned, but that's because the history of hemp had been suppressed. So Herer cobbled together an exhaustive compendium of original sources in his 1985 book, *The Emperor Wears No Clothes*, that mapped out how cannabis as a drug and hemp as a fiber, fuel and food were eliminated from modern culture. The industrial giant DuPont, for example, had acquired the patent for nylon fiber (made from oil) in 1936 and needed hemp fiber—then the most-used fiber—out of the way, and lobbied hard for its suppression. According to Dupont's 1937 corporate report, this was an important element of the "social reorganization" it was trying to bring about with its new synthetic products.

Herer's book has become the bible of the hemp movement, and there's no need to repeat all his points here or in his great salvos at Rainbow Farm. Suffice it to say that hemp was so important to the United States of America that one of the first acts of government in the new Jamestown Colony, Virginia, in 1619 was to order all households to grow hemp. For over two hundred years, U.S. taxes could be paid in hemp. It was the top crop for textiles, rope, maritime supplies, paint, paper, soap, lamp oil and industrial lubricant until the early 1900s, and you could even eat the high-protein seed cake. Until aspirin was first marketed by Bayer in 1899, cannabis extractums were also among the most widely prescribed medicines.

It wasn't called by its Spanish name, "marihuana," until Bureau of Narcotics chief Harry Ainslinger needed to racialize the push for crim-inalization in the 1930s and so aligned the weed with bloodthirsty Mexicans.

What Jack and Ed had twigged on their LSD perigrination is that many of the products that have replaced hemp, whose manufacturers often pushed for hemp's prohibition, have turned out to be world killers. Synthetic fibers, for instance, have created a powerful thirst for oil and filthy refining processes and landfill-choking mountains of non-biodegradable waste. Wood-pulp paper drove the wholesale mastication of global forests. Cotton has destroyed arable lands and necessitated massive use of herbicides, pesticides and fertilizers to feed the hunger for cheap textiles. Deforestation and the oil economy are the principal contributors to worldwide desertification and global warming.

The obvious solution? Go back to hemp! Pantagruel indeed, un-leashing this information is the ultimate Pantagruelism, with Herer as the intoxicated herald reeling in the Rabelaisian half-light between irony and a bloody critique. So the foolishness of Herer's patchwork compilation lays bare a truth that is so self-evident—"inherent," as Chris Conrad said that same day—that a government agent of a certain youth would think he made it all up. But year after year, Herer's facts grew more solid. The cannabis plant was an ideal renewable resource; some varieties grow as tall as twenty feet in a season and could easily provide herculean annual amounts of fiber, pulp, oil, soylike protein, biomass fuels such as ethanol—and all without one smokeable leaf if it had to be that way. It could make everything from composite woods to fiberglass to plastic to porridge. African countries could grow it and reclaim their deserts and feed their people in one fell swoop; the menace grows everywhere—"from the equator to the Arctic Circle, from the desert to the sea"—with a minimum of agrochemicals and equipment.

Henry Ford knew all about what hemp could do. In the 1930s, Ford was running a biomass conversion plant in Iron Mountain, in Michigan's Upper Peninsula, turning crops like hemp and cornstalk into methanol, creosote, charcoal fuel and the precursors to plastics. At his Dearborn plant, Ford's engineers made a car unveiled in the December 1941 issue of *Popular Mechanics* that was fabricated almost entirely out of these products. There was a steel tube frame underneath, but the body and interior were comprised of plastics created from wheat straw, hemp, and sisal bound with a synthetic resin, which was tougher and lighter than steel. Plus, it could run on ethanol. (Now we know it could have also run on hemp oil.) Ford said he believed that one day he would "grow automobiles from the soil."

Which was exactly what Herer was ranting about: Plant hemp and stop cutting down the trees and pumping oil and literally reverse global warming overnight! Make millions upon millions of new jobs and save the farmland and still have the world's highest standard of living and, yes, get completely baked.

"Marijuana should be the most sacred plant, and wherever there's a bare spot on earth, *plant marijuana! Get your seeds and plant it everywhere!*" he roared.

The pig farmers and factory rats and closet hippies were thrilled to be getting a dose of this. This was more than just a legalization rally. This was a new sustainable vision for reorganizing life on Earth.

Chris Conrad even had a name for it: The New Hemp Order.

Following in Herer's giant footsteps, Conrad was a magna cum laude graduate of Cal State Dominguez Hills who had devoted his life to Johnny Appleseeding the facts about hemp all over the globe. He too gave a cracking speech that afternoon, voice bellowing, microphone blapping, and he touched on something deeper.

Hemp would save the world from ecological disaster, yes, but it would also save the soul of a nation. Wrestling with raw truth was supposed to be the promise and the responsibility of being an American. But now the tail was wagging the dog so violently it was hard to hang on. Who was the number one contributor to campaigns that pushed for "three strikes" laws and stiffer mandatory minimum sentences for pot? Prison guards, and by a big margin. Indeed, the late 1980s, early 1990s had seen the rise of a "prison-industrial complex" and the number of prison guards increased in California (for example) from 1,800 in 1977 to over 28,000 by 1997. It wasn't the American people who were stuffing the new prisons with potheads, it was the industries who made a buck off it.

Hemp had been all but wiped from the history books, but the *pleasure* in educating ourselves wasn't hard to regain, Conrad argued. The truth was revealed by planting a hemp seed and watching it grow.

"And the plant grows and it flowers and the flowers produce those wonderful cannabinoids," he railed, "including THC, tetrahydrocannabinol, on the tricombs of resin glands of the flower of the cannabis plant, that connect with the receptors of the human brain, *and remind us why we are here! Why indeed, do we take the risks that we do?! To stand firm in the name of freedom and justice!* And it reminds us that this planet can heal and it can grow back. And once you've seen the inherent logic of the natural order of regrowth and rejuvenation, it can never be taken from you! And it's important that we go forth from here, determined that *we shall grow hemp in Michigan!!!*"

Receptors on the brain? The critique went deeper still.

Conrad was one of the chief prophets of a new way of thinking about pot, and it was based on some very new science. In 1988, only nine years earlier, Allyn Howlett and William Devane at the St. Louis University Medical School had identified a cannabinoid receptor on the brain. It was the first step toward answering an essential medical question: did THC, the psychoactive agent in marijuana, release dopamine in the brain in the same way as heroin and other opiates or speed or coke?

Dopamine is the neurotransmitter that carries the message of extreme pleasure from neuron to neuron in the brain. It's the flood of clarified joy across your brain at the moment of orgasm. If you think about what you'll do to get laid, you know why neural pathways that trigger dopamine release are called the "brain reward system."

Dopamine was why dope was called "dope." It was also the key to the way that we thought about addiction. Since opioid receptors were discovered in 1973, it's been accepted that all drugs that can be abused are those that lower the threshold of the electrical stimulus required to release dopamine. Cocaine and amphetamines, for example, block the reuptake (or elimination) of dopamine and so the body, thinking it needs more, keeps making more of it. Opiates like heroin or morphine work on three known receptor sites by mimicking what are called opioid-peptide neurotransmitters, which increase dopamine activity. The strong reinforcement of a jolt of dopamine can directly affect behavior. This is the neurochemical definition of addiction.

We've grown up reading about the studies in school: Lab rats will starve to death in order to keep pushing that little bar that gives them another hit of morphine or cocaine (or, by the way, caffeine or nicotine). Cannabis was made a Schedule I drug in 1970, with abuse potential on a par with heroin, because it was believed it worked the same way. After the user was hooked, dopamine deprivation would allegedly send the pot smoker into craven, *Reefer Madness* desperation. Well, every pothead in the world knew this wasn't true.

It turned out the heads were right. By the early 1990s, studies on the cannabinoid receptor indicated that pot isn't dope. It didn't have any reinforcing properties and didn't inspire addictive behavior. Rats and other animals ignored a regular dose of THC and they'd actively avoid big doses. They hated it. These studies poured into the scientific press and medical journals.

By 1997, it appeared that weed worked differently than dope because of the location of cannabinoid receptors in the brain. They weren't part of the same reward system that produced addiction. As Jon Gettman wrote in 1995:

Marijuana is distinguished from most other illicit drugs by the locations of its brain-receptor sites for two predominant reasons: (1) The lack of receptors in the medulla significantly reduces the possibility of accidental, or even deliberate, death from THC, and (2) the lack of receptors in the mesocorticolimbic pathway significantly reduces the risks of addiction and serious physical dependence. As a therapeutic drug, these features are God's greatest gifts.

God's gifts, indeed! The Pantagruelism was becoming a rout. "The Lie" was thickening like chicken fat in the fridge. Pot wasn't addictive. Plus, to this day, there has never been recorded a single death attributed solely to ingesting cannabis, and here, apparently, was the reason why: Pot couldn't shut down your breathing or heart like dope could. You literally couldn't overdose on grass.

The very biochemistry of cannabis begged the big questions. The metaphysical loomed over the science. Why do humans have cannabinoid receptors? Or even opioid receptors? Whether you believe humankind was fussed together by a Creator or a series of evolutionary adaptations, these receptors are there for a reason. (By 2004, an article in *Scientific American* would herald the discovery of endocannabinoids, the "body's own marijuana," and find that all vertebrates produce them, which means they've been part of human evolution for at least 500 million years.) We'd cultivated pot for over ten thousand years exactly because THC would easily bind to our brains—all the science was supporting its historical uses: It killed pain; it worked emotional centers of the cerebral cortex to produce powerful antianxiety properties; it reduced spasticity; it fought nausea; and, as a kind of cosmic bonus, it stimulated motor areas of the brain and memory centers so you got stoned, got the munchies and forgot your troubles.

If the most recent research pans out, endocannabinoids may just be the neurochemical key to religious joy itself, the spark of transcendent ecstatic experience from which all religions are born—the burst that caused Mohammed to receive revelations after fasting on the mountainside or Joseph Smith to reenvision the twelve tribes of Israel or Gautama Buddha to feel the holy brain-body flood of of all-accepting enlightenment, or even which zapped Saul of Tarsus on the road to Damascus and raised him up as a Christian.

Timothy Leary, the shrink, thought that spark meant your brain itself is God. Or else it just *knows* God. Either way, ganja and humankind and Higher Intelligence were walking the same cosmic trail through the dirt.

In truth, there weren't many at Rainbow Farm who took it this far. For Joe Bag O'Donuts who didn't quite catch the cosmic wave, weed was just a safer pain killer than nasty Vicodin or Oxycontin, and a healthier party alternative to alcohol and especially to hard drugs like heroin, coke, meth, or even nitrous oxide.

But a preacher can transform any gathering, and there were a lot of weed-touting shamans at Rainbow Farm. For the pot mystics, the ability to feel cannabinoids was a gift, and so bliss consciousness was communion with God or Yahweh or Jah or Allah or Jehovah or Krishna or Brahma or Ahura Mazda or Buddha or whatever ancient pagan deus seemed to fit the bill, Crom or Osiris or Minerva. It made sense that only a loving, all-powerful manitou could sprout a seed out of the ground that could relieve suffering.

The best part was that it grew as a grass. As in Psalms 104:14 "He causeth the grass to grow for the cattle, and herb for the service of man." The mystic connection flowed up out of the incandescent grass, no different than the timothy and bluegrass and clover under their bare feet, or the native Michigan prairie that poked through the years, the little bluestem and pan sedge, the Indian grass and bottlebrush and wild rye. The weed was luminous with sucked-up sunlight and that light would bathe your soul, activate your bullshit detectors and come on like a truth serum.

"You guys, remember this," said Herer in closing, "This is the greatest battle the world's fighting right now . . . the fight to relegalize pot. And how silly they're going to look in the end, when they see all the points; we saved the world, and got it away from these industrialists who were going to poison us and end our existence for a profit. And we, a bunch of Deadheads, potheads and freaks, saved the world."

Just another Sunday night camping out in the car. Max, who's all ready to bask in the afterglow of what's going to be another in a series of shows up here, and a personal victory for him again . . . Very safe-feeling environment . . . No police action leaving or coming, no roadblocks . . .

—*Notes made by Jay Statzer at three thirty a.m. on Memorial Day, Hemp Aid '97*

Cass County Prosecuting Attorney Scott Teter said in his first meeting with me that it wasn't his choice to go after Rainbow Farm. It was just his job.

"I'm on one side and I'm going to enforce the law that he does not agree with and is violating. That puts us head-to-head," he said in his courthouse office in downtown Cassopolis. "Unfortunately, there's not a lot of other ways around that. I understand that he did some positive things with the community. It has nothing to do with whether they were good people, bad people, or whatever. They made bad decisions. I took an oath to do something about it."

Teter had only been in office five months when Hemp Aid '97 came down, and there didn't seem to be much he could do about it. The year before, Max had run up against Teter's old boss, Margaret Chiara, who

had since moved on to become the U.S. Attorney for Michigan's Western District, and had beat back the need for permits at the last moment
by getting R. J. Tavel on board as the show's educational nonprofit sponsor, thus exempting them from the Woodstock Laws.

But when you experienced the high revival-meeting tenor of Hemp
Aid, and knew a thing or two about Teter, it didn't take much to see
where he and Rainbow Farm would butt heads. It could break down
into a wrestling match over moral authority.

Teter was an ambitious thirty-four-year-old conservative, and he was
elected on a law-and-order platform promising no quarter for child
abusers, statutory rapists, drunks or dopers. One of his first successful
acts was a billboard campaign that read: "If your sex partner is under
sixteen, they won't be when you get out of prison." This had won the
praises of local church folk and letters of commendation from the state,
and landed Teter a spot on the nationally televised *Today* show. Because
he knew his Christian morality would play to enough of his base, he
was fairly open with the media about his opinions. At his press conference following the election, he announced, "I believe I was guided by
the Lord."

But being a born-again didn't make Teter a good ol' boy. He didn't
have the charisma of a happy warrior. He was a good-sized, athletic-
looking guy, big enough to be a forceful physical presence, but he pro-
jected only a grim air of authority. He bore down on the details of the
law, and people referred to him as a "law-and-order man," or when they
were being less kind, a "ramrod." Others said he was just doing his job.
He didn't mistreat anyone before the bar, but his imperious style rubbed
people the wrong way and he was reportedly kept at arm's length by the
set of families who had run the court for almost a dozen years. Mark
Herman, an attorney and a fourteen-year Cass County courts veteran
who was the juvenile court administrator and referree—a judgelike official who hears child-protective-services orders, pretrial matters and
dispositions that can be handled without going before an elected
judge—says Teter clashed with the three sitting judges in Cass County,

Dobrich, Dodge and Deats, all former prosecutors who would not tolerate being told how to run their court. Similarly, he had a poor connection with Sheriff Joe Underwood.

"The prosecutor is the chief law enforcement official in the county, and Scott Teter was a kind of bull in a china closet," said Herman. "He wasn't the kind who would call up and go, 'Hey, Joe, what do you think of this?' He's the kind to go, 'This is what we're doing and this is how I'm doing it.' And if Joe didn't like it, too bad."

Judges are elected just like prosecutors, but in the hierarchy of the courts, they don't like to be challenged. "In Scott's defense, he's probably about the first prosecutor that stood up and said, 'I'm going to do it my way,' " Herman added.

The Teter family were pillars of society in Edwardsburg. Scott's dad, Jack, had a 120-acre horse farm and became a county supervisor under his son's watch, and his mother Marian was a prominent Realtor. Brother Jay Teter was a country and western artist and would have breakthrough hits early in the new millennium with the songs "Cowboy Ride" and "Football, Beer & You." Jack had been an RCA studio musician and evidently even played on some of Elvis's tunes, and Scott exhibited some of his father's showmanship.

"He's all bluster," said a local attorney who didn't want to be named. "He talks a good case, but then it falls apart in court."

"Scott's an arrogant sonofabitch that jumps in front of the cameras every chance he gets," said Lorraine Jaffee, a local foster-parent advocate who'd crossed swords with him many times. Pouring energy into child welfare issues was good, she agreed; at last someone was going after deadbeat dads. But she and other advocates like her friend Velma Pierce, who were constantly in the courts fighting to get children returned to their parents or to foster parents who wanted to adopt, claimed that Teter simply defied logic when it came to parents he didn't like. Jaffee and her then-husband, a reporter for the *South Bend Tribune*, had once lost four foster children they were set to adopt in a demonstrable error by child protective services, and it had to go all the way to the governor, and a judge in a different county, before they got them back, and Teter fought them every step of the way.

Still, it wasn't the prosecutor's job to be popular. All those people could be wrong; he could take it. Like his family, Scott was a member of the Community Baptist congregation, and that's where he drew his support. He sang in the choir. He was antiabortion and hard on drunks. He went after the bad guys that looked and acted like bad guys. Believers didn't have to fall in love with him in order to get behind his agenda.

"Tom flaunted Scott Teter's authority," said Rose King, a well-known Cass County ambulance technician who also owns the Hilltop Laundromat. Her laundry was the site of a gruesome shotgun double-homicide that made national news—the Hilltop Shooting—which was also handled by Teter, and though she wasn't his biggest fan, Rose thought he'd handled that case alright. She thought Teter was pretty much bound to take a singular course of action at Rainbow Farm. "We're trying to get our young people off drugs in Cass County, and it was just sending the wrong message," she said.

By May 1997, he turned his attention to shutting down Hemp Aid. He didn't have to wonder what was going on; Max had put Hemp Aid ads up on his Madd Maxx Web site and they'd fliered half of Michiana. Doug said that right away the farm started getting threats on the answering machine. One of the neighbors came down to the farm one night and said, "We heard cops talking in town and they're not gonna let this go down. They're gonna have the road blocked."

One of the state troopers became a regular on their answering machine, always insulting them the same way, calling them "pickle suckers."

They gave copies of the phone messages to the farm's attorney, Don France, and filed a complaint with the Michigan State Police. Tom dictated a letter saying, "Your officers should have better things to do with their time than leaving threatening phone calls in the middle of the night."

But despite the hostile atmosphere, Teter didn't go cowboy over there and bust up the hemp revival. Instead, he took his cues from the

Michigan State Police and hung back. There were the usual holiday so-
briety checkpoints out on M-60, but there was no roadblock, no raid,
and that can probably be attributed directly to the darkling menace of
those half dozen men and their families who turned up from the Michigan Militia.

That microcorps of Michigan Militia was the source of a lot of dread
and ruction among the pacifistic hempsters over the weekend—Jack
Herer didn't like it much, and Chris Conrad had to spend a lot of time
talking Jesus with Scott Ploehn before the two of them came to respect
one another.

But the Militia's armed revolutionary ways didn't bother Gatewood
Galbraith. He didn't care about the guns. Hell, he'd rather be armed,
and he didn't care who knew it either. Nobody wanted to be the
speaker to follow one of Gatewood's speeches, because, even more than
heroes like Herer and Conrad, he had the orator's gift. Words blew out
of him like out of a Baptist on fire, he was a tall drink of Kentucky water in a suit and tie and a black cowboy hat, a real Southern guerilla
with a lawyer's lexicon and a mountain drawl tumbling like honeyed
sand. He was a perennial candidate for governor in Kentucky, and
would even pull 15 percent of the vote as the Reform Party choice in
1999, and he liked the security of the Militia. Galbraith was billed as
"The Last Free Man in America" and nobody could bring it home to the
blue-collar voter like he could.

"Your generation, you are involved in a great struggle, and if you do
not learn to be free, you're going to end up being a slave," Gatewood
growled, stalking the Hemp Aid stage on Saturday afternoon under the
walnut trees. "This generation has one of the greatest challenges presented to it of any generation in human memory. And that is to stand up
for individual rights, as an individual, at a time when the government
(pronounced 'guv-ment') and the corporations seek to enslave you.

"I have one question to ask you," he continued. "And here it is: Did my father's generation hit the beaches of Normandy and Iwo Jima so'd I'd have to piss in a cup to hold a job in America?!"

Hell no! came the roar. Oh, the hippie gods were not only smiling, they were raising the little hairs on the backs of Tom's and Rollie's necks.

"Why, *hell, no!*" Gatewood answered himself. "How many people in this group have to piss in a cup to hold a job?"

About one-third of the people in the crowd shouted or waved their hands.

"There's a lot of you that do, because you gotta have a paycheck and because you got family. But that is wrong. That is a violation of your civil liberties. That is a violation of your privacy. The first thing I'm going to do as governor of the state of Kentucky is I'm going to ground every one of those national guard helicopters in the air! This is America, not Afghanistan! And we're not going to treat our people like we're an occupied country. We're going to cultivate and enlighten and educate and uplift the people. Not make them slaves of the corporations, where they have to prove biological loyalty by peeing in a cup."

The crowd roared and coughed its medicated approval. That southern curl just got right under your rib cage and sunk into your injustice organ. Gatewood shouted that he was against the New World Order. He was against corporate globalization. He was against the rise of the information society, where everyone is constricted by their Social Security number and credit report and a handful of stealable PIN codes. He was against the New Deal and most of President Lyndon Johnson's Great Society. And he repeated the mantra of the weekend, the movement's own mantra: They had to take the country back.

By force, if necessary.

"I'm a conservative in the Barry Goldwater sense," said Gatewood years later, interviewed from his office in Kentucky. He had a big hippie following, having been on the cover of *High Times* in January 1991 with his good friend, Willie Nelson, but he was only bound to nonviolence insofar as others were nonviolent to him. "I'm all for individual sovereignty and personal property and the basic freedoms of the Constitution. I'm anti-Fascist. In fact, one of the reasons for my successes here in Kentucky is I married up marijuana and the militia. I didn't see reason for those two to be disparate or operating against each other. Same kinds of basic sovereign rights give you the right to own arms . . . [and] to smoke natural herb in the privacy of your own home. They're both conservative issues as far as I'm concerned."

The 1997 Hemp Aid was the first of six appearances Galbraith made at Rainbow Farm. A widely sought speaker, he thought the farm had the best-organized event in the country.

"I have a picture sitting about three feet away in my office, of me holding an M60 with about 500 rounds of ammunition around my chest. Fuck these Nazis, brother," Galbraith said. "I ain't afraid to die. I went in the marines in 1956; I recognized that I've got to put my life on the line for something I believe in, even if then it was a false belief, but now I get to choose what I'm gonna fight and die for. So when I see somebody like Tom who shares those sentiments, you know, damn, there's very few of us around."

After hours, when Herer, Conrad, Elvy Musikka and militiamen like Ploehn and Carter joined Tom and Rollie for drinks and talk up in the farmhouse, the risks were openly addressed.

"Tom and I had conversations about what the county's reaction to him was," said Galbraith. "We knew he was under investigation. At that time, we knew that they were arresting folks when they left the premises and we knew that he was rankling a lot of people."

For all the tension and flaming rhetoric, the festival was an unforgettable flash of peacefulness, a lingering satori. This time there were no Pig Fuckers. There was no slashing heavy metal or bloody bare-knuckled boxing or demolition derby. There was only the drifting tendrils of sticky chronic and smokers lined up at a voter registration booth and a crowd around Max's Hemp Museum. Folks were strategizing with Herer and Conrad and Musikka and the party rolled 24-7. Hemp Aid '97 was a success, and many regulars still consider it the best-organized and most hassle-free festival ever held on Rainbow Farm.

Max had worked hard to secure the name Hemp Aid, and had met with Willie Nelson twice just to make doubly sure it was okay to use it, since it was a spin-off of the name of his festival, Farm Aid. A hemp advocate himself, Nelson approved, and though he never appeared at Rainbow Farm, Tom thought of him as one of their elders. Max, of course, wasn't taking any chances. He put his paperwork in and later he received an official service mark registration from the U.S. Patent Office dated October 20, 1998. Max Baer Robinson owned the name "Hemp Aid."

They had needed to establish a culture of both resistance and nonviolence, and with a minimum of guidance it had flowered of its own accord.

A line of vendors stretched away from the bottom of the bowl back toward Pemberton Road, spicy steam rising from Bob File's Pure Pork sandwiches and sausages and his neighbor Oli Olafsson's vegetarian feast and a procession of other food vendors. Kegs were fast emptied at a buck a cup. Bongs and pipes and hemp clothing and rainsticks and frisbees and jewelry were trading hands, often by barter, and Max's vast libraries of free hemp and marijuana literature were carried off into tents and car camps. Wright Spry had sunk a well and set up an open-air shower that could accommodate four people at once on a slight rise above the Rock Camp, and at any time four naked beauties were part of the entertainment for everyone—you couldn't help but look. The water wasn't heated, so getting clean tended to be a brief, loud affair.

In fact, there was a fair amount of skin showing, mostly women feeling free to nude up and take in the sun or dancers of all sexes jiggling to Johnny Socko, Catman and the All-Niters, Buddha Quest, the Rozen Bombs or any other of at least fifteen acts that showed up. There was a giddy feeling of first-time liberation to the place, and a lot of folks could only imagine they were supposed to be acting like hippies or strippers—but despite the electric waft of pheromones that charged the place with a sense of promise—play your cards right and you might *get some strange*—it wasn't quite a free-love fest. The Files and Olafssons and dozens of other people brought their kids. It took on a blue-collar family vibe somewhere between Woodstock and a union picnic.

The nights held more promise of adult satisfaction—you never knew what you might run into out in the bushes—and the rain only encouraged the fun. As a storm soaked that first Saturday night, a couple of brave souls who'd been struggling to climb the slick grass on Deadhead Hill stripped off what was left of their clothes and began bombing down the slope on their asses. A Kalamazoo ska band called the Mad Butchers entered hippie legend when the rain cut their power but the band played on as best they could, with the horn section playing completely naked. Derrik DeCraene took one look at this developing scene and got on the radio to Doug and Moe and the crew—"Hey, Whoaboy or somebody? I need some big sheets of Visqueen up here, on the double!" Within minutes was born one of Rainbow Farm's most enduring and beloved traditions: the Hippie Slide.

It was rough sledding, really, sliders would end up with the worst strawberries on their hips, women with entire ass cheeks a deep purple, from greasing up with Palmolive and a hose and slapping down the plasticked hill in the buff, bouncing over rocks, sticks, woodchuck dens, what have you. Guys made muscleman poses and girls twirled their nipples and shook ass for the crowd. The only object was to see who could slide the farthest, and the only rule was you had to be naked. Derrik would judge them for style and distance and at future festivals he'd give away prized T-shirts that said things like: I Survived the Hippie Slide at Rainbow Farm Campground, Vandalia, Michigan, and Nuts, Butts, Tits & Spliffs.

Bands started playing as accompaniment, and in 2000 the band Leftover Salmon would improvise a jam called the "Hippie Slide" based on the New Orleans chant made famous by the Dixie Cups, "Iko Iko," along with the chorus of Sir Mack Rice's "Mustang Sally" changed to "Slide, hippies, sliiiiiiiiide!" Leftover Salmon had a strong national following on the post–Grateful Dead circuit, and Derrik had hoped to put out that jam as Rainbow Farm's first commercial release.

The farm drew the madness out of people, too. Characters emerged from the smoke to let their particular trips run full bore.

One of the regulars was a girl named Speedy, for instance, a pretty good-looking girl, too, by all accounts, who shucked her clothes after dark and would spend the night running. Just running and leaping around the camp in the nude, high on weed or meth or life or whatever, and this got up the interest of some of the men, so to speak, and the joke was that you could have her if you could catch her but as far as anyone knew no one ever did.

If you didn't have a nickname when you arrived, you'd have one by the time you left. Regulars had names like Parkin' Mark and That Guy and Buzz Daily and Hippie—tall dedicated smiling Hippie, a real grassroots foot soldier—or Jim Crosslin's good buddy who had been known for twenty years only as Cockroach (his good friends called him Roach). Some of these private, countryfied folks didn't have many other friends, but they sure liked Tom and Rollie. They'd give you a name, give you a tent, put you to work. As Roach's wife, Kim, said to me, "They got women's shelters and Tom's was like Tom's shelter, you know?"

Legends were born. Rev. Right Time & the First Cousins of Funk became the first band kicked out of Rainbow Farm, for hijacking a golf cart. Tom and Rollie's weed supplier had developed some grass so good that farm employee Dayved Watts, whose nickname was Whoaboy, called it "closet bud."

"Why do you call it closet bud?" *High Times* editor Steve Hager once asked him. "Because you're growing it in a closet?"

"No, because you get some and put it on the shelf in your closet and it's so good you get high just knowing it's in there," said Whoaboy.

One of the vendors ended up in a tree. A security guy and videographer named Curtis Greene and others had to talk him down, gently, gently, and then he was none too happy about it, and so they duct taped him to a chair until the medics could deal with him. Another kid got thrown off the farm and ended up naked on a neighbor's porch, so a cop who'd grown up with Derrik DeCraene brought him back to Rainbow Farm and dumped him there.

They even had the church representing. For three shows, evangelicals came out and set up their own tent in Vendor's Row, witnessing to the stoned. One show, the crew had the church contingent cooking hotdogs for those who'd run out of money, just to bring them some customers. "We got plenty of lost souls up here," Tom told Doug, "might as well let them have a few."

This was political work in itself, of a kind, but real ballot work was getting done, too. They were registering loads of voters, and someone had ginned up petitions for a medical marijuana initiative, copied almost word-for-word from the Proposition 215 legislation that had passed by a landslide the previous year in California, and folks were lining up to sign it.

But the thing people were doing most was smoking weed. It was a pot festival and they weren't hiding it. They were blowing that gage by their tents, in their cars, laying on the grass, eating vegan stir-fry, talking politics at the NORML table and at the Hemp Museum, walking through the woods, swimming in the pond, wading in Kirk Lake, picking leeches, picking ticks, swatting skeeters, with their heroes, with strangers, with narcs, with people they didn't even particularly like, they were cooling out anywhere and with anyone and at any time.

"A local lady told me who Tom was, and that they were smoking hemp out there," said Sondra Mose-Ursery, a large, calm, no-bullshit lady who was then in the fourth of her five terms as mayor of Vandalia. "I told her, you don't smoke hemp, it's a fiber. But she said anyway they were having 'pot parties' out there.

"So I went out there and talked to Tom. And Tom explained the politics of the place and that they were supportive of an initiative to legalize marijuana.

"I was turned away first because I didn't have ID. I went back out

there the next day, and I didn't smell any marijuana. I didn't see anyone passing anything or having sex. I saw a lot of people watching a
concert."

"We took our grandson up there," said Rebecca Kitner from the KC
Pizza. "We'd walk around the whole place, there wasn't no reason to
keep him away from there."

"People said they saw sexual acts and all that, but we never saw any
of that," said her son, Jerry Cocanower. "I talked to someone from the
South Bend Police Department up there one time. He said he was just
checking it out. He wasn't in uniform."

The closest neighbor, who lived in what was really the only other
house on that stretch of Pemberton Road, was a solitary man named
Carl "Butch" McDonald. His family had helped set him up in a simple
but tidy cinderblock house on a few acres just on the southern edge of
Tom's property. Butch wasn't that old—only in his late fifties when Tom
first moved onto the farm—but he was in ill health, having had a stroke
and bypass surgery. One of the first interactions he had with Tom was
when he sold him the 1932 Farmall tractor with the tricycle front end.
The tractor ran great, like they do, you see sixty-year-old tractors for
sale in *Wheels and Keels* every day, and did a lot of the heavy hauling on the
farm. Butch himself was a gruff man of few words, but he liked Tom
and became a regular at their cook-outs and their festivals, where he'd
mostly just sit out of the way and nurse a beer. When I talked to him he
said he thought the festivals were "fun."

After dark on Memorial Day, after most of the campers had drifted out or
were still trying to get their cars started or their heads on straight, Tom sat
at the kitchen table with Doug, Rollie, Moe, Derrik and Amy as they
counted up the money. It didn't seem possible, but there was only two
thousand dollars left over for Max and R. J. Tavel. Tom's cut was
two thousand dollars, too, so he threw that in their pile and took nothing. Moe says he took five hundred dollars of his cut and threw that in

with Max and Tavel, too, hoping they wouldn't feel slighted and the farm could keep a good reputation in the activist community.

Max says it happened differently. "When I left the property after the event, I was handed two thousand dollars and promised we would divide the rest of the money in two weeks after we had time to recuperate. I asked Tom what he was going to do with his share and he said, 'We're going to Disneyland!' "

Tom was joking but Max wasn't laughing. The gathering around the table got very tense. With an official count of over two thousand people on the gate at thirty dollars a pop, they had at least sixty thousand dollars to work with, plus vendor fees (they kicked back 10 percent of their take to the farm). Max had expected to get a quarter of the total, and a quarter for Tavel's FIJA group. But Rainbow Farm barely made it into the black on the show. They spent about twelve thousand on Jack Herer alone, after his fees, hotel, airfare, entourage and expenses. Galbraith came up from Kentucky, Chris Conrad and his wife, Mikki Norris, from California and Elvy Musikka from Florida. Tom wasn't cheap: He gave everyone deluxe treatment if he could swing it. Plus they had lights and sound gear, a massive bill for Porta Pottis, paid medical staff, a rented ambulance, a million-dollar insurance bond, improvements in water, electric, and RV hookups that were done on a rush and staff payroll. Thousands went to just miscellaneous petty cash—taxis, runs to the hardware store, ice, you name it.

Max and R. J. thought they should get paid before the contractors and talent, but it didn't work that way. They left the room for a minute, then came back and raised holy hell. Some words were exchanged, but the one thing Tom would not abide was somebody yelling at him in his own house and he threw them out. He told them to go home and cool off, get some rest, and they'd talk about it later.

Tavel thought for sure Moe and the others agreed they'd been screwed. "They were hurt or incensed by the niggardly sum of money Tom was 'donating' to FIJA to say thanks for all my support of him," he wrote to me in an email. Nobody else at the table, however, was storming out in protest.

"Hemp Aid was never intended to be the commercial event Tom turned it into," Max said. "It wasn't supposed to be Pepsi-Stock. It was meant to be a fund raiser for the relegalization movement in the Midwest, and particularly to help the Hemp Museum expand, improve and become more mobile to attend even more hemp and nonhemp events, just like Farm Aid is to the farmers. Tom knocked the wind out of my activist sails for a long time by ruining this event and ripping me off for thousands of dollars, my time and labor, and almost my honor. In my opinion, he did more to hurt the movement by taking away much needed funding that was raised in the name of legalization and built a private campground."

Everyone was quick to credit Max for contacts and lots of legwork—it was because of him, and only him, that they had pulled in Herer, Conrad, Musikka, Galbraith and Steve Dillon of the Libertarian Party in Indiana, among others. But, by many people's accounts, he ran around on acid half the time and that didn't help keep things orderly. For instance, Max had put his own Indiana phone number on the Rainbow Farm flier and, though Tom gave him money to pay his phone bill, the phone was cut off on the day the festival began. Jack Herer was stranded at the airport—partly because the phone number didn't work. "What the fuck kind of festival is this we're going to, your goddamn phone's disconnected!" Herer yelled when Doug finally paged him at Midway airport.

Max and his pal Jay Statzer, with whom he'd tried to face down the police at Independence Camp, also made arrangements for speakers, bands and equipment that overlapped plans put in place by the paid entertainment coordinator, Derrik DeCraene. Some of those bands were pissed later because they didn't play or hadn't signed contracts or hadn't been paid when others had. Derrik was too hyperorganized for that kind of slop, and didn't want Max or Jay involved. Statzer was there as a contributor and ad rep for a magazine called SLAM—Street Legal

Arts and Music—and later would be a Michigan contact for the medical marijuana group, Cures Not Wars.

"I told Moe halfway through that show that I didn't want to work with Max no more," Doug said. "I told Tom that day, 'He's fucking you over and you better watch him. I don't trust him.'" Derrik said the same. Moe was more equivocal, respectful of Max's reputation as the creator of the Hemp Museum, which he genuinely admired.

After Hemp Aid '97, however, the bottom line was that Max was out, and he was livid.

Max came back up to the farm a couple of weeks after Hemp Aid '97 and he had the flier all ready for Summer Fest '97 that fall. Tom had asked him to come back for the production meeting, as they'd already rolled some of the Hemp Aid profits into insurance and equipment rental for Summer Fest. As far as Doug or Moe or even Derrik knew at that time, Max was still part of the decision-making crew. But Max showed up with this flier and passed around a mock-up to get some feedback; Tom grabbed it and stared at it a minute. It had The Hemp Museum in huge letters and then Rainbow Farm in smaller type. Tom got that look in his eye.

"What the fuck are we promoting here, Max?!" Tom shouted, slapping the mock-up down on the table. "The Hemp Museum or Rainbow Farm?"

Max tried to protest.

"I don't know if you've fucking noticed, but this is Rainbow Farm where you're sitting now, not the Hemp Museum. We have events whether the museum is here or not. I'm happy to have it, Max, you're a big part of this, but this is a Rainbow Farm show—*not a Hemp Museum show!*"

Moe thought, Oh no. Here we go. He looked down at the table, saying nothing.

It turned into a fight. Max wasn't going to take that kind of shit. The two men barked at each other for a few minutes, and then that was it. Max was out and he never came back.

"Tom told me to bring the computer, which he had donated seven months before to myself and to the Hemp Museum, back to the farm because he wanted to have it upgraded for me. I did almost all the Internet work for Hemp Aid on that computer. When I arrived he took the computer in the house, told me there wasn't any more money and told me I was no longer going to be a part of Rainbow Farm events," said Max.

"I know why," he added. "He loved the fame, money and power."

"The man I met was all business promotion," said Tavel. "Side door libertarian, not an idealogue, born out of convenience and not commitment."

Through Statzer, Max published a public break with Tom in a tiny little editorial literally printed in the margins of *SLAM* magazine. But the pot activist community is small and everyone saw it. This was enough to have some Indiana activists boycotting Rainbow Farm for a year or two. Statzer, however, was back to Rainbow Farm in subsequent years, manning the activist tent.

Statzer wanted to be where the action was, and the action was now at Rainbow Farm. The event and the name that Max had helped establish stuck fast. Ben Masel thought it even threatened his Weedstock events over in Wisconsin.

"Well, he was running his events on the same day I was," said Masel, who was careful to say that he respected Tom and Rollie and their event. "There's only so many top speakers and they're hard to get. Tom was willing to pay top dollar. I ran into Doug once at Windy City Weedfest in Chicago and I told him to propose to Tom that we stagger the events so we wouldn't be splitting the crowd. That message got relayed to Tom, but evidently he wasn't interested."

Every year from 1997 to 2000, Rainbow Farm would host major festivals on Memorial Day and Labor Day weekends, plus a lot of smaller events in between.

"For years, decades, Hash Bash had been the one and only marijuana event in Michigan," said organizer Adam Brook. "But suddenly there was Rainbow Farm. Rainbow Farm really took over as the center of the movement for Michigan."

County prosecutor Scott Teter had a nightmare on this hands. Hemp Aid was a hit—a drug festival protected by the Michigan Militia. Even if the worst that was happening out there was misdemeanor pot possession, it really looked bad. What the hell to do?

He got a break. In June 1997, three members of Ploehn's North American Militia unit, Bradford Metcalf, Randy Graham and Ken Carter, were arrested on conspiracy charges. Graham and Carter had been Rainbow Farm regulars. Ever since McVeigh had been caught, informants had been worming their way into the Michigan Militia, and one of them claimed the trio was plotting to blow up the federal building in Battle Creek, an IRS office in Portage and the crowded highway interchange of U.S. 131 and I-94 outside Kalamazoo. They were also taped on the phone plotting to kill the informant. The feds were frequently taping the Militia at that point. Max Robinson showed me a letter from the feds informing him that one of his conversations with Ken Carter had been recorded.

Of course, one of the points of being in the Militia was to be armed, and when ATF agents raided Metcalf's place they found more than two dozen rifles and semiautomatic weapons, including a sniper rifle and a silencer, plus three weapons the government said were illegal machine guns and the belted ammunition for them.

It would be more than a year before the men would finally be convicted, with Metcalf getting forty years in prison and Graham getting fifty-five. Ken Carter turned state's evidence and got three years, but died of natural causes soon after being released.

This was heavy stuff, and Teter would be dipped in shit before he'd let that kind of thing continue at Rainbow Farm. Unbeknownst to him, Tom and Rollie and everyone at Hemp Aid were already one step ahead of him. Even before Hemp Aid '97 had ended, the crew had decided that it would be the last festival they'd do with the Militia.

It could be that guys like Herer and Conrad got to Tom, or the fact that the militamen themselves talked constantly about expanding their operations there. In late night talks with camp security, militiamen described how they could arm the perimeter at Rainbow Farm with everything from automatic weapons to bazookas to trip-wired mines, setting up hidden camps with advanced communications equipment, night vision gear, the works. You know—*if things got bad.*

That kind of talk had a negative effect on people.

"I'll tell you what, I was a gun nut, and I was excited that the Militia was going to be out there," chuckled Adam Brook. "I thought everybody was going to run around up there, armed. I thought we could bring guns. But I was up there and saw that wasn't the message Tom and them were going for at all."

After that spring's festival was over, Brook mentioned to Tom he'd like to do some target practice up at the farm, but Tom nixed that idea. "Tom was like, 'Nope, I really can't have you doing that. I got people and kids around here all the time, and we have to be more responsible than that,'" added Brook.

Maybe he just didn't have the money to pay the Militia. For the second show in a row he'd promised to "donate" two hundred dollars to each man but then couldn't pay it. Max was incensed. He said that at one point some of the militiamen asked if they could go through the trash to recycle the aluminum cans—doesn't seem their speed, but sometimes the facts are weird—and he claims Tom let them, saying that could be their donation.

By the time Ploehn and others had settled in at home after Hemp Aid '97, Tom and Doug had sent them a letter explaining that they were grateful for their help but thought it best that Rainbow Farm make other security arrangements for future shows.

Later in the summer, the farm was contacted by Tom Wayne, the newly elected executive officer of the Michigan Militia Corps Wolverines, to inform them (as he told me), "That's not the Michigan Militia. That's some splinter group. Please don't consider them Militia, because we're a legitimate political activist group and those guys aren't." With the investigation of Carter, Metcalf and Graham churning, Ploehn had been voted out and his meetings at Speeds came to an end.

"I believe marijuana is acceptable for medicinal purposes. I've been watching it for years. I'm a Vietnam veteran," said Wayne. He just wasn't for smoking 24-7. "If the Militia ever had gotten into a combat situation for whatever reason, the last guy you want is the one smoking a joint in the middle of the woods. I mean there's a time and place for everything and that's not one of them."

Ploehn would come to the shows in the future and was even a speaker at Hemp Aid '98. They'd get in on guest passes. They were not persona non grata.

"We made a clean cut, and we made it as public a cut as possible because we did not want to be associated with the Militia or anybody militant," said Doug. "We wanted to be a peaceful organization, and that was primary. But we weren't allowed to be that first show; we had threats from the police and they were ready to shut us down."

Still, Teter didn't know the Militia were gone. In fact, it served the farm's security interests if the police suspected they were still there, so Tom and the others did little to disabuse them of this notion. If the authorities were afraid of the Militia, let them be afraid. Cultivating that fear turned out to be a very bad mistake.

THIRTEEN Collars for Dollars

PROSECUTOR TETER NEVER WENT out to Rainbow Farm to see a festival firsthand. "I didn't need to," he told me later in his office. The evidence he sought would make it unnecessary to interact with Crosslin in any way. Civil forfeiture was so widely used in drug cases in the mid-1990s that if Teter played his cards right he would never have to address Rainbow Farm's message or their popular ballot initiative or the idea that they were supported by some of the county's most prominent citizens. All he had to do was tie Crosslin to one felony and he could sell Rainbow Farm right out from under Tom, guilty or not, and no judge in the country would bat an eye. That would be the end of it.

So, on May 10, 1998, Teter sent a short and relatively polite registered letter to Tom at the farm, placing him "on notice" that he'd received a lot of "Warrant Requests"—meaning informal complaints—about Rainbow Farm and that he could prosecute for infractions including noise, trespassing, littering and "multiple violations of the controlled substances act." There was no mention of shutting down the show, but it was there in thinly veiled language, as Teter said he supported Tom's right of peaceful assembly but added: "If your assembly infringes on the enjoyment of your neighbor's property I will have no choice but to prosecute you pursuant to the Cass County Nuisance Ordinance."

There was also no mention of forfeiture. Not yet. The letter goes on to admonish Tom to instruct his guests to abide by the law, and invites Tom to contact him with any questions.

Tepid as it was, the letter said a lot about the oncoming conflict between Teter and Crosslin: There had been complaints, so evidently not
all the neighbors were on board; Teter was going to prosecute any bullshit charge he could find; all Teter had were bullshit charges. Noise
complaints? Litter? The worst he had was misdemeanor possession.

And so Teter was hanging back. He didn't have the felony yet. And
then there was the matter of the Militia. In Teter's mind, the prosecution
of Tom Crosslin and Rainbow Farm had already become a potentially
deadly conflict.

"We had made a decision several years ago that, no, for misdemeanor
use of marijuana, I was not going to marshal five hundred troops and go
in and provoke a violent confrontation to either have some of our people hurt or some of their people hurt," he said.

Later, in an interview with the *South Bend Tribune*, Teter said he had
never busted up one of the festivals because he wanted to avoid a "bloodbath."

No one had weapons at Rainbow Farm, not even the Militia, so it
was only Teter who thought he had potentially violent hippies on his
hands. But it wasn't hard to see where he got the idea. It seems clear in
hindsight that the violent overtones to this conflict started with the
simple reputation of the Militia. That reputation may have prevented
Teter from charging in there with his sheriffs and state police to casually molest the dopers, but it also set him on a martial footing. Wrongly,
he thought the Michigan Militia were there because Crosslin and his
people wanted a showdown.

As was his habit, Teter never talked to Tom about it. In fact, the two
men never met face-to-face until years later, when they were in court.
He avoided Tom like they were two ownerless dogs that know if they
cross one another they'll have to fight.

That was not Tom's way, however. Upon receipt of this letter, Tom did
what he always did: He got in the car and drove down to Cassopolis to
set up meetings in person with Teter and Sheriff Underwood. He stopped

at both offices. Neither man would see him, and neither would set up a meeting. Tom took the letter to his attorney for farm matters, Don France, who kept an office in the nearby village of Marcellus. They talked it over and Tom decided, fuck it, he was going to ignore it. France counseled it was best not to antagonize the prosecutor. Tom understood his job was to cultivate the support of his neighbors and not pick up that felony.

Teter admits he sent a narc to Hemp Aid '98 and to the fall festival, Summer Fest, which was renamed Roach Roast in a contest on the Rainbow Farm Web site, but Tom and the crew expected as much. They weren't against cops. They just had to leave their guns at the gate and get a tour.

"Ben Masel in Madison, Wisconsin taught me that you never let the police on your property," explained Adam Brook. "You keep them at the gate until the event coordinator can meet them and have that person walk them around. And you get a group of drummers with hand drums to follow behind the cop as he's walked through the venue. You hear the drumbeats coming and you look that way, and sure enough, that's a fuckin' cop! People would come up and say, 'Oh, I really appreciate that, man. I hid my bag because I heard the drum.' "

But Teter was trying to snag a fish, so he sent his men in sub rosa. And they came up with nothing. There was nothing going on there except a bunch of citizens smoking weed. As Teter put it in a Rainbow Farm time-line released later: "Confidential informant discloses open use and distribution of controlled substances at the festival but insufficient evidence to prosecute."

He tried to shake the tree in other ways, too, by setting up state police roadblocks on the corner of Pemberton and Black. The troopers couldn't prevent anyone from coming down the dirt road, technically, but they could reduce the road to one narrow lane and stop each car to get a peek inside, pull them over for fix-it tickets, do whatever they could to get a reason to search the vehicle. For a lot of heads, that was enough to scare them off. They felt the burden of the weed they were carrying and drove right past Pemberton Road and never came back. The farm got a lot of feedback from these people through the underground, and it was clear there were hundreds, maybe even thousands of people who wouldn't come to the farm because of "Checkpoint Charlie." Tom was always angry about this, as the roadblocks may have prevented his festivals from making money.

This was frustrating for Teter, too, since it did him no good to bust some pimply faced kid selling hits of blotter acid or a bag of weed. By 1998 it was already pretty clear he was angling for forfeiture—bust Tom for distributing and take the whole farm. For many of the Militia members, the threat of seizure was exactly what they were protecting Rainbow Farm against, and what they'd come to protest.

Teter didn't have many options for finding a felony that would stick. Rainbow Farm didn't grow pot, and they didn't sell pot, so they couldn't get them for manufacture or distribution. He only had one available strategy at that time, and that was to tie Tom or Rollie to small-scale sales as the owners of the property.

Promoters of rock festivals and similar events, however, were protected from this kind of prosecution. In cases stretching back to the jazz clubs of the 1950s, but proliferating in the festival-laden 1960s and '70s, the courts had consistently come down on the side of property owners and promoters: Even if a business owner had some knowledge that drugs might be used at his club or festival, that didn't mean he knew specific individuals who were coming specifically to break the law. In other words, the owner wasn't aiding and abetting a specific crime. Promoters or venue owners had only been busted when they were specifically involved in selling drugs to customers, or taking a cut from an in-house dealer.

The 2002 Illicit Drug Anti-Proliferation Act—popularly known as the RAVE Act, after the House version of the bill, which was named the

Reducing Americans' Vulnerability to Ecstasy Act—would be written specifically to change all that. It would expand the crackhouse law to make promoters and landowners liable for drug use, even on rented property. But in 1997 there wasn't any RAVE Act.

"Wasn't going to happen," said Doug. "Even with Tom and Rollie stretching the rules on so many things, that was the one iron-clad law: No selling dope. That was the one thing we knew we'd get busted for, so it was strictly forbidden on Rainbow Farm for management, staff, contractors, bands and vendors to sell anything illegal."

What narcs saw instead was a party, and a damn good one. The music, now with a professionally rigged sound-and-light show, would start at noon and go until midnight. The county ordinance said it had to stop at eleven p.m., so they'd wait for the cops to show around then and someone would radio to Derrik and he would let the band finish their last few songs. The routine was that a few days later in the magic mail they'd get a notice of a five-hundred-dollar fine for having broken the noise ordinance and they'd pay it.

When the music was over, most people would wander back to their camps to chill. There was always a big crowd, however, who wanted to go all night. To keep this crowd from roaming the countryside or, god forbid, flooding into the smoky little country bars of Vandalia or Cassopolis—the invasion of the hairy freakies—the farm in 1998 started to put up a circus tent where they could take the late-night party indoors at a lower volume. This evolved quickly into a kind of exotic erotic zone behind walls of dank canvas where even drum circles got naked and loose. Brooklyn's famous Bindlestiff Family Circus played Hemp Aid '98, and during the day they moved through the crowds performing their well-known brand of family entertainment, including acrobatics, walking on stilts, rope walking and western whip tricks. They made the kids laugh. After midnight in the big tent, however, it was strictly adult, and they put on a decadent X-rated show featuring anal fire eating and vaginal plate spinning. Yes, one of the acrobats stood on her head and inserted a plate-spinning stick in her vagina and kept the plate spinning by kegeling. It was like an erotic Olympics, and who wouldn't want to be naked when the acrobats themselves were skinned up? Tom didn't quite get his *Caligula*-style orgy, but things were moving in that direction.

Then it would break down into a steamy, hypereroticized rave—with Robert's dog, Thai Stick, running back and forth all night snapping at the dots off the disco ball. Local DJs and techno musicians would bring their own gear and spin all night to a frenzied gang of younger partiers who knew they'd been set free of not only any intervention by the fuzz but also the conventions of raving, which usually meant no nudity or overtly sexual acts. Clothes were peeled off as the music intensified and the radiant bodies pushed the temperature up inside against the grassy chill outside, the heavy oxygen of the country air thickening under the tent with the smoke of BC bud and homegrown hydro and all-I-got Mexican and pheromones and shameless lust. Fornication in the rave tent itself was discouraged, but the bushes and tents were close at hand. There was a reason people came back to Rainbow Farm time and time again, and it wasn't all about the politics and the weed.

But what was there to bust? It was consensual behavior between adults on private property. There might have been some hits of Ecstasy floating around, but Tom and Rollie weren't dealing.

Instead, Teter was working another vein, albeit a very very thin one. His informants told him that vendors at the festivals kicked back 10 percent of their proceeds to Rainbow Farm. This was a potential weakness. If he could get one of the contracted vendors for selling dope— someone selling printed frisbees, for instance, who also moved a few shrooms or weed on the side—that might be enough of a connection to Tom's wallet.

In the early 1990s, Michigan developed a reputation as a place where the limits of civil forfeiture were tested, sending several cases to the U.S. Supreme Court—where the cops won time after time, and took those victories as encouragement for their libertine interpretation. A certain *Midnight Express* ethic gripped the state. Michigan's prosecutors and local fuzz aggressively pushed the logic of asset seizure all the way out to the limits of constitutionality and then beyond, out into a cop fantasyland where even thought-crime might cost you your life's honest work.

That's what it cost Edwin Dews and his wife, Joanna. Dews was a middle-aged ex-marine living in Durand, Michigan, just west of Flint, who was no fool when it came to drug law and government power. As the owner of three Rock-A-Rolla record stores, he knew right where the line lay between music culture and drug culture, what was legal and what was not. Or he thought he did, and so did the attorneys and accountants who'd helped him set up his thriving businesses. He had never received notice there was anything wrong with his inventory. But that was all before the day in 1994 when the local dope team, the BAY Area Narcotics Enforcement Team—BAYANET—came down on his operation like a sky-choking cloud of flying monkeys.

There was no warning and no exchange of niceties; teams of men sporting tactical jumpsuits and automatic weapons ransacked the Rock-A-Rolla store in Flint, plus a vast warehouse there in Genessee County, then two more stores across the line in Saginaw.

The charge was not selling drugs but drug paraphernalia. In the back of each Rock-A-Rolla store, under a huge suspended sign declaring "No Minors" and identifying the store as a licensed tobacco shop, the Dews offered a wonderland of bongs, pipes, papers, incense, marijuana legalization pamphlets, books by *High Times* columnist "Ask Ed" Rosenthal, all the truck any ordinary head would need. There was little doubt some of it was used for smoking pot—dual use, some head shop owners call it, for tobacco, weed, or any other herb you might want to smoke, illegal or not—but there was no pot involved in the case, nor drugs of any kind. The stuff had been for sale there for years and years, and represented about 5 percent of the space and the sales in the store. The Dewses' bread and butter was selling CDs.

The BAYANET squad shook down the store, then turned their attention elsewhere—the Dewses' home. They swarmed into the house, too, and took everything they could find there. Again, no drugs. But there was a safe in the basement, where Mr. Dews kept a gemstone and rare coin collection, which represented his life savings. The state police eagerly helped themselves to that stash.

Michigan has a fairly reasonable paraphernalia law, which, like its obscenity law, requires that the state notify a legitimate retailer when an item might be considered illegal and give them a period of several days to get a ruling from a judge or else to simply remove it. The Rock-A-Rolla raid was a Michigan State Police operation, but Dews got no warning. When this was brought up in the first minutes of his first hearing, the judge vacated the state case and immediately handed the file to a waiting U.S. attorney, who declared it a federal case, in which there would be no notification provision.

Dews had no defense in federal court and lost everything. He and his wife lost two million dollars in property—the stores, the warehouse, the inventory, the gemstones, *everything*. Over a vanload of bongs and incense worth a couple of thousand dollars. One of the defense attorneys, who was a conservative Republican antidrug guy, said it was the worst miscarriage of justice he'd ever seen.

"I'm a past chief of police, so I've been on the other side," said the attorney, Robert Greenstein. "Where a confiscation case is had, for weeks afterward you hear talk about what percentages are going to which department. It's just a source of income. Don't let anyone tell you that that's not how it works, because I know for a fact. That's what starts revolutions, or people burning down their buildings and people getting shot. I think the whole thing was just a disgusting shame."

Shocked to tears by the whole thing, Joanna Dews blurted out in court, "Welcome to Nazi America!"

Tom Crosslin knew about these kinds of cases. Speakers like Galbraith and Tavel and Dillon—hell, all of them—were well educated on forfeiture, and for the libertarians who partied there it was one of their principal antigovernment gripes. The farm had been in touch with a national organization called Forfeiture Endangers American Rights, or FEAR, then headquartered in Washington, D.C.

One of FEAR's former Michigan members, now speaking only on condition of anonymity because marijuana activism would cost him his job, said that most of the Michiganders who called him for help had the same story: "They find a roach in your ashtray, they pull you out of the car, take all the cash out of your wallet, take anything of value in the car, take your wedding ring, and then dare you to do something about it. You have to post a cash bond to get that stuff back, often more than the stuff is actually worth. So there are no charges, because they figure you're not going to report it. And there's no accountability—that cop just puts that stuff in his pocket, including your dope, and walks away.

"People would ask me what to do," he added, "and I'd tell them almost every time: Just wash your hands of it. Walk away. It's too expensive to try to do anything about it, and you won't win anyway."

Brenda Grantland, a nationally known criminal defense attorney and founder of FEAR, knew about Rainbow Farm. Farm employees had been in contact with FEAR at their offices in Mill Valley, California, prior to 2001, and during the standoff someone informed her office that they might need representation.

"I thought Rainbow Farm was going to be a major issue for us," says Grantland. "We were going to do a major campaign around it. I was aware of what was happening after about the second day. But then 9/11 happened and it all just went away."

Asset forfeiture, as it's called, has been part of public law since biblical times, but the U.S. Congress first made it available to drug warriors as part of the Comprehensive Drug Abuse Prevention and Control Act of 1970—the same bill that created the Shafer Commission, whose recommendations to legalize marijuana Nixon ignored. The new law, 21 USC § 88, is a civil statute aimed squarely at busting mass shipments of drugs, primarily by organized crime. The idea was that the feds would seize the drugs, buildings, and conveyances used to transport drugs, sell them, and plow those proceeds back into crime fighting (through the General Fund). Every state in the union quickly passed its own state forfeiture statutes. Michigan's (MCL 333.7521) is modeled very closely after the federal law.

Right away, however, prosecutors figured out that the burden of proof in civil cases is so low that they could pretty much snatch whatever they wanted. In civil cases, they only had to have "probable cause" to seize property—the same level of nonproof required to get a search warrant. In a 1974 case that was upheld by the Supreme Court, an expensive leased yacht was forfeited after customs agents found one joint on board, thus establishing that the "innocent owner" was not protected from losing property and that the forfeited property had no value relationship— known as "proportionality"—to the seriousness of the crime. For one joint, you could lose a house or business worth millions of dollars.

In civil forfeiture, all our usual rights and protections are flipped. Property doesn't have any rights, only people do. For instance, in order to retrieve forfeited property, the owner has to prove by a "preponderance of the evidence"—a much higher standard than that under which it was seized—that the stuff was not used in a crime. The thing is presumed guilty and must be proven innocent, a usually impossible task.

Plus in Michigan and a few other states, the defendant had to post a bond, usually 10 percent of the value of the item seized, and hire his own lawyers to fight the forfeiture, as there's no provision for a court-appointed one. The U.S. Department of Justice reports that as many as 80 percent of these cases go uncontested.

Still, before 1984 these seizures were relatively rare. There was no direct incentive for law enforcement; the money went into the General Fund. But when Reagan heated up his War on Drugs in the early 1980s, he unleashed the forces of greed to help drive drug prosecution. His Omnibus Crime Bill of 1984 established funds for forfeiture monies at the Department of Justice (DEA, FBI, ATF) and at the Treasury Department (Customs), letting them keep the money they made.

The bill also extended this privilege to the states, making forfeiture a bonanza for local cops. By the mid-1990s, forfeiture was a one-billion-dollar-a-year industry, and is now a major source of law enforcement funding at all levels, from village police units to the Department of Homeland Security.

The practice is also rotten with corruption. A 1991 series of articles in the *Pittsburgh Press* reviewed five hundred federal cases and found that 80 percent of the people whose property was seized under civil forfeiture were never even charged with a crime. Most just gave up trying to recover their property. In state and local cases, the percentage was presumed to be even higher. Though overall seizures have fallen slightly in recent years, the result of federal reforms in 2000 and 2002, forfeiture is a growth industry. The tactic is so lucrative that there are now over two hundred federal statues authorizing forfeiture for other crimes, not just drugs. By 2000 you could lose your property for things like making a false statement on a bank loan application, or for failing to report to the IRS the purchase of money orders of over three thousand dollars within twenty-four hours.

The SWET squad that operated out in the area around Cass County, for instance, lived off forfeiture revenues. State police budget documents obtained through FOIA reveal that in 1999, for instance, SWET received $930,000 directly from forfeiture and restitution. Of that, $30,000 went to investigations, $78,000 to vehicles and another $27,000 went to specialized equipment rentals. Almost $300,000 of it went to paying other governments in their Southwest Michigan district, like Cass County, for their police services. This was the high time for forfeiture, the late-1990s, and in subsequent years those numbers would drop.

It took a lot of busts to scrape up that kind of loot. FEAR's Michigan activist said that the average value of a seized car, for instance, was listed as $25; the average amount of cash found during drug raids was $50. These weren't drug kingpins they were going after.

After some conscientious politicking spearheaded by Illinois senior senator Henry Hyde, some of the provisions of forfeiture were rolled back in 2002. But by then the practice already had a deadly track record.

"When somebody called me, the day before or after Labor Day, about Rainbow Farm, my first thought was, 'Oh, are we going to have another Donald Scott situation here?'" said NORML's Allen St. Pierre.

Like pot activists all over the country, Tom and Rollie had also heard about the Donald Scott case in Ventura County, California, a fabricated forfeiture prosecution that had turned deadly. Doug, Moe and others acknowledged that this case struck a fair dose of fear in everyone on the farm.

"It was the kind of thing where you never knew from day to day: Was this going to happen to us? Was somebody just going to kick the door in and shoot us?" said Derrik DeCraene.

That's exactly what happened to Malibu-area bon vivant Donald Scott. In 1992 Donald Scott was a colorful, cantankerous sixty-one-year-old millionaire, heir to a fortune made by his grandfather selling Scott's Emulsion, a health tonic once popular in England. Scott had swanned around the Hollywood scene in his early years and dated French-born film star Corinne Calvet. His friends included Clint Eastwood. Scott and his third wife, Frances Plante, lived on his gorgeous Trail's End Ranch in Ventura County, 250 acres of coastal big trees, grasslands and high mesquite chapparal and some of the last open space left in Southern California. The ranch was a private inholding nestled in the Santa Monica Mountains National Recreation Area just across the Los Angeles County line, and had been openly coveted for years by the U.S. Park Service and other agencies. The property held several important archaeological sites dating back to the area's native Chumash people, a history that Scott treasured.

On several occasions, the Park Service, state agencies and environmental groups had approached Scott to buy the property, but he wasn't interested. Scott suspected there might be a development deal or something else hidden in their agenda. "But Scott would never negotiate with government officials, whom he distrusted," reported the *Los Angeles Times*.

So we know now, a task force of local officials got together with the Los Angeles County Sheriff's office and found a way to simply take the property. All they had to do was *accuse* Scott of growing pot. You think this can't happen in the United States of America, but that's just how it happened.

In September 1992, according to a devastating series of stories by local publisher Anne Soble, writing for the *Malibu Surfside News* (affirmed by the *Los Angeles Times* and other papers), a state game warden and an employee of the California Coastal Commission, an extraordinarily powerful agency controlling development on the coast, dropped in on the Scotts and brought a six-pack of beer. They asked for a tour of the Chumash sites on the property, feigning archaeological interest, but the Scotts refused because the trails were frequented by rattlesnakes. Plante, Scott's widow, thought later that they were looking for weed.

According to a seventy-three-page report released by Ventura County district attorney Michael D. Bradbury, entitled "Report on the Death of Donald Scott," released March 30, 1993, on two separate occasions U.S. Border Patrol agents made illegal, surreptitious incursions onto Trail's End Ranch to look for dope, but found none. Lacking any evidence, Los Angeles County Deputy Sheriff Gary R. Spencer "filled his affidavit in support of a search warrant for Scott's two-hundred-acre Malibu area ranch with false and misleading statements," according to the DA.

The most outrageous were attributed to a DEA agent, who hovered over the ranch in a helicopter looking for weed. The district attorney's report reads: "[The agent] had been unwilling to let his so called 'sighting' be used as the basis for obtaining a search warrant until Spencer 'used purported statements of [an] informant to induce [the agent] to agree to use his name in the warrant.'" The report continues: "the almost unavoidable conclusion to be drawn from [the agent's] change of heart is that he was either lying or not sure that he saw marijuana."

The story concocted by the warrant was so preposterous it defies reason. A NORML spokesman summarized it like this: "At one point, they sent over a helicopter with the then-expert from the DEA and the California Narcotic Officers' Association to fly over this guy's house and the guy filled out an affidavit which led the next day to the police raid on the guy's house. This guy had something like 120-foot-high, I can't remember whether they were eucalyptus trees, I mean these were huge trees. And the claim from the government was that this guy had hoisted marijuana plants to the top of the canopy, through a sophisticated pulley system!"

Of course, there was no such treetop pot farm, no pulley system, nothing. Donald Scott didn't grow pot and didn't have any pot on his farm.

The next morning, between seven and nine a.m. on October 2, 1992, an assault team kicked in the door of Donald Scott's house. A phalanx of flak-jacketed sheriff's deputies, DEA agents and U.S. Park Service officers, all shouting and brandishing automatic weapons, shoved Frances Plante through her kitchen and into the living room as she screamed "Don't shoot me! Don't shoot me!" Scott, who evidently heard the commotion but was unsure of who was in the house, searched his bedroom for a Colt .38 snubnose revolver he kept there for home defense. According to accounts in the *Christian Science Monitor* and the *Independent*, a British publication, he'd been up drinking and had taken a Valium, and was still fuzzy. He came downstairs with the gun over his head, asking what was going on. According to Plante, the officers told him to lower the gun, and as he did they shot him at least three times, leaving him to die unattended in a pool of blood while they searched the premises. Scott's gun was never fired. They found no trace of marijuana anywhere on the estate.

A deputy involved with the raid figured they could make the forfeiture stick if they could find as few as fourteen marijuana plants. In any case, they'd get a huge chunk of change just holding it for a while, as the estate was worth at least $5,000,000, which means the bond alone would be $500,000.

But they never got the Scott estate. Unlike most victims of forfeiture, Frances Plante had enough knowledge, enough help from the Ventura DA's office (pissed that L.A. sheriffs had executed this raid in Ventura County without informing them), and enough dough to raise holy hell, and the results were a searing indictment of all parties involved.

The Ventura DA's report on this killing included copies of a parcel map to Scott's ranch, handed out to deputies just before the raid on the property, with hand-drawn dollar amount values marked out on all the neighboring parcels, one of them at $800,000. They'd had the properties assessed. The Dope Team knew exactly how much the property was worth, and could do the math themselves and figure out how much this would net their departments.

Bradbury's report reaches an explosive, damning conclusion: "The Los Angeles County Sheriff's Department was motivated, at least in part, by a desire to seize and forfeit the ranch for the government. . . . Based in part upon the possibility of forfeiture, Spencer obtained a search warrant that was not supported by probable cause. This search warrant became Donald Scott's death warrant."

"Oh, it was a very, very disturbing case," comments Allen St. Pierre. "Almost, in my mind, gave carte blanche for exactly what happened years later, in this situation at Rainbow Farm. Not one nanogram of marijuana, paraphernalia or cultivation was found. Nothing was found. And they shot this guy [Scott] dead. But nobody went to jail. The principals involved in this not only did not get punished, they ended up staying on the hierarchy for better jobs. Which set the table, at least psychically, for these kinds of actions all these years later."

When Teter became the county prosecutor in 1997, forfeiture frenzy was peaking. In Michigan, in particular, some of the most troubling aspects of forfeiture had been reaffirmed by two precedent-setting cases that had just gone to the U.S. Supreme Court in 1996.

In 1992 a Michigan case called Ursery (no relation to Vandalia mayor Sondra Mose-Ursery) established that civil forfeiture is not, in fact, double jeopardy.

The Bennis case was even more puzzling. On October 3, 1988, John Bennis of Royal Oak, Michigan, was caught making it with a prostitute in the front seat of his car, convicted of indecency and fined $250. Then the cops seized his car as a "public nuisance." His wife, Tina Bennis, was half owner of the car, and had not only paid for part of it with her babysitting money but used it to cart their five kids to school. The Supreme Court, however, was not moved by her interest in the car, and in 1996 handed down a ruling with far-reaching implications, saying that law enforcement could seize jointly owned property without any regard for innocent parties who might be harmed.

This is what Teter was talking about when he wrote in his letter that he'd prosecute under the "nuisance" statutes.

Down on the farm, however, they were acutely aware of being on shaky footing, and made a genuine effort to keep any such link from emerging, even inadvertently.

"Our credo, right from the start, is that there were no hard drugs on this farm," said Doug. "We believed in partaking of marijuana privately, responsibly. We didn't want hard drugs. We didn't want people selling drugs up here."

Moe nodded and added, "Tom's motto was: 'If you're not getting high enough on marijuana, then smoke better marijuana.' He was absolutely against hard drugs, and he'd either throw the drugs out or throw the person out if he found them."

The Hemp Aid '97 flyers made it plain: "DO NOT BRING: Firearms, fireworks, nitrous, bad attitudes, or ANY bottles!" Like every one of their flyers, in a box at the bottom it said, No Hard Drugs.

A big wooden sign at the entrance to Rainbow Farm also spelled it out: "Using or selling drugs of any kind is illegal. Anyone found with hard drugs on Rainbow Farm will be evicted." Their Web site said the same thing.

The Midwest, then as now, was absolutely rife with cheap, crappy methamphetamine—called crystal methadrine, meth, speed, or crank, and produced using a number of slightly varying recipes—and that tended to cause problems. Campers who were on it would get aggressive and paranoid. Also particularly nefarious at the time was nitrous oxide, N_2O, better known as "laughing gas." This is the same stuff you used to get at the dentist's office. Those who had access to medical supplies could get it by the scuba-sized canister, but it was also available through food-service dealers as "whip-its," small cartridges used in whipped-cream dispensers. It was usually dispensed by filling party balloons.

"We hated that stuff most of all," said Derrik. "Nitrous just made people stupid, and it was dangerous. You just couldn't tell if somebody knew what they were doing or were just going to flop over in an over-dose, like shut down their respiratory system or something.

"We had one band that came in, and they were unpacking backstage and doing their thing, and suddenly I get word that one of the roadies, or one of their guests, has set up a nitrous tank. I go over there, and go, 'Hey, man, what the hell are you doing? You can't just bust that stuff out here. Put it away.' I'm trying to be cool to him, because it's a pretty major band, one of the biggest ones we had. So the guy puts it away. But later in the evening, somebody tells me again that he's filling balloons from this tank, so Tom goes over there and he's hot. 'You're going to get this fucking place shut down, you sonofabitch,' he's saying, and we sent him packing. He was making a big stink, 'The band's not coming back here, you guys are uncool,' that kind of thing, but we didn't care. Fuck you for jeopardizing our safety, you know?"

Doug was particularly hard on the kids who showed up hoping to sell trips.

"One of my security guys came to me one festival with a brown paper bag full of mushrooms," Doug recounted. "I would've loved to just hand 'em out to everybody. But I couldn't. And I made a big show of it: There was a burn barrel out behind the building, and we'd just been burning some trash. And I dropped that bag into that burn barrel. And I said, 'Now, any government agents out here watching, I want you to see what we do with people who sell drugs at Rainbow Farm. We destroy 'em.'"

It was late 1998, and mayor Sondra Mose-Ursery was sitting in her Penn Township office, a little brick building in Vandalia, when Tom Crosslin came in for the first time.

"It was a few days before Christmas, and a lady was in here asking for help, looking for a new coat and toys for her kids," she recounted, giving the flat, dead-eyed look of a lady who suffers no fools. "Her husband was in jail. I didn't know Tom then, but he was in the hallway. I asked him to wait, and said, 'I think this is real important,' and he said, 'I do, too.'

"Tom was asking about houses for sale in the village. But he said he overheard what the lady wanted and offered to help. He asked how many families need help in the area around Christmastime. He said, 'I know how good that makes a kid feel. I saw it in my own family that a few toys at Christmas give kids a lot of hope, and how disappointed those ones were who didn't get anything.'

"I found four or five families needed help. Tom took it further. He offered to buy a toy for every child in the village. I said, 'What? This man is nuts.'

"He said we'd jump in his red truck and go into Elkhart and have us a time. I wasn't about to get in no truck with him and go nowhere. I didn't know who he was, right? So he offered to let us Xerox his driver's license, and I had my assistant, Pat, take down his license plate. Then I said, 'Okay, now I trust you.'

"We went into Elkhart. We bought toys, remote control cars, train sets, dolls, tea sets, all kinds of stuff. Then we got back and Tom said, 'We forgot wrapping paper.' I said, 'Are you crazy?' He said, 'Well, I bought all these toys, the least you could do is wrap 'em.' So I got some other ladies together and we wrapped 'em and labeled them boy and girl, by age.

"Then Tom said, 'I remember how great it was when my uncles used to give me a dollar bill. I'm gonna give 'em all a five-dollar bill, too.'

"I said, 'I want you to hand out those five-dollar bills.' But he didn't want to do that. He didn't want anyone to know who did this.

"Afterward, he bought two houses here in town, fixed them up and sold them to needy families. He also sent out his crews to clean up an old dump alongside Bonine Road. Didn't ask nobody if it needed to be done. Just went out and did it. He done a lot of things needed doing around here."

Another one of Tom's gestures that made an impression around Cass County was one Amy called the "peanut butter sandwich story": Robert came home from school one day and hopped off the big yellow school bus in front of the farm house with a long face. He was seven years old and in the first grade. Amy asked him, "How was school today, Robert?"

"Fine, except all I had for lunch was a peanut butter sandwich and some Kool-Aid."

"Why only that? What about the rest of your lunch?"

"Well, I was supposed to get the hot lunch, but it wasn't paid for."

Tom paid for Robert's lunches in advance and when he called the school the next day he wanted to prevent this kind of screw-up from happening again.

"How many kids there don't take the hot lunch?" Tom asked the school secretary. She told him about ten to fifteen weren't on the program. Poverty was no stranger to the schools in Cassopolis, and it wasn't a stretch to figure the hot lunch was the best meal some of those kids would get.

"I'll tell ya what, I'll give you a blank check for all the meals that aren't covered in Robert's class every month, and you just fill it out. Give everybody hot lunch."

Amy saw those checks and remembers that one of them was for $140. Chump change, maybe, but not when you just don't have it. What is clear in all of these stories is that Tom didn't do what he did with an ulterior motive—to buy good will. And if he did, he miscalculated.

"Man, we cleaned up dumps, we stopped people from dumping, we did so much stuff, environmentally. But half the time they were trying to prosecute us for it," said Derrik DeCraene. "No matter how much I do in this community, I can't get an 'Atta-boy' to save my life."

FOURTEEN A Blood Feud

RAINBOW FARM HAD THEIR best show ever booked for Hemp Aid '99: a Memorial Day weekend with the king of all stoners, Tommy Chong. The tall, hairy half of the comedy duo Cheech & Chong, Tommy Chong had written and directed a series of late-1970s films including *Up in Smoke* which were among the highest-grossing of the time for Warner Bros Studios. The duo's comedy albums like *Big Bambú* and *Cheech & Chong's Wedding Album* were platinum standards in burnout humor. Chong was a mainstay of comedy circuits, while Cheech Marin by that time had quit the duo for full-time acting gigs on TV series like *Nash Bridges*. Because Rainbow Farm had a festival vibe, Chong decided he would come with a blues-rock act put together with his sons, billed as Chong and the Family Stoned.

Perhaps even more significant, Tom and the crew had managed to get *High Times* to the show.

"We tried for *years* to get *High Times* to even take our calls, much less attend our festivals," said Doug. "We kept getting the cold shoulder. It was a source of major frustration. So one day, Tom and I both got editor Steve Hager on the phone, finally. I just confronted him, 'What is the problem, Steve? You obviously sense a problem somewhere here, because you're ignoring us.'"

Hager laid out some of his concerns, and right away he said, "I know Max Robinson to be a freedom fighter and a friend of Jack Herer." After some discussion, it turned out that Max had put a bug in Hager's ear that Rainbow Farm was nothing more than a bunch of "money grubbers." They tried to argue the point, telling the truth about how Max and R. J. had taken home all of the profit there was from Hemp Aid '97, but Hager was defensive on behalf of the activists he already knew.

Tom and Doug were pissed and told Hager to go cover Max's next festival and hung up. After a series of phone calls and emails, however, it became apparent that High Times might be missing an opportunity. "So anyway, he called us back," said Doug. "Here's the deal that Steve Hager made: 'I'll come out and cover your event, you pay my expenses for travel and my expenses while I'm there, you pay me three thousand dollars to speak at the event and you hire the Cannabis Cup Band to play at your festival for three thousand dollars and pay their expenses.' When all was said and done, it cost us ten thousand dollars to have a half-page article in High Times magazine about our Hemp Aid '99 festival. Plus the advertising, which we paid for separately and wasn't cheap."

With Chong and High Times on the way, the place needed rapid improvements. They had to put a roof on the little stage, open a store, put in permitted campground sites, get better sound. Chong was going to sell a blizzard of tickets, and the moment he signed a contract their little production went from costing tens of thousands of dollars to hundreds of thousands overnight. They upped the ticket price to sixty-five dollars, knowing even then they might not recoup.

Rainbow Farm sent out riders to paper the Midwest with fliers. Moe, Amy, Rollie and little Robert gave out five to ten thousand at Hash Bash. Tom paid gas and food money to drivers headed to Chicago, Madison, Detroit, Indiana, Ohio, New York and Kentucky. One person with a trunkload of fliers would hand off whole bundles to activists he met along the way, which would then continue traveling south, west and east. A bunch of them got into Canada, mostly to Windsor and Toronto. This show was going to be a whopper.

That ramped-up activity did not escape Scott Teter. He'd read the fliers and realized he couldn't wait for Tom to make mistakes anymore.

On March 24, 1999, he sent another certified letter to Tom. Unlike the letter from a year earlier, this one presented a major threat. Acknowledging that the farm had been under "surveillance and investigation," Teter proclaimed that he now had hard evidence of drug violations, including distribution, which was a felony. It did not say this distribution was connected to Tom or Rollie in any way. This would have been an extremely hard case to make, since neither Tom nor Rollie nor any of their licensed vendors sold or distributed drugs, as far as they knew, but it didn't sound like a bluff. He concluded the terse letter with: "The use of your property for this purpose will subject it to civil forfeiture pursuant to MCL 333.7521 et seq; MSA 15.14(7521)."

A few nights later, in the chilly dark of March 29, Tom stalked his kitchen, raging. Rollie's stony, seated presence seemed to feed his rage, as he yelled lines for Doug to type in his response to Teter.

He'd finally arrived at the point where Rainbow Farm was going to work: Tommy Chong on the way; *High Times* covering; local and maybe national press sure to attend. He had probably fifty thousand dollars or more out on deposits for the festival already. He hadn't, so far as he knew, commited any crime more serious than a misdemeanor, and here was Teter saying he was going to seize his farm.

Neither Tom nor Rollie could type, or for that matter even write all that well, so Doug typed, complete with misspellings and an opinion wrongly attributed to drug czar Barry McCaffrey, due to the enormous pressure of Tom's fury. Doug cautioned the bar fighter, "Tom, are you sure you want to say it like that? That can be interpreted a lot of ways, it makes us look like we're being a little inflammatory."

Tom snarled back, "Hell yeah! That's exactly what I want to say. And that's the way I want to say it."

Grover T. Crosslin
59896 Pemberton Rd.
Vandalia, MI 49095

March 29, 1999

Scott L. Teter
Prosecuting Attorney
Cass County Courthouse
Cassopolis, MI 49031

RE: Your letter of 3/24/99

Mr. Teter:

I want to make sure that you think about a few things before you take any further actions towards your threat to seize my property. That threat was taken very seriously by me and my neighbors who I have been speaking with after receiving your letter. They have expressed grave concerns over your threat as well. I do not grow, sell or distribute marijuana on this farm. I do not condone or encourage the use of any drugs. They are not allowed on this farm. I distinguish the difference between marijuana and hard drugs and our government now does too.

What will it take for you to understand that the events at my farm are peaceful gatherings of people to demonstrate against bad laws and form a foundation from which to change those laws. Our government is set up with certain freedoms assured to the public for this very reason, so the people can change government when government stops serving the people. Mr. Teter, the fact that you don't care for our politics does not give you or any government agency the right to disregard our rights to assemble and petition our government.

Remember, we are pacifists, we do not allow weapons on our farm. We are striving to bring about peaceful change from within the system of laws set up for that purpose. However, as John F. Kennedy once said, "Those who would deny a peaceful revolution, demand a violent one." How will history judge you? A politician who helped force a violent revolution, or a man of virtue who allowed a peaceful change?

Our friends at the Michigan Militia have their ideas of how we should handle your threats, but as I said, we are pursuing a peaceful change to the laws that are now threatening our communities (and my own family) more than ever. Your bad attitude over this whole thing concerns me, and out of fear for what you might do to take my property, I am asking my Militia friends to provide an un-armed witness team to document with video cameras any and all actions you or any other government agency may take against us.

I have discussed this with my family and we are all prepared to die on this land before we allow it to be stolen from us. How should we be prepared to die? Are you planning to burn us out like they did in Waco, or will you have snipers shoot us through our windows like the Weavers at Ruby Ridge? Maybe the Governor can call in the National Guard for another Kent State. The American people took those government atrocities very seriously and I assure you they will feel the same about any violent actions you may decide to take against us.

The federal government has just received the results of the IOM [Institute of Medicine of the National Academy of Sciences, 1999] study on marijuana that refutes all of the previous lies and misinformation our government has fed us over the past 60 years. Drug Czar William [sic] McCaffrey and conservative columnist William F. Buckley along with over 100 mainstream newspapers are calling for the end of the drug war. Yet people like yourself continue to turn a blind eye to truth and reason.

You could be reasonable about this situation and help us in our efforts to make positive changes in these bad laws and make a smooth transition into a more compassionate and rational society with regards to its handling of the drug problem. You have a golden oppurtunity [sic] with us to do just that and be seen as a politician with a future in the new millennium. It seems that you prefer to be a hard ass prosecutor and totally disregard all good sense here.

They way I see it, you have no choice. You either work with us, or you will be replaced. Consider Dan Lundgren, former Attorney General for the State of California. He chose to disregard the will of the people in their desire for legalized marijuana in California, and he was voted out of office by the very people he refused to listen to. The same can happen to you. The county of Mendocino in California has a new prosecutor and sheriff. These two men were voted in because of their openly pro-marijuana positions.

Mr. Prosecutor, we have the support of the working man and woman in Cass County and you don't. Your support of our efforts here will win you the next campaign. Continue to fight us and you will show the voters of Cass county that you are just another dinasaur [sic] politician from the 20th century on the verge of extinction. You have the oppurtunity [sic] to help us change the world in a positive direction or you have the oppurtunity [sic] to continue the path your [sic] on and have the blood of a government massacre on your hands.

It's your choice. If you choose to send out your secret police, I hope you are standing there on the front line to witness the results of your actions.

Sincerely,

[signed]

Grover T. Crosslin

Teter, for his part, took one look at that letter and saw little more than the words *Militia* and *blood of a government massacre*. And that was all he needed to see.

The prosecutor explains his misinterpretation with cool rationality: "He sent me back a two-page letter that basically said, 'We take your threats very seriously. I turned them over to my friends at the Michigan Militia. They want to come pay you a visit. And if you ever attempt to come on to this property, the ground will run red with blood before you move my family out.'

"Well, that sort of set the tone that we weren't going to be able to talk this thing out."

Of course, this was a radical misinterpretation, and clearly not what the letter says. But Teter got ready for war. Tom was not fully aware of it, but his legal dispute with Teter had turned into a blood feud.

The county threw any number of injunctions at Rainbow Farm in an effort to keep Hemp Aid '99 from happening, but each revealed that the farm had more support than either side knew. On April 23 county administrator Terry Proctor sent a letter to Crosslin saying this Chong show was almost certainly going to violate the county's "large gathering" ordinance, and questioning the validity of their 1998 501(c)(3) sponsor. Tom sent letters back via Don France confirming that they'd clear up the sponsor issue. A county judge gave Teter his injunction on May 6.

After the donation dispute with R. J. Tavel and FIJA in 1997, Bob Fitrakis stepped in as Rainbow Farm's nonprofit sponsor, the editor of a then-twenty-eight-year-old radical community newspaper called the *Columbus Free Press* out of Columbus, Ohio. Published under the familiar lefty slogan, "Speaking Truth to Power," the Free Press was a classic liberal vehicle, "awaiting the rise of the next left mass movement." While the libertarians present at Rainbow Farm were digging metaphoric foxholes for their personal defense against a big government assault, Fitrakis and the paper's nonprofit foundation, the Columbus Institute of Contemporary Journalism, were preparing for a socialist-flavored utopia. Fitrakis, a college professor himself, marveled at the polyglot political culture that came together there.

"Yeah, that was half the fun of going out there," he laughed. "The one year I was out there, you had the Democratic gubernatorial candidate, Jeffrey Feiger, there. You had the Libertarian Party. You had the Green Panthers. You had everyone from the U.S. Marijuana Party to people who were far more libertarian. Everyone got along perfectly. It was one of the most wholesome, thoughtful, nice environments you'll ever be in. There was a tremendous sense that no one should sell hard drugs or illegal street drugs. It was a great place.

"I mean, I was one of the founders of the Democratic Socialists of America," he added. "I had come out of the Human Rights Party of Michigan, which was the antiwar, left-wing student party out of Ann Arbor. I'd also been a cultural sympathizer of the White Panther Party, John Sinclair's party. In fact, one of the last times I was at Rainbow Farm, I had the privilege of being there with John Sinclair. He was one of my original heroes. It really was an alliance of the left and the right. You'd say, 'Man, these people have a *very* individualistic property rights perspective, or they've got a *militia* here, but nobody really bothered anyone at that farm. It really was the Rainbow tribe across the political and cultural perspective."

For Fitrakis, the unique political structure of Rainbow Farm was also shocking in its origins: These people were as agrarian as a Maoist dream and had come out of the blue-collar grassroots.

"I've got a Ph.D., I've got a J.D., I came from Detroit, I mean it was just always surprising to me, to see these people coming out of Elkhart and Nappanee and rural Michigan, and they were all pot smokers! But there was something about *pot* that created a sense of community there and brought people together there that, under normal circumstances, wouldn't talk to each other."

Evidently, the Columbus Institute had failed to file a statement of continued existence and their nonprofit status had lapsed briefly in June 1997. "A filing error," says Fitrakis, and for the next week, Fitrakis barraged the Cass County court with documentation. Hemp Aid was only a few weeks off when the county was satisfied and the "large gathering" injunction was lifted.

Teter had another one waiting. On May 21, only a week before the festival, he filed on behalf of the County Health Department to stop the festival because the farm was not a licensed campground.

This injunction caused a fair bit of panic. Their campground had always been a campground in name only, not as permitted by the state. If anything, it was a "primitive" camp, with no facilities other than two pitcher pumps, the cold-water outdoor shower and ten thousand dollars in Porta Pottis on the day of show. One year earlier, in May 1998, on the day before Hemp Aid '98, Rollie had filed with County Health for a campground construction permit, filling out the required separate forms for the county and the Environmental Health Department. Rollie was the nominal president of Rainbow Farm, Inc., and much of the paperwork on the farm was under his name. Earlier that year, Doug, in his official role as manager, had begun working with a county engineer on water and septic plans for a large service building to be built along Pemberton Road—to be replete one day with shower rooms and bathrooms. On the same day in May 1998, Rollie applied for a campground license.

Tom got a deal on a huge new pole barn in the summer of 1998 and plopped it down in the old garden site. It was massive, a sixty-by-eighty-foot metal structure on a cement pad, which would be extended to become sixty by one hundred feet. By Hemp Aid '99, this was to become the Rainbow Farm camp store, farm office, and a coffeeshop called The Joint.

Attorney Don France, an RV park owner himself, was helping Tom get permits, but the state wasn't satisfied with their campground plans until January 1999, and even though they already had a camp store by then they only got preliminary camp construction approval on April 20, 1999, to build everything else (420! The smoker's code number for weed). They were approved to build a sanitation station for RVs and thirty-five modern campsites in a group area. They would add shower rooms, bathrooms and a laundry onto the camp store building. They also had approval for twenty-five individual marked sites, which they built. None of these were to have individual water or electrical hookups—they were trying to preserve the farm's open grassy fields.

Eight days before Memorial Day weekend 1999, however, the camp sites weren't in yet. Only the big new double-pump field well had been sunk.

Because the sites hadn't been finished, they didn't have the campground permit. It seemed like Teter had them. The amount of money Tom had laid out for the show would break Rainbow Farm and send it and Tom's Services, Inc. into bankruptcy. Then came a quiet call from someone at the county.

"We had the complete support of the Cass County Health Department," said Doug. "I had one guy tell me, 'Look, Teter's been down here going through our files, and it would be a good idea if you fill out a couple of these forms for temporary permits and we just keep them on file.'"

Doug and Rollie rolled down to Cassopolis and filled out the paperwork. Without Teter even knowing about it, an inspector ran out to the farm and the temporary permit was approved. On May 27, the day before Hemp Aid '99, Teter had to lift the injunction.

"Teter was pissed," Doug chuckles. "Can you imagine? Someone from your own government tips off the hippies and helps them out?"

Hemp Aid couldn't be stopped at that point. The most successful show Rainbow Farm would ever stage was on.

"Rainbow Farm was what I envisioned America to be," said Tommy Chong, "a lot of tents with people selling headbands and tie-dyed stuff and pipes. Nomads and gypsies traveling. Bands playing on the stages. And people camping out. It was utopia."

Tommy Chong talked about playing Rainbow Farm while sitting in federal prison in Taft, California, in November 2003, in the middle of a nine-month stretch for selling bongs with his face on them. It was a coordinated sting run by John Ashcroft's Department of Justice, targeting Chong specifically. In court a U.S. prosecutor said as part of her argument that Chong was a bad example because he made fun of drugs and cops in his movies. Sitting there in an outdoor visitation area, with a cool breeze off the Central Valley desert, you didn't have to know anything about the First Amendment to see in this funny grandfather with a deep purr for a voice the evidence of a drug war gone off the rails into total paranoid fantasy.

"That place was unique," he added about Rainbow Farm. "I thought it really was a sign of the times. I thought we were heading in that direction. I didn't know we were headed the other way. It was hippie-land. That's what I loved about it."

Chong had been working up a rock band with his sons (two of his six children), Paris, on bass, and Gilbran, on drums, so they tried out that power trio on the Rainbow Farm crowd. Chong and the Family Stoned played some Cheech & Chong favorites like "Earache My Eye," the acid rock send-up attributed to Chong's alter ego, Alice Bowie: "My mama talkin' to me try to tell me how to live / but I don't listen to her 'cause my head is like a sieve." They did a little "Up In Smoke," a reggae version of "Summertime," a Jazz Crusaders tune, and even a punk song. In between came the famous stoner banter—*"Dave's not here, man!"*—and of course, there was a virtual hail of joints on stage.

"Everybody wants to say they smoked with Tommy Chong," he smiles.

The Chongs didn't camp—they'd be mobbed, he acknowledged—but while spending hours in the farmhouse talking to Tom and the crew, Rollie got excited about Paris's new venture, a company called Chong Glass that would make Tommy Chong bongs. Damn the Dewses' case: Rainbow Farm was already in the bong business and they were going in deeper. Rollie put in a preorder and the farm was the only venue in the Midwest selling them, and they sold like mad.

In the house that weekend, Chong saw shades of things to come for Rainbow Farm. "One of the guys, he was one of the guys workin' there, who was an ex-Vietnam vet—do you know which one that was?"

He was talking about Jimbo, or Big Jim Collett.

"I think so. Yeah. Yeah. Yeah. He used to kind of freak me out a little bit, with gun talk. I couldn't go there. I'm totally a pacifist.

"That's what these law enforcement people live for: someone with a gun. Because then they got an excuse to blow 'em away."

When Chong met him, Tom seemed to have it all under control—the hippies, the Militia, everything. But later, it would start going cockeyed, for all the usual reasons.

"Well, it's always money," Tommy said. "See, when you're paying money for acts and stuff like that, it's very tough to make it. That's a tough business."

Later, during the summer of the standoff, Tom would call Chong for help. He wanted to put together a benefit for legal bills. He even offered to sell Chong the farm.

"I would have loved to have owned that property. It was a great piece of property. In fact, that was one of Tom's offers. 'You want this place?' " he laughed. "But I learned. No, no, no. I wouldn't go near it! With the way it is now. It'd just be more stuff for the federal government to come and take, if they feel like it."

Jimmy Lee Collett and his wife Guynel were locals from Cassopolis who started coming out to the festivals early on, bringing their baby daughter, their teenage daughter and her boyfriend and Jim's brother, plus a posse of assorted friends from their family home down in Tennessee. They were experienced campers and came to inhabit Rainbow Farm for the summer months. They often bartered their festival tickets and camping fees in exchange for services. It wasn't long before they were invited to join the festival crew.

Jim's brother was paralyzed from the waist down and had been in a wheelchair for several years by the time they got to the farm. He had sunk into a depression and Jim brought him out to the farm to try to pull him out of it—which worked. He would haul himself down to the wooden porch in front of the store and hang there all day, talking to the throngs of customers and keeping an eye on the action. This was a key vantage point for watching the front gate and for anybody trying to sneak in along the front fencerow, so the crew gave him a radio and made him eyes and ears for the Peace Police.

Guynel Collett was a trained EMT and registered nurse at Elkhart General, and during the festivals she manned the medic cart. There was no end to the injuries big and small, from cut feet, campfire burns and spider bites to the vendor who had a heart attack and one particular partier who either overdosed or had a severe allergic reaction to drugs. Guynel took her work seriously and was well connected in the county, and they never lacked for professional medical care or ambulance service at the farm—despite the fact they had to hire it out of Edwardsburg.

Jim was a big, powerful man with a military background who looked like one mean sumbitch, but whom everyone at Rainbow Farm found to be a kind of southern sweetheart. He was pretty stoic and gentle, but could turn on the vibe—the this-might-be-your-last-breath stare—when that was needed. He was also one of the Peace Police.

The Rainbow Farm crew knew some of Big Jim's history—once in 1995 he'd gone ballistic in a jealous rage and the police ran him in on charges of assault and battery—but since he was pretty sweet to everyone at the farm they didn't consider it any of their business. On the contrary, farm organizers could put that dark streak to use from time to time.

Derrik got to know Jim Collett a bit and liked him as much as Doug did. Jim, he said, was like a lot of the people on the farm, motivated by love. He believed that prosecuting potsmokers was a witch hunt. "Jim would have done anything for Tom," Derrik said.

Derrik DeCraene had a nickname for Jim; he called him The Biter.

"One time, after we had the office in the store building, just off The Joint, a guy came into the room back there and he was hot. Whatever it was about, Jim was just sitting in there reading the paper as this guy started cussing me up and down. But he left and I turned to Jim and said, 'Damn Jim, I thought I was gonna have to have you bite that guy.' And Jim said, really matter of fact: 'I'd'a bit him, too.' After that, I called him The Biter."

Sometime during the festival season of 2000, Jim would start spending a lot of time on the farm, maybe because things weren't going so well at home, and one day he rolled up with a travel trailer, a twenty-eight-footer or so, and parked it behind the store on the north side of the building. He lived in that trailer much of the time, and had a little camp back there with his own fire pit and outdoor furniture. Jim was a fixture on the farm, and that trailer was there until the nasty end.

By Doug's count, about 2,800 to 3,000 paid tickets came through the gate for Hemp Aid '99. But the real number, with guests and freebies, staff, family members, plus a dozen speakers and almost twenty local bands and their guests and an almost unstoppable number of sneak-ins, came close to 5,000. Having Chong and *High Times* in the house gave everyone an enormous kick in the ass. They all puffed up a little with the feeling that their farm was more than just a bucolic little temporary autonomous zone. They felt connected to something bigger. Their utopia was part of a movement.

The Rainbow Farmer having the best time of all was Robert. He and his pals didn't have to know anything about legalizing marijuana, because the spectacle itself was like a boy's paradise.

Robert was nine years old at Hemp Aid '99. His hair was cut in a little rattail hanging off the back of his head, and he had his own golf cart. He was a king among his classmates at Frank Squires Elementary school; a gang of friends from Vandalia came out to the farm almost daily. Tubby was the son of Dwight "Dinky" Vowell Jr., a festival volunteer from Vandalia; Matt was the son of Dinky's brother-in-law, Ronnie, who was also a volunteer and nicknamed "That Guy." Other regulars in Robert's crew included Tammy Brand's son Dairik and another Vandalia boy named Jamie. Tubby was the smallest but the most aggressive, and Matt was a kind of peacemaker, and they had plenty of tools for mischief at their disposal. The farm had golf carts, motorbikes, ATVs, rope swings, miles of trails for BMX biking, two videogame setups in Robert's room, and there were always sodas in the fridge and snacks on the grill.

During Hemp Aid '99, Robert was rolling around in his golf cart, with a couple of buddies on board, when he pulled up to Moe at The Hemp Center—the farm's new version of the Hemp Museum.

"Moe, we need a job," he said.

Moe was only too happy to delegate. "Alright. You got a cart. I need somebody that can go around and find a trash can that's more than half full. You come right back to this tent and tell Amy where it's at."

The rest of the day, they were up and down the place like army ants.

They reported on the barrels and Amy wrote them down. "Okay you guys, we're gonna go find some more," he'd bark. When the boys discovered the barrels were full of aluminum cans with a ten-cent deposit on them, their mission changed.

"All them cans we're looking at are ten cents apiece, you know," said Jamie. Soon they had a huge stash of cans behind the recycling center. Moe went back in the grass one day and said, "Man, who put all those cans in the weeds back there?"

"Them are ours," said Robert fiercely.

Teter wanted state and federal help to deal with Rainbow Farm. On April 6, 1999, he'd seen Bill Clinton's drug czar, retired army general Barry McCaffrey, deliver an address on national drug control strategy at Notre Dame, and McCaffrey's message had been unequivocal: Fight the activists and the medical marijuana advocates, as they're a threat to the continued criminalization of pot. Teter had already begun meeting with then State Attorney General Jennifer Granholm, a Democrat serving under Republican governor John Engler, about how to best use the Dope Team resources. Those meetings expanded into a statewide, multiagency task force, formed specifically to strategize around Rainbow Farm. That group came to include not only Teter, Sheriff Underwood, Granholm, other county prosecutors and representatives of the state police, but also federal prosecutors and agents of the DEA and FBI. Teter acknowledges the meetings happened, though he would not answer requests for details about who was there and what was discussed. (FOIA requests for information about this task force through the Michigan State Police and state attorney general's office were denied, indicating there were no relevant records.)

On Memorial Day 1999, undercover SWET officers were in the crowd at Hemp Aid looking to score.

"Our officers, literally within ten minutes, made their first buy," said Teter. "Standing right in the road. And they proceeded, from that point, over the next several gatherings, they bought every single drug on the market but heroin. They bought opium, they bought prescription drugs, they bought meth, they bought crack, they bought hash, they bought uppers, downers—I mean, it wasn't limited to a few people smoking marijuana."

That weekend, officers bought blotter acid and grass. In 2000 they would begin some targeted buys, building cases against specific individuals. At Hemp Aid 2000, they bought marijuana and LSD from a kid named Mike Royal, and hash from a James Schmidt. At the July 21, 2000, *High Times* WHEE festival on Rainbow Farm, they bought more pot from Royal, LSD and hash from Schmidt, coke from Andrew Rasmussen and meth from Aaron Brown. This went on and on, right up until the last Rainbow Farm festival on April 20, 2001.

But none of this was linked to Tom. There was no RAVE Act and he wasn't violating the crackhouse law. Teter was trying to build a case against the property, basically, in order to support a forfeiture action, but it was a stretch.

"The Constitution specifically protects your right to assemble and the right to free speech," Teter acknowledged. "You can discuss all those issues, you can lobby for those issues, you can get legislation, as California has and a number of other states for those issues, and there's nothing illegal. In fact, our system encourages that.

"The concern is, at one point, the gatherings took on a different connotation. It became: 'Come to this property and use, distribute, and deal any narcotic that you choose to.' And in Michigan, if you use property in violation of the Controlled Substances Act, you make that property subject to forfeiture to the state. I explained that to him in the letter. It was a matter of individuals dealing, individuals using, individuals distributing narcotics on his property."

But, legally, the forfeiture wouldn't stick if they couldn't attribute to Tom direct knowledge of—or profit from—the sale of drugs.

Teter continued: "So then the question was: Was he aware of it? Through our investigation, what we verified was: Because of the open and obvious dealing that we saw, when we sent in undercover officers, there's no way you could not know of it."

But the Rainbow Farm policy clearly stated all drug use was illegal.

"Right," quipped Teter. "And that's simply not the case, from what we observed. When I sent in undercover officers and confidential informants, at one point, Mr. Crosslin was driving around with a golf cart right in among the dealers and people yelling, 'Get your dope. Get your dope here!' It was a flea market for narcotics, in effect. I mean, they had booths."

If Tom really said these things, no evidence was ever produced. And by "booths," Teter meant the vendors—whom he often referred to as "dealers." That made a lot of legitimate businessmen pretty pissed. Especially because he never linked any of them—not one—to drug sales on Rainbow Farm.

"There's no way in the world that was gonna happen," laughed Derrik. "First of all, our vendors didn't sell drugs. So they pop some kid with a bag of weed to sell to pay for his gas money there and back, so what? That didn't have anything to do with us or our contracted vendors. We're glad to bust him, get rid of the liability."

Besides, the staffers had a pretty good idea who the narcs were even if some of the young partiers didn't.

"I had 'em pegged," said Derrik. "I parked 'em right by the ticket-booth and we watched 'em all weekend. They came out, I'm sure at the taxpayer's expense, with a huge-ass motorhome, coolers of beer. Like that didn't stick out like a sore thumb. Here's all these hippies in beat-up VWs and with gray tape on their vehicles and stuff, and here they are in their big-ass RV, partying like hell. They had probably six or eight guys in there.

"They made the biggest mess of all of our campers. They would leave beer cans everywhere and they would party and drink and sit up on top of their motorhome and just be the biggest horses' asses the whole time."

Derrik also thought it was fine for the narcs to see people smoking.

"We didn't have anything to hide. Yeah, people were smoking pot out there. Yeah, it was against the law, but it was a public defiance, a civil disobedience. Hash Bash is the same thing; people gather on the Diag and smoke pot right in front of the cops in bright daylight!"

Jay Statzer, not at all adverse to smoking when and where he could, was impressed by Crosslin's sincerity about not allowing drug sales on Rainbow Farm. "One time I was sitting around with Tom at Vendor's Row, and casually mentioned that if we could find some hash I'd love to smoke some hash with Tom," Statzer said. "So this high-school-aged kid standing around there disappeared, he must have been a runner, because he comes back with a quarter-gram of hash. And I was about to buy it so I could smoke it with Tom, and Tom intervened. Instead, he busted this kid. He said, 'Nope, you can't do that here. You can't sell drugs on Rainbow Farm.' He almost kicked the kid out. And I guess if the deal had gone through, we both would have been kicked out—and I was going to smoke it with Tom!"

The SWET investigation spent a lot of money and time, but their work never produced much evidence that hurt Tom. No charge was ever brought against any owner or employee of Rainbow Farm as a result of this work. And although the investigtion was exhaustively detailed in Teter's eventual forfeiture filing, it wasn't the crucial finding that allowed that forfeiture to go forward. It was a fishing expedition and the big fish weren't biting.

"Shit, Tom was frustrated to see all that money slipping through his hands!" Doug acknowledged. "Every show, there's thousands of people there, and lots of 'em are smoking weed. You just know someone's making money. But we didn't even talk about it. It couldn't be us. They were just waiting for something like that."

By Hemp Aid '99, it seemed that money was not going to be a problem much longer, anyway. Despite the ongoing state police roadblock for each show, which might have cost them as much as fifty thousand dollars in profit each time, Tom was feeling confident. Big Brother and the

Holding Company, Janis Joplin's old band, was lined up for Roach Roast, and they were talking to Mike Clarke from the Byrds Celebration (a version of the Byrds put together by drummer Clarke) and to Mickey Hart, the drummer from the Grateful Dead. The crowds were building.

The best revenge is living well, and Tom would take revenge when he could get it. Somewhere along the way, he'd located an incredible deal on a white 1976 Rolls-Royce Silver Cloud, somewhat long in the tooth but still a fine luxury ride for when he didn't feel like bouncing along in the red pickup. He took the High 1 vanity plate off Jerry Stone's old motorhome and put it on the Rolls. The car had an eight-track tape player in it and Tom had located a few old tapes; his favorite was a greatest hits collection by Patti Page, so any cruise in the Rolls meant drifting through the bean fields listening to "Tennessee Waltz." Tom had also purchased a maroon 1974 Jaguar and put a plate on it that read HEMPME2.

They even had use of a limo to ferry around the artists and speakers. A Kalamazoo limo driver showed up at Hemp Aid 2000 willing to trade his services for two tickets to the festival and gas money. He drove a few of the musicians back and forth to their hotels, and even if it only lasted one show it sure looked good.

At one point, Doug found himself literally swimming in cash at the farm. He'd been working full-time as the manager of Rainbow Farm since 1997, and he was the only one who knew how to handle large amounts of money. When he worked at the bank, each night his safe had had three to five million dollars in it. Down on the farm he finally had to hire three or four people whose job was just to count and recount each other to keep tens of thousands from going missing in a farm economy that worked mostly off a blinding flurry of cash payouts.

"At Hemp Aid '98, we had a lot of cash crammed into the safe," he recalls. "It was packed in there tight. It would take me, all by myself, a good twenty-four hours to count all that money and package it up. Everybody wanted to know where we stood, and I said, "Well I don't know until we count the cash and that's a big job.""

"Well, let's get some people that are gonna do it," said Tom.

"Who do you want in a room with potentially seventy thousand dollars in cash?"

"You, me and Rollie and Derrik and Jerry Stone."

"Sure, I guess," said Jerry Stone. "But why do you want me in on this?"

Ever impatient, Tom said, "We just need help, man."

"Okay, what the hell."

"This is when we had the office down in the basement of the house," Doug continued. "We had a big, long table, and we just crammed shopping bag after shopping bag full of cash into that safe, and I was just pulling them out and emptying them right on the table and there was a mountain of cash there that we were literally swimming in and playing in and having fun with. Just because it was something we always had dreamed of: being able to dive into a pile of twenty-dollar bills. We spent a long time that day locked up in a room counting cash."

By Hemp Aid '99, even that was too risky. At sixty-five dollars a pop, they had so much money sitting around it was begging to be stolen. So they hired a Brinks truck to come make pickups and go straight to the bank. Each run cost five hundred dollars.

This was a mark of legitimacy for Doug: "It was cooler than hell when the Brinks trucks pulled up at the festival. They'd come out with a fucking dolly, with bags all packaged up and a gun. We figured that sends a message that we're managing it properly. If you were thinking about robbing us, you waited too long; it's gone."

FIFTEEN The Personal Responsibility Amendment

GREG SCHMID SAT HOME in Saginaw on election night in November 1998, watching the midterm results roll in from all over the country. He was the kind of guy who would stay up all night on election night to find out exactly what happened with every race, and he paid special attention to the ballot initiatives. At thirty-eight years old, he was a life-long Republican and partner in one of the most successful constitutional law firms in the state, Schmid & Schmid, based in Saginaw and specializing in ballot initiatives. His father, Allan Schmid, had written the 1978 Headlee Amendment, a conservative coup when it passed, which limited the amount that state tax revenue could increase each year. The firm had also successfully placed term limits on Michigan state legislators.

Referendum politics can be a bad bug, and the activist who works this so-called "fourth branch" of government can get hooked on its apparent purity, needing to touch that raw, chaotic voice of the people. In a democracy sometimes compromised by its representatives, nothing can be more tempting than calling on that ultimate authority to settle a question. But it's a branch not exercised that much, considering how relatively easy it is to buy signatures today, because activists can spend an astronomical amount of money only to misjudge the will of the people.

In 2000, for example, Amway president Dick DeVos, a longtime education activist and a member of Michigan's Board of Education, put a finger in the wind over in Grand Rapids, in the heart of southwest Michigan's Bible belt, and decided the time was right for vouchers that would allow public funding for private religious schools. He and Wal-Mart heir John Walton and the Catholic Church spent about fourteen million dollars getting a voucher initiative onto the ballot and fighting a war in the press, but still found out they were dead wrong at the polls, where it failed badly, 69 percent to 31 percent. The damnable thing about referendum politics is that it requires giving the people what they really want.

One thing that people really wanted, in state after state, was medical marijuana.

Marijuana was not Schmid's issue. But he was well aware of California's 1996 medical marijuana initiative, Proposition 215, which had passed by a landslide 57 percent. Medical marijuana was the perfect issue for a ballot initiative—popular with the citizens but too hot for legislators. Five states and the District of Columbia had medical marijuana initiatives on the ballot in 1998, and they all breezed past but one.

"When the Washington, D.C., election results came out on the Internet, the result kept saying 'not released,' " Schmid noted. "And I noticed the next morning that it still said 'not released.' It kind of got my goat a little bit that they would not publish the results of an initiative vote."

Because the District of Columbia is not a state, but is governed by Congress, Representative Bob Barr, a Republican from Alabama, had pushed through some language prohibiting the federal government from spending money to print the results of the vote, which turned out to be 71 percent to 39 percent in favor of medical marijuana.

"So I looked into why they couldn't release this vote, and it just made me madder and madder. I determined right then and there that I was going to do a marijuana initiative," Schmid said.

Bucking the trend, however, Schmid decided not to make it a medical marijuana initiative. He wanted a sweeping constitutional amendment legalizing all weed. Believing he had a hot ticket, he flew out to

Washington, D.C., in early 1999 to present the idea to leaders of Americans for Medical Rights, the group financed by millionaires George Soros, Peter Lewis of Progressive Insurance and John Sperling of the University of Phoenix, looking for one million dollars to hire signature gatherers. He was turned down cold. The AMR told him the only thing that would work was a California-style medical marijuana statute, not an over-broad amendment, and said, "We don't spend our money on things that we don't think are going to be successful."

Schmid, knowing Michigan's deep libertarian streak, thought otherwise. Emulating the tactics of professional wrestler turned independent Minnesota governor Jesse Ventura, who did a lot of his campaigning via the Web, Schmid posted his petition online. He had to get state congressional approval to do it, as this was the first ballot initiative ever posted for signature online in Michigan. It was called the Personal Responsibility Amendment, and it fit on one sheet of paper.

The PRA did more than California's Proposition 215; it drilled right to the heart of every major cannabis issue. In short, concise language it established pot as legal medicine, relegalized the hemp industry, decriminalized small-time possession and stripped the cops of the corrupting "collars for dollars" incentive driving drug asset forfeiture. In fact, it required that all forfeiture proceeds would go to drug treatment and domestic abuse centers.

It was easy to see that Schmid was over reaching. The polls in Michigan were in Schmid's favor, running 75 to 80 percent prolegalization, he said, but many influential state lawmakers feared full decriminalization, and cops were not going to give up their death grip on those pools of easy cash.

"So I understand that. I got a little Machiavelli in me, right next to my Don Quixote side," said Schmid.

Schmid has since become a state coordinator for NORML, but NORML wouldn't touch the PRA. Schmid waited for a nonprofit political sponsor. In April 1999, he finally got a response.

Rainbow Farm would sponsor the PRA.

*   *   *

To the crew on Rainbow Farm, Schmid and his PRA were a sign from God. Someone had put their collective thoughts on paper. It was the most concise definition of Rainbow Farm's mission any of them had ever seen. Plus it amended the state constitution. Tom was elated.

Unfortunately, amending the Constitution by initiative also meant that it needed 302,711 verified signatures (10 percent of the total voters in the last gubernatorial election), gathered within a six-month window of time, to get on the ballot. A regular statutory initiative, which would simply put a law on the books or change the tax code, might only need 60,000 to 80,000, but it could be overtuned by the legislature. With the number of signatures that get automatically disallowed to account for fraud, the PRA would need close to 400,000 signatures—with no funding, and an all-volunteer team of signature gatherers. Once again, Rainbow Farm was doing it the hard way.

Schmid appeared at Hemp Aid '99 and gave his spiel. He brought masses of petitions and trained Rainbow Farm volunteers to collect valid signatures. Schmid was training volunteers all over the state, establishing local activism chapters. He came back for Roach Roast '99 and finally in January 2000, after a number of long organizing meetings at Rainbow Farm and other venues across the state, the PRA petition drive began. It was the first time that Michigan's marijuana movement had organized around a single statewide initiative.

To kick things off, Doug helped Schmid put together a February fundraiser at Kalamazoo's gorgeous old State Theater, with its baroque gilded façade and supernumerary flourishes, headlined by hiphoppers Buddha Fulla Rymez—who were farm favorites, with their dope-inflected swagger, and would later do some recording with Eminem—and featuring presentations on the PRA and on Hash Bash by Adam Brook. Tom was too tapped out at the time to fund it, so Doug fronted the $2,500 to rent the theater out of his own pocket. The hippies who showed up only donated $500 at the door, so Doug and the fundraiser lost $2,000. "That day I donated $2,000 to the PRA," he laughed later.

For farm supporters whose actions had been limited to passing out literature, going to Hash Bash, and maybe joining former Yippie Dana Beal's once-a-year Million Marijuana March, the PRA provided new legislative focus. Sheli McNeill had been running the activist tent at Rainbow Farm for two years, presenting the sprawl of groups like the November Coalition, Michigan NORML, Cannabis Action Network, Cures Not Wars and others. She was twenty-two or twenty-three when the PRA was launched, and was out on the road going door-to-door with Rollie.

Sheli also embodied the mixed politics that, oddly, could connect with those voters in southwest Michigan.

"When I was in high school, I was more about civil liberties. We were protesting abortions," Sheli said. "And that's how I got into it, basically, knowing that people's liberties were being taken away. I smoked pot my whole life. Then it came to the point where I've dedicated the past five years of my life fighting for marijuana civil liberties."

Just to clarify: McNeill was propot but antiabortion. The civil liberties she saw being taken away were those of the unborn. But she didn't see any conflict in these positions.

"I believe that everything has a right to life, and I believe that everything has a right to liberty. And if those two conflict with each other, then I don't know what to say about that, you know? In a lot of ways, I am liberal, especially when it comes to gay rights.

"Besides being prejudiced against hard drugs," she added, "I would say we were definitely liberal."

The PRA politicized Shayla Salzman and Casey Brown for the first time. They were barely in their early twenties and on the road in 1998, following Phish in their Volkswagen van, when they made what was supposed to be an overnight stop at Rainbow Farm and stayed for two years. During Roach Roast '98, Shayla had become the camp store's first manager. In 1999 and 2000, Shayla and Casey would go out with Sheli McNeill gathering signatures for the PRA.

"The biggest thing about the farm is that you were important when you were there," Shayla said. "I was helping change the world for my type of people. You would have redneck hunters and vegetarian hippies and punk rockers all sitting in a circle around the campfire. People that you would normally never even talk to, not even look at, here they are, sittin' next to you, and you're makin' best friends with them."

The PRA had no paid staff. Campaign donations trickled in in increments of twenty and a hundred dollars. Their entire campaign was done for twenty-four thousand. It couldn't get more grass-roots. *High Times* wrote about it.

"California wasn't that easy, and California had a very well-organized pot movement. But Michigan's a hard state," said *High Times*'s Steve Wishnia. "They needed 300,000 signatures to get on the ballot. That means you need a thousand people getting four hundred signatures each [a certain percentage get thrown out]. That's a lot."

The campaign gave Rainbow Farm a renewed sense of purpose. They were doing more than raising consciousness. Now they had a ballot initiative that could change the law. Marijuana could save the world!

Six months later, by the 2000 deadline, they were short.

"Our petition drive went through July 10, and we got 250,000 signatures out of nowhere, which was a miracle. We knew at that point it was worth doing over, because we had never gotten that kind of response from a volunteer initiative," said Schmid.

Encouraged, Schmid started over again in 2001, this time kicking off the drive at Hash Bash in April rather than sending petition gatherers into the worst of the Michigan winter. Rallying to the PRA's surprising strength, NORML decided to make a show of support. NORML cofounder Keith Stroup came out for Hash Bash to address a crowd of six to eight thousand people. The day before the event, Schmid helped organize a National Symposium on Prohibition Reform Advocacy, with seventy-five to eighty statewide movement leaders.

In the first week of May, Dana Beal led the Million Marijuana March, actually four separate marches in Traverse City, on the capital steps in

Lansing, in a big public park in Battle Creek and on downtown Hart Plaza in Detroit. The signatures were pouring in from PRA chapters all over the state.

They wouldn't make it, but Schmid believes that, by the spring of 2001, the PRA had become a real threat to state authorities. Even after the attacks of September 11, even after all that would happen on Rainbow Farm, they would get 288,000 signatures.

"That's what you call a near miss," said Schmid. "We would have needed a lot more, maybe 100,000 more, I'm not trying to spin ya. But I think we would have made it."

It's too simplistic to say that the feud between Teter and Tom was caused by the growing popularity of the PRA, but Schmid and others contend that it contributed mightily to the bad attitudes of the county administration and the state police.

"[Tom] made himself popular in that community, so when he said things, people believed him. He wasn't fringe," said Schmid. "But he was, at the same time, bold about his beliefs in personal freedom. He had what Johnny Cash called that 'lean and hungry' look; he was dangerous to them, because he would articulate freedom issues from gun control to marijuana reform and any consensual adult act."

Just to complicate matters, Soros and his Americans for Medical Rights came blowing into the state that same year, having done their polling and finding that Michigan was, indeed, ripe for a marijuana initiative. They spent over $1 million to hire signature gatherers and put a "treatment instead of incarceration" initiative like California's Proposition 36 on the 2002 ballot. Schmid offered to help consult on the Americans for Medical Rights initiative, but they said they had it all smoothed out. That initiative was later thrown out by a hostile Michigan Supreme Court on a technicality, a matter of misnumbering some paperwork.

SIXTEEN What's Your Entheogen?

TOM WAS LEAN AND hungry, alright. He'd thought he was on his way to some serious money in 1999, but by 2000 he was feeling the first pangs of starvation as a result of Scott Teter's injunctions, narcs, letters and especially the roadblocks. If the PRA passed, it would solve a lot of those problems, but it wouldn't give him the satisfaction of seeing Teter defeated. Tom wanted him voted out of office. Inspired by the example of Mendocino County, California, where locals had elected pot-friendly authorities, he and Doug had put the word out that the farm was looking for candidates to run for both sheriff and prosecutor in the fall 2000 elections.

A decent candidate for sheriff materialized and came up to the farm for a few serious discussions about what it would take to back him. The sitting sheriff, Joseph M. Underwood Jr., was popular and uncontroversial and probably couldn't be unseated, but even a long-shot bid would send a message to the county that Rainbow Farm wasn't going to take this shit forever. Tom and Doug and Derrik put even more effort into working up a candidate for prosecutor, but kept coming up empty-handed. They must have approached every attorney in a three-state area, and even went up to the University of Michigan in Ann Arbor to talk to young law students, trying to find one on the verge of graduating who shared their views on legalization. By late summer, with the elections approaching, they hadn't been able to find an attorney willing to move to Cass County, and then the candidate for sheriff pulled out, too, so in the end both Underwood and Teter would run unopposed.

That summer, however, Rainbow Farm saw a burst of political stump-
ing. Politicians of all stripes were hungry for the important swing votes
that would be cast by fringe Republicans and Democrats, Independents,
Greens and "bluenecks" who hung out there. Democratic gubernatorial
candidate Jeffrey Feiger came by the farm and networked a bit with the
crew in his unsuccessful bid to supplant then-two-term Republican governor John Engler. Feiger politely declined to speak publicly at the farm,
intimating that the drug and Militia overtones were a little too hot for
him. That pissed Tom off a bit, but Feiger did agree to speak at a rally
thrown by the farm in Vandalia. In the park near the mayor's office, down
on Christiana Creek, Tom put on a well-attended rally and handed Feiger
a campaign check for a thousand dollars. Finally, he figured he had at
least one politician in the state that was on his side.

The Libertarian Party, the Greens, the Peace and Freedom Party, the
U.S. Taxpayer Party, the Reform Party, the Natural Law Party and all manner of spin-off partiers' parties were less afraid to be associated with
Rainbow Farm, and a lot of their candidates turned up for speaking en-
gagements and shook hands with the campers or appeared at one of that
summer's five big events—their biggest season ever. "Marvin Marvin"
Surowitz, a pot activist who spoke at many Rainbow Farm events as the
founder of the Save Our Constitution/P.A.R.T.I.E. Party—People's Alliance to Reform, Transform, and Improve Everything—appeared as the
Libertarian Party nominee to the University of Michigan Board of Re-
gents, a statewide office. Michael Corliss, the chair of the Libertarian
Party of Michigan, which was drawing an increasing percentage of the
vote in the Great Lakes state, came out on September 3 to give a well-
received speech in his run for the U.S. Senate, as did another Libertarian,
sixth U.S. Congressional District hopeful Bill Bradley. John Galt Jr., who'd
launched his own festival in rural Pennsylvania called the Summer Sol-
stice Hemp Happening, or sshh, "a gathering of the peaceful tribes, of the
earth people, the politically disenfranchised, and oppressed," swung by
in his bid for U.S. president. Hemp Aid that year saw a fervent political
pitch from Tom Ness, the longtime editor of the alternative Detroit

music-and-politics paper, *Jam Rag*, and the Green Party candidate for U.S Senate from Michigan.

None of this, however, meant much to the pols in downtown Cassopolis. Even Feiger was pretty fringe, when it came right down to it. So Tom drove the point home with a little well-aimed tax revolt that touched Teter directly.

Shayla Salzman was at her job managing the Rainbow Farm camp store when Tom and others rushed into the coffeeshop, excited by a bit of local political news. The word was that the county fathers were planning a vote to extend a short-term tax in order to renovate the county courthouse, where Teter kept his airless little office. In 1990 a tax with a ten-year sunset had been voted in to build a new jail and sheriff's office complex out on Highway 62 toward LaGrange, and the ten years were up. The new offices were built, so county commissioners were set to meet the next day and extend the tax to shift work to the courthouse.

Tom was incensed, and got staffers on all three phone lines to alert the public.

"Tom thought that was bullshit, because there's nothing wrong with the courthouse," said Shayla, "and we just got in the phone book and called every person in Cass County and said, 'Hey, did you know that they're voting to continue the tax increase today to build a new courthouse?' And we called so many people that day that they ended up voting it down. There was a huge article in the paper about how they were so surprised that this vote had been turned down, and how nobody had even known about the vote until anonymous callers called the public."

This kind of behavior was bound to create some bad blood. Despite their blunt approach, naïveté and frequent ineffectiveness, Tom and Rainbow Farm were hard-working political agitators. They were figuring out how to turn their beliefs into votes.

Sweet, avuncular, white-bearded and Casey Jones–hatted Stephen Gaskin, long rumored to be Saint Stephen from the Grateful Dead song of the same name—"Saint Stephen with a rose / In and out of the garden he goes"—but which lyricist Robert Hunter denied, had a message never heard in any other presidential campaign. He was running for president in 2000, as a candidate for the Green Party nomination, which ultimately went to Ralph Nader. Gaskin was right in there with Herer and Conrad in his hemp message—Marijuana Can Save the World!—but he had another interpretation of the prohibition lie and how it functioned: He thought banning cannabis was not just corporate control of consciousness, but the political repression of liberal humanism. On July 14 at the *High Times* WHEE fest (World Hemp Expo Extravaganja) at Rainbow Farm, Gaskin first delivered what he called his "Hippie State of the Union."

I come to a conclusion that gives me no satisfaction.

When the crime is so minor, having marijuana, and the punishment is so unreasonable, taking people's homes and years of their lives as well as a very real twentieth-century shunning, one is forced to look for deeper motives.

I have come to believe that it is not the proscription of a substance but the systematic oppression of a certain kind of people. There have been a whole series of decisions made, on local, state and federal levels to the effect that any committed liberal persons are undesirable and are to be banned, interdicted, harassed, discouraged, arrested and pee tested. It is a blatant use of police power to frighten and intimidate millions of people into giving up a heartfelt spiritual practice and lifestyle. As Jello Biafra of the Dead Kennedys said, the war on drugs is ethnic cleansing, American style.

Ethnic cleansing brought up images of massacres in Bosnia, but these words articulated what Tom felt was happening to him in Cass County. His efforts to give voice to a cannabis-friendly majority had made him an undesirable. And because he was an undesirable, a horrid ganglia of mandatory sentences and forfeiture laws could be used to obliterate him. As Gaskin said:

The oppression to which I refer is for the purpose of keeping these millions of people off balance to minimize their political power. All those 500,000 pot smokers doing time are out of the political process, present but not able to vote. The urine test is the loyalty oath of the 1990s. The hippies are this season's Jews, this season's Reds, and Newt is this season's Joe McCarthy.

Tom paid special attention to what Gaskin said because the sparkling sexagenarian teacher understood what it was like to have property on the line. Gaskin, too, lived under the specter of seizure.

Gaskin was a lefty and a communitarian from the days in the sixties when that meant something that could get you killed, and private property was a concept that his collective had wrestled with for decades. But the cosmic joke was that its manifestation had been in real property, a six-and-a-quarter-square-mile chunk of kudzu-clad gold called The Farm located in Summertown, Tennessee.

In 1967 Gaskin had been leading countercultural rap sessions he called the Monday Night Class as a writing teacher at San Francisco State College, when the explosion of the hippie movement swelled his class to almost 1,500 weekly attendees. Invited to tour the phenomenon, Gaskin and his wife Ina May (now a best-selling author and teacher of midwifery and natural childbirth) and their friends formed a bus caravan that traveled for months and finally bugged out of San Francisco for good when they discovered their nirvana in the rolling foothills south of Nashville and founded The Farm in 1970.

Gaskin was a big-time doper, too. On the back cover of his best-known book, *Cannabis Spirituality*, he's pictured holding a prize-winning bud from the Cannabis Cup in Amsterdam. He was busted for growing pot on The Farm in October 1970 and took it all the way to the Supreme Court, lost, and served jail time in 1974.

The Farm was proof that real-world paradise could be spun from the raw esoterica of pot mysticism. It was not only one of the longest-surviving intentional communities in the country (thirty-six years in

2006 and counting) and one of the biggest, at one time supporting over 1,500 people; it was also a model for the promise of Americanism.

Gaskin's principal texts, far back before his exposure to Buddhism and socialism and hippyism, such as they were, were the Declaration of Independence and the U.S. Constitution and the Bill of Rights. Enshrined in those inspired documents was a beautiful guarantee: the promise that no one would get in the way of your grand spiritual experiment—after all, weren't the Puritans on one of those trips, too?—and no one would strip you of your property, the thing that most rooted you to the earth. This was just about as graceful an expression of humanism as had ever been written, he thought, and facilitated the pursuit of spirituality. It also left the door wide open to a liberal or left-libertarian definition of private property: choosing to live and own communally.

Gaskin said something very powerful in his talks with me: "I tried to tell folks right down the line that a true spirituality cannot ignore politics. And that politics has got to be informed by spirit.

"Politics is 'Hooray for our side.' And a really spiritual one realizes that, after the election's over, we're still gonna be here. I consider our original Declaration of Independence and Constitution and Bill of Rights as an attempt to bring spiritual values into the political world. That's why I feel so badly about how the right-wingers are just tromping all through that stuff, saying, 'This is only man's law. You don't have to obey nothing but God's law.' But the best wisdom of the best people is worth paying attention to."

The Framers, he said, knew what they were doing when they limited Congress's power to police morality. Because those powers could be used to demonize a population. No matter how strongly we feel about moral issues, it was un-American to use the law as a tool of ethnic cleansing.

His message was utopian, but it was grounded in real blood and dirt. Gaskin had a favorite saying for it: "Utopia is a Greek word meaning 'nowhere,' and we have a zip code."

Gaskin spent a lot of time with Tom, talking about how to organize his venue, talking about the law, talking crowd psychology and political action. The Farm had survived two civil forfeiture actions and a lot of the issues Tom was confronting.

"They were so idealistic," said Gaskin. "Tom was a guy who came on to be a hippie late in life and sometimes they're a little over the top, like a reformed drunk or something. Like a born-again. I had a very good feeling with those guys all the way along the line."

The bottom line for Gaskin was that they had to remain committed to nonviolence. They had to disavow the Militia and stop all the machine-gun posturing. If the militiamen weren't carrying guns on the farm, don't call them militia. At Hemp Aid '97 Gaskin had seen the psychological effects of the Militia's presence and counseled Tom against it. Back when Gaskin was leading the Monday-night sessions in San Francisco, on the day after the Kent State shootings there had been howling in the auditorium about how it was time for armed revolution. Gaskin had shouted it down, knowing this was the way to slaughter. He hadn't changed his mind thirty years later.

"You've got to have credibility to move with. If you slide off into violence, bad violent talk and crap like that, you lose your credibility," he said. "I'm an excombat marine, man. I've done combat in Korea. I've carried dead friends out of the rice paddies. I haven't got anything romantic about hardware and guns.

"Like Chekhov says," he added, "if there's a pistol on the wall in Act One, it will be fired by Act Three."

There was more to Gaskin's rap. The way to peace and real communication was not just through nonviolent protest and effective politicking, but through the weed. It was fun to listen to this coming from Gaskin—he came off like the mischievous, friendly grandfather that he was, a countryfied American, wrapped in the flag, wearing Levi's and filled with homespun wisdom. Not a hint of irony in it, either. He counseled that you could find a route to peaceful living by following the high of cannabis itself.

He taught through small stories—he'd written down a whole book of them, called *Amazing Dope Tales*—in which he held out smoking rope as a sacrament, and not a secular one, either, a Holy Communion with the green and giving Earth as an intelligent entity. Like Amerindians from the Huichol to the modern day intertribal Native American Church, hundreds of thousands of native users cutting peyote buttons off a cactus for a mescaline-driven vision quest, marijuana was the naturally occurring bringer of expanded sight, one of the few you could just grow in your own backyard. An herb! More technically, an *entheogen*—from the Greek, "that which causes (a person) to be in God." This is a word mostly used in reference to hallucinogens like LSD, but it's appropriate to use it here in reference to weed because it refers to ritual use, shamanistic use, which Gaskin and a lot of the heads on Rainbow Farm saw as their devotional.

This was meditative practice. It wasn't just about getting stoned, it was about the state of stonedness, a diminution of the combative spirit and enhancement of the perceptive, the empathic, a proactive opening and acceptance of other wills working around yours. Pot could be used for getting giggles out of the TV, or pure apathetic oblivion, but it could also be like the rainbow connection, drawing the green of the great cosmic laugh into your body in tight-chested huffs. It could be a sacrament in a new communion of saints. Weed didn't have to carry the metaphoric and allegorical weight of the body and the blood; like the wheat kernel in the bread, or the grapes in the wine, it was the actual stuff sprung straight out of the dirt, no doctrinal contamination required, and it changed your consciousness.

Gaskin was a lighthearted creature in person, quick with a joke, but this business of "being in God" was part of a reform program he wanted to make real in the world. In his book, *Cannabis Spirituality: Including 13 Guidelines for Sanity and Safety*, he advocates the use of marijuana as a perceptual engine, a transmuter of souls, but he didn't worship the weed itself.

In fact, some heads were a little disappointed that the book didn't contain more about the science of THC and cannabinoid receptors in the brain, but Gaskin's sacramental use took the chemistry for granted. It had more to do with human potential and the mind and a Gaian critique. Puff only worked because the human mind worked, and the human mind was a part of evolved life, of Gaia, and that immutable was the source of all. His was Mother Earth connection as ditchweed, ripped straight out of the wormy earth with clods still hanging on the rootball.

This ethnobotanical program was about reclaiming both God and man by first taking God out of heaven and placing Him or Her or It on Earth, to still the war drums of apocalypse pounding among fundamentalists everywhere and disrupt the culture of the afterlife (a culture of death) and foster a commitment to life right now, and, second, by giving people a chance to evolve into a new culture. THC could make you completely vulnerable and fairly truthful, ready to acknowledge the motivations of the person next to you and to address them. It fostered a kind of default tolerance. Where every soul was chosen and worth saving. So people could really talk.

Tom might have been a big, bar-fighting hillbilly but he aspired to this consciousness. When Gaskin connected the Gaian headspace of a ganja high and the Gaian substrate of the dusty dirt beneath his sandals, it really hit Tom in the spine. He had realized long before meeting Gaskin that his property had something to do with his sense of God, and his attachment to the land was not avarice and jealousy and exclusion but something bigger, something that moved him emotionally. He knew that smoking up helped him to linger over every oily chunk of peat on his place, every cedar waxwing, every *Rana catesbeiana*, the American bullfrog, and Gaskin helped him know he didn't have to look any further for a path to God.

Whether he could get to that closeness of communication with Teter and the cops was another matter. The shared experience on Rainbow Farm was just not clocked that well by outsiders, and especially law enforcement, whose training was to isolate crime and ignore the rest. In their clumsy, corrosive response to the place, the authorities didn't want to know about Rainbow Farm's spiritual program, or its political intent, proving again they didn't even really understand what America was all about anymore.

High Times editor-in-chief Steve Hager understood. He'd been intellectually consumed with cannabis spirituality for a long time—Gaskin was one of his heroes—and he thought Tom was starting to get it. He'd been hesitant about Tom's motives in the beginning, but in the September 1999 issue of the magazine, he and his staff listed Rainbow Farm as fourteenth on the list of twenty-five Top Stoner Travel Spots in the world.

Like any homespun entrepreneur with a fingernail grip on the American Dream, Tom's strategy was grow or die. He hoped that the size and quality of his operation would buy him some measure of unassailability, and he was always looking to expand the company town. In 1999 and early 2000, the crew put a sixty-by-twenty-foot extension on the camp store and added shower rooms, bathrooms and a coin laundry. They built out The Joint with an espresso bar and two pool tables, plus a beautiful plank porch all down the front of the store facing Pemberton Road. They doubled the size of the farmhouse. Everything was brand new and well made.

But the truth was Tom couldn't afford what he was building on Rainbow Farm. Despite occasionally swimming in cash he was very rapidly drowning in debt.

Tom and Doug knew this, but another man who had a pretty good idea was Scott Teter. On April 21, 1999, only a month after the infamous letter first threatening forfeiture, Teter commissioned a guy named Dick Thompson to run an asset forfeiture investigation. In this case, justice is certainly not blind; the prosecutor was going to know exactly how much Tom was worth before snatching it.

He was worth a lot, it turned out, but he was increasingly leveraged. The thirty-four acres of Rainbow Farm and its improvements were worth enough that, in the space of one year, Tom could take $250,000 in equity out of it. Tom and Rollie also controlled three companies: Rainbow Farm, Inc., Tom's Services, Inc. and a rental properties holding company in Elkhart County. Tom had fifteen rental properties there, valued at $188,000 by Thompson but later sold individually for prices totalling hundreds of thousands more than that.

In July 1998 Tom had been forced to take out a mortgage on the farm itself—something he swore he'd never do. He'd picked up a note from First Chicago NBD Mortgage for $142,500. Then he picked up a second mortgage on the farm on March 8, 1999, again with NBD, to build out the camp store. This one was for $50,000. He was far from being done, though. On October 4, 1999, Tom took out another mortgage to buy a neighboring parcel, incurring another $17,000 in debt.

South of the farmhouse, just up a two-track on the other side of Mount This, was a twenty-acre property fronted along Pemberton Road between Tom's parcel and Butch's parcel that had belonged to a guy known only as the Goat Man. Tom couldn't get around the east end of his marsh without cutting through this parcel, and his walks took him past it every day. Owning it would give him more nice group wilderness camps and a road all the way around the marsh.

The Goat Man was a figure that had all but disappeared from the country: an honest-to-God hermit. His real name was Mr. Douglas and he'd been a college professor; he had a wife and a daughter in Chicago. But at some point he'd retreated to this twenty acres of swamp— "Unabombered it," one of the neighbors joked—and simply parked his old 1950s sedan in the weeds and that's where he lived. One year a church came by and built him a shack, a shingled eight-foot-by-eight-foot box with a door, and he shared it with his goats. Jokes aside, he was a purposely innocuous man who spent his days building a land bridge out into the swamp, filling a wheelbarrow with hard clay from the south side of Mount This and wheeling it out to the water's edge, leaving big mysterious holes in the hill. One or two times a week, he used to get a hot meal from Minnie Davis, whose house once stood directly across the street from Rainbow Farm.

Maurice Williams had known the Goat Man, but the hermit was long gone by the time Tom made the scene. Douglas had evidently been struck by a car and killed while riding his bike into town in the rain. His property had been sold to a Dowagiac fellow named Bill Yuhas and his grandson, Toby Yuhas, who bought into it for hunting access to the swamp. There wasn't a snowball's chance in hell that Yuhas was going to sell to Tom.

The two were at odds almost from the moment Tom showed up. Doug said that he and Tom were driving past the property one day and a couple of Yuhas's men were there on the shoulder pulling trash out of the back of a truck and throwing it into the ditch. Tom was pissed. Stories differ, but Tom and the men either had words or he just called the sheriff on them. Yuhas was cited, but a judge later threw out the case because it was ruled he was on private property.

Toby would later have his own run-in with Tom and his crew.

"I was back there one day duck hunting in the swamp, way back, and suddenly those guys were shooting at me," Toby said. "I don't think they knew I was there. I was all in camouflage and sunk halfway up in the water. But I did get hit with a BB in my hand. It was spraying out over the swamp. So I told the sheriff about it, and a deputy went down there and told them they'd better keep their bullets on their own property."

Tom never did come and see him or apologize for having shot at him, even by accident. But even then, Toby said, he wouldn't characterize it as a feud or anything. They just didn't deal with one another. The guys on the farm thought differently and based most of what they knew on their interactions with the old man, Bill.

"The guy next door hated Tom. Wouldn't sell it to him," said Dayved Watts, better known as Whoaboy. "He was a prick, though."

Tom approached Yuhas through his attorneys, trying to buy the twenty acres, and was turned away. Then Doug tried to buy it, but Yuhas found out he was affiliated with the farm. Moe then tried, using the pseudonym

Mojo Risin'. As if that wasn't a dead giveaway. Finally, a most unlikely suitor, Whoaboy eased his way in under the name Rare Earth, LLC, a land corporation backed privately by Tom.

Whoaboy was a tall, wiry Rainbow Farm security man and Moe's longtime friend from Elkhart—the two of them had lived for years together in a wilderness camp up north in Michigan. His high cheekbones made him look like a pale Indian with long brown hair streaked with gray pulled back in a ponytail. He'd acquired his nickname on a trailer factory crew, when he'd worked too fast and one of the other guys chided him, saying, "Whoa, boy." The name stuck. At Roach Roast 2000, Whoaboy would marry his then-girlfriend, Michelle, right on the old stage up in front of a crowd of festivalgoers. Forever after, her name would be Whoagirl.

Whoaboy and the future Whoagirl met with Yuhas.

Whoaboy said gleefully, "I told old Bill, 'We just got married, the kids are all raised'—we didn't even have kids, we weren't married at the time—'we're looking for a place that's quiet, where I don't hear traffic, I can just sit out on my porch and not be bothered.' He bit hook, line and sinker. Proceeds to tell me, 'Oh,' he says, 'You'll love it there, it's so quiet, nobody ever comes around there, you'll never see traffic.' And he knew the whole time that this concert venue was next door. He's thinking he's fucking me. He was getting over on this hippie. I was gonna get burnt by my own kind. And I'm sitting there thinking in my mind, *well, you go ahead, stupid.*"

The day after they'd signed the paperwork—the ink was barely dry—a man with a bulldozer was out there cutting the Wilderness Camping Road, aka Goatman Road, right into Rainbow Farm. When Yuhas saw that equipment and dozens of volunteers out there pitching gravel, he knew he'd been had. Whoaboy almost felt guilty about it, but just almost. He was fiercely proud of what was happening there.

"I've never done nothing in my life where thousands of people gathered from thousands of miles away and they all wanted to be me," he said. "Rainbow Farm is the accomplishment of my life."

For his part, Toby Yuhas wasn't much preoccupied with how the farm was purchased, "under false pretenses," as he put it. He was worried about what happened in the end.

"None of that means that I approve of what happened to those guys out there, though," Toby added. "They got a bad deal. I don't think everything that happened back there has ever come out. I think it was wrong how they were killed there.

"If you felt that people ought to be able to do what they want on private property, then you didn't like it," he added. "If you're one of them that thought it was all about drugs, then maybe you feel different. I didn't like how it all happened."

In late 1999 Willie Nelson headlined a fundraiser for Gatewood Galbraith, who was running for Congress from Kentucky in the 2000 election (in which he would pull a startling 27 percent of the vote). It was the third such benefit Willie had played for Gatewood over the years and the rangy Libertarian lawyer rented out the Red Mile trotting track in Lexington, Kentucky. This was the home of the Kentucky Futurity, the final leg of the trotting horse triple-crown, and ten thousand people showed up including Tom and Rollie.

"Tom and Rollie attended the little party that Willie and I threw prior to the concert," said Gatewood, "and I was real pleased because I held Tom in high regard and Rollie, too. I was just tickled to death that they were able to finally meet."

The room was crowded and Gatewood was trying to keep too many people from swarming Willie, but he let Tom and Rollie spend a few minutes getting to know him.

"I think that Willie took my word that Tom was a present-day hero, which is pretty much how I described him," said Gatewood. "He was laying his life on the line."

This was the kind of company Tom wanted to keep and he had to have facilities to woo them, so he went right on buying things.

In the spring of 2000, Tom was offered a pretty good deal on the Bonine Mansion, a grand and shabbily aristocratic 1840s red-brick Geor-
gian manor house and Underground Railroad stop with a cupola and
airy parlors with twelve-foot ceilings. Everybody knew the place, sitting
just a couple of miles west of Vandalia on the corner of M-60 and
Calvin Center Road surrounded by miles of flat dirt beanfields.

James E. Bonine had come from Indiana to settle in Cass County in
1841, and his descendants later became Michigan state senators and
U.S. congressmen. He purchased the land in 1837 and built the imposing
house on what was, by 2000, an isolated, two-acre woodlet of spreading,
ancient white pines that droned in the dusty wind. The carriage house
and barns sat across the dirt road, on a corner plot that is now a feed
store, and the two were connected by tunnels that were used to hide former slaves.

Tom sold a few of his remaining properties to get the Bonine house,
and the Rainbow Farm crew eagerly set about converting it into a bed
and breakfast, the Rainbow Road House, which made business sense
because they could put up bands and guest speakers there. Tom was
deeply taken with the Underground Railroad history of the property
and talked to reporters about it. The first thing his crew restored was the
cupola tower, where they kept a light burning 'round the clock, then
they rehabbed a bedroom for Tom and Rollie and one for Robert.

Derrik DeCraene didn't like the looks of the wet, cobwebbed tunnels
in the basement. "I've shone a light back into those tunnels," he said.
"It'd take a better man than me to crawl in there, I'll tell you what."

"I stayed in that mansion," said Stephen Gaskin. "Rollie brought it
up to that sheriff, because he was black. He said to him, 'Here were are,
restoring this mansion that's a key piece of the Underground Railroad,
protecting that heritage, and you're giving us nothing but shit about it.
Shame on you.' "

For Rainbow Farm, this was a symbol of respectability and class that
put out the right message about their intentions. They weren't trying to
turn Cass County into a squat for jobless hippies. They had a well-

appointed campground and a Rolls-Royce and now a mansion, too. Rumors went around that Tom was making millions up at the farm, and folks regarded him as either an exploiter or an eccentric or a cult hero.

People called Tom "paper rich and cash poor," but he was rapidly growing poor in both. "When I first met him, he had fifty-two rentals," said Derrik. "But him and Rollie had worked for ten to twelve years pretty hard to develop that. He had a lot of rent money comin' in. But if we needed a new tractor, he'd go out and just sell a house. And as time went on, his houses depleted down into the single digits."

The problem was, the festivals just didn't pay.

"The most financially successful [festival] was probably either Roach Roast '99 or Roach Roast 2000—we made the most off those," said Doug. "We made more money at the gate on Hemp Aid 2000 than we did any show by far—we brought in about $180,000—but we spent about $180,000, too. We made $2,000 or $3,000, maybe."

By spring 2000, they were looking to shave ten or fifteen grand out of the budget because that would be their profit margin for the whole year. They could cut back on the green room and limos and such, but they couldn't seem to increase their draw past 2,500 or 3,000 people, which was their break-even mark.

At every show in 2000, the state police would continue the tactic they'd perfected in the early years there: put two squad cars nose-to-nose, cutting off all access to Pemberton Road, with just enough space for cars to pass through one at a time. It was like swimming a herd of wildebeest through the crocodile-infested river; a certain number were just going to get taken down. A lot of heads grew scared of the water and stayed away.

This tactic was crippling Rainbow Farm. If the cops couldn't shut them down legally, they'd do it by intimidation. At hemp festivals all over the country, it was often the same story. The organizer of the Indiana Hemp and Freedom Fests, the former Geri Guthrie (now Twitty), said they lost sixty thousand dollars on their last event in 1999, and largely because of roadblocks. She knew her crowd numbered twelve to fifteen thousand, but the Indiana State Police put nine cruisers on the main entrance, so she never got more than a few thousand through the gate.

Tommy Chong was right: It's always the money. At the full height of their powers, with the county rocked back on its heels, the Rainbow Farm dreamers packed their 2000 summer schedule with great shows and high politics and lost their ass.

In a sober late-winter meeting before that season, which left them all feeling a nervous thrill, they agreed that their ambitions required renting a massive new stage setup, complete with stadium-sized sound and lights, and plunking it in the flat of the field down by the Rock Camp.

According to Derrik, Tom and Rollie gave him an "anything-you-want-to-do policy" with the entertainment equipment, and he had a wish list all drawn up. For Hemp Aid 2000, he rented not only a huge stage with deluxe lights and sound but also big video screens for both sides of the stage, coordinating a four-camera shoot with a live video mix. With two stages, it was like a Hempapalooza, and the cost was enormous. But they'd kicked open the door to the A-list.

Merle Haggard and the Strangers played the farm on June 11 in an effort to reach out to the local blue-collar and agricultural crowd. One of the greatest songwriters in country music, Haggard was a shit-kicker icon representing an authentic lineage back to Hank Williams and Jimmy Reed. Haggard's straight-ahead blacktop anthems were everything beautiful about a man fighting, losing, going to jail and seeking redemption. Tom was more excited about that show than almost any other at Rainbow Farm.

Hag's bus pulled up in the grass by Rock Camp and Tom and Rollie strode out to greet him, accompanied by Derrik, Moe, Amy, Doug and others. The first thing he said as he stepped down to take Tom's hand was: "I can't believe they haven't killed you boys already."

Haggard's image crossed over both sides of the culture war; even religious conservatives could get with his leather-vested, man's man persona, and they streamed in, the cars bearing "Try Burning This One" flag bumper stickers lining up in the hayfield and dudes in cowboy hats and their ladies in denim tight as Saran Wrap. Plus there were the hippies. It was a mix made in hell if it were in any other promoter's hands, but at Rainbow Farm this was viewed as a triumph; Haggard was going to let them touch just a little bit of the terse rural skeptic who ironed a crease in his jeans.

He played "Rainbow Stew" in honor of the place and also "The Fightin' Side of Me," which might have been the intro and outro music of Tom's personal movie. But everybody was ready to hear the big hit, the one song that had taken on a delirious new meaning, the one that in 1969 was construed as an antihippie anthem, "Okie from Muskogee," and when he did play it those opening lines rang out over the treetops with a deep irony and a shattering of irony all at once: "We don't smoke marijuana in Muskogee . . ."

The folks in Carhartt jackets and cowboy hats started nodding in concordance as the Strangers laid down their bulletproof sound, glowing in the assumed admonition—See? Merle is going to clear up all this drug nonsense and get the country man back on the righteous track—but then around them came the cheers rising up from the dewy grass as the Hag barked it out with a special emphasis— "maaarrreeeeeeeewwwaaannnaaaaa"—burning joints and bowls held aloft like hippie censers in a salute to change. Then some of those cowboy hats and factory windbreakers grew still, and the pointy boots stopped tapping for just a minute. What the shuck was this? It was still a shit-kicker anthem, but it was the world that had changed; it was still alright to love America, to Love It or Leave It, but part of loving it was understanding that conservative thinking had moved on. As Haggard was fond of saying during the concerts of this era, "Well, that song don't mean what it used to," but it still did, too, what a beautiful thing, and it wasn't long before the cowboy shirts with their nacreous buttons were bouncing again, *what the hell.* What had once been an indictment of seemingly treasonous hip-pieisms had become a paean to rural attitudes since evolved.

Unfortunately, there were only about five hundred people there to see it. That was about a tenth of the crowd they had expected. Rainbow Farm simply hadn't had the money to buy ads in the big city papers in Chicago or even South Bend. In fact, they'd almost completely aban-doned any notion of promoting the show, other than a rash of local fliering.

Afterward, Haggard and his band sat around the fire at the Rock Camp until the wee hours of the morning playing guitar and waiting for one of the bus drivers to sober up. "He wrote a song while he was up here and he performed it. It was about legalization. Which totally freaked me out," said Doug.

The receipts from the show were pitiful, but Tom owed Haggard $10,000. He borrowed it from Pops, who was at the show that night, and swore he'd get it back to him after their scheduled *High Times* event in July.

But the *High Times* World Hemp Expo Extravaganja (WHEE) would turn out to be a similar bust. The fest was the kickoff for *High Times*'s North American Peace Tour and took place over the July 14 weekend, with the Byrds Celebration, Hager's Cannabis Cup Band, speakers led by Gaskin, and campout mayhem. Hager also had a three-man camera crew there making a documentary that has not yet seen the light of day.

"They actually had three [WHEE festivals] in the summer of 2000," said *High Time*'s Steve Wishnia. "I think one was in Washington State, one was in upstate New York and one was at Rainbow Farm. Tom lost a lot of money on the one at Rainbow Farm."

The math was simple, Wishnia said. Tom overspent, so had to over-charge, asking fifty dollars a head. But the venues report it differently. All three festivals that summer charged the same, by agreement before-hand, and all lost money. Plus, Teter was there with his roadblocks and his SWET motorhome action team, who bought pot, LSD, hashish, co-caine and speed, but made no arrests. Whatever the cause, Rainbow

Farm lost another ten grand. Again, Tom went to friends and borrowed the money.

On the Tuesday morning after Roach Roast 2000, Tom strode into the farm office down in the store and just blurted out, "Doug, I need to pay my debts, give me $40,000 out of those receipts." Doug felt the adrenaline rush through his body. The banker ran the books clean, it was all shown to the IRS, and according to his ledgers the corporation only owed Tom $10,000 for equipment deposits and the like. Tom loaned money to the corporation as needed; those legal loans were all there on the ledgers, so that was not unusual. But Tom had promised that Doug and Derrik would be able to touch some of the Roach Roast profits for their own personal money for the winter.

Tom was in no mood to hear about it. "No," he said, "I've got to pay off $40,000 right now." He seemed panicky. He said he had some personal debts. What he wanted was his $10,000 and then a $30,000 draw off the corporation. But there was only $35,000 clear from the festival. After some tense discussion, he demanded at least $30,000, end of discussion. After he left the room, Doug collapsed in a state of exhausted, bitter disappointment. For an entire summer of sprinting on the farm, both Derrik and Doug would each make $2,500.

Derrik was pissed and wanted to know where all the money went. He knew they'd cleared money on Roach Roast, with Big Brother and the Holding Co. headlining. So Derrik and Rollie turned on Doug and accused him of embezzling the money. Tom had warned Doug not to talk about this to anyone, but for once Doug wanted Tom to take responsibility. Doug's hands were clean—it was all there on the books, and Rollie and Derrik could figure it out for themselves if they simply looked at the cash payouts in the ledger. But Tom sat there in silence letting Doug fry, and Doug didn't say much, either. Derrik thought Doug was hiding something, but it was a matter of pride. Tom had been an honest man, but something had changed.

Tom and Doug talked afterward, but he didn't like the sound of what Tom was saying.

"We're all gonna work for nothing this winter," said Tom. "We're gonna do whatever it takes to make money. I'm gonna have to do some of things that I know how to do in order for us to survive."

Doug didn't know what Tom was referring to and didn't care to speculate. He had a mess of his own to take care of: In 1999 Doug's dad had retired and moved to a Moose Lodge retirement home in Florida, leaving Doug the family home in Elkhart. He had hoped to use his cut of those Roach Roast proceeds to make mortgage payments and keep the place.

"I gotta go, then, Tom."

"I need you here," his friend said. Tom had put Doug in an impossible situation, but he still felt abandoned; his money man, the guy who kept the books, was leaving during their worst-ever crisis. "If you leave now, Doug, don't ever come back. We're finished."

"It doesn't have to be that way, Tom," Doug said, caught flat-footed. He just wanted three months to get caught up on the house payments. But by the following Monday, he was fired and stood accused of stealing twenty thousand dollars. Tom sat shamefaced in their final meeting and let Doug take the heat, neither man revealing that Tom had drawn the money himself. Doug pulled together a box of stuff and rolled through Vandalia in his tired car with the air smelling like burning leaves and broke off all contact until well into 2001.

Some of the tribe went with him, too. Shayla and Casey were close to Doug and they split, moving into Three Rivers. Moe and Amy and Whoaboy left that summer, too—Moe had been drunk while fliering at Nelson Ledges in Ohio and got in a fight there, so Tom gave him the heave-ho. Derrik became the new manager and he mostly had Big Jim and tree-tall Hippie and a serious young militant named Travis Hopkins there to hold the place together, plus a small cloud of teenage hangers-on. As the winter deepened and Tom's mood soured, some of that cloud just drifted away.

SEVENTEEN Betting the Farm

ON SATURDAY, APRIL 21, 2001, a seventeen-year-old high school junior named Konrad Joseph Hornack was apparently driving back to his home in Eau Claire, Michigan, at around ten a.m., in full daylight, when he ran a stop sign and into the path of a school bus carrying the Eau Claire High School varsity softball team. The impact crushed Hornack's Chevrolet Cavalier, killing him at the scene, and tipped the bus over leaving the driver and six of the kids on the bus with minor injuries.

The accident occurred at the intersection of Watson and Hillandale Roads, out in the sticks near Sodus, a township in Berrien County along the St. Joseph River about forty miles from the farm.

What wasn't immediately reported, but was made part of Scott Teter's case, was that Hornack died wearing a Rainbow Farm wristband, indicating that he may have been at the farm's 420 festival the night before.

No one at Rainbow Farm remembered Hornack being at 420, their very successful Earth Day festival, which drew 1,000 to 1,500 partiers at twenty-five dollars apiece and made the farm enough money to pay for band deposits and promotion for Hemp Aid 2001, getting them out of a real hole. State police investigators never went out to the farm, to anyone's knowledge, to show them photos of Hornack or try to get any information about what happened. But Hornack's best friend, Danny Petertil, told detectives they'd both gone to Rainbow Farm that night and got high on LSD and smoked pot. There wasn't any indication that Hornack may have been high or drunk at the time of the accident, but Petertil said Hornack had left the festival, alone, at two a.m. What he did during the eight hours between then and the accident is unknown. A pack of Zig-Zags, a copy of *High Times* and a sleeping bag were found in the car, and he was driving on a restricted license as the result of a DUI.

Weeks later, Lt. Joseph Zangaro, Michigan State Police SWET section commander, held a press conference and showed a gruesome eight-by-ten photo of a mangled hand with the Rainbow Farm bracelet still attached.

"That bracelet on his wrist," said Zangaro, "it's a hospital-type bracelet. You get these at the festivals to prove you have paid your admission."

Advertisements and fliers for Hemp Aid 2001 turned up that same weekend at Hash Bash, as usual. The success of the 420 event put the farm back on its feet, somewhat, and Derrik and Tom made an all-out push to get roughly ten thousand dollars in band and equipment deposits out and get Hemp Aid organized on the double-quick. There had never been any question that the show would go on, only what kind of show it would be under Derrik's new austerity program. Now they went ahead, reenergized. Rainbow Farm would survive.

Teter felt he couldn't wait any longer. Hornack's grotesque accident was too much to ignore. So he began crafting a search warrant, but it didn't have anything to do with drugs. It was the old Eliot Ness routine: He went after the farm for tax evasion.

Just before Hemp Aid '99, a full sixteen months before Derrik took over, Teter had cultivated a confidential informant (referred to in his paperwork as CI 2314—CI for Confidential Informant) who worked a cash register in the camp store. Of course Doug and Derrik know who it is now but decided this person should remain nameless because this info set into motion a chain of events that the informant could not have foreseen. According to court documents, the cashier reported that no employee payroll taxes were being withheld.

There was no reason to withhold payroll taxes if no one was on the payroll. Everyone on the farm, including Doug and Derrik, were seasonal employees paid as contract labor and issued 1099s. The farm was registered with the state and paid all its sales and use taxes on schedule. Doug's shift reports were all there for every cashier, and all the 1099s were in order. In the fall of 2000, Derrik had wanted to build a little more security for the workers so he contacted H&R Block in Edwardsburg to get himself and a few other folks on full time and began paying payroll taxes in 2001.

By then, however, state treasury investigator Deanna Ward was already building a case against the farm, using the testimony of CI 2314. SWET provided Ward and Teter endless estimates of how much money was changing hands at the farm, in terms of festival receipts. It made for a pile of documentation, but once again, none of it indicated any obvious tax crime by Rainbow Farm. All they had was the kind of hyperbolic speculation that comprises the art of the search warrant. No one ever contacted Rainbow Farm's two accountants to check the records.

Then came a lawsuit that gave Teter another window into farm finances.

After the season closed, security chief Mike Long, who owned a construction business in Edwardsburg and hired over one hundred people to do security of the farm, sued Tom Crosslin and Rainbow Farm for $10,000, which included the approximate value of a trip to the Cannabis Cup in Amsterdam he claimed Tom had promised him as a bonus.

Mike Long and his brother, Bill Long, called Doug that winter asking him to sign a statement swearing that Tom had promised them a trip but then never delivered. Doug demurred, saying again that when he had paid them in September they were paid in full, and if they pressed this claim they'd just bring unwanted scrutiny to the farm, and maybe give authorities a reason to search the place or subpoena evidence. Mike Long told him that it was a matter of principle. "A person should follow through with his promises," Long said.

No trip to Amsterdam was listed on any contract and Long lost in court. The only reason it's significant is that the suit made it appear that some Rainbow Farm contractors were being paid in cash or in kind—maybe some not contracted of all but working only on verbal agreements. According to many farm regulars, Teter may have had other sources on the farm, too, reporting that folks were getting paid under the table. (The Longs were evidently pretty freaked about events that happened later. When I first called Mike Long to ask about their relationship to Teter, Mike's wife Missy picked up the telephone and yelled into it, "We've already lost enough on account of Rainbow Farm. You call me up wanting me to talk some dirt about Scott Teter? Why would I want to cut my own throat?!" Then she hung up.)

On May 8 a warrant in the form of a six-page affidavit by Deanna Ward was approved and signed by a district judge in Lansing. No one in Cass County approved any raid. In fact Derrik DeCraene, who was pretty good friends with a couple of deputies in the sheriff's department, says only one Cass County officer was present when the raid did come. It was an outside job from start to finish.

The warrant contained the standard descriptions of the house, indicating all windows and entry points, and listed the camp store as "the business."

There were five pages of transactions listed, estimates of gross receipts made at Rainbow Farm and an explanation about the tax registration form dated April 6, 1998 and signed by Rollie. None of it indicated any intentional illegality. In fact, they'd never find anything wrong with the taxes on Rainbow Farm. Notably absent from Agent Ward's affidavit was any mention of the quarterly payroll withholding and unemployment taxes being paid by H&R Block since Derrik had taken over, or the 1099s for contract employees all the previous years.

Property to be seized was listed as: "Financial and accounting records from 1998 to the present including all payroll records," etc. The word marijuana did not appear in the document.

At the same time, however, Teter's office put together an exhaustive complaint for forfeiture, listing fifty-eight causes for drug asset forfeiture—none of them having anything to do with taxes or the farm's legitimate campground business. The eighteen-page series of SWET anecdotes are so overwhelming they verge on the comical.

The subject stated that he did not know of anyone selling beer but that he was selling "shrooms," referring to the hallucinogenic mushroom psilocybin. When asked how much he was selling them for the subject replied, "an eighth ounce for thirty." Detectives asked to see the mushrooms and the subject reached inside the tent he was sitting in front of and produced a bag of mushrooms. Detectives could see inside the tent when the subject opened the flap that he had several such bags in the tent. . . . At this point the detectives asked the subject if he would mind if they rested at his location. He stated that he did not mind and the detectives and the subject, who identified himself as "Joel" sat and made small talk. During this time, "Joel" reached inside the tent and produced a bag which contained a marijuana bud and placed the bud in front of himself. "Joel" stated that he was also selling marijuana and that this particular bud was his "showpiece." Detectives noticed that there were two Rainbow Farms [sic] employees who were sitting on a golf cart who were watching these events. Shortly thereafter, the Rainbow Farms [sic] staff members came over and informed "Joel" that he should not be openly selling drugs where anyone could come by and see it. The staff advised that "Joel" should conduct such transactions in a more discreet manner. The staff advised that for all they knew there could be ten undercover cops in the campground.

Every entry is like this. SWET officers are buying Honey Brown beers from an unlicensed vendor, "ganja balls" that looked like Rice Krispy treats from some kid walking around lugging a cooler full of them, ounces of weed, doses of liquid and blotter acid, grams of red opium and hash, eighth-ounce bags of weed from some player in a black stretch limousine who kept the bags under his baseball cap, quarter-grams of coke, half-grams of crystal meth. There is tale after tale of Tom stopping by in his golf cart to blow some gage with festival goers.

It was all about drugs, not taxes, and drugs were what they expected to find. By itself, these cases weren't enough to take the farm, but if the

SWET boys could find drugs in the farmhouse it would be pure overkill. Teter needed just one score from that house. Not too many prosecutors are going to have a massive forfeiture document ready just in case they find drugs on a tax case. Nor is a tax case usually resolved by a massive tactical raid. He already knew what he would find there.

Derrik DeCraene had just dropped off to sleep when the taxman came. He'd been up all night patrolling the back property at Rainbow Farm for crackheads. This had become a serious problem on the farm; coke freaks buying their rock down in the parking lot of Mr. D's convenience store and then looking for a place to smoke it up, usually while parking on the Kirk Lake access road. Derrik and Doug had told the cops about this repeatedly, but no one ever came out to help them.

Travis Hopkins, who by then had been made head of security, had some kind of court matter regarding his son that morning, and other farm regulars were just worn out, so Derrik cut them loose and rolled around the farm until about five a.m. in his golf cart. Then he crawled onto his office couch in a pajama bottom and crashed. He heard Travis, who was sleeping elsewhere in The Joint, leave at about eight a.m. He opened one eye when he heard the crunch of tires and fast-moving footsteps on gravel outside, thinking it was Travis coming back. Then the door crashed open and men swarmed in.

This was no tax action—it was a full-blown drug raid. Ten or so state troopers in full assault gear and ski masks swarmed him, guns drawn. Some of these men may have been on Rainbow Farm before, but Teter's "bloodbath" talk had worked its evil magic. He looked up and their gun barrels were shaking.

"Who are you and what are you doing in this building?!" one of them barked.

He stared into the barrel of an assault rifle. "Don't shoot me."

"What's your name?!"

"Derrik DeCraene. I'm the manager of Rainbow Farm. This is my office."

For the longest moment of his life, he thought this was it. He would be the next Donald Scott. That finger would just squeeeeeeeeeze the trigger and it would be over.

Derrik blinked at them as they continued to repeat their questions. Then he got his wits about him.

"Man, here's what I'm going to do," Derrik said in a kind of forced calm. "I'm going to put this arm down real slow, and I'm going to sit up, and I'm going to put my pants on. I'm unarmed. You just tell me which way to go."

As they hustled him to the door, the masked men drilled him. "Where's the drugs? We know there are drugs."

"What do you mean?" said Derrik.

"Where's the drugs? You know, the dope?"

"Dude," said Derrik, who says that a lot, "you might be able to find a joint in this building if you try, but I don't know what kind of dope you're lookin' for, you know?"

Outside, he blinked in the blinding summer sunlight. Around him was a war zone. Officers in assault gear were everywhere, moving around squad cars and SUVs and paddy wagons and command vehicles. It was all state police. Sheriff Underwood was nowhere in sight. As Derrik watched, the tactical squad brought Tom and Rollie out of the house and turned them over to uniformed troopers, and Tom was hot. They stood him against the house for a moment, covered by officers with rifles shouldered, firing-squad style. It was too much for Tom.

As a big uniformed officer tried to get Tom into a squad car, the Rainbow Farm owner unleashed a two-minute tirade on all the troopers present, screaming at the top of his lungs. It was all captured on video, and the trooper shooting that video even snickered a bit when Tom turned his anger on Lt. Ott, the commander from the state police post in nearby White Pigeon.

"You don't want these sons of bitches in here spying like that!" Tom roared at an officer off-screen. "I hope you all go to hell! All you motherfuckers. I hope that. All you sons of bitches. Fuck this, you Nazi motherfuckers! You hear that, you Nazi sons of bitches?! *Fuck all you Communist maggot motherfuckers! Fuck you all! Motherfuckers!* I hope you all fry in hell, you Nazi motherfuckers! Especially you, Ott! You got the balls of a gnat. What kind of Nazi are you? That's fucking Hitler shit! 'I was only following orders!' While you were killing fucking kids. Nazi sons of bitches. You're all fucking Nazi motherfuckers. And shame on you, [mentions another officer]. You motherfuckers are all gonna die! Motherfuckers! Nazi sons of bitches! *Nazi motherfuckers!!* All you sons of bitches will rot in hell! I'll personally guarantee it, you motherfuckers! 'I was only following orders!' That's what Hitler's bullshit was! You punk motherfuckers! All you punk sons of bitches!" Then, to another officer who was cracking up, as he was pushed into the car, "Laugh, you fat little fucker."

Rollie stood silently by the side of the house. He was put in a separate car, his head down.

On another part of the lawn, Derrik saw to his dismay that cops were rounding up the campers in the four or five sites occupied that night, including well-known Washington State pot activist and Rainbow Family scion Gideon Israel, who had been a speaker at three festivals in 2000 and was staying in one of the farm's tiny cabins. They'd pulled another couple out of their tent, making the woman stand in the grass half naked while cops searched their camp. Afterward, that couple mentioned to Derrik, "It's nothing personal, but we'll never come camping here again." Down by the front gate, farm employees showing up for work were being detained. They put Derrik alone on a hay wagon behind the store. He immediately thought of Robert and relaxed some when he realized the boy had already gone to school.

The assault team then ransacked the store, grabbing up the bongs and penis-shaped pipes and paraphernalia, plus T-shirts, Frisbees, rolling papers, the works. Finally one of the cops came out with his mask rolled up to show his face.

"Oh, we found your dope. Your ass is going to jail," he said to Derrik. He held up a joint in a baggie. It was old.

Derrik had a quick temper and he was starting to get lippy. "It ain't mine." The trooper turned about eight shades of purple and Derrik recoiled, thinking the guy was about to bust him one in the teeth.

"What the fuck you mean, it ain't yours?"

"Dude, that ain't mine. Where'd you find it?"

"In that building."

"That building is property of Rainbow Farm." No matter whose joint it was, that put the possession charge on Tom and Rollie. Derrik saw the writing on the wall. Tom and Rollie were going to jail. Somebody was going to have to bail them out and keep the place open.

Treasury agents came over to talk to Derrik on the hay wagon. They wanted to see those tax records. Just the day before, he had received the latest 1038 forms in the mail from H&R Block for payment of payroll witholding tax, and they were literally sitting in plain view on his desk.

"Fine, let's walk down to my office. My 1038s, I just got 'em, I do 'em quarterly, they're on my desk. Haven't even filed 'em yet."

The woman looked at him, stunned, and said, "What do you mean?"

"Well, I still have the stuff, it's fresh on my desk. I just got 'em back."

The woman hesitated. "You do your own 1038s?"

"Well, yeah, I run this place. It's my responsibility to keep track of that shit."

"Oh."

Evidently, no one from the treasury department had thought they'd find this. The payroll taxes for about a dozen employees, at least the 2001 taxes, were all taken care of. Derrik provided treasury agents with a few documents but they left a lot of the pertinent files listed on the search warrant—which were right there in the file cabinets—and split without any further questions.

The warrant used to conduct the raid was a complete sham. During the four months that followed, DeCraene was never interviewed about tax preparation, nor was Doug or anyone else. No one ever called their payroll accountant at H&R Block, nor their previous accountant in Elkhart. There was never any audit. Most of the available records were never removed from the Rainbow Farm office. Later, some ended up with Sharon Keener and some with Tom's brother Jim and his wife, Miriame.

The SWET troops found just what they were really looking for. It happened so quickly—they knew right where to look—they probably just told the taxman to stay the hell out of the way.

When Tom and Rollie were out of the house, troopers went straight to the basement and hit paydirt: Behind an unlocked door, they found a fairly major grow room. Rows of tiny starter marijuana plants two to twenty-four inches high were jutting up from trays of Grodan rock-wool sitting on metal stands. The walls of the two rooms, in the new added-on section of the basement, were covered in foillike silver, and standing floor fans circulated the air. Grow lamps hung overhead and stood on stands with their ballasts, and tubes for a hydration system ran to black plastic tanks under the trays. A tank of CO_2 stood in the room, used to push the plants to grow faster and bud out harder. Timers, grow food, jugs of chemicals and gardening paraphernalia lay everywhere.

Even eleven-year-old Robert knew what the plants were and how they were grown: he later referred to them as "clones." The female cannabis plants were cloned to create strains of identical weeds, then grown under precisely controlled temperature, Ph, light, CO_2 and food conditions to optimize the THC in the buds.

These plants wouldn't bud until September, though—they were only a few inches high. But there were at least three hundred of them, by state trooper count. And that would be more than enough to bring down Rainbow Farm.

Tom and Rollie sat in their separate squad cars and fumed. The troopers obviously didn't consider Tom dangerous, because they took the cuffs off in the car. He angrily flipped off a Michigan State Police cameraman. His head began to droop.

The grow room was new. Tom and Rollie had only built it over the winter, and the very few farm employees who knew about it considered it a grave mistake. Teter didn't even have to allege that the weed was for sale or distribution; it didn't matter. Manufacture is a felony in itself. It would have been impossible to prove that it was for sale anyway, since none of it was ever sold. It was allegedly their second crop in the grow room, and the first was barely enough for Rollie's voracious habits.

"I told them I thought this was the single worst idea I'd ever heard in my entire life," said Derrik. "Here they are, the most high-profile pot activists in the state of Michigan. We are a major thorn in their side; they're just looking every day for a reason to nail our ass. And they're going to grow pot in the house. What a dumbshit plan.

"I said to Tom, 'Have you ever heard the term "betting the farm"? Well, that's what you are doing with this. You are literally betting the farm on this one.' "

The troopers seemed to know it was there. Betrayals matter, but Derrik said it would not have been hard for word to leak.

"There were slip-ups," he said. "There was one instance where we were sittin' out—we had this little bay, like a garage area, where we repaired golf carts. We were burnin' one at the picnic table one day and Rollie comes walkin' down. And a couple of hands from the local farm was up there. Farm kids, they're not real stupid when it comes to plants. So Rollie reaches into his coat and pulls out this bud that's about a foot long! And I mean, this son of a bitch was *green*! This one particular farm kid, man, I could just tell by the look on his face that he was—*boing!* [eyes pop out]— boy, you don't just pull out a bud like that, you know what I mean?"

The cops stopped their investigation of the house and went back to Judge Dodge to get a drug search warrant. Everything stopped for several hours while this took place.

While everyone waited for that to happen another unmarked state car came down the dirt road and pulled in. Inside were Teter and his boss from Lansing, Michigan State attorney general Jennifer Granholm. Just swinging by to take a victory lap.

This much is true about every bust that happens anywhere: It's not like on TV. The cops don't know who anybody is and weirdness erupts all over. At about ten a.m. the cops started talking about how they were go-ing to have to shoot Thai Stick because there was no county deputy there to deal with the dog, so Derrik risked getting himself shot to grab the dog and take her back to his hay wagon. Later, a van pulled up in the mid-dle of the bust loaded with take-out from McDonald's and almost all the officers present stopped guarding their dangerous prisoners and sat down in the shade for lunch. Derrik went up to a sergeant who had taken up residence in the ticket booth, complaining that all his people were hungry, too, and the sergeant told him, through a mouthful, "Like I owe you shit." After a few more minutes on the hay wagon, Derrik decided to just act like an American with rights. He walked up to the nearest cop.

"Dude, am I under arrest?"

"Well, we don't know yet."

"Well, you got my name and contacts and if you lose that I'm in the phone book, so let me know. I'm gonna take off."

Then he walked down to his tiny Ford Probe and got in. Seeing Der-rik make a move, about five other detainees rushed the car and squeezed in. They were dragging the muffler in the dirt as they bounced out the gate. Gideon Israel, a big man pushing three hundred pounds, ambled out the gate down to Butch's house and paid Butch ten dollars to give him a ride into town. No one did anything to stop him. That was the unofficial end of the raid.

Tom was charged with manufacturing marijuana over two hundred plants (a fifteen-year maximum sentence), felony firearm possession (two years consecutive), possession of a firearm by a convicted felon (five years) and maintaining a drug house (two years). Plus he was a repeat offender, so many of these maximums would be increased under sentencing guidelines. If convicted, he was looking at as much as twenty years in prison.

Except for the five-year firearm charge, Rollie was charged with the same. But he was a first offender and probably faced much more lenient sentencing—maybe a couple of years.

The guns were ordinary stuff you'd find in any Michigan household that has guns, but they were trouble for Tom. In the bedroom closet upstairs were two loaded 12-gauge shotguns. In the attic, accessible only through a door in that same closet in Tom and Rollie's bedroom, troopers had also found a Ruger 9 mm semiautomatic pistol in a case with a full magazine in it. Teter's indictment referred to the 1995 assault on Pearl Mills as the felony that precluded his owning a gun, but it should be pointed out that the case was pleaded down to a misdemeanor, so this charge wouldn't apply. However, he had another felony on his record from a robbery committed during his motorcycle gang days in Indiana twenty years earlier, and it's unclear if the ban on owning a gun had ever been expunged.

On that same day, the law descended on the four small-time dealers that SWET had been tracking for years on the farm, but whom no staffer at Rainbow Farm would have been able to identify. Michael Royal was thirty-seven and from Defiance, Ohio. James Schmidt, twenty-nine, traveled to the farm from Lake Zurich, Illinois. Aaron Brown was a twenty-two-year-old from nearby Allegan, and Andrew Rasmussen, twenty, lived in Bay City. These hapless souls were just faces in the crowd at the farm, selling their weed, coke, meth and what have you to pay for their vacations; SWET had some of their deals on videotape.

"It appears that these festivals were little more than an excuse for drug dealers to peddle their wares from a carnival booth instead of from a street corner," attorney general Jennifer Granholm wrote in the press release—once again, wrongly identifying these kids as registered vendors. Their sales were not done from any booth.

Teter also was quoted in the press release: "These people were basically thumbing their noses at Michigan and federal drug laws and the local law enforcement agencies in the area," he said, adding, "We are now working with the State Police Tax Enforcement Team to investigate possible tax violations on the part of Rainbow Farms [sic] and its proprietors."

Derrik went back to the farm in the pit of the afternoon so that someone would be there when Robert got off the school bus. There wasn't a soul in sight except for Thai Stick running around loose. The police had left the lights on and the doors banging open in the warm spring breeze. The store, he said, was "ransacked." For some reason, the cops had seized Jerry Stone's old motorhome and trundled it off as evidence, never to be seen again, though other cars and tractors were left alone. There was only the quiet of the late spring, with the blackbirds tootling and the biting flies and peepers just starting to pick up in volume.

Gideon Israel and a friend cautiously returned to the property going the long way around, down Quaker and Kirk Lake Streets. If they saw cops they were going to breeze right on by. But only TV vans were there and Gideon ended up speaking to many of them. He slept in The Joint that night while Derrik guarded the house.

There was a note on the door of the store. It was a court injunction for a public nuisance abatement and a temporary restraining order on the campground. The campground and store and The Joint would eventually reopen, but Rainbow Farm was barred from having any more festivals. Hemp Aid 2001 was officially canceled.

Teter also had filed that day, May 9, for forfeiture of Rainbow Farm.

By arrangement with the state police, Robert got off the bus that day with the children of Oli Olafsson, an attorney who was a lifelong friend of the Files. Olafsson and his wife, Barbara, were rehabbing the old elementary school on the Bivouac property into a home on the outskirts of Vandalia. They had three kids around Robert's age, who were all friends of his from school. Oli and his family were also regulars at the festivals.

Four days after the bust, Derrik bailed Rollie out of jail, a $10,000 bond on $25,000 bail. With Rollie's signature, as president of Rainbow Farm, it was easier to scrape money together for Tom. They hocked the

Rolls-Royce to an acquaintance for part of the money and finally got together a $25,000 bond on his $150,000 bail.

On the night Derrik and Rollie got him out, Tom stomped up and down in the house, already talking about how they were going to have to defend the farm when the pigs came around to collect their forfeiture spoils. Teter's career, he swore, would be ruined. What he couldn't do with lawyers he'd do with popular support, and what he couldn't do with support he'd do with the Militia. When it came right down to it, there'd be a hell of a firefight.

Derrik tried to get him to ease off a little. "Man, get some sleep. Your mind's crazy. You've been in jail for a week. Think about it tomorrow. We'll talk."

He never got the chance to cool down. On May 15, only one day after Tom had come out of jail, Derrik and Rollie were sitting on the front porch waiting for Robert to get home from school. The bus came up the road and blew right past without stopping. Rollie jumped up, confused, and got on the phone to call Dinky and Oli, to see if he'd gone over there. But neither one of them had him, so he called Sam Adams Middle School in Cassopolis. When he came back out, his face was ashen. Robert had been taken out of school by the sheriff by order of Child Protective Services, petitioned by Teter, and had been turned over to the state Family Independence Agency. No one had called Rollie to even let him know.

Passive, stoic Rollie came apart. He rang the Cass County FIA office, his normally flat voice rising with rage. He could lose the farm, he could even go to jail for a few years, but he couldn't lose Robert. "Who the fuck you guys think you are, just taking my kid?!" he shouted into the phone. "You can't do that! I haven't been convicted of a goddamn thing!" He rifled through the house for his wallet and keys and he was down the dirt road in his lemon-yellow VW bug on his way to the FIA.

In truth, Teter had a defensible position regarding Robert, but it smelled badly of purposely aggravating Crosslin and Rohm. Technically, the cause of action was listed as "neglect and abuse," but even a casual observer could see Robert hadn't suffered any of that. Teter and the FIA people spoke with Maria Jones, a counselor at Sam Adams, on the day they took Robert out of the school. She reported that the boy had no problems at school, "until recently because of the publicity surrounding his father." He'd never talked about any issues with drug use, nor was he a drug user. He was, she said, "a pretty good kid," good attendance, good behavior, always nicely dressed. A kid, in other words, who had no problems at home or at school and was getting along fine.

Why, then, did they just give the kid to a sheriff's deputy? Mark Herman, the Cass County probate court referee, says he ordinarily would have seen a case like this, but Judge Dobrich had stepped in to handle it herself, and she felt she had good reason to do so. The way that Robert was removed was standard procedure, he says, but the case for removal was a judgment call, a gray area.

"Marijuana possession and use—maybe," Herman said, "you have to hear the particulars, as to whether or not you believe the child was in danger." The FIA's own standards for drug use as the basis for an NA case are unclear: Children who test positive for drugs at birth, for instance, indicating a drug-using mother, are not automatically removed from homes. This is considered insufficient evidence. "The first section of the juvenile code says services should be provided to any juvenile that comes before the jurisdiction of the court. Services should be provided to the child preferably within his or her own home," Herman notes. The procedure was to have a meeting within twenty-four hours about how to remedy the conditions that put the child in imminent danger—in Robert's case, the marijuana and the guns. But up at Rainbow Farm, those conditions were already cleaned up a week before Robert was taken. The imminent danger was gone.

Teter himself acknowledged that a marijuana charge was not grounds to remove a child from the home. "For a regular marijuana charge, no," he told me, "but we were concerned about the weapons. They were loaded and propped up against the wall in the bedroom closet."

The gun charge could have been disputed in court, which would have left manufacturing pot as the whole basis for neglect and abuse.

Judge Dobrich was unable to comment on the case, but spent some time explaining that, legally, there had to be some findings that the child had been placed in harm's way. The standards are "imminent risk" and "failure to protect." Dobrich was kind enough, and is highly respected by the people in the community. But the inferences she made in approving the removal were clear: The danger lay in the loaded firearms and open pot smoking in front of the child, along with a "high potential of violence." This is the end result of Tom's misunderstood "blood of a government massacre" letter and the county's fear of the Militia. Neglect, then, is a relative term.

The small-town connections, however, were so tight and impenetrable that child advocacy workers around Cass County called it a "courthouse mafia." The head of Child Protective Services was Cindy Underwood, the sheriff's wife. Judge Sue Dobrich's husband was a former honcho in the sheriff's department, and was then chief of police in Dowagiac, where about 70 percent of the cases coming through the county juvenile system originated. Forty-third circuit court judge Mike Dodge had been there since 1982 and his wife oversaw community corrections for the sheriff. And so on. Local foster-care advocates say they were pleased that their county family court was so active (they were winning awards these years for removing so many children, placing a record percentage of them in adoption), but priorities got blurry; many claimed police business leaked into the job of protecting children and keeping families together.

Robert had been through this before. In April 1997 he had been removed by Child Protective Services because someone reported that Rollie had been smoking weed in front of him. According to an interview with Tom done by Jay Statzer that summer, they got Robert back right away just by changing Rollie's address to one of the houses in Elkhart.

This time it wasn't going to be that way. The day he was removed, Robert was placed in foster care with Robert "Ted" and Debbie Steele. He was the former chief of police in Edwardsburg, and the couple had a nice place, a fairly big house with seven other children. It was a good placement, and the Steeles were firm and trusting with Robert. On that first day, Robert and Ted got to know one another by picking up car parts at AutoZone. Derrik and Travis visited him there, and even Robert would later say he felt okay with the Steeles. But those first nights were dark. The eleven-year-old, tall for his age but wiry and talkative and still a very little boy, sat up all alone in his own room and worried about what would become of him. Without his dad, he was up for grabs. He knew the court wouldn't let him go back to Leslie. He saw himself bouncing through foster-care homes like this one for the rest of his teenage years.

Melody Karr, who worked with Cannabis Action Network up in Mesick, Michigan, a tiny rural crossroads about four hours north of Rainbow Farm, called her friend Trena Moss, another longtime PRA petitioner, NORML contact and plumbing contractor from Allen, and said they ought to get down there to protest Robert's removal. They were sure there'd be a huge turnout.

They were on the courthouse lawn in Cassopolis on the morning of Rollie's first court appearance, but only five people showed up. Moss had her big sign from the PRA that said "End the Assest Forfeiture Nightmare" and "Peace With Honor in the War on (Some) Drugs."

"I guess in my own naïveté', I thought there would be hundreds of people there to protest this," said Moss. "I honestly did. But it started to rain. And this was in May. It was so cold. And I remember we stood there anyway, damn it.

"That was the moment when I pretty much threw all caution to the wind and said, 'I'm standing up for what's right and I don't care.' That was it for me. When I went home, I took out my shotgun and my shells and I kept them near my bed for several months after that. Because what we saw in court, it was so unright. The injustice was so great that I guess I didn't even feel safe in my home after that. I want you to know, though, that I'm completely nonviolent. It's my religious belief not to do anything violent. But at the same time, I don't know how I can explain how disgusted I am."

The Steeles brought Robert down to the FIA offices in Cassopolis.

Rollie's long hair was washed and he was wearing some clean jeans and a button shirt, trying to be respectful of the legal process. He swore he would toe the line to get Robert back, and would abide by any reunification plan. Then the boy rushed into the conference room and clutched his dad. The two of them sat down in a chair, Robert on Rollie's lap, and he asked his boy if he was okay. Father and son sat there for a long time and just sobbed.

The summer came but not with its usual wet. The still air hung with a languid humidity, and the heat came on as the long, mad nights shuddered with heat lightning and the sickly green glow of tornado weather, but not a drop of rain would fall for almost three months. Tom didn't have the money to keep the road oiled and dust coated the azaleas and wild rose in the ditch. As the heat intensified and crops struggled, the chronic dryness stilled the trees and put a rattle in the rye and ghostly wisps on the timothy. An ugly black torpor set in at Rainbow Farm.

On coming out of jail, Tom had already changed. Part of his optimism and love of problem solving had slipped. He all but ignored the charges against him, shrugged them off to focus on the idea that Teter was going to seize his farm. That he himself had brought this on with his grow room contributed to an evil, roiling mix of hatred and guilt. When he had a shred of hope, Tom was a man of great focus; but now, hopeless, separated from the child that gave him joy and reminded of his error every day by Rollie's presence, he became obsessed, and especially with the idea that this county prosecutor who appeared to have no special skills, no natural power, no charisma, no courage, would strip him of everything he'd built. In fact to an outsider he seemed anything but powerless, nothing really irreversible had happened yet, but Tom acted as though he couldn't mount a defense.

He needed Old Saint Stephen or Chris Conrad or Gideon Israel or one of the true channelers of the hippie gods then, but he held them and their phone calls at arm's length. Instead he started to drink. He drank and smoked with only a few clueless kids and Travis and Hippie and Big Jim around to remind him of his horror and his rage.

The pacific oooohhhhhhmmmmm of cannabis did him no good then. This was the test, if ever there was a test for Tom Crosslin, and what he saw in his stony visions was a peaceful acceptance, sure, but it was not the blossoming of ahimsa, or nonviolence. Instead he saw a message he had to deliver, starless and Bible black. The natural perspicacity of cannabis threw open the heart of the matter before him as if his heart and Teter's and the beating core of the law were chunks of living lucite and what he saw there sucked out all his fear. Tom simply knew the forfeiture would never happen. At least, not while he was alive. Maybe this was the truth of his being in God, or maybe this was a moment beyond God when horror was all there was to accept.

The law was no deterrent when the punishment was so great it threshed all the fear out of a man. Tom had become a dreadful enemy: a loving, well-intentioned man who had looked into the heart of the law and found himself erased.

The day after Robert was taken, Tom, Rollie and Derrik drove into Kalamazoo to meet with an attorney, Randy Levine, at Levine & Levine, a top criminal defense firm. Levine saw it was going to be a spectacular gig but needed $150,000 just to look at the case. Driving home, Tom grew more angry when he realized he just wasn't going to have the resources to put on the righteous show trial he wanted.

Tom growled about how he'd done everything he could do to communicate with Teter, then referred again to his favorite quote from JFK: "Those who would deny a peaceful revolution, demand a violent one."

"But if they want their revolution, well, they're gonna get one," he told the passing farm fields as they rolled down Highway 131.

"Well, dude, I've done what I can," said Derrik, finally saying what was on his mind. "You guys are able to do whatever you want as free people, but I'm not gonna be no part of nobody's revolution. 'Cause there ain't never been a revolution in history without a shit-ton of blood spillin' first."

Tom looked at him. "Well, then, gather up your shit and cover your tail, 'cause it ain't gonna get any better," he said.

During the hour drive from Kalamazoo to the farm, Derrik realized his mind was really made up. This five-year period of his life had ended. When they pulled into the farm again that afternoon, he cleaned out both the farm office and the production office—all his posters and band paraphernalia, souvenir laminates and contact files, music and audio gear—and threw it into cardboard boxes. It was May 16.

Tom came out and joined in, distressed, and kept throwing more and more stuff into Derrik's car, even stuff the former manager didn't think he should take.

"We had a good relationship when I left," said Derrik. "They were like, 'Hey, man, we respect you for your decisions and we'll be friends, and if that's what you got to do to follow the course of your fuckin' life's path, then by all means do it.'"

Tom kept throwing things into his car, saying, "You take that. Just take it." Some of it was very personal stuff that Tom and Rollie wanted to make sure would get to Robert—photographs, clothing, other memorabilia that belonged to the two men, but mostly from Rollie.

They were cleaning house. It was the last time Derrik would see Rainbow Farm.

Later that same night, Derrik wandered back into his own place, a modular home in a kind of rural minipark on the edge of a swampy lake. He'd been expanding the prefab into a full-size home, but it was all framing and wires. He stood in the middle of the room with boxes in his hands. It was like seeing the place for the first time.

"I'd worked so hard, easily sixty to eighty hours a week up there, for so long, man, I didn't know what to do," he said. "I came home that day and I sat here and I thought, 'Who in the fuck am I? And what am I? And where am I now?'

"I was really weird for about a year. In fact, it was a good year and a half within us getting raided there, I would not sleep without pants on. I thought, I'm never gonna be caught by a bunch of cops sleeping naked or in my underwear or anything. It does some shit to ya, psychologically. There's some members of my family suggested that maybe I should get some counseling. For trauma-type guidance. Like I could afford a therapist."

Other employees stayed on through the summer. Nikki Lester, the willowy hippie chick in her twenties, had been working in the store since the beginning of the year, cashiering, ordering inventory, keeping the coffeeshop in supplies, doing odds and ends, sometimes even collecting eggs from the henhouse. Derrik had just shown her, the night before the raid, how to fax the time sheets to the H&R Block lady in Edwardsburg and take care of the payroll.

A few days after Tom and Rollie got out of jail, Tom came by Oli's school building where Nikki was living with her boyfriend Buggy Brown, and asked if she'd come and clean the house. Nikki came down to Rainbow Farm and spent about four hours picking up the cops' rubber gloves and the contents of all the drawers and cabinets they'd emptied. She'd never known anything about any grow room, though she had been Robert's babysitter for some time. "But I know I had a problem and I still do to this day of blocking out reality," she said.

Nikki was very close to Robert, and was sometimes responsible for seeing him off the bus, getting him something to eat, playing ball, getting him to play dates with his school friends. During the raid, she had realized that Robert might be nabbed so went down to the jail for Rollie to sign a note letting Robert stay at Oli's.

"Then he wanted to go down to the farm real quick, so I took him down there," Nikki said. "When he was sitting in the car, he was crying and stuff. He asked me, 'Did they go in the basement?' Immediately I'm like, 'Oh gosh. Don't tell me, Robert, were they growing?' He's like, 'Yeah.' I said, "Robert, you're eleven years old and you're very loyal to your father and Tom to keep a secret like that.'"

After Robert was removed to foster care, Nikki never saw him again.

David Guest, who would later go on to sign Tom's and Rollie's wills, was hanging at the farm and working there on a regular basis that summer. Travis and Big Jim were there—Jim mostly holed up in that old travel trailer he had parked behind the store. Smiley, rawboned Hippie had made his camp in the woods for years and this last summer occupied one of the little wooden cabins. Travis was living and working at the mansion a lot of the time, working fast with Rollie to finish a couple of upstairs bedrooms and a bathroom so he could pass home inspection to get Robert back. Rainbow Richie was doing some work at the farm, too.

Buggy Brown was staying close to Rainbow Farm, and not just because he was Nikki's boyfriend. He believed in the mission of the place and the hemp movement. He didn't care how outrageous it got—he had an outrageous personal story himself, having grown up distrusting the law and government as the child of Hare Krishna parents on the notorious New Vrindaban commune in the northern panhandle of West Virginia. He had worked for many years raising money for the International Society for Krishna Consciousness, or ISKCON, and his parents even sent him to study with Krishna mystics in India. The first time I met Buggy, he urged me to read the fantastically pulpy true-crime book, Monkey on a Stick, written by two reporters from the San Jose Mercury News and the New York Times, cataloging a legacy of murder, rape, child abuse, fraud and international drug smuggling centered at New Vrindaban. The scandals finally brought down many of the lavish, gold-plated communes and centers started by the ISKCON founder, His Divine Grace A. C. Bhaktivendanta Swami Prabhupada. Several of the 1970s-era leaders of ISKCON ended up either dead, disappeared in India or serving long prison sentences.

Buggy had escaped the worst of this early period of ISKCON cult development, but in many ways he was a Krishna refugee. He still found himself working booths in malls for Krishna-based businesses, and while working for one such business he met Oli Olafsson. Though Olafsson had a thriving Grand Rapids practice as an attorney, he ran a lucrative side business selling ceramic potpourri pies—potpourri fragrance holders sculpted to look like hyperreal apple pies—and Buggy had moved up to Michigan with Nikki in May 2000 to help with the business. In the mornings and evenings he worked the dairy at the File's farm.

Despite the tensions, the campground continued to work its magic and there were campers on the property almost every day. Omar Alham started living in a tent at Rainbow Farm after some friends turned him on to the place just before the fourth of July. Omar's dad lived in Egypt and the kid was in and out of contact with the county juvenile authorities. Despite a definite pall on the farm, the summer air was still charged with pheromones and dope and sweet music, and Rainbow Farm was a great refuge.

A new kid came around that summer, one of Omar's friends. His name was Brandon Peoples, and his girlfriend, Shelly Routley, lived down on Quaker Street across a long block of cornfields and woodlots. Peoples wasn't tight with any of the long-term Rainbow Farm warriors—Nikki carded him once when he bought a water pipe that summer and knew his name, anyway—but he was there long enough to get his nickname, and everyone called him Bones.

Rainbow Farm's mission was still clear, it was still utopia in full effect, even under threat of forfeiture. Maybe even more so, for guys like Travis and Jim. They responded to the threat. It brought out the fight-or-flight instinct in them.

"Travis felt like he had some importance being there, you know?" mused Nikki, who was later briefly Travis's girlfriend. "Tom and Rollie, they welcomed me and I think that's the same with Travis. They welcomed him in and they treated him with respect, and they made him feel needed."

Rollie, for his part, was in the grips of a kind of sublimated hysteria, doing whatever anyone told him to do to get his boy back. The finished rooms in the mansion gleamed, immaculate in comparison to the rest of the place. Travis lived in what had been a servant's quarters up the back stairs from the kitchen, and Tom was with them most nights; in fact, Tom and Rollie were almost constantly in one another's company despite FIA requirements that they split up.

One of the other conditions was that Rollie quit smoking weed, and he did try but without much support. He attended meetings about his habit, which was described by several people as involving as many as thirty bowls or joints a day. He was screened for pot regularly at Woodland Addictions Center as part of his bail and often tested positive. At a July 19 visit, for example, he admitted to counselors that he still smoked "one joint of marijuana per day." The center noted that his " 'strong denial and core attitudes regarding marijuana' puts Roland in poor risk for long-term abstinence."

A big part of the problem was that Tom made no effort to quit at all, and neither did anyone else. Rollie was surrounded by pot smokers; every night at the store, Travis, Nikki, Tom, Omar, Rainbow Richie, David, Big Jim, this guy Niles who sat around and played guitar and anyone else who happened to be there—there were always stragglers— sat outside on the picnic tables and smoked up. He was doomed.

Early in the summer, Tom and Rollie held a yard sale at the mansion to raise a few bucks. It was down to that. Derrik rolled by to bullshit with Tom and was shocked by what he saw. Tom sat in a lawnchair with a hat pulled low over his eyes and the blank hint of a grin. To Derrik, he seemed deep in the grip of antidepressants, lit by a kind of permanent twilight. It may have been only the untrustworthy light of shame, but Tom was no stranger to Prozac—he'd sometimes handed out the pills to Doug and Moe during festivals just to keep their mood up.

"How's it going? Shit going on?" Derrik chirped.

"Hey, yeah, what's up, Derrik?" Tom said, as though he'd just noticed anybody else was there at all.

They talked, but they didn't really talk. Tom's despondent mood had grown so much worse. It was as if, Derrik said, "the energy and the enthusiasm and all that had just been sucked right out of him. He wasn't a let's-take-on-the-world-type dude no more.

"But at that point, they'd taken away his license for business, they'd taken away his family, *everything*, man. So they came to the point where they were yard saling it. It was awful."

Jim and Miriame Crosslin stopped by the mansion in the evenings. Tom didn't say much and he drank. Jim was scared by it. Tom wasn't, everyone said, suicidal. Suicide wasn't in his nature. But he was depressed. Carrying through with his pledge to resist the drug war put him on a short path, and he could see where it ended. His only concern was for Rollie and Robert, even while his plan to resist the forfeiture would put Rollie at risk.

Melody Karr and Trena Moss were out collecting signatures for the PRA that summer, which was somewhat diminished without Rainbow Farm but still plugging away, when they stopped at the mansion over the fourth of July with Karr's three kids. Tom invited them in for coffee. While they were talking, he'd just walk over to the window and sigh, distracted. They had to go on to Battle Creek to work the Balloon Fest for signatures, so Karr's youngest son, John, stayed at the mansion with Tom and Rollie. She was a little worried about him misbehaving and adding to their troubles, but they assured her it was fine.

"When I got back, Tom pulled me aside and said, 'I know you were kinda worried if the boy was gonna behave or not, but he was really good and helpful, and I hope you don't mind if I give him this.' It was a scanner radio," said Karr. "He said, 'I don't have any cash or anything, we're kinda broke, but I've got this, and I think he'd like it.' They gave him a couple toys that were out in the yard. It was kinda like if he couldn't see his own son, he was enjoying being with another kid."

"Tom told me something that I'll never forget," said Moss, who had lost her daughter in a fire. "He said that we were lucky because God had our child, but the Nazis had theirs."

In June Tom found a new law firm, Vlachos & Vlachos in Kalamazoo, who agreed to defend him for fifty thousand dollars. Tom managed to raise half of it as a deposit and they went to work. In one of the first meetings with attorney Dori Leo, a former prosecutor for eight years in Kalamazoo, Tom made it plain that he didn't have much faith in the courts.

"Tom was very defiant," said Leo. "But Rollie, my impression of him was more that he was scared. I think Tom was well aware of what was coming down the line because as he was up on his property at one point, he made an eerie statement to me. He said, 'You're gonna be the last one to tell the story.'"

She thought some of his charges could be beaten. She thought the tax warrant was questionable, and knew that forfeitures had been success-fully resisted. One of the most knowledgable about this was Judy Osburn, who had cowritten the bible for the antiforfeiture group, FEAR, the *Asset Forfeiture Defense Manual*, and had helped on some sections of *The Emperor Wears No Clothes*. These resources were available but Tom didn't have Leo aggres-sively pursuing this angle. She felt that Tom had already given up.

"As a matter of fact, the day I was supposed to meet him, the day everything started, he was supposed to bring me paperwork that was going to be a major step towards helping resolve the case," she said.

Tom's attempts to find help were hesitant, tentative, almost like he didn't want anyone to talk him out of his course of action. He called Tommy Chong and asked him to buy the farm. He called Gideon Israel a couple times that summer, and the old hippie from Rainbow Valley tried to take Tom in an entirely different direction.

"I said, 'Tom, I think you should be looking to get out of the coun-try,'" he said. "'This looks like a slam dunk.' And he would just get real adamant, like, 'No way am I leaving the property. Under no circum-stances.' And then I'd say, 'Tom, I just don't think it's going to work out this time, because everything's so stacked and they're so evil.'"

Gideon Israel (born Jeff McMonigle) had been through all of this before—exactly this. His Rainbow Valley festival site was a forty-three-acre parcel fourteen miles outside Olympia, Washington, where Israel and a partner had put on sixty-five peace-and-love festivals between 1986 and 1997, with crowds as large as five thousand people. He'd been shut down for a pot sale and LSD possession and his land was seized. But he'd only spent six months in jail; he thought Tom's case was of a differ-ent magnitude.

"Me, I'm feeling real sick about everything, because I know where this is heading," said Gideon, High Times's 1999 Freedom Fighter of the Year. "I read then that Tom had a couple prior felonies, and then I read there was a pistol involved, and I started advising them: This is very, very serious."

Like a lot of people in the pot movement, he didn't like militias and he didn't like guns.

"There was no major hippie movement in Michigan and the Midwest," he explained. "I could noticeably tell they were more Detroit oriented, which was to me much more aggressive, harsher stoners. I'm a die-hard nonviolent."

"I was working on his big house up to the day he died," said Joe Evans, the former proprietor of Joe's Lounge, who was then seventy-three and doing plaster work in the mansion. "Every day, there was Tom, he was saying this about the government and saying that. I said, 'Man, they gonna kill your ass.' He said, 'I don't give a damn, I'm not afraid to die.' I said, 'They don't mind shooting your ass, either.'"

August 16 was Robert's twelfth birthday, and Tom and Rollie were allowed to send him gifts. But time was working against Rollie and Robert. As the heat of the rainless summer set in for real, day upon day of towering hot breezes scorching the fields and raising dust storms, Tom got restless. He told several farm supporters at the mansion that he was in the supermarket one day and ran into some state troopers. He told them he'd see them in hell. "Oh, we won't be taking you to court, then," the trooper allegedly told him. "We're taking you to the morgue."

On August 17, the day after Robert's birthday, both the weather and the stale waiting broke. A massive thunderstorm rolled across the state bringing a soaking rain. (The U.S. Department of Agriculture would later declare eighty-two Michigan counties disaster areas eligible for emergency farm loans due to drought.) But it was also the first day of a makeshift two-day "festival" on Rainbow Farm, in open defiance of

Teter's injunction against gatherings on the property. Tom and Rollie set it up via word of mouth, and there were anywhere from twelve to eighteen people present, but few of them were farm employees. None of the original utopians were around—no Doug, no Moe and Amy, no Whoaboy, no Derrik, no pot movement people. That history had been tied off and discarded.

Two of those attending the festival were Teter's narcs. They reported that Rollie and Tom were both smoking weed. Holding a festival violated their injunction and smoking pot was a bond violation.

There was no music, no speakers. The little group of partiers stood around on the old stage looking out at the dry, mowed field, listening to a boom box and smoking weed and drinking beer and shooting the shit.

Tom felt a change come on, a strange clearheadedness. Maybe it was the rain. He'd just made up his mind what he was going to do.

An advertisement appeared afterward on the Rainbow Farm Web site announcing a Labor Day festival. It wasn't called Roach Roast but bands and speakers were promised.

Teter pounced, like Tom knew he would. He sent a letter to Tom and Rollie in the third week of August, announcing that their bond was under threat of revocation. They would be due in court at one thirty p.m. on Friday August 31, with the assumption being that they would return to county jail.

The prosecutor followed that letter with an accelerated schedule regarding the forfeiture. Tom hadn't been anticipating that until their trial, but the first hearing on the forfeiture claim would be directly following the bond hearing, the same day. Teter was squeezing them. That letter arrived early in the week of the hearing—the kids at the farm said they remembered a sheriff's deputy serving papers on Tom—giving them only a few days to prepare a defense. There was no way Vlachos & Vlachos could even begin to be ready by then. As Brenda Grantland of FEAR pointed out, the only thing you could do was go to the judge and ask for more time, saying it wasn't fair, which usually worked. Dori Leo told Tom they'd just go to the hearing and "see what happened."

"Tom knew it was all over, and if he went to court they were going to issue order after order," says attorney Don France. "That's why he acted the way he did."

Vanessa Hunckler was 18 and working in a hippie T-shirt shop in the muggy Mississippi River town of Quincy, Illinois, a place called Terra Wear Unlimited. Needing to break out of her hometown for a stretch, she and two guy friends got on the Amtrak on August 22 and made a nine-hour trip through Chicago to Kalamazoo hoping to work and party at Rainbow Farm's Labor Day show. Tom sent Hippie into Kalamazoo to pick them up.

Nessa was an artist and had taken the job at Terra Wear to learn how to silkscreen. She and the store's owners had gone up to Roach Roast 2000 and fell deeply under its spell. Nessa had been to Hemp Splash in New York and festivals in Oregon, but Rainbow Farm was the only place where she felt no hostility and none of her stuff was looted. It was a cool fresh stretch of green grass where she could dance and be a sexy young kid with her dreadlocks splayed all around. She called Quincy "a living hell."

She had just stepped out of the shower at Rainbow Farm that first night and was drying off in front of the store, working on her hair, when Omar came sliding through the gravel in the powder-blue Hempulance. He got one eyeful of her and his vision swam.

"He had dreadlocks at the time and he had all kinds of beads and stuff in his dreadlocks. And I had hemp wraps, with different colors of thread and charms and beads, so the first thing we started talking about was our hair," said Nessa. "Then it was, 'You want to go start a fire?' We set up a tent, and we just hung out. Just went riding around playing bumper cars on the golf carts out in the field and stuff like that."

They made it that first night and were together constantly afterward. But there was a funny vibe at the farm. An unbearable, moonish light came off Tom, like he was gray from worry. Rollie's high chuckle had been crushed and he seemed to be constantly on the verge of tears. There was some question that the Labor Day festival wasn't really going to happen. Nessa felt like her new life might be yanked out from under her.

On Wednesday morning, Omar and Nessa came out of their love nest and down to the showers to find trucks backed up to the store and everything being hauled out of it. "We were like, 'Tom, what's going on?' And he was like, 'Well kids, it's over. There's not gonna be a festival. They've messed with us too long. You guys are gonna have to go home.'"

Tom bought Nessa's two friends train tickets out of Elkhart and back to Quincy. Nessa had made her break with that place and decided to stay with Omar.

Court papers in hand, Tom got on the phone and started calling people, telling them to come get their stuff. Along with Travis and Jim, he and Rollie crammed some of the nicest stuff into the mansion—the best furniture, Robert's entire bedroom, all the files and computers from the office, their farm and hemp memorabilia, all the expensive tools and equipment. They puttered the old Farmall up there and garaged it. Most important, Rollie gave Travis a ring with a horseshoe on it that he knew Robert would want, and looked him straight in the eye and told him under no circumstances was anyone else to have it. It was for his son, and his son only. He knew that earnest, seething Travis would take this as a sacred trust, and he did, sitting over their most precious possessions like a gnarling dog. Tom settled what debts he could, doling out supplies and equipment—bongs and pipes, hemp clothing and gear, ATVs, minibikes, golf carts, tools, the jukebox, the espresso machine, the pool tables, audio gear, four of the six wooden cabins. It all had to go.

Tom gave Dwight Vowell Sr. the contents of the store in one of those deals. Whatever was left by Thursday, he would take it all away, including the shelves, the cash register, the coolers—the lot. Mr. Vowell would later set this stuff up in the back of a tattoo shop in Cassopolis and try to sell it off as Rainbow Farm memorabilia but it was a short-lived enterprise and he later left town.

Already by Tuesday the trickle of folks turning up for the Labor Day party had turned into a steady stream. Tom had to stanch this flow, so they got on the Web site and posted a new notice: "The Labor Day event has been cancelled. Bad Government has again intervened, and the campground is closed. Stay tuned for further developments. We thank you for all your support. We love you!"

Tom shuffled through these tasks dutifully, grateful for the distraction, phasing in and out of rages and sullen drunkeness like clouds passing over the surface of Kirk Lake.

But poor Rollie seemed lost. There was his boy, only a few miles away in Edwardsburg, gearing up to go back to school in a few days. Robert was going to play trumpet in the school band and he also had floated the idea of playing football. His mother was against it, but others thought the boy would be good at it, including Mayor Mose-Ursery, who had tried to talk Tom into letting him play rocket football the year before. Rollie helped with the unburdening of all that had comprised Rainbow Farm, but every so often he was overcome and had to sit down or walk away.

Rollie rolled by Robert's school in his Beetle, casing the building to see if there were a way to snatch Robert and split. Tom had left the option open for him. In fact, as Tuesday rolled into Wednesday, Tom began to insist. He had made plans for Rollie to take what was left of their money and dash. But Rollie wasn't dashing without Robert, and he didn't know where he would go without Tom. Rollie grew panicky and disoriented, and people like Nikki who were close to him could see it.

On Monday August 27, Tom called Doug and told him he'd closed the farm. Doug drove up from Elkhart Wednesday afternoon with a heavy heart, through the heat shimmer hanging over the suddenly replenished swamps on Calvin Center Road, hoping he could talk his friend out of anything foolish.

He parked down by the store and Tom came out to meet him, giving Doug a bearhug. The two men walked out onto the property they had groomed from Maurice Williams's old derelict Maple Leaf Farm, Tom's soft and countrified version of pagan Rome, and stood on the old wooden stage smoking cigarettes to keep the mosquitoes off.

"They're puttin' it to us. They got a hearing Friday," said Tom, handing Doug the papers. "Read this."

They were papers to revoke bond and to hear an order on the forfeiture of the property.

"Man, that's off in the future," said Doug. "They can't do the forfeiture that fast."

"No," Tom said, "They lumped these both together."

Doug read them again.

"Well, what're you gonna do?"

"Well, I'm not going into court. If we go into court, they're throwing me into prison and throwin' away the key. The judge signs that order and the state owns my property. I go to that hearing, I've lost."

"Well, what're you gonna do?"

"I'm not going to it," said Tom. "I'm giving Rollie the opportunity to make up his mind and go or get out of town or do whatever."

"You know what's going to happen if you don't go to that hearing," said Doug.

"Yep, I know exactly what's gonna happen." He hesitated. The peepers howled in the trees down by Kirk Lake. "I'm trying to get Rollie to leave town and we've got about nineteen hundred bucks and I just want him to take it and get the hell outta here."

"Tell him to come to my house, then. I'll do whatever he wants. Go to Canada, Mexico, whatever. Him and Robert both. But, shit, aren't your lawyers able to do anything to postpone this?"

"Fuck them, I paid them twenty-five thousand dollars and they can't do anything about getting Robert back—they're telling me, 'Go to this hearing, and we'll discuss it in court.'"

Tom chuckled. "They can't help me. I'm gonna help myself."

Then he stuck Doug with some sentences that would give him plenty of bad nights. "Doug, I've lived a good life," he said. "I've done everything that I've wanted to do in my life. If I die tomorrow, I'm ready. I'm not scared about dying. I just don't want Rollie around here to go through all of that."

After this speech, Tom realized Doug might try to intervene. He warned him to stay away. It was to be Doug's job, he said, to make sure the real story got told, and to see after the new wills he was writing up giving everything to Robert.

That was about the last thing Doug wanted to hear. He didn't want to be involved with Tom's money anymore.

"Yeah, I know, that's going to be a shitty job, but I just don't want my family or anyone else to come in here and start grabbing everything we built for Robert," Tom argued.

After a bit of silence, Tom remembered some of his own strategy and he started talking about how he was booby trapping the trails, planting antipersonnel mines around the farm and wiring up explosives to take off any invaders. He'd been telling people this all week, firing up the troops down at The Joint with drunken boasts about how he was going to have the whole place rigged to pop. Doug had some inkling this was just bravado. Tom didn't have these materials. He was just saying it to keep everybody away from the farm, and he hoped that word would get to the cops and maybe keep them out, too.

"I don't want to have to kill anybody, Doug," Tom said. "I'm not out to kill the police or to fight with the police. I'm just not going to let Teter take it away."

In the end, the two men held each other.

"I'm sorry, Tom," Doug said.

"I love you, Doug," Tom said, then added, "Do you forgive me for the things I did and the things I said?"

"I never held any of that against you, from day one," muttered Doug. "Things worked out the way they worked out, you know, there's no hard feelings."

They walked slowly back down the two-track to the store.

Rollie knew what they were talking about. Doug asked him why he didn't do what Tom asked and split; he would help him leave the country. Hell, he might even come with him.

"I can't live without Tom, Doug," said Rollie quietly, looking straight at him. "I just can't live without him."

"Well, what about Robert?" pleaded Doug.

"I'll lose Robert, the way things are goin'. But I just can't live without Tom."

Doug got in his car and the sky was black. On the drive back to Elkhart the stars shredded the scrim hiding heaven. The street lamps and mercury lamps were far apart, and in the darkness between them time seemed to be accelerating. Doug wanted to slow it down. But there were long stretches where there were simply no lights at all.

Rollie obviously hadn't completely made up his mind about staying with Tom. On Thursday morning, his yellow Beetle pulled up outside Sam Adams school. He got out and approached one of the staff, telling them he was Robert's father and that the boy had forgotten his homework at home. Couldn't he come out and get it? When the teacher said she'd take it to him, Rollie said he must have left it at home, and drove away.

That night, Nikki left the farm just as the crew started to drink and smoke in earnest. They proceeded to get roaring drunk outside the empty camp store building.

"Travis and Jim were saying, and Tom and Rollie, too, about how they were gonna be heroes," said Omar and Nessa. "They kept on saying that, how they were gonna be heroes."

EIGHTEEN Death on Mount This

Friday, August 31

TOM MAY HAVE SET in motion his revolution, but neither he nor Rollie regarded this with the stillness of monks. Maybe the long arm of the law would somehow hit them with beanbags or tasers or gas and they'd wake up in leg irons. Maybe they'd win—cause a mutiny among some astonished county deputies and bring a flak-jacketed Teter to the table with an apology—"Okay, boys, we'll stop the forfeiture action. Now let's talk." Whatever was going to happen, Tom and Rollie—and Jim Collett, too, for he had stayed on after everyone else had left—were determined to live, and did a lot of living in these compressed minutes, the kind of clear-eyed living of gamblers who have set in motion events that can't be stopped.

They did everything they could to get innocents out of the way. When they sent Omar and Vanessa out the gate that morning, and later Buggy after the fires started, they told them to spread the word that anyone turning up out there was liable to get shot.

At around eleven thirty a.m. on August 31, Tom walked down the trail that went up over Mount This, following the power line, and across the old Goat Man parcel to Butch's house. Butch McDonald was sixty-three by then and it took him a minute to get to the door, but when he opened it he was shocked to see Tom dressed head to toe in camo and carrying the Ruger assault rifle with its big protruding clip.

"They got us up against it, Butch," said Tom.

"What you want me to do?" said the neighbor. He talked like a surly old cuss but he and Tom got along famously. He said he considered Tom "a real good neighbor."

"I think you better clear out and go to Pam's while we get this settled out. I don't want you to get hurt."

"Alright Tom, I'm clearing out."

They didn't sit around and visit long. If Tom said go, he'd go. He said that after Tom left, he "threw his truck in reverse and got out of there," leaving the house locked and heading toward his daughter, Pam's, place.

Mrs. Cox, the neighbor on the corner at Pemberton and Black, also got a call from Tom telling her it might be a good idea to "get a hotel for the weekend because it's gonna get ugly up here."

By twelve forty-five p.m., Newberg Township and Penn Township fire department vehicles sat with sheriff's vehicles near Pemberton and Black, lights flashing, as people gathered there to stare up at the sky to the north. By then, Derrik's production office was reduced to a series of iron beams and some smoking black debris. Tom, and perhaps Rollie and Jim but certainly Tom, was moving methodically from structure to structure and burning down Rainbow Farm. Smoke billowed above the trees and loud thumping explosions set off each new fire—Tom might have been using some kind of accelerant like lighter fluid to ignite them, but the buildings had also been packed with bales of dry straw. A forensic chemist later determined that none of his twenty-four debris samples tested positive for gasoline. The ticket booth in the main drive and Doug's cabin up on Mount This were both gone. Sometime between noon Friday and noon Saturday, nine of the structures on the farm would be burned—everything except the house. The camp store, Tom's pride, the greatest thing he'd ever built, wasn't particularly easy to burn, with its metal siding and concrete floors, but once the wood roof went up it melted and collapsed, burning Jim's trailer, too. The thick black smoke could be seen from every direction for ten miles. All the neighbors saw it and knew: That right there is the end of Rainbow Farm.

Mrs. Cox put her seven-year-old child in the car at noon on Friday and drove down the road to see what was happening to Rainbow Farm. She saw Tom pacing back and forth in the yard dressed in his camo and cradling a rifle and the buildings burning, and he waved her out of there, telling her to get away.

Sheriff Underwood's office was on notice about this already. During the week, he'd received some information from one of the neighbors, saying Tom had come by telling them to clear out, that "all hell's going to break loose this weekend."

Up at the farmhouse, the three men were expecting that hell to come pouring over the hill any second.

Every lazy wobble of a leaf in the heavy maples was a gesture. Every crow whose wings creaked, flapping down the power lines from Mount This, was an omen. They watched the road to the south and the woods around it because that's the way the cops would come, and during the early part of the day cars did roll past but it was mostly neighbors sneaking a peak. The afternoon heat on August 31 and the acrid smoke of the fires held the presence of men, the heat signatures, the outlines of men they were sure were in the trees on the edges of vision. They re- lied on Thai Stick to find them, walking her through the grass and the edge of the trees but staying close to the house, waiting for the assault. She barked, she stopped and froze, her eyes focusing on movement in the road that would turn out to be a squirrel or a civilian's car, and no assault ever came.

In fact, there was no cop within three-quarters of a mile of Rainbow Farm and for good reason.

At just after noon on Friday, several passers-by drove past the farm on their morning business and called in to report that the "pavilion"— which seemed to mean the camp store—was on fire. Then came a call to Cass County 911 from Butch's nephew:

R: Cass County Central
A: Uh, yes, sir. My uncle lives up there by Rainbow Farms.

R: Uh-hm.

A: And, uh, in fact, they just had a fire call come for the, uh, over the radio, because of a pavilion's on fire.

R: Uh-hm.

A: But, Tom Crosslin?

R: Um-hm?

A: . . . came down and told my uncle here, about a half hour ago, to get the hell out of there, because there's going to be trouble because Tom and a bunch of other people are all dressed in camouflage attire. Okay. And I've called up to Cass County before when uh, my uncle . . .

R: What's your name?

A: My name is Bob McDonald. Carl McDonald is my uncle, he lives right next to Tom.

R: And they said there was going to be problems, huh?

A: Well, here's the deal. My uncle also told me, and I called the police about it, that he's acquired .50 caliber guns.

R: Okay.

A: Fifty caliber, because he said the bullet's about like, uh, six, seven inches long.

R: Alright.

A: And he told him that they wasn't going to take them alive, so with the fire burning there, I don't know, it might be some kind of ploy.

R: How long ago did he tell your uncle this?

A: Um, I just, oh, probably ten minutes ago. And then I heard this fire call, 'cause I brought my scanner on.

R: So your uncle just heard it today?

A: Yes, just a half hour ago.

R: Okay, that's what, that's what Crosslin told him, right?

A: Yes, sir. And he was in camouflage uniform then, as well as other people there.

R: Okay.

A: And they got them standing around the woods with camouflage uniforms, so I don't know, just be careful, and I just wanted to tell ya anything that could help you guys out.

R: 'Preciate it.

A: Yes, sir.

R: Thank you.

A: You bet. Bye.

No one knew what to make of this except maybe Jim Crosslin. Jim had seen the guns and yeah, there was a big one. Sometime in August Tom had scraped together the money to buy weapons, and he wasn't concerned about who knew it, either; he was so proud of them he rushed right over to Jim's house to shoot them off: two brand new Ruger mini-14 semiautomatic assault rifles, chambered for the .223 military round, with 30-round banana clips and many boxes of ammo.

"If somebody comes, they're gonna be in for a nasty surprise," Tom said.

Then, said brother Jim, there was the big gun. A gun that Tom referred to as the "elephant gun" because "it was big enough to take down an elephant." It may have been a big-game gun like a Weatherby .460 or some ungodly Nitro Express caliber like a .577, but those African buffalo guns would be fairly rare. It may have been a .50 caliber rifle, he didn't really know, but they shot it that day in the back field and it was all a man could do to hang on to it. The shells were huge, just as Tom had described them for others. But it was a bolt-action rifle and not a machine gun, that much Jim knew for sure.

David Koresh's followers on Mount Carmel in Waco had a .50 caliber machine gun that kept the FBI and ATF at bay for a long time during their conflict, and this was a detail that Tom would not have missed. Maybe he thought the words ".50 caliber" were a kind of magic talisman. But whatever the "elephant gun" really was, it was no bluff.

That talisman power worked instantly. The next calls on the dispatch tape were warnings to deputies to stay out of the area, and what rang down the line, in radio calls to sheriffs, fire, ambulance, state police, and finally the FBI, all across the state, were the words: ".50 caliber machine gun."

Neither local sheriffs nor, really, the Michigan State Police had any way to deal with a .50 caliber machine gun. They could involve the local National Guard with the help of the attorney general, but if it was really going to get hairy they were going to need the feds.

Sheriff's deputies pulled in to Oli's schoolhouse and rapped on the door. His school parking lot stretched out along Black Street, mostly empty, and though Oli didn't like it much, the officers informed him they would use this big chunk of blacktop as a command post.

Sheriff Underwood called dispatch en route to the scene and was told that no one had called Rainbow Farm and they didn't have the number handy. "That's nice," he joked. "I wish they'd wait 'til I was off work." Once dispatch had looked up the number, he called. The phones were out. None of the three men there carried cell phones—only a satellite phone would get decent reception. When Buggy went home to his apartment at Oli's place, he informed the cops that the phone lines at Rainbow Farm had burned down. He was cagey, though; he didn't tell them how many men were there or how exactly they were armed. Big Jim, in particular, was never mentioned.

Teter waited until one thirty, then paged the courthouse to make sure Crosslin hadn't shown. He went back to his office and worked up arrest warrants for Tom and Rollie. He wasn't going anywhere near Rainbow Farm. Dori Leo, however, left the courthouse and rushed to the roadblock, trying to negotiate a way to get her cell phone to Tom. Undersheriff Larry Gorham was on the phone to Michigan State Police captain Richard Dragomer, the district commander in charge of nine county posts, including White Pigeon, the closest state police post, which had answered many calls to Rainbow Farm, and the local SWET team. Dragomer was very familiar with Tom Crosslin and said his men and tactical teams were on their way.

At about the same time that afternoon, with no one out at the farm but Tom, Rollie and Jim, a news helicopter from Channel 16 WNDU-TV in South Bend dipped low over the farm, getting live footage. Pilot Richard Voigt had flown for thirty-two years including taking choppers into combat in Vietnam, and his cameraman, Eric Walton, scanned the scene looking for any people down below. For Rainbow Farm supporters, this TV coverage was the first they saw of what was happening to their beloved dream. Moe and Amy were watching. Doug was watching. Travis was watching. The Crosslins who weren't at the roadblock or the command center and half of Elkhart were watching.

The Steeles were watching, too. They had retrieved Robert from school and were trying to keep him away from the TV, but their phone was ringing off the hook and Robert was bouncing off the walls. By the end of the first day the Steeles and county caseworkers had felt it best to let Robert know what was happening.

After the helicopter had circled over the farm for a few minutes, sheriff's deputies reported hearing as many as fifteen shots from a high-caliber rifle and the helicopter was ordered out of the area.

The FBI later interviewed pilot Voigt, and he said he only found out he was being shot at after a call from his dispatcher. He'd been flying at about 1000-1200 feet above the deck and saw no one and felt nothing. When he landed at the South Bend Airport, however, he found a hole in his right-side horizontal stabilizer, a small fixed wing on the tail boom of the helicopter. It went in one side and out the other, as if shot from below. Federal Aviation Administration inspector David Kepple stated he thought the stabilizer had been hit by a jacketed military round, which Voigt thought looked like a .22 bullet but which a St. Joseph County sheriff's deputy later described as being exactly like a bullet hole from an AK-47 (which is a bigger, .30 caliber round).

When word of this reached Underwood, he called in the feds. Shooting at an aircraft is a federal offense and the Federal Aviation Administration would involve the FBI. He got on the phone with special agent Roy Johnson from the FBI office in nearby St. Joseph, Michigan, and apprised him of the situation, and Johnson would come out to the command center later that afternoon.

In the meantime, the county set up a perimeter and tried to get some information on who was out there on the farm. Roadblocks had been set up well away from the action, blocking off both Pemberton Road and a stretch of Black Street (to secure their command post). Underwood, who knew Tom, was in no hurry to march out there or to flush him out. He'd never had the overheated relationship with Tom that Teter had. It was clear that Tom cared about the neighbors, having warned them to get out, but then he'd shot at a helicopter. Underwood had a shooter on his hands, and he had to know a few things.

Along with Undersheriff Gorham and detective Robert Babcock from his department, Underwood met with Buggy immediately after the copter was shot and asked him to be an intermediary. They needed somebody to go back to the farmhouse, ask Tom what he wanted, get him a phone and get a little intelligence.

Buggy told them immediately: "I'm a pot smoker. Is that going to be a problem?" The cops brushed this aside. Buggy spent the next four days as the primary link between the authorities and Tom and the whole time he had a big bag of weed and a pipe in his pocket.

Buggy was a bright and quiet man, powerfully built with shoulder-length brown hair, hooded eyes and a stubble of tough beard on a square jaw. He minded his own business, and the idea of being the eyes and ears of the law did not sit well with him. But he also thought Tom's armed stance was incredibly bad for the pot movement. He figured he could modulate this conflict, give the cops something to go on but not enough to encourage them to storm the place and save his friends' lives.

"I told [Underwood] I had no problem going back out there," said Buggy. "I'd already been out there once, and despite being told to leave, that just didn't bother me. I felt safe. Under no threat, or anything like that."

Buggy took some questions from the sheriff, and a deputy drove him down to the intersection at Pemberton and Black. From there, he walked the three-quarters of a mile to the farm. They all judged that it was too risky to send anyone back there in a car, as whomever was on the farm might open fire without knowing who it was. Buggy would make ten trips back to the farm over the next four days.

He carefully approached the house and Tom came out to meet him in the shady front yard. Nobody shot at him but they didn't let him into the house, either. Tom was in a surly mood and tried not to say anything.

"Nobody's coming back here," Buggy assured Tom, respecting his fear but trying to draw him out a little. "They're hanging out at the school and I've been sent back to find out what's going on and what you want."

But Tom wasn't hearing most of this. He was in a calm but black mood, possibly smoked-out and filled with the specter of his burned buildings. He would barely even speak. After Buggy talked for only a few minutes, Tom told him he better leave. But he didn't say he couldn't come back. Buggy walked back empty-handed.

By then CNN was taking live reports from South Bend's WNDU-TV and other TV crews had set up at the command center. Echoing all over the schoolhouse lawn were reporters repeating into their cameras that Tom and Rollie were wanted on drug charges and no one seemed to know what was at issue. There was little mention of the farm's politics, the forfeiture, or even the removal of Robert. This was incredible to farm supporters and family members—hadn't anyone filled them in on what was happening here? Could eight years of very public Rainbow Farm actions and history be reduced to one sentence that made Tom sound like a druggy lunatic? Pot activists from around the state jumped in their cars and started making their way to the farm to set the story straight.

Buggy had chores to do for the Files, then returned to the command center. By this time, Dori Leo was there and the new plan was to get a phone to the farmhouse.

So Buggy made his second trip of the day, this time carrying Dori's phone. Tom and Rollie let him in the house on that trip. It's unclear whether he saw Jim or not, but Jim was still there. They actually tried to use the phone and Tom talked to Dori for a minute but the reception cut out and then the battery went dead. This didn't do anything to help Tom's mood. Buggy sat there, frustrated, trying to talk to him.

"What am I supposed to tell them?" he asked Tom. "Who are you willing to talk to or let out here?"

"Nobody," Tom said. Then he thought about it. "Robert. I'll talk to Robert."

There were four rifles in the house, as far as Buggy could see, and he reported this to the Sheriff. They wanted to know makes and models but he said he didn't know. Still, this is more than just the rifles he'd seen Tom and Rollie carrying earlier. There were regular-sized boxes of standard ammo, black in color, roughly six inches by four inches by one inch. No big boxes, nothing that looked like .50 caliber.

They sat on the front porch and Tom said the cops had to stop sending people down the road. There were still quite a few vehicles moving, he said, and he was sure some of them were police in civilian clothes. If the cops put on a big "show of force," he said, that was just going to make it worse. He wanted everyone to leave them alone.

Buggy told them what had come out on the news about the helicopter getting shot, and Tom wanted to clear that up. He asked Buggy to make a correction to the reporters at the school.

"He apologized for that—with no indication of who actually shot at it. Because he had no intentions of hurting or threatening any civilians or anything like that," Buggy told the reporters. Tom had thought that the WNDU helicopter was police because it was blue and yellow, and it wouldn't have been shot at if they'd known it was press.

He wasn't going to hesitate, though, to shoot at the cops.

Before he left, Buggy joked that he would bring his friends breakfast, trying to establish some kind of continuity. Fine, Tom said, and gave him an order for McDonald's.

"That gave me some hope," Buggy said, "because it was clear they were planning on being there in the morning."

Buggy walked out again and went to work around four p.m. doing the evening milking at the File's. Sometime that afternoon the sheriff cut off the power to the farm. But it didn't make any difference, because Tom and Rollie had generators.

Nikki, who also lived at the school with Buggy, was in on some of these early meetings with Buggy and Underwood.

"Numerous times, they asked: What would it take to let it come to an end tonight?" she said. "And Tom sent back the message: 'Send Teter back here and you can be at home fucking your wives tonight.'"

While Buggy was at work, Underwood and the Michigan State Police let two more cars go back, against Buggy's advice.

Jim and Miriame Crosslin drove back to the farm and just pulled right into the driveway. They all cracked a few beers on the porch and after some pleasantries Jim asked Tom and Rollie point-blank to come out with him, to give themselves up. "It's just too late," said Tom. So they all sat there in the slanting late afternoon sun and smoked two joints and drank beer. Jim had brought some—he likes his Busch—but Tom wouldn't hear of it. Even on a day he thought might be the last day of his life he insisted on playing the host. "Naw," he said, "I got plenty of beer in here. We'll never drink it all. Have some of mine."

He did have plenty, too, so Jim drank it. Cases of beer were stacked up in the kitchen. He seemed to have a fair amount of weed, too. But they didn't let Jim poke around in the house. The generator was running in the basement and the TV was on. When Jim and Miriame had pulled up, Tom and Rollie were watching their own farm burning on the news.

"What about Robert?" asked Miriame.

"He would rather go visit you in prison than the cemetery," said Jim.

"You talk like that, I am going ask you to leave," said Tom, looking at Rollie.

So they sat there and chatted about old times for what must have been an hour. Tom asked them to go, and Jim didn't know what do to. He gave his brother a long hug. It had always been Tom's show but Jim sure as hell didn't want it to end.

When Jim and Miriame left, they stopped at the command center. Rollie, they said, had informed them that they had "fifty Militia members in the woods around the property." Jim told them the house was "wired with C4" (a high explosive), and that he had seen wires running through the house while he was in there drinking beer. Others later confirmed the presence of an orange cord running along the baseboards and around the windows.

Jim and Miriame also relayed that Tom was "extremely sorry" for the shooting of the helicopter and wanted the apology delivered to WNDU.

The sheriff had one more trick up his sleeve. He let Tom's mother, Ruby, go out to the farm, along with her husband, Luther Batey, and the pastor from their church. Luther was dying of cancer and this was a straight-up sympathy play. But Tom wouldn't have it. He was furious that his mother was endangered that way, in the minutes before sunset, and he wouldn't talk to them. He hugged his mom and told her he loved her, then turned them right around and sent them back down the road.

He left them with a reiteration of his warning: "Tell Underwood or whoever that anybody else comes down that road tonight gets shot. That clear? Nobody else."

Night fell and an intense quiet dropped over Rainbow Farm. Tom and Rollie and Jim were listening to the woods, but intermittently they would fire up the generator to watch TV for a bit and run the lights, which created quite a racket and obliterated their ability to hear any interlopers. Then they'd cut it again and sit in total darkness, drinking, taking shifts sleeping, watching the darkness for the assault that never came.

Once in a while, Thai Stick would bark, and reportedly the men let fly a few rounds into the darkness during the night. Shooting at shadows.

Saturday, September 1

During the night, Michigan State Police established an observation post in the woods in view of the house. This wasn't a simple tiptoe to the top of the nearest hill. Troopers crawled into the woods draped in camo and with faces and hands painted, probably pissing their pants all the way, expecting any second to meet up with these reported fifty Militia members, landmines, trip wires and possibly a .50 caliber machine gun. It was the horrible, sweat-blind, blood-in-your-ears business of men hunting men in the dark, with certain bad odds that someone would end up dead. It was reported that random rifle shots and "explosions" erupted throughout the night. Bad blood began to boil. Officers cursed Tom Crosslin for putting them in the path of random gunfire and worse, just as he was in the house cursing them for wanting to kill a guy who was standing up for their rights. The night was heavy and sleepless with biting mosquitoes and dread.

One thing troopers needed to know was how many people were on the farm. If Buggy knew anything, he wasn't saying. The men on Rainbow Farm would have viewed it as a serious escalation if these "snipers/observers" (as they were called) were discovered in the trees. The woods around the farm bent back like the oiled jaws of a bear trap, and Tom and company could feel it. As far as they were concerned, if a SWAT team was out there they weren't coming to arrest anybody. They weren't just repo men. These were the exterminators.

The observers didn't find any fifty Militia members in the woods. But they didn't just find Tom and Rollie, either. After a long, good look at the house, during which time the lights would fire up and figures were visible inside and outside, they counted three persons. There may have been more, for all they knew, but clearly Tom and Rollie weren't alone. When word reached the command center, a frantic search began for all other known employees and supporters of Rainbow Farm who were present during the May 9 raid.

Almost everyone had already been located on Friday—people like Nikki and Buggy and Travis were close at hand, and most of the others were reachable—except for Derrik DeCraene and Jim Collett.

Deputies went to DeCraene's home on the swamp outside Edwardsburg and found the place deserted. At around four a.m. on Saturday morning, September 1, the FBI started calling every DeCraene in the state of Michigan. Derrik's ninety-two-year-old grandfather got a call. It couldn't be good to be awakened by an FBI agent looking for your grandson in the dead of night. The few calls received by relatives made their way to Derrik's mom and then to friends.

"I was dating a girl about an hour or so north of here," Derrik said, indicating north of Vandalia. "I was up at her house, staying there for the weekend, or for a couple of days, whatever the case may be." They hadn't been watching TV.

"I get a call up north from one of my buddies, saying, 'The FBI is searching the state for ya.' So then I have to call everybody in my family at that point, at four thirty in the morning, and tell them, 'Yeah, it's all good. I don't know what the fuck's going on, but I'll try and get a hold of these people.' "

He called the number his mom gave him, an agent from the Kalamazoo office of the FBI, and got him at that unseemly hour. "Are you aware of the situation that's going on?" the agent asked.

"Well, yeah, I'm just now catching up to speed on whatever they're putting on the news. Other than that, that's the most I know," said Derrik.

Word was relayed down the chain of command that Derrik wasn't the third man on the farm. But they asked him to come in. Derrik packed up that morning and made his way south.

Melody Karr was out late on Friday night and came home to her place in Mesick to find a message on her machine from Trena Moss, saying there was trouble on the farm. Karr had been planning to go to the farm that weekend for the Labor Day campout, and had even talked to Rollie a week before. She only found out at the last minute that it had been canceled, so the mention of "trouble" had her worried sick.

"Well, are you going down there?" she asked Moss.

Moss didn't know what to do. They were prosecuting these boys for pot, and the two of them were pot activists. Anybody down there might be putting themselves in the way of an arrest. "I told Bill I wouldn't," she said, referring to her husband.

"I don't know what we could do, but I kinda feel like I really need to go there," said Karr.

"Yeah, okay. I'm gonna flip a coin," said Moss. She prayed to Jesus, saying, "If you want me to be there, heads I'm going, tails I'm not." It came up heads.

"He only made it come up heads 'cause He knew I was going no matter what it said!" she laughed.

Similar conversations were going on all over the Midwest. Quite a few phone calls got through to Dwight Vowell's place. By Friday afternoon, it seemed clear that a whole raft of people were going to show up. The cops wanted them away from the main barricade at White Temple Road and Black Street, so Dwight had a solution. He owned a piece of property right at the city limits where White Temple hit M-60, only a couple of hundred yards from the barricade and Oli's school. It was just at the edge of town and the most visible spot available, right under the big white bulb of the water tower, and if protestors wanted to put up tents there and make a camp, that was fine with him.

When Karr and Moss showed up around one p.m. Saturday afternoon, there were already people at the M-60 camp. Dinky, his nephew Darrel, Travis and another guy named Johnny Muday were waving handmade signs at passing cars and talking to the occasional reporter. Travis was supposed to be watching the stuff at the mansion, but occasionally Nikki or someone would spell him for a few hours. Karr pulled in and pitched a tent. She wouldn't get home again to her job until the second week in October.

Over the next two days, the camp would swell, with perhaps two dozen people camping there and locals popping in and out at all hours. They kept a fire burning at night and the neighbor let them run power and water off her house. She even brought them a TV so they could see the news. At one point, Robert's school bus driver stopped by to express support.

For the most part, the protests were civil. They held cardboard signs hand-lettered in paint and magic marker that read Free Tom Now and War On Peace, Stop Murder Now and Honk 4 Freedom. Travis and Darrel had a battery-powered bullhorn and they would witness to police within earshot, shouting, "It's a campground, not a compound! Don't kill our friends!"

But there were times when things got hot. A supporter from Kentucky got arrested down at the barricade after he told one of the troopers to go fuck himself.

One by one, however, the reporters drifted over to the camp and got a taste of the larger story, hints at the years of conflict on Rainbow Farm and the burden of the forfeiture statutes. Still, with so many details about the developing standoff itself, newspaper and TV reporters were looking mostly for emotional outbursts. Early on a novelist from Chicago turned up to get the inside story for *Rolling Stone*. Karr and Moss and their crew from Traverse City ended up doing a lot of talking.

"Whenever we saw cameras or a reporter coming our way, we intercepted them," Karr said, "because if we didn't, they ended up cornered by the drunkest, most belligerent asshole out there and Tom and Rollie just didn't need that."

At sunrise, Tom popped off a few rounds from the Ruger to let everyone know he was up and at 'em. Jim and Pops could hear the shots in Vandalia. The first time they heard them they were worried, but later it was a reassurance, a signal from Tom that said, "I'm still here."

Midmorning Buggy drove to the farmhouse in his white '91 Toyota van with bags of food from McDonald's. Tom and Rollie looked pale and their eyes were bloodshot, having endured a long night of beer, coffee, cigarettes, dope and sense-numbing paranoia. Buggy asked again what could be done to end this but he and Tom didn't chat long. During Buggy's visits to the farm, Rollie was always there but rarely spoke. That wasn't unusual for Rollie; he generally let Tom do all the talking anyway, but Rollie seemed completely detached, unable to even utter a word, especially his son's name. Tom, however, brought it up. He said at last that he wouldn't be able to do any negotiating until he'd talked with "our son" Robert.

Buggy brought this back to Agent Johnson and the others at the command center. This was not what they wanted to hear. Putting Robert on the phone might be giving them a way to say good-bye. Johnson, whom Buggy described as a "profiler," had essentially taken over as Buggy's chief contact at that point, and he agreed they could simply wait. Let Tom cool down.

Teter showed up on the scene Saturday morning and tried to get in on the debriefing after Buggy came back from his first visit. The prosecutor immediately spied Nikki hanging around nearby—she lived there, of course—and barked, "What's she doing here? She's one of them!"

Buggy overheard this and looked up from the debriefing.

"If you don't get rid of that guy right now, I'm all done. I quit," he told Johnson.

Teter was urged to go and he did leave. Just the sight of him sent the family members and farm supporters into a rage, and that was hurting negotiations. He never came back. It was understood that he'd be kept informed by phone about any major developments. At that point, Underwood became the official media spokesman.

That morning at five past eleven, two troopers from a state police "emergency services" squad—a SWAT team—crawled to the observation point and stayed out there for several hours, getting a good look at all three men walking on the road in front of the farmhouse. They referred to them in a written report as "Camo's ball cap mini-14"— meaning camo-wearing guy with a baseball cap carrying the Ruger mini-14—"Camo's 'doe rag' AR-15"—someone with a bandana on his head carrying a Colt AR-15 assault rifle—and "Camo's Ball Cap 'Long Gone'"—a transliteration from "long gun."

At this point, identifications were still shaky. It stands to reason that the third man would have been identified as Collett after direct observation by officers, but no mention of him appears in either of the three-inch-thick FBI or Michigan State Police reports until later that day. Collett would be identified that day, but agents would still be unsure there weren't more people at the farm. The FBI agent in charge was still making it a priority to get a third person ID'd on Monday, after Collett would be out of the picture. It's still unclear whether or not other people, never named, might have made brief forays into the farm.

According to the Michigan State Police aviation section, officers had heard what they thought were chainsaws buzzing on Rainbow Farm during the night and they needed to know if the boys had dropped trees in the road to block assault vehicles. There was no plan yet to launch an assault, but the Michigan State Police SWAT commander was putting one together. It seems likely that what they were hearing was one of the farm's generators, but a fixed-wing police airplane took off from Niles airport to check it out.

After circling the farm at about 2,000 feet and having difficulty seeing anything because of the dense forest canopy, the Michigan State Police pilot made one final pass at low altitude, flying at about 1,000 feet above ground right up Pemberton Road from the south at 138 miles per hour. Gunfire erupted from the farm and Lt. Mike Risko from the Paw Paw post reported a volley of shots fired and told the plane to pull out of there. It wasn't hit.

Officers decided they needed armor, so Agent Johnson and Captain Dragomer called in at least two light armored vehicles, or LAVs, which are part of the armory for Michigan State Police emergency support teams. The standard General Motors LAV III wasn't going to do much good if Tom and Rollie really had a .50 caliber machine gun up there, but it would stop the .223 Rugers or AR-15 they'd seen the men carrying. The LAVs were delivered by truck to Oli's house, and bounced off their carriers in a puff of black smoke. Rainbow Farm supporters and family members who had gathered there saw these things—which many of them later called "tanks," but these LAVs had no guns on them—and their hearts sank. Oli's yard was full of helicopters and troop transports and several SWAT teams, and now these camouflaged eight-wheeled assault vehicles; with every escalation, the place was taking on deeper aspects of a military operation. It was looking more and more like Waco.

Derrik showed up at the command center and was ushered into a room at the school. He thought they were going to ask him to do the negotiating that Buggy was doing, but talk moved in another direction. It started out friendly enough, but it quickly got ugly.

"They wanted a bunch of information from me that I couldn't supply," Derrik said. "Apparently their biggest problem was that they had tried to shut off Tom and Rollie's electricity to make their conditions more miserable, but they still had power at the house. And they were asking me stuff like that, and I was like, 'Man, I don't know. I've been gone for like a couple months.'"

Who had Tom and Rollie been talking to? Had they been stockpiling food or supplies? Had they been acquiring weapons?

"Dude, I've been gone since May fifteenth, and here we are September one. You're asking the wrong dude. If you want to know about our payroll or taxes or somethin', that kind of info I'm privvy to."

That line of questioning petered out. But another guy came in to talk to him and he wasn't sure if this man was FBI or state police or what, but the attitude changed.

"They wanted me to tell them that Tom and Rollie were sellin' pot," said Derrik. "Well, the truth was, they weren't. They never fuckin' sold pot. Nobody on the staff sells pot. If you need pot, somebody will *give* you some. So I told told them that: 'You might as well go on their taxes and hope that you find a loophole that I missed somewhere. Because you're barkin' up the wrong tree. They're not drug dealers. They're pot smokers. And they're just a little bit pissed off right now.'"

More people came into the room. They put warm bodies around him and the room got too tight. Derrik could see what was happening. They were going for the big justification for this whole prosecution: They'd have it if they could get the testimony of the former Rainbow Farm campground manager that the staff there were dealing drugs. And they weren't taking no for an answer.

"So then they put you in the spotlight and let the bright lights shine, have a couple guys lean over the desk and go, [shouts], 'We know that you're privy to this information! You've seen everything that goes on, here! We can make your shit a living hell!' And they give me the rigmarole about how they could threaten my security, too, which I really don't care to discuss."

As had happened with the woman from the Michigan State Treasury Department, the shouting stopped once they got the details and realized that Derrik had been filing the farm's taxes correctly.

"All they needed to know was that I had my 1038s prepared for the IRS. That's all they needed to hear, that I even knew what that form was, they were freakin'," he said. "Once they heard me say that, they were like, 'Oh, fuck.'"

Derrik was cut loose but told not to disappear. He was pissed about the threats, but tried to keep some perspective. He wanted to do what he could to help Tom and Rollie. Later that same day, they called him back in to the command center.

The second interview session was a little less acrimonious. A Michigan State Police detective asked him, "What can we do to ease the tension in this thing here?"

Derrik is the kind of straight shooter who says exactly what he thinks even when he probably shouldn't. "Well, those guys have been holed up in there and they're probably not real comfortable," he said. "Send 'em some pot."

His interviewer snorted, "What? You're—let's be real here, dude."

"I am being real. They're pot activists. Smokin' a joint's not going to make 'em wig out no more than you guys pointin' your guns at 'em and driving your armored vehicles up their driveway. If you want to provide an olive branch, go in your little evidence room and pull out the finest sack of green you got and ship it up there as a token."

At this point, the officers present laughed him out of the room. "Dude, you're a loon. Get the hell outta here. Go home."

Sometime during that Saturday afternoon or early evening, a most remarkable thing occurred: Jim Collett walked off Rainbow Farm and disappeared. And it wasn't even that hard to do. There were over one hundred law enforcement officers deployed on this deal, but the perimeter itself was more than porous—it didn't even exist beyond a couple of armed officers and a squad car on four checkpoints on the roads. Straight out the front door to the east of the farmhouse lay miles of unpoliceable swamp owned by the Department of Natural Resources, leading eventually to Savage Road. Off the back of Rainbow Farm's property, to the west, northwest and southwest, lay Kirk Lake and the Files's property. The beans were thick and the corn was almost ripe, reaching far above a man's head, and there were two-tracks all through this property.

However Jimbo did it, he walked out and away. Tom and Rollie were alone on Rainbow Farm.

At about five p.m. that night, a sheriff's detective named Todd Younts reported from his position at Born and Black Streets that he was taking rifle fire from the intersection of Pemberton and Black, just 150 yards over a low hill from where he was parked. Somebody had walked down to that intersection and sent two shots in their direction. The deputies hid behind their patrol car and then pulled back to M-60. Perhaps this was cover fire under which Jim slipped away, or maybe this was Jim shooting his way out, but no law enforcement ever reported Jim as having shot anything.

The evening took a strange twist for Jimmy Lee Collett, though. Later that night he was picked up by the Cass County Sheriff's Department and held in Cass County jail on an unrelated charge. He was wanted on an outstanding warrant out of Indiana for criminal confinement with a weapon, a Class D felony.

That same night, Cass County detective Bob Babcock interviewed "Jimmy Collett"—as he was called in a Michigan State Police report on the event—in the local jail. He admitted he'd been in the residence at Rainbow Farm. More, he told Babcock he'd witnessed Tom "wiring the house to explode," using propane tanks, gas cans, bales of straw and orange detonation cord inside the house. He said that a hundred-pound propane tank had been set up right by the stairs near the kitchen, and furniture was propped up against doors and windows, and a huge amount of clothing and paper scattered over the floor.

On September 7 Jimbo was turned over to the Elkhart County Sheriff's Department and was later convicted of the confinement charge and sentenced to eighteen months in an Indiana prison with credit for 103 days served and equal good-time credit. After some months, he got parole and a year and a half probation.

Maybe all this was by design or just a warped twist of fate. He served his time for family issues and was never tied to the Rainbow Farm investigation. Collett had a record in Michigan, the 1995 assault, but he was never listed as a suspect in several thousand pages of investigation documents. Maybe they let him go in exchange for a little information. Contacted in Kentucky, his only comment to me was, "The story of Rainbow Farm has already been told."

Buggy went back out to the farm two more times that day, but little progress was made. There was no phone and Tom simply wasn't doing anything until he and Rollie could talk to Robert. Buggy left the farm in the twilight, listening to the crystalline *eee-oh-lay* of a thrush as the last rays of sun backlit the clouds of bugs and the shifting dust. With state snipers/observers watching, Tom and Rollie fired about ten random shots into the darkness that night.

Sunday, September 2

The FBI's special agent in charge, John Bell Jr., showed up early Sunday morning, September 2, from the Detroit office. After discussions with

Captain Dragomer, he agreed to formally commit federal agents and resources to the situation—prompted by the shots at the helicopter and the Michigan State Police plane. But Bell didn't immediately bring in new tactical forces that changed the situation much at Rainbow Farm. He didn't roar in with tanks to insert gas through the walls or other heavy ordnance. State police already had snipers out and had their light armored vehicle, which they hadn't used yet, and so that's right where he left things.

It's hard to know how far the FBI was prepared to go with this. Because of ongoing lawsuits over what took place on Rainbow Farm, FBI personnel have not been made available to interview for this book, so all we can know is what they put in field logs, reports and legal documentation acquired through discovery and FOIA.

Both Sheriff Underwood and Prosecutor Teter, though happy to have federal help, later expressed concern about the FBI taking over the situation. To Underwood the Rainbow Farm people were at least familiar faces, his neighbors, and he was determined to wait this out. He was the locally elected cop; he had to live with the results.

Teter thought they were going to leave him with a bloody mess.

"That was my fear: that they'd take over," he said. "I've talked to other people who've had the FBI come in on one thing or another, [and they said] the FBI comes in and basically tells everybody else, 'Get the hell out of the way, because we run it now.' But that was not my experience. Granted, they have their own operational manual that they follow. And it's pretty strict, in terms of what their procedures are and what they do with their manpower. They direct themselves."

Teter stayed close to his office and the sheriff's office throughout the weekend. Bell and other agents kept him up to speed.

"They were real thorough about at least making sure that I knew what was going on," said Teter. "At some point, I'd be responsible to answer."

One thing is clear: Bell and Dragomer agreed to not rush Rainbow

Farm. The report of FBI investigator Robert Sligh in Memphis states: "SAC Bell and MSP agreed that no assault plan would be developed at that time. Rather, the purpose of the tactical plan was to contain Crosslin and Rohm, develop additional intelligence, and attempt to negotiate a peaceful resolution."

The Bureau had taken lots of flak after the disasters at Waco and Ruby Ridge, and their approach to armed standoffs had changed somewhat by 2001. There was no official policy memo sent around that Justice Department watchers were aware of, but FBI director Louis Freeh acknowledged during the 1996 confrontation with the Montana Freemen that the agency used "a fundamentally different approach" than was used at Waco or Ruby Ridge. Two years later, after five of the Freemen were convicted in court, U.S. Attorney General Janet Reno's office issued a statement saying, "During the standoff, law enforcement authorities implemented new procedures adopted by attorney general Janet Reno and FBI Director Louis Freeh. The standoff ended peacefully." That tactic, presumably, carried over in 2001 to President Bush's just-installed attorney general John Ashcroft and acting FBI director Thomas Pickard as well.

But what did it mean that they would *contain* Crosslin and Rohm? Obviously they weren't talking about sealing off the area completely, because Big Jim loped right on out of there *no problemo* and other people would prove their perimeter was porous at best. With the Freemen, the FBI had set up on the fence, in plain sight of the occupants, and gone no farther, effectively sealing off a mile-square area. On Rainbow Farm, however, the state police and FBI method of containing Tom and Rollie was like tightening an invisible noose. Snipers ignored the perimeter but surrounded the house while hidden in the woods. Sooner or later, the men on the farm would feel the rope. And then you'd have a confrontation.

The local feel of the standoff changed quickly with the FBI's arrival. Tactical teams pulled in from Detroit and all over the state. It was inevitable that some of these men would have a minimum of information: The floor plans of the house. What breed of dog. Which is their gun hand. An entire life can get reduced to this. Justice Department agents came in from Washington, D.C., including a hostage negotiator who had worked similar situations in the past. Cass County forces were less and less involved.

Underwood and some of his detectives stayed on at the school but sheriff's deputies turned the roadblocks over to the state police. It was an FBI/Michigan State Police show after that.

Faithful Buggy turned up with another McDonald's order and drove to the farm at around ten a.m. Bell and Johnson and others had filled him in on a new plan. Officers were going to try to set up speakers close to the house so they could inform Tom of their movements, even if he wouldn't talk to them. Then, agents were going to hardwire a phone, running a new line in from the corner. They asked that the men please not shoot at officers or phone guys setting this up.

Buggy blew a joint with Tom and Rollie and relayed all this while they ate. Tom's mood was deteriorating. By now, there'd been a lot of shooting at what he thought were cops moving around in the woods, at helicopters, at airplanes. That was only going to end badly. Buggy sat with them and tried to get some small promises, but Tom wasn't giving them. He wouldn't commit to using any such phone and asked Buggy not to come back again that day.

Early that afternoon, state troopers ran the LAV down the road to the farmhouse to set up the speakers and to try to drop a cell phone, possibly by chucking it onto the lawn wrapped in what they called a "mitten." They didn't get very far. The speakers were set out and as someone inside the LAV tried to hail the house at two fifty-two p.m., six shots were fired. A loud "Fuck you!" was heard coming from the house, followed by another twelve to eighteen rounds. Tom or Rollie or somebody was shooting at the LAV, hitting it, sparks flying and lead ricocheting off into the woods. They also shot at the speakers. The officers didn't return fire but spun around and headed out, chased by one last shot at their tails. The speakers were unusable. The plan to drop the cell phone was abandoned. Observers heard music blasting in the house later that evening.

Between six thirty and seven thirty that night, the FBI's SWAT personnel deployed to the woods for the first time. State police and FBI had decided to split the duty in twenty-four-hour shifts, so there would be no mix-ups in assignments, techniques, radio protocols and all the rest. FBI special agents Richard Salomon, Michael Heffron and Jeffery Peterson were dispatched to an observation post on top of Mount This designated Sierra 1. Snipers also established positions called Sierra 2 and 3 in the same stretch of woods south of the house. The trees and underbrush were dense up on Mount This, and unless you were on the two-track, you could only see some of the house and yard. But you could also see parts of Pemberton Road and the main trail that went to Butch's house.

So there were at least three FBI snipers, probably some of the best shooters around, who could have hit Tom and Rollie and Thai Stick at any time as they moved around in the house and yard. But they didn't. They waited.

Salomon, Heffron and Peterson squatted in the woods until about four thirty a.m. Monday morning and were off until eleven a.m. That morning was characterized in their logs by a "lack of activity." Only about "10 shots" were fired from the farm that morning.

It's a mark of a well-loved man that, when he's up on the ledge, scores of people turn up who think they can talk him down. Hundreds of people felt close to Tom and Rollie, even people who really didn't know them all that well, like Buggy. All day long, calls came in to the command center from people who were just certain that they could talk Tom and Rollie out of that house. Leslie Pletcher called at nine forty-five a.m. to tell them she was Rollie's ex-wife and would "like to talk him out." Tom's sister, Shirley, turned up at the school wanting to go to the property, and her boy Jon and Larry's son Benji were ready, too. Pops had come by and was turned away. Jim and Miriame's son, Boss, sat at the barricade all day Saturday, Sunday and most of Monday, not even leaving to eat or drink, having people shuttle food to him, just on the offhand chance he might get in to talk some sense into his hero, his Uncle Tom.

It wasn't just family. Adam Brook thought he could have talked him out if he'd been allowed in. Same with Ben Masel, who'd barely even met Tom. Stephen Gaskin said he was "sick over it," and, "I know that he would have listened to me if I could have got there." Tom's old truck-driving buddy Phil Overholser said, "If I'd a known it was happening, I know I could have talked him out of there." Nikki was sure she could have appealed to them for Robert's sake. And on and on.

At the very least, people thought they might be able to persuade Rollie to leave.

Across the block on Quaker Street, Brandon Peoples—Bones—felt he was the one. He would talk to them. He had only been to the farm for the first time that summer—Omar had picked him up one day when he'd had a bad fight with Shelly and they both went to Rainbow Farm to fish for bluegills in Tom's pond. That's what people went there for, to cool out, to think. Over the summer, Peoples had developed a strange love-hate relationship with the place. He was a rabid homophobe—acquaintances say he was just incredibly raw about this—but he was drawn inexorably to Tom. Brandon seemed to indicate that Tom had some answers for him, for something gnawing away at him. Tom would smoke a bowl with you and not judge; even a kid like him was welcome. The community needed this guy, Brandon needed him and he was going to try to save him. Early in the morning, he was pacing around the Routley's house, where he was with Shelly, then he went back to bed for a while, trying to make up his mind what he was going to do.

Monday, September 3

At his eight a.m. briefings the next morning, John Bell reiterated that they still needed to "ID subject #3," their third man. This is confusing, as Collett had already been interviewed in jail. Maybe someone else was out there, who later left. Agency profilers were busy building a psychological work-up on Crosslin, and they decided to go out to interview Tom's mother right away that morning, dispatching an agent named Ramirez.

Buggy turned up with the McDonald's breakfast as usual, and agents had planned to wire him with a microphone so they could hear his conversation with Tom. But for whatever reason—Buggy didn't suffer law enforcement group-think too well—at about eleven twenty he started out to the farm without getting outfitted, much to the agents' frustration.

Out at the house Tom's fatigue had turned to rage. The LAV had scared him—now they had tanks and an assault was imminent!—and he described to Buggy how he and Rollie had blasted the machine and how the sparks flew. The speakers in the woods were an outrage—were they going to play heavy-metal music to keep him up all night like he was Manuel Noriega? He suspected there were agents in the woods even then creeping in on him.

But most of all, Tom said, the fuzz were pissing them both off by not letting them talk to "our son" Robert. Robert had to be involved now or they were just stuck. And thanks for breakfast.

Out at the Steeles', Robert agreed that morning to make a tape recording and write a letter to his dad to let him know he was okay, but agents reported he didn't want to go to the farm. Special agent Andrew M. Bartnowak, an FBI hostage negotiator out of Detroit, went out to see Robert, made the recording and carried it back along with the letter. In his beautiful, shaky handwriting, all print, no cursive, with scribbled-out corrections and misspellings, it read:

From your son Robert
Hey dad please come out so no one gets hurt
I love you a lot we can do all of he fun things
we did befor O.K. dad I love you a lot!!!!

You remember all of the good things we
use to do like playing paint ball wars
or playing bumper cars on the golf carts.

I am safe and O.K. I am in good shape
in tell you get out.

Love Robert

Agents Salomon, Heffron and Peterson returned to their hilltop post at around one p.m., just after Buggy split. They came and went in a real-tree hush and Buggy never saw them, but they saw him. They made whispered radio contact with the command post and told them only one of them could get reception out there and they had to move around a lot up on Mount This to stay in contact.

Soon the radios popped with new information: Several observers reported they had a visual on a new subject walking into the farm through the back fields, a young man, shortish, skinny, blond haired, eighteen to twenty years old. He didn't appear to be armed. They needed an ID.

Nobody could help the feds much with this because nobody at the farm really knew Brandon Peoples. Maybe Nikki or Derrik could have picked him out of a photo, if they'd had a photo, but Buggy didn't know him at all and around the Tactical Operations Center, or TOC, as Oli's schoolhouse was now called, his identity remained a mystery.

"I left around one or two p.m. I saw and talked to some police officers by two armored cars and then walked through the woods," Brandon told the FBI later. "Riley [sic] and Tom invited me into their house."

Brandon had left the Routley household on Quaker and just walked in through the farm paths and woods—*barefoot!*—which took him about an hour and a half. He saw some men cutting hay and then ran into a couple of armored vehicles with four to eight officers standing around in camouflage, some of them in helmets and vests. He motioned to the

LAV there and said, "Do they float?" and the men laughed. He went on his way making like he was just moving down the road. At some point he ducked into the fields and stole onto the farm.

He didn't even know Rollie's real name—thought it was Riley—and the men were none too happy to see him, but Tom told Brandon he had "balls of steel" to have walked through all those cops, and barefoot, and invited him in. The deal was he could stay for a while, maybe help them make a run down to neighbor Butch McDonald's house for food, but then he'd have to go. Tom and Rollie told him that it was no game, that there was shooting going on, and how they'd nicknamed the LAV "Sparky" because of the way the bullets bounced off when they shot it. They didn't want to be responsible for getting him killed. Tom showed him around the house and told him to be careful of some wires because the house was rigged to burn. One wire ran from the back door to some pillows behind the couch in the living room. He also told him the lawn and the trails were mined and that he was damn lucky he made it all the way to the house in one piece. Brandon told the FBI he saw a wooden crate in the living room with the words mines explosives printed on it. The bit about the mines and trip wires turned out to be a ruse, and maybe the part about the house being rigged, too, but Brandon believed Tom and was scared by the prospect of having to make his way back to Shelly's.

It was just the three of them, then. Tom told Brandon there had been another guy, but "he took off when the shooting started." Brandon was shown a photograph of Collett two days later and acknowledged that he'd seen the guy ten to fifteen times at the Rainbow Farm store that summer.

Meanwhile Buggy was driving big spools of wire up and down Pemberton Road helping the Verizon worker put in a new phone. Verizon would later mail Rainbow Farm a bill for nine hundred dollars for this; Doug sent the bill to Teter. Buggy drove out to the farm and dropped a spool of wire in the yard, then went back to the junction box on Black

Street and began walking the wire out. When he ran out of wire halfway to the house, he realized he should have dropped the spool at the halfway point, so he walked to the farm to retrieve it. He came into the house around two thirty just to let the guys know what he was doing. Tom said that was fine, he'd talk on the phone so long as they'd get Robert on there. Brandon saw Buggy and Buggy saw Brandon, but Buggy didn't know the kid and he told agents when he was pressed that he'd never seen this kid before.

Buggy was busting his ass to save his friends and it was wearing on him. He wasn't too thrilled to see some other kid show up out there, though it might make Tom think twice about shooting at anybody. He finished wiring the farm end of the phone at about three thirty and went back to finish it up at the other end.

Tom and Rollie were drinking beer and smoking some weed Buggy had given them but Brandon didn't join in. He'd smoked with them down at the store during the summer but he was seeing already that it was time to get out of there. The skies were darkening with a real heavy summer thunderstorm. Tom told him, okay, it's time go to Butchies. He gave Brandon a pair of hemp shoes to put on his feet and told him to keep them, a souvenir of Rainbow Farm.

Brandon said Tom and Rollie made it sound like Butch had stocked his place for them, but Butch said later he just happened to have a few things in the house. Tom picked up the Ruger and made sure he had a shell chambered. He warned Brandon to stay right by him because the trails were mined. Brandon declined to carry a gun but carried a feather for good luck.

Rollie stayed in the house with Thai Stick, in touch with Tom via two-way radio.

They went up and over Mount This with Tom struggling a bit up the steep and sandy trail, walking within twenty yards of the three agents frozen up on Sierra 1. Agent Peterson had moved into a fairly visible position near the campsite in order to get better radio reception, and he suddenly whispered into his radio that Crosslin and unidentified #3 had just passed their position, heading south. He had almost been seen and he quietly moved to better cover after they passed. At Butch's house, Tom went to the front door, which was secured by a large silver lock, and just shouldered it in. Brandon said it gave way so easily he thought it had just been pulled closed.

Inside, there were five cartons of cigarettes sitting on an end table. Tom fished two black trash bags out of the kitchen, double-bagged them, and they threw the ciggies in it along with coffee, coffee filters, hot dogs, a twelve-pack of Miller Lite, some frozen steaks, bread and other food. Tom took a look around the place. There were guns everywhere, unlocked, at least one of them loaded. It was well known that Butch was armed; guns had been stolen from his place at least twice in the eight years he'd lived there. There was a dummy grenade sitting on top of one of the dressers in plain sight. Tom picked up a .22 varmint gun from a gun cabinet and offered it to Brandon. "Don't you want to stick around and have some fun?" he joked. Brandon turned it down. Tom took none of the weapons or ammo. He picked up the coffeemaker and Brandon carried the food and they headed back up the trail.

Butch and his daughter, Pam McDonald, later said it was robbery. It was a ninety-dollar Bunn coffeemaker and they wanted it back. In an interview, Butch and Pam wouldn't say that it was Tom that came and got this stuff. All they knew is that some sumbitch kicked the door in and robbed them and the door cost eighty dollars to fix. Doug said that he came over later and bought Butch a new door.

"If I'da known he was coming over, I woulda left the door unlocked," Butch rasped.

They went up and over the hill, breaking a sweat in the dead heat of the afternoon, deer flies and mosquitoes worrying their necks. They were too preoccupied to notice any agents squatting in the woods. Tom and Brandon hauled their swishing, clanking loot down the slope and into the house. The agents on Sierra 1 whispered that the men were back in the residence.

Around four thirty, Buggy showed up again at the farmhouse to announce that the phone was in. They burned one and then he and Tom dialed the command center. The negotiator, Andy Bartnowak, got on the line. Buggy went to hand the phone to Tom but Tom refused, saying he meant what he said: He'd only talk to Robert. He'd have to talk through Buggy, so Buggy stayed on with Andy. Tom barked, "Tell them I will talk to the FBI only after I talk to Robert." Andy said that wasn't going to be possible, they were going to have to start somewhere else. Tom flew off the handle, shouting comments heard on the other end of the phone. "Fuck these motherfuckers, who are they to put stipulations on me?!" he shouted. "They're the ones that took my kid away! Fuck the FBI! Hang that shit up!" Buggy hung up. Tom told him it wasn't his fault, he knew Buggy had worked hard to get that phone in there, but he was going to have to take it all back out. Tom told him he wanted to have a "heart to heart with Robert." That sounded like it would be a good-bye speech, as far as Bartnowak was concerned. "Just get that shit out of here, I'm not talking to them," Tom said.

Buggy drove back, dejected, with the phone in the car. He left the phone wire laying in the road. Dark clouds were tumbling in the sky overhead, but there was still little breeze on the ground. Nothing was moving, and there was no reason to think anything was happening in the woods. But by the time he rolled back to the TOC at the school—a drive of maybe five minutes—the Detroit FBI's Blue Team, their assault backup, blew past in the LAV. Followed by the paramedics.

According to FBI interviews with Brandon and the shooters, it happened like this.

Just as Buggy left, Rollie said, "Well, what did the neighbor have stocked for us?" Tom went through the bag and realized they'd brought the coffeemaker and coffee but forgotten the coffeepot at Butch's house.

Tom asked if Brandon would go back on his own to get it (pretty strong evidence the trail wasn't actually mined). He'd be safe, he assured him. No cops were looking for him. Brandon said there was no way he was going out there to tiptoe through the trip wires. Besides, he said, he was going to have to leave soon. Tom was sweated by the walk and didn't want to go, but he was desperate for the wake-up of that hot coffee. Quickly he made up his mind. Okay, they'd go back to the house together and then Tom would walk Brandon off the property safely.

They went out the door at five seventeen. As they went up the hill again, Brandon still carrying his feather, he was literally walking in Tom's footsteps, feeling less and less secure about the mines allegedly on the trail. He was more aware of the distance this time, counting the minutes before he could get out of there, growing paranoid. They walked the two-track to where it joined the finished gravel camp road, through thickets of dogwood and raspberries and massive azaleas and clouds of gnats, then up through Butch's yard. Again, Tom shouldered the door in. Brandon carried the coffeepot with the words "Bunn Pour-o-Matic" on the side as they pulled the door closed and made their way back.

They came up to the top of Mount This at about five twenty-three. The distances were relatively short, the trips were quick. Tom stopped then and bent down. Brandon thought he tied his shoe. Tom needed to stop and rest; he was winded. The lack of sleep and the constant diet of beer and weed were slowing him down. At the bottom of that hill was coffee waiting to be made.

Suddenly Tom stiffened. "Shh," he said to Peoples. "Did you hear that?" Brandon was standing directly behind Tom, looking down, having been watching his footprints in the dust. Tom touched his two-way radio and said to Rollie: "Incoming." As Tom crept forward a few strides toward a small campfire ring, where Rainbow Farm's Peace Police had camped, Brandon grew frightened because Tom was walking off the trail. He took two, three steps, trying to walk exactly where Tom walked.

Tom moved into the campsite holding the Ruger in both hands, looking down into a trashcan there, studying the ground. The agents were only ten yards away but the undergrowth was thick and they were well camouflaged. He looked right at Agent Peterson but didn't see him, then turned away. The agents said in their report they hoped he would not make them out and they'd just let him walk away. But Peterson said he was watching Tom's face from close range as he moved slowly around the campsite, walking directly toward Agent Salomon. Peterson took advantage of a moment when Tom slipped behind two trees to readjust his gun hand. When Tom was visible again, he saw the flash of recognition flicker across his eyes, then Tom froze on Agent Salomon's position.

"Almost instantaneously, Crosslin began to raise the mini 14 and lean forward in a shooting position with his index finger in the trigger guard," Peterson wrote in his report. "Certain that Crosslin was about to fire on SA Salomon, SA Peterson began to squeeze the trigger of his M-16. Before he could fire, he heard two almost simultaneous shots and Crosslin dropped, almost falling on the youth."

Peterson was carrying an M16 A1 .223 rifle, Heffron an M4 .223, and Salomon was carrying a Bureau-issue .308 sniper rifle. Heffron's shot evidently passed through a small tree and shattered, with fragments hitting Tom under the arm and in the gun hand.

Tom never squeezed off a shot.

Brandon heard someone shouting "FBI! FBI! Put it down! Stop! FBI!" But he didn't remember that until days later. If Tom did raise his gun, Brandon never saw it.

But he felt what he didn't see. And what he felt was Tom's head exploding in a cloud of red. Salomon hit Tom almost between the eyes.

Salomon's .308 slug blew Tom's entire brain out the back of his head, sending bone shards and blood raking across Brandon's face where he stood, immobilized. Tom was dead before he hit the ground. Brandon fell, in hysterics, screaming, "I'm hit! I'm hit!" Peterson and the others rushed up to cover him, shouting, "FBI, show us your hands, show us your hands!" Brandon didn't know what do to. He was covered in blood, maybe his own, hunched on his hands and knees behind Tom's body. He shouted to the agents that he was "going into shock." He was so horrified that he went into a kind of paralysis; he couldn't move. Agents were shouting at him and he couldn't seem to make out what they were saying. After long minutes, what seemed like an infinitely folded eternity packed into an instant, Brandon managed to straighten up into a kneeling position and raise his hands, shaking violently.

He stayed like that, shuddering uncontrollably, unsure whether his own head had blown up, too, looking down on Tom's body, Tom's brain laying in the leaves about two feet to the side, until Heffron came around and put handcuffs on him and pulled him away.

At five twenty-five the call came. Shots fired. Five thirty, two subjects down and shot, medical en route. Five thirty-three, one dead, one in custody.

Jim Crosslin watched the helicopters buzzing his house all weekend and tried to distract himself by cutting wood both Saturday and Sunday. Boss was waiting at the barricades at Black Street and White Temple Road, so if anything happened he'd know soon enough.

On Monday night, around nine p.m., Miriame saw a county car pull into Pops's place.

"When Tom was killed, they did not bother to tell us," said Miriame. "They sent somebody to tell Ruby and she found out at six something and we did not find out until almost the nine o'clock news was coming on—when they told Grover. I found out because I had a scanner here. They were down at Grover's and I told Jim, 'Let's go, something's going on.'"

"There wasn't no reason to kill my Tom," Ruby said. Over a period of months she constantly postponed giving me an interview, often saying she couldn't meet because she needed to get her hair done, unaware perhaps that she'd said the same thing the day before. "They coulda wounded him or shoot to maim. They shouldn't have antagonized him so. Why would they put people in the woods like that?"

The rain was imminent, the first drops were falling, and Karr and a few others at the White Temple barricade ran back to the M-60 camp at around eight p.m. to cover up the neighbor's TV, roll up car windows, and get clothes and other equipment into the tents.

As they walked up, they saw it on a TV news break: Tom Crosslin, owner of Rainbow Farm campground, had been shot and killed by agents of the FBI.

"It was getting dark, but it was also stormy," said Karr. "But you've got to understand: at that point in time, in that situation, you're seeing signs everywhere, right? I mean, everything had significance. And as soon as we came back and told everybody that Tom was dead, the skies opened up. I mean, like, *that second*. The rains came down, everybody was soaked to the skin in five seconds. The lightning was horizon to horizon, nonstop. It was *apocalyptic*.

"And we're standing out there going, 'Yeah, see that? That's for *you guys* over there'—the cops. And the cops are standing there with their riot guns, thinking, 'Are these people going to rush the barricades?' There were some people who were saying, 'Yeah, let's rush the barricade!' And there were some of us that were going, 'No, there's no point in everybody getting killed.' There was a really tense few moments there."

"Me and Boss were so pissed, we went down there screaming and yelling at them," said Jim Crosslin. "I seen one state trooper—"

"Had tears in his eyes," added Miriame.

"—had tears in his eyes," finished Jim. "He knew it was wrong. He was crying when he was coming at us to keep us back and he knew something went wrong. They murdered my brother, that's what was wrong."

The scene at the barricades spun out of control. Jim was screaming "Murderers!" at the federal agents; Boss was screaming, Shirly was screaming and then Pops showed up and there wasn't much worse than that: the old, angry father of a suspect who's just been shot and killed. A patriarch in his seventies with some moral authority, and bereaved, and he's angry at you. Pops was livid, and just his presence made officers nervous. At ten thirty a call went out looking for any additional state troopers to report to the barricade, as there were twenty-five angry people there, a bunch of press and only six troopers to deal with it. Soon some county sheriff's deputies rolled in for backup, none of them too happy about it.

Tammy Brand, whose son, Dairik, played with Robert just about every day, came pushing to the front. The police tried to hold her back like the rest but she finally managed to get herself heard.

"Robert just found out they killed Tom and he wanted me to come up here and tell 'em not to kill his dad!" she shouted to the police.

That stilled everything for a moment, but the police were on edge.

"They wouldn't talk to her," said Karr. "They were like, 'Get back, get back.' And we were trying to say, 'Look, no, she's not one of us! She's just a normal person!' She really needs to talk to you guys.' And eventually they did let her in to talk to 'em.

"And we just stood out there in the rain and stared at them. And they stared at us, you know? I remember one officer in particular had his riot gun and was looking like he wanted to use it. But most of them looked like they really didn't want to be there, in my opinion. It was the county boys. They were like, 'We just kind of inherited this shit.'"

Just after dark, a full harvest moon rose blood red in the east over the black thread of M-60, sending the protestors into a frenzy. The whole world was reduced to one overwhelming dollop of pathetic fallacy. Doug was in Elkhart and he saw that moon and just sat out in the rain and wept.

A news photographer took a picture of Nikki, fallen to her knees between some squad cars, with her head in her hands.

While the wailing rose up and an all-out riot smoldered, Moe Yonkers slipped out of the knot of protestors and away. At ten forty-five, a call came in to command that a guy possibly named Johnny Mo got out of a vehicle on M-60 and ducked into the underbrush, walking toward the farm.

It was either the bravest or stupidest thing Moe ever did. They'd shot Tom and probably wounded this other kid, the hawk was out, but he knew Rollie simply wasn't going to shoot anybody. That's all there was to it and there wasn't a person interviewed for this book, including Teter and Michigan State Police lieutenant Mike Risko, who did a lot of the talking, and Underwood and others, who didn't feel exactly the same way. Without Tom, Rollie was no threat. Moe was going to go in there, get Rollie to put down that gun, and walk him out of that house, and that would be the end of it. If they were going to shoot him in the back while he walked, so be it.

He didn't get that far. The fuzz were on him the whole way and let him tire himself out making his way to Black Street, then picked him up there and brought him in to the command center. Moe was among a chorus of voices who emphasized to the officers there that Rollie wouldn't shoot anybody. Use Robert to talk him out. He just wants to stay close to his son.

Brandon was kept at the command center for at least an hour. He was examined by paramedics who found he'd taken a bullet fragment to the shoulder and a gash to the neck from a piece of Tom's skull, plus had scratches on his face. They let him clean himself up a little, but he was still sitting there with Tom's blood and brain matter stuck in his hair and on his clothes. He shook badly as he told the agents the stuff Tom had told him—how the yard and trails were mined and strung with trip wires, how the house was rigged to burn and filled with bales of straw, how he'd seen a wooden crate printed with the words mines explosive but that it was full of rifle cartridges in boxes. All this was relayed to officers in the field. Brandon was taken down to the sheriff's office for booking.

Later that night, Peterson got together with Salomon and Heffron, and wrote in his report: "Peterson noted that each one voiced the same hope that Crosslin was going to turn and go the other way, the same as he had done previously. SA Peterson opined that they had actually let Crosslin get too close to them for their own safety but they all maintained the hope that he was not going to see them and would go back to his residence."

Salomon and Heffron, the shooters, did not write out statements, on the advice of their attorney. Their weapons were taken away, as is standard bureau procedure.

At six thirty or so the Michigan State Police took over and the FBI left the woods.

Rollie was an infant in his sudden lonesomeness; the pensive and sexy long-haired boy who needed to be taken care of, who was in thrall to love, who had been abandoned by his father and mother and left behind a thousand times in his cold dreams was abandoned then finally for real. The night lost all texture, it couldn't be known, it gaped before him holding nothing. He sat in the house he had built with his own hands, but it was not his house, clutching a gun he carried only reluctantly, faced with death for a cause that was worth dying for only when the words came from his lover's mouth. Tom's words had been full of life, and now that there was only dying to do they ceased to nourish. His own desire shimmered in and out of view. He was himself for the first time in a dozen years, just Rollie, and he had to decide who that would be.

He hadn't been in much steady contact with the Livermores, though they had come to Roach Roast 2000, their first festival, and his half-brother Nick Rohm had been up three or four times since 1998. His stepbrother, Rob, who was Rollie's age, was a regular, and was as close to him as anyone from that family. Which wasn't terribly close. And Rollie's biological parents were figures in the distance, mute at best, threatening at worst. He had run into his real dad, Bob Rohm, at the supermarket once in Elkhart. "Look, Robert, there's grandpa," he'd said out loud to Robert, but the elder Rohm didn't respond. He just walked past like he didn't see them. Rollie's mother, Cheryl Lynn, had phoned a couple of years earlier to tell him she was moving back to Elkhart, but Rollie had told her not to show up at his doorstep after she'd thrown him off hers. Not long after that, Cheryl died of a chronic illness, leaving him the only things she'd ever represented, an empty space and a bill. Her family had asked Rollie to pay for her funeral but he refused, though he did attend it out of respect.

Only the dog was his that night. He sat petting Thai Stick, the Rottweiler grinning and anxious for Tom to return. The whip-poor-wills talked on the powerlines about beginnings and ends. The moon came up waxing full and red between the storm clouds over the trees along Pemberton Road, and then there would be no night, no relief, only continued life in fey, reddened half-light.

The Livermores were alerted to what was going on early in the weekend at their home in Rogersville, Tennessee. They talked to the FBI negotiator on duty and he thought they might be needed to get Rollie out. It's a long drive, and, according to the Livermores, they were assured nothing would happen until they got there.

The rest of the official account came in two versions, both supplied by the Michigan State Police. One was what Livermore would call "their ninety-thousand-page story"—the report released to the press in January 2002. The other hot source was a pair of tapes, debriefings of two snipers/observers, sergeant Daniel Lubelan and trooper John Julin, made by lieutenant Joseph Zangaro on Tuesday September 4, 2001. These tapes were often at odds with the official story and it made a difference, since they were the only men who saw Rollie run. And the ones who would shoot him.

State troopers rolled up to the house in an LAV that night and Rollie did not shoot. If he'd ever shot his Ruger, he wasn't shooting anymore. Just like Moe and everyone else said. Troopers tried to talk to him through the loudspeaker on the vehicle, but Rollie wasn't coming out. He was scared. The troopers were scared, too: they had the briefing from Brandon about mines and trip wires, and the specter of that alleged .50 caliber. At five past ten, Rollie picked up a thrown radio and got on it, agreeing to accept a phone. Just before midnight, Rollie picked up a Motorola cell phone dropped in the grass by the front porch and dialed it. On the other end was a state police negotiator, trooper Bob Anaya. He was in a mobile command post set up at Pemberton and Black, sitting around a little table with a tactician, Sergeant Diane Oppenheim, and psychologist Dr. Richard Smith. Rollie started talking.

They didn't talk long but it was established that they would talk. It seems that during the next few hours, Rollie might have fallen asleep. Deep silence fell over the scene.

Sergeant Lubelan and Trooper Julin set up early that night in the line of walnut trees that would have been right behind the grand stage during a show, with a clear view of the backyard. These two, about 175 yards from the house, were all that secured the route west past Kirk Lake and into File's property. Lubelan set up behind a tree with a .308 Remington 700 sniper rifle, and Julin set up close by with a .308 caliber Harrington & Richardson M14 marksman rifle used by the marines. They were both well camouflaged and settled in for a long night. Other snipers/observers covered other vantage points on the house.

At about three twelve in the morning, troopers in the LAV were advised to do something to wake Rollie. They shot three 37 millimeter "baton" rounds into the front windows, breaking them. One of the canisters from these rounds was later found on the dirt road, a 37mm Practice Ferret Inert Powder Barricade Penetrator from Defense Technologies. These don't make any smoke or flame, though they do get hot. At least four 12-gauge beanbag rounds were also fired, two through windows and two through the doors. Rollie immediately got on the phone and asked why he was being shot at. Anaya told him they were just trying to wake him. They talked for a good spell. Rollie said he'd thought it over and he'd come out if he could see Robert in person. After some discussion among the negotiating team in the mobile unit, it was agreed. They'd get Robert out to the farmhouse and Rollie would surrender at seven a.m.

The radio call went back to command at three forty-five a.m. Ten minutes later, Robert's caseworker at the Family Independence Agency was contacted and she set off to fetch Robert from the Steeles'.

Robert knew by that time that Tom was dead, and that changed the situation. He hadn't wanted to go out to the farm before, but with Tom dead he did. Ted Steele rode with the boy and kept close to him in the car. He was the only support Robert had; he was only twelve years old, and couldn't imagine what he was about to face. The boy was anxious, but full of hope, and kept saying he just wanted to get there in time, just wanted his dad to be safe.

They pulled into the school at five forty-five and Robert met with another negotiator, state police sergeant Dave Wood, and prepared to go back to Pemberton and Black. They were going to be driven back to the farm in the LAV, and Steele was coming with him. They caught a lift down to that intersection and were still down there where the dirt met the buckling blacktop, with troopers drinking their morning coffee and frogs and birds chattering in the cattails as they scraped the sweet air, when the negotiators in the mobile unit told Rollie his boy was there and was coming out. It was six a.m. on the dot.

State police lieutenant Jerry Ellsworth, a trooper in charge of the assault team that was going to make the arrest, was on the headphones during the six a.m. call with Rollie. "Rohm sounded as if he had been sleeping and was quite groggy. His speech was very slow, at a low level, and punctuated by sighs. Trooper Anaya continually had to advise him of the agreement and we were giving him time to get cleaned up so that he could come down and talk with his son at seven a.m. During this discussion Rohm was saying 'okay' and 'uh huh' as if he understood the process. . . . It was at that time that a noise was heard indicating he laid the phone down on a hard surface but did not hang up. . . . Rohm now could be heard walking back and forth in the house. All of a sudden a crackling sound could be heard as if he was crumbling up a piece of paper near the phone or was standing near a fireplace. It was determined by the sound that he had set the straw bales at the window on fire."

While they were loading up, Robert pointed at the trees on Mount This. There was smoke.

At five past six, snipers whispered into their headsets that the upper floor of the farmhouse was on fire. Robert and the troopers held up at the intersection, and within a few minutes heard gunfire, random at first, but then increasing numbers of shots. They thought it was Rollie, but it was the ammo going off as the house burned. Within fifteen minutes, the house was a ball of flame, and black smoke belched into the sky. The .223 ammunition was popping off in every direction.

Robert and Mr. Steele were tucked into a squad car and rolled out of there. Robert was going out of his mind with worry, crying, wanting so badly to stay and find out what was happening to his dad. He still held out hope that he would be arrested alive as they drove westward toward Cassopolis.

Rollie burst out of the smoke-filled house through the sliding door to the dining room at six thirty-five, on the west or back of the house, trotting through the backyard carrying the Ruger, looking disoriented, with Thai Stick stopping on the back porch. Fire marshals would later determine that Rollie had started that blaze.

The scenario made less and less sense over the next few minutes. As Rollie left the house, walking and running back and forth in the backyard with the Ruger in his hands, there was still no reason to think he was anything but terrified. The state police were forced to treat it differently. As reported in their log: "6:20hrs. Roland Rohm's son is sent home with foster parent Mr. Steel [sic]. Father did not honor agreement."

The state police's Lieutenant Risko says that no tear gas was used on the house and the baton rounds used were not the kind that could start a fire. "The fire marshal said it was arson. I don't know how much more specific I can be," he said.

"After the report of the glow coming from the second story of the home, a short time later, Rollie came out of the house, ran to a position away from the home," continued Risko. "At that point, the [LAV] moved in, and with loudspeakers—he was holding his assault rifle at the time—and over the loudspeakers they were telling him to drop his weapon. He refused. He ran back, they think possibly for the dog."

Thai Stick came out onto the small porch off the kitchen and, according to the depositions of the two snipers, froze there. Rollie had run out to a small spruce tree twenty yards from the house, just descending the round of the hill, but then walked back for the dog. They reported that he set the gun down in the grass and had to use both hands to get the dog off the porch, possibly because she was blocked by or tangled in the railings. The dog was let loose, then Rollie picked up the gun again and jogged across the lawn to the tree, crouching there. Lubelan and Julin were told "not to let Rohm leave by any means."

He sat there for a few minutes, watching the front driveway. The LAV came up that concrete drive and rounded the north end of the house, looping right toward Rollie. The driver, interviewed later by the Michigan State Police, claimed he couldn't see through the smoke and was being directed by the snipers, lurching forward in halting advances. At some point, two officers reportedly stuck their heads out of the top hatches of the vehicle so that Rollie could see them.

"They thought that maybe they could get him to throw down the weapon," said Risko. "When you're not being spoken to from an unseen voice behind a big megaphone on an [LAV]—maybe if he saw the men, they could convince him to put down his weapon. But instead, he brought it up and pointed it at one of the officers, at which time our officers in the field had to take him out."

Lieutenant Ellsworth was in the LAV, on the microphone, repeatedly telling Rollie to drop his weapon. He couldn't see Rollie. On his radio, he told Lubelan and Julin that if Rollie raised his gun, to "eliminate the threat." Seconds later he heard shots.

Both snipers reported that Rollie had shouldered the gun and pointed it at officers in the armored vehicle, but that is a matter in dispute and the subject of a lawsuit. If he had started the house on fire, maybe he had decided at last who he was and this was it. But he never got a shot off.

Julin took either eight or ten shots (official counts varied) and all missed. Lubelan shot once with the Remington, sticking the bullet through the stock of Rollie's gun and through his upper chest near the heart, putting him down. He shot again as Rollie fell back and hit the ground, with the bullet running through his left leg, allegedly exploding a lighter in the left front pocket of his camo cargo pants, and up through his body, exiting near his stomach. He rolled over and lay under the pine tree face down, dying in the grass.

Ellsworth ordered the LAV up to the house, then the arrest team jumped out and used the vehicle as cover to approach Rollie. Ellsworth jumped on Rollie's back, handcuffed him, then flipped him over, pushing the Ruger away. Rollie was already dead.

The house burned till not a stick was left and fell into the basement. No mines exploded. No .50 caliber ammunition went off, nor was any big gun ever found. It's unknown whether the "elephant gun" was ever actually there. None of Tom's big armaments or mines or trip-wired booby traps were ever found.

The Livermores arrived from Tennessee just a little after seven a.m., blurry from the night's drive, and presented themselves at the barricade. An ambulance came through going toward the farm. They could tell by the look on the face of the first cop they talked to that it was already over, and John Livermore was furious. He didn't want to be here with these people, he wanted to be able to get Rollie out of there and settle this and go home. As they were ushered back to an FBI agent, he shouted, "You said nothing would happen before we got here!" Gerry was heartbroken. She felt some of the life rush out of her. She had been his mother, probably the person who had worked harder than anyone else to save her sweet Rollie, and in the end none of these men could wait for her.

The news went out more quickly this time. Protestors stayed on Dwight's corner in their tents under the scrub elm, where the water tower pressed the name of the place—Vandalia!—into the clouds and they waved at passing cars all day, some of them in tears. People rolled past to shout obscenities, call them hippies, tell them to get a job, tell them Tom and Rollie deserved to die—same old shit. Their signs changed then. They said, Tom and Rollie Were Murdered and They Killed Them and Waco Ruby Ridge Rember [sic] Rainbow Farm. But that place was gone.

NINETEEN Steal Your Face/Steal Your Farm

The swimming hole looks inviting under the blue sky . . . Come back at dusk, however, and the pond turns black—as dark as death—or on the contrary, a restful dark, a dark to savor.

—Edward Hoagland

ROBERT'S CASEWORKER FROM THE Family Independence Agency and a couple of others came out to the Steeles' to give him the news, and they let Ted and Debbie break it. Robert flew into a cold rage as they told him, lashing out, punching not at the people in the room but at the couch, the walls, at anything that would take the punch and not punch back, although that might have been welcome relief. He bloodied his knuckles and left little spatters here and there.

He needed Leslie then. He asked for her and asked for people from the farm, for Travis and Derrik, he liked those guys, they didn't quit, they were there at the end. But it didn't happen. He wasn't allowed to see anyone other than his FIA counselor and the Steele family for over a month after his father was killed, and he didn't share all of his rage and fear with the Steeles. He wasn't allowed to join the mourners at his father's funeral or even to know where he was buried. Child protective services and Judge Dobrich and Teter decided it was better to keep the twelve-year-old away from those people.

* * *

It's hard to get beyond that feather. It was in the FBI interview notes: "Peoples carried a feather for good luck." So much turned on that. Brandon Peoples might be dead if he'd agreed to carry that .22 back from Butch's house. He got rough treatment anyway. Rainbow Farm supporters were a conspiratorial lot and their paranoid brains were just acrackle. The rumor went around that Brandon was a plant, working for the police, sent in to walk Tom into an FBI ambush. But his friends know that's not the case. He hushed up, it seems, under threat of arrest. Besides, a liar doesn't just conjure up an inspired, life-saving detail like that feather.

Late Monday night, after being grilled for hours by the FBI and the Michigan State Police, during which time his story didn't waver much, Brandon walked into the Routleys' house on Quaker Street. He was still wearing the blood-spattered clothes. Omar and Nessa were there with Shelly, Brandon's girlfriend. She'd been going to Rainbow Farm since her band played there in 1997.

Before any of them could ask, Brandon said, "I don't know what happened," waving them off. Then he went about changing his shirt.

Brandon has never talked to a reporter about what happened out on Rainbow Farm. Evidently, he's never revealed details to anyone except in the brief, coded version that he spit out that Monday night to his friends. He has been interviewed three times, however, by the FBI and by farm supporters and by a lawyer who later deposed him for a wrongful death suit, and the stories are all about the same: he just didn't know if Tom had shouldered the gun.

Or, he was pretty sure he didn't know. It had happened too fast.

Omar said, "I know what happened. Yeah, and he did implicate the truth: that Tom never raised his gun. He had it at his side and Brandon was walking behind him.

"Anyway, I could never ask Brandon about this again," added Omar. "No one can. But I remember what he said the first night—except for that coffee pot detail. They were walking and Brandon couldn't have been any more than five feet [from] Tom, and they opened fire on Tom.

He couldn't fire on them. He didn't have a chance to even raise his gun. He never fired a shot."

This seems to contradict Agent Peterson's report from the FBI, but Omar and others present say Peoples was not insisting his own version was right. He kept repeating over and over that he didn't really see it—or that he couldn't *say* that he really saw it.

He had bloody wounds on his forehead and his neck and his shoulder. He looked down and noticed the blood on the hemp shoes Tom had given him that day.

"I'm going to keep these shoes forever and I'm never going to wash that spot out," he told them.

"He said, 'Don't ever speak of this again with me. Don't ever bring it up around me. I'll tell you what happened this once and that's it,'" said Vanessa. "After that, he just got real weird because it traumatized him."

"So we all cracked a beer and moved on, you know?" said Omar. "We stopped talking to him about it."

Brandon was interviewed privately by Rainbow Farm supporters and their attorney on Sunday September 9. In handwritten notes, an examiner says: "He was eventually put in a car and taken to the police command center. He was questioned there, then told not to speak to anyone or he would be charged with aiding and abetting a felon in the act of a federal crime and other charges he couldn't remember. He was then released."

Afterward, their friend Brandon was not the same. After a while, he stopped really being their friend and didn't talk to Omar and Vanessa anymore—or anyone else. He broke up with Shelly but still lives in the area.

Omar and Vanessa went over to the Routleys' about a month after the shootings, after the memorials were over and everything was still and the October cold was setting in. They saw Brandon sitting at the kitchen table rolling a toy car back and forth, and he hardly acknowledged them at all. "It was like he had retrograded," said Vanessa.

One day he took the blood-stained pants and shirt and the hemp shoes that Tom had given him and burned them.

"It's a sick society," John Livermore told WNDU-TV on the day Rollie was killed. He was a big man in his fifties, wearing a flattop and sunglasses, tears streaming down. "If you got somebody that is an obstacle, that's a thorn in your side, you just go ahead and kill 'em. That's all I got to say."

Later, years later, Livermore would have a lot more to say, when the investigations and reports came out. The FBI and the Michigan State Police did their own reconstruction of events. Attorney General Granholm's office announced it would be involved in the investigation. The sheriff's department was investigating. The Libertarian Party was investigating. A small-government group called Taxpayers United was investigating. Teter was investigating.

Teter, in fact, was leading the whole investigation. It was his job to bring charges, if any, against the snipers, so the thousands of pages of reports, affidavits, photographs, surveillance and evidence video, autopsies, reconstructions and logs from all these agencies ended up with the farm's archenemy. The heads all thought it was the worst possible joke.

The Crosslins and Livermores, seeing the writing on the wall, did what they could on their own.

At seven p.m. on Wednesday September 5, the police quit Rainbow Farm and allowed the press and family in. John Livermore, Doug Leinbach, Rev. Steve Thompson—a pastor who was the leader of Benzie County NORML up by Traverse City—and dozens of others were on the scene, and the first thing they found were about forty-eight fresh beer cans, thrown in the basement and laying around the hollowed-out foundation of the house. The only people who'd been allowed on the place until then were the police, so they must have had themselves a little victory celebration.

Then there was the shock of that foundation itself: There wasn't one shred of debris inside. The FBI had taken every charred stick. The foundation of the house didn't even look scorched: the words Let Freedom Ring jumped off the basement wall right where Derrik had painted them. The clean orange dirt smelled like sassafras root.

Livermore got all kinds of ideas from what he saw. He thought the scorch marks found in the debris outside indicated that the cops had blocked the doors and burned the house down. He thought Rollie had been handcuffed and then executed. Obviously, his version was greatly at odds with official Michigan State Police and fire marshal reports. But he tried to get witnesses and corroborating forensics.

On the night the standoff began, August 31, Michigan Militia Corps Wolverines commander Tom Wayne got a call from federal agents at his home in Galesburg, Michigan. "Someone called the Militia—me—and asked what I was going to do about it," he said. "It was Labor Day weekend on a Friday evening. Come on now, how am I going to get anybody? Everybody's out with their family. Not that we'd do anything anyways. They wanted to see where I was so they could go ahead and do the rest of what they had to do."

Using resources provided by Illinois real estate tycoon Alex Magnus, a well-known benefactor of right-wing causes who had funded several Waco and Oklahoma City bombing investigations, Wayne helped bring in forensic pathologist and medical examiner Dr. Ronald Graeser, O.D, to look at what was left of Rainbow Farm. Graeser had been medical examiner for four Michigan counties over twenty-three years and had famously done forensic work around the death of Branch Davidian Jimmy Riddle in Waco.

Just after 9/11, Wayne and Graeser were on Rainbow Farm taking measurements in a cold rain, checking shot angles, searching for any stuff left behind. Graeser was planning to compare his reconstruction to autopsies and reports from Cass County medical examiner Dr. Robert Knox and from police and FBI, but Teter embargoed all those reports for three months. At the Livermores' insistence, Graeser examined Rollie's body. They had already had a second full autopsy performed by the Oakland County Medical Examiner's Office, signed by deputy chief M. E.

Kanu Virani, and all three examinations were quite similar, but they only made sense if Rollie was a left-handed shooter.

This was the subject of furious debate, because Rollie's mini-14 was a right-handed gun. Tom had been hyperconscious of Rollie's left-handedness, and everyone agreed he would have bought him a gun with the slide and ejection on the correct side. Graeser had found the sniper's positions in the fencerow down by the Rock Camp, and, for a right-handed shooter the angles were all off. There must have been somebody else shooting at him—a different sniper or the guys in the LAV. Whatever it was, the scenario appeared different from what had been released in the press briefings. In fact, they couldn't even tie Rollie to the Ruger, because it had not one fingerprint on it.

When Teter finally released his meticulous report on January 7, 2002, a lot of these details were cleared up. It was no surprise to learn that he'd cleared all the officers of any wrongdoing. These were, he said, cases of "justifiable homicide."

Teter's report acknowledged discrepancies from what had been reported before. Tom had been shot more than once, but the second shot, from Heffron, broke apart as it passed through the small tree and peppered Tom in the back of his gun hand, his shoulder and his side, lodging in his neck. In fact, the entry wounds under the right arm and in the back of the gun hand bolstered the agents' case by indicating he may have had his gun arm up in a shooting position.

Rollie's case, which was so much more questionable, was partly clarified for Graeser by one fact: According to the police, he shouldered the gun on the left. He was, they said, a left-handed shooter and aimed the right-handed gun from the wrong shoulder.

"There is no way the cops could have fabricated a scenario that fit perfectly with all the measurements and forensics that I had done independently, or to have justified their action by making up that left-handed detail. I was confident it happened pretty much like they reported it," said Graeser.

John Livermore had been shooting with Rollie and swore he shot right-handed, which threw all the angles off. Then, there was the matter of his balls. Both second and third autopsies noted that his testicles had been removed and were missing, with no explanation. Rollie's body showed a three-inch-by-three-inch abrasion on the inside of the left leg, right up into the groin. In the first autopsy, it was called a burn (explained by the exploded lighter in his pocket), but subsequent autopsies called it an abrasion. Like a kick in the nuts from a hard boot. Livermore thought the state was hiding evidence that Rollie had been alive when he was arrested, beaten or kicked, and then killed.

In late 2002, the families hired attorney Christopher Keane to pursue wrongful death suits. In discovery, he acquired the taped debriefings of Lubelan and Julin, and found a potentially explosive inconsistency in the story of Rollie's shooting. In the official Michigan State Police report, Lubelan was reported as saying he held the crosshairs of his scope on the "mass of [Rollie's] body." On the tape, however, Lubelan clearly said he "held on his back." He repeated this in a later deposition. Rollie was shot from the front to the back, so this didn't stack up.

Keane then brought in one of the nation's top ballistics experts, Luke Haag, and Charles Morton, a master criminalist who had been a witness for the defense in the Ruby Ridge case. Morton's partner in an investigative firm called Forensic Analytical, Dr. John Thornton, came out to gather evidence twice on Rainbow Farm. Thornton had also headed up a crime lab, and for twenty-four years was a Professor of Forensic Science at the University of California at Berkeley.

They were the tops in their field, the pros, and Keane dropped Tom's case right away, saying it just wasn't a slam dunk. The official report on Rollie, however, clashed with those debriefing tapes, with shot angles and with autopsy reports, among other problems. Most notably, there are conflicting reports about if, when and why two troopers stuck their heads out of the top of the LAV. This action guaranteed death for Rollie, as snipers Lubelan and Julin were under orders to shoot if their team members were exposed to risk. As this book went to press that case was scheduled to go to jury trial.

Graeser, however, didn't need to have more proof to know something went wrong up at Rainbow Farm. He wrapped up the whole story and put a bow on it.

"Here you have an expensive farm burned down, a child deprived of his father and his home and removed to foster care, and two productive men dead," he said. "Is it worth that, to prohibit someone from smoking pot? I don't think so. Obviously, this is a flawed policy."

After the shootings, farm supporters were under heavy surveillance. When they were out at Rainbow Farm, radios and men were easily overheard in the woods. When they were on Dwight's M-60 camp, men were walking through the junkyard fifty feet away, setting the sheep there to bawling. At night these troops flashed lights at one another from both sides of the busy road.

Melody Karr and another Traverse City–area activist, Adam Zielony, were driving down Black Street en route to Cassopolis for their morning coffee, he thinks it was early on Thursday September 6. Instead of cutting over to M-60, they took Black straight through Vandalia. Suddenly they counted ten canvas-covered National Guard trucks pulling out of a side street carrying troops. Although Zielony said it was hard to tell how many people were in the trucks because they were covered, they were shocked to think that that many truckloads of troops had been surrounding them for the forty-eight hours since Rollie was killed. The trucks pulled onto M-60 and rumbled out of town.

Jim Crosslin asked Doug to pick out some music for the funeral and he went deep into his memory and found some songs that he and Tom had admired over the years on a homemade cassette almost thirty years old. The songs were from the 1971 album LinkWray, and he cued up "Fallin' Rain," "Fire and Brimstone" and "Ice People." The first song began playing as rain spattered on the roof of the Walley-Mills-Zimmerman

Funeral Home and Crematory in Elkhart and thunder shook the place, with good old rockabilly Link in his inward 1970s Van Morrison or Leon Russell mode and that country guitar chugging and his suddenly eerie lyrics hushing, "all that is left is the fallin' rain."

About five hundred people tried to cram into the place and it was as good a portrait of Tom's life as you were likely to get—the family, the hippies in their full regalia like a lost clown troupe from a Day-Glo circus, contractors and friends in their best Sunday suits paying respects, heroes like Gaskin and Brook, other promoters like Rob Robinson from New York, the band Buddha Fulla Rymez—sister Shirley DeWeese even brought the dog, Thai Stick, which padded over and put its head in Doug's lap. The vibe was black and a lot of people were scared stiff just to be associated with Rainbow Farm anymore, but once they were all together they felt a modicum of safety. There were a few reporters, probably even some narcs. Being there was better, many said later, than waiting for the raid at home.

They exited the funeral home to two more Link Wray tunes, "God Out West" and "Crowbar." The rain let up when they got outside and for a long moment bright sun broke through, making first one huge rainbow and then a fainter second one, a double, and everyone just stood there gaping, pleased with this as some kind of sign.

There were a few people who had to rush out afterward. Travis had been doing his damnedest to guard the mansion but someone had already broken in and grabbed Rollie's glass pipe collection and some posters. Souvenir collectors fluttered around the farm like avaricious moths, awaiting an opportunity. Melody Karr and a group from the Traverse City area were camping at the farm for the same reason. Someone had tried to take the campground sign and the magic mailbox. The flag had been found on the ground with a bullet hole in it. Even pieces of the stage had been looted. It turned out Travis was too late: During the funeral someone broke into the basement again and stole all his power tools.

Tom was cremated and the Crosslins took the ashes. After the service, a crowd ended up at Pops's again for a wake, packed into the house and the garage, trying to stay out of the rain. At one point Hippie came over to Omar Alham and whispered "six up!"—Rainbow Family code for cops or narcs—in reference to a couple kids that had come uninvited. It turned out they weren't cops; they just thought this might be a good opportunity to sell some acid to the bereaved.

Rollie's funeral was on Tuesday September 11, 2001, just a few hours after the whole country watched the Twin Towers go crashing to the ground in New York City. Despite the electrifying fear that ran through the country as a whole, and which about tripled and quadrupled the paranoia attending many of the farm supporters, the event went on as planned. Most of the same people came.

About an hour before the funeral, the Steeles brought Robert in alone to say good-bye to his beloved dad. He left a big wreath of pink, blue and yellow flowers on Rollie's casket that read, "To My Best Dad—Robert." The folks who showed up an hour later found it there in the empty room and the tears that came then could have floated an ark.

Gerry and John Livermore were handing out information pamphlets outside the funeral home because many people in town didn't even know what it was about. "We stopped this one woman," said Gerry, "and she says, 'I think they deserved to die.' I'm going, 'How can you say that? You don't even know these people.' 'Well, they had drugs.'"

Rollie's body was put in an above-ground tomb in a cemetery in Elkhart, in case it was needed for further investigation, but the FIA didn't want Robert to know about that, either. Robert's maternal grandparents, the Rogers, finally took him down there one day months later, just so he'd know where to find his dad when he needed him.

Pops Crosslin never did want to talk to me for this book, but Doug took me over there one day and Pops let us in. We sat there on an Indian Summer afternoon in 2001 in the sunroom on the back of his house, drinking coffee with his wife, Mae, looking out at the pond. He was in his seventies and made it clear he didn't care much for marijuana, didn't think it was that meritorious as a cause, and added, "I don't believe in homosexuality, but it isn't much of my business, either."

He was grieving still, worn out by the loss of his son, worn out by years of Tom's constant agitation and then worn out by his sudden absence. He loved Robert and was heartbroken he hadn't seen him. The boy had been there a lot over the years and his pictures were all over the neat, well-appointed prefab house.

"They murdered them boys, plain and simple," said Pops in his deep Tennessee curl. "There's no other way to look at it."

At that time, there wasn't anyone he blamed more than Teter. If he hadn't pushed the way he did or had been more communicative or had brought in a third party to mediate all this, the conflict might have come out differently. But Teter was too stiff. And so was Tom.

"Tom wasn't gonna be pushed, though," he reiterated.

"He could be real ornery," nodded Mae.

"With all these governments that were involved here," he said, flat and serious, "I can see why you get these militant militia and whatnot training every day. They're training for situations exactly like this!"

He looked at Mae and added, "And if I was any younger I'd be out there training with them myself."

It was a cold night that same November just after the killings, our breath freezing in little clouds, and Doug was looking for a party. He wasn't much in the mood for drinking and smoking, but it was a gathering of the tribe, which he needed as badly as anyone. Winter was coming on, and the red oak leaves scratched cardboard brown in the air above Elkhart's scrappy south side. We drove up to two houses and peered in the dark windows. The Rainbow Farm survivors had heard a reporter was coming and they had moved the location of the party several times during the afternoon.

"These are real trusting people," said Leinbach, not being sarcastic. "But they just need some time to heal. They've been scared half to death."

When we finally walked into the party, the look flashed around the room. It's always the worst part of my job, but the best, too. *Don't talk to that guy. He could be a cop.* It's a miracle, really, that it continues to work, but slowly their paranoia faded. The house was a comfortable two-bedroom job, all wall-to-wall carpet, big home entertainment center, broke-in couches. Everyone in the place was getting stoned. Hippie was watching the TV despite the live music spangling out of a back room through the kitchen. Sheli McNeill was there, Casey and Shayla, Travis. A giant floor-to-ceiling bird cage stood in the corner with the door open and a beautiful white cockatoo talked to the house full of guests. The place was near where Tom used to party with his biker club twenty-five years earlier.

On an enclosed porch off the back of the house was the full-fledged manifestation of Rainbow Farm: ten or so regular acolytes wailing away on their instruments, singing their redemption songs. The porch was outfitted as a makeshift rehearsal studio with a full Ludwig drum kit and a PA and everyone was laying in. As we entered, they were playing a tune by Three Doors Down, and Derrik was seated at the drum kit, hollering, "This is like Stevie Ray Vaughan's house, here, man. Grab a guitar." The owner of the house sat in, Doug, too, and Travis, and Chuck Jacobs from Goshen. Derrik's assistant on the farm, "Bongo Bob" Phillips, was there on his congas. They leaned into the tune, "Loser," as a fat joint went around the room, the smoke growing so thick you could practically see the sound waves booming off the PA, singing: *Cause I'm a loser and sooner or later you know I'll be dead.*

The libertarian utopia, the way Tom imagined it, was totally impossible, and yet it had happened despite Teter or anyone else. I had been reading philosopher Robert Nozick's 1975 National Book Award winner *Anarchy, State, and Utopia*, trying to make sense of the politics on the farm, when I came across a passage which described the thing in a nutshell, the impossibility of freedom and the inexorable need for it in one paragraph:

The conclusion to draw is that there will not be *one* kind of community existing and one kind of life led in utopia. Utopia will consist of utopias, of many different and divergent communities in which people lead different kinds of lives under different institutions. . . . Utopia is a framework for utopias, a place where people are at liberty to join together voluntarily to pursue and attempt to realize their own vision of the good life in the ideal community but where no one can *impose* his own utopian vision upon others. The utopian society is the society of utopianism. (Some of course may be content where they are. Not *everyone* will be joining special experimental communities, and many who abstain at first will join the communities later, after it is clear they are actually working out.) Half of the truth I wish to put forth is that utopia is meta-utopia: the environment in which utopian experiments may be tried out; the environment in which people are free to do their own thing; the environment which must, to a great extent, be realized first if more particular utopian visions are to be realized stably.

Well, Tom had tried to draw the hard outlines of the meta-utopia, but, despite the promises of the Constitution, it clearly hadn't been established yet.

Doug was painting for a living. Derrik was starting a promotions company and writing new music. Shayla was waiting tables at Bennigans, waiting for "something else to be important." Casey had painted a picture of the Grateful Dead skull-and-lightning-bolt logo, which is called Steal Your Face, on the old Rainbow Farm stage, and had written under it, "Steal Your Farm." Buggy had a job in an Elkhart factory. Nikki was with her folks in West Virginia. David Guest had disappeared. Rainbow Richie was milking cows. Brandon was wigged. Like Whoaboy, Moe and Amy were back doing construction, and were in and out of town, once gone to Oregon for a while. But they had a glimmer of a dream: they wanted to revive The Hemp Center and start taking it to festivals.

Vanessa and Omar got married and when AP quoted her in a story about Rainbow Farm her real father saw it in Texas and they were reunited. The couple were headed down there, where their daughter would be born.

The big German shepherd in the party house was barking and the cockatoo was *coughing* in emulation of all the potheads hacking away, and the lady of the house produced a huge pan of comestibles and the twelve-packs of beer kept rolling in. They played Bob Marley, the Grateful Dead's "Box of Rain," James Taylor. Stuff everybody knew on guitar. The words that put you back together if you sang the right pieces. Shayla sat on Sheli's lap and laughed to tears, and out in the front room the TV had everyone in stitches, and the laughter got tangled up in the music and the party went over the line into something mystical, too. Hippie came back there, with his long gray hair and black leather motorcycle jacket, and I thanked him for letting me hang out that night, and he said, "Hell yeah, man. That's all we do!" The cold night pressed in as condensation on the blackened windows, and somewhere in the transition off the Grateful Dead, Doug and the man who lived in the house got an idea together, a bit of synchronicity, and started playing Van Morrison's "Astral Weeks," struggling at first and then everyone plugged in and found the groove and the stoney, sunburst, radical green churchyard poetry began pouring out. Rainbow Farm was alive. And marijuana could save the world.

EPILOGUE

Robert Rohm lived with foster parents for a little over a year, then was adopted in late 2002 by his maternal grandparents, the Rogerses, who had already adopted his half-sister, Candy Duvall. Rev. Denny Rogers and his wife, Evelyn, were core leaders of a Christian community called Voice Ministries in Osceola, Indiana, and Robert became active in ministry programs. He eventually got a few of the keepsakes that Tom and Rollie had set aside for him, including Rollie's horseshoe ring, which he wore on a chain around his neck. As of this writing, he was a smiling, handsome sixteen-year-old with short blond hair and snapping blue eyes. The court also recognized him as the sole heir to Rainbow Farm.

In 2002, Prosecutor Scott Teter agreed not to seize Rainbow Farm on the condition that the farm and all of Tom Crosslin's and Rollie Rohm's properties were liquidated in order to settle significant debts. The farm itself was sold in 2004 to a real estate group that intended to parcel it off for luxury homes. Teter did not finish his term, but took a job in the attorney general's office in Lansing. Medical marijuana initiatives passed in Ann Arbor and Detroit in 2004. Robert said he didn't much follow what had happened to the farm in the aftermath of the shootings, nor the lawsuit, but that he missed his dad, saying, "My dad was kind and gentle." Overall, he said he wanted to put Rainbow Farm behind him. "It's my past; I don't really care about some of my past. Some of it's cool, some of it's not. I'm going to focus on the Lord, work and school and see where the Lord takes me."

ACKNOWLEDGMENTS

I would like to express sincere gratitude to the people who appear in this book and who are too numerous to thank, in particular Jim and Miriame Crosslin, Gerry Livermore, members of the Crosslin, Rohm, and Livermore families and the many who chose to remain nameless but still provided me with background notes. All of the material in this book not gathered by direct observation was culled from exhaustive interviews with witnesses over four years, corroborated news items, court documents and thousands of pages of reports by law enforcement. I am deeply indebted to Doug Leinbach, without whose long memory, attention to detail and infinite introductions this book couldn't have happened. Also essential were the contributions of Moe Yonkers, Derrik DeCraene, Max Robinson and Chris Keane. Special thanks to Jay Statzer, Chad Rea and ElVee for superb archived recordings and photographs, and to NORML for research. Thanks to the Marijuana Policy Project for a vital research grant. Hats off to Dana Adam Shapiro, formerly at SPIN, Chris Napolitano at Playboy and Amy Scholder at Verso Books for early support of this story. Eternal gratitude to my assistants, including Jane San Buenaventura, Kate Petre, Marnie Castor, Shelly George, Eleanor Barbour, Idan Ivri, Rhiannon Aarons and Rob Holland. Big thanks to Karen Rinaldi and Kathy Belden at Bloomsbury U.S.A., and Sloan Harris at ICM. And to the people of Cass County, Michigan, who were generous to a native son.

INDEX

A NOTE ON THE AUTHOR

Dean Kuipers is the deputy editor of *Los Angeles* CityBeat and the author of *I Am a Bullet* and *Ray Gun Out of Control*. His work has appeared in *Rolling Stone*, the *Los Angeles Times* and *Playboy*. A native of Michigan, he now lives in Los Angeles.